ETHNOGRAPHY IN ACTION

ETHNOGRAPHER'S TOOLKIT
Second Edition

Jean J. Schensul, Institute for Community Research, Hartford, Connecticut
Margaret D. LeCompte, University of Colorado, Boulder

PURPOSE OF THE ETHNOGRAPHER'S TOOLKIT

The second edition of the **Ethnographer's Toolkit** is designed with the novice field researcher in mind. In this revised and updated version, the authors of the **Toolkit** take the reader through a series of seven books that spell out the steps involved in doing ethnographic research in community and institutional settings. Using simple, reader-friendly language, the **Toolkit** includes case studies, examples, illustrations, checklists, key points, and additional resources, all designed to help the reader fully understand each and every step of the ethnographic process. Eschewing a formulaic approach, the authors explain how to develop research questions, create research designs and models, decide which data collection methods to use, and how to analyze and interpret data. Two new books take the reader through ethical decision-making and protocols specific for protection of individual and group participants in qualitative research, and ways of applying qualitative and ethnographic research to practical program development, evaluation, and systems change efforts. The **Toolkit** is the perfect starting point for students and faculty in the social sciences, public health, education, environmental studies, allied health, and nursing, who may be new to ethnographic research. It also introduces professionals from diverse fields to the use of observation, assessment, and evaluation for practical ways to improve programs and achieve better service outcomes.

1. *Designing and Conducting Ethnographic Research: An Introduction*, Second Edition, by Margaret D. LeCompte and Jean J. Schensul
2. *Initiating Ethnographic Research: A Mixed Methods Approach*, by Stephen L. Schensul, Jean J. Schensul, and Margaret D. LeCompte
3. *Essential Ethnographic Methods: A Mixed Methods Approach*, Second Edition, by Jean J. Schensul and Margaret D. LeCompte
4. *Specialized Ethnographic Methods: A Mixed Methods Approach*, edited by Jean J. Schensul and Margaret D. LeCompte
5. *Analysis and Interpretation of Ethnographic Data: A Mixed Methods Approach*, Second Edition, by Margaret D. LeCompte and Jean J. Schensul
6. *Ethics in Ethnography: A Mixed Methods Approach*, by Margaret D. LeCompte and Jean J. Schensul
7. *Ethnography in Action: A Mixed Methods Approach*, by Jean J. Schensul and Margaret D. LeCompte

ETHNOGRAPHY IN ACTION
A Mixed Methods Approach

Jean J. Schensul and Margaret D. LeCompte

A division of
ROWMAN & LITTLEFIELD
Lanham • Boulder • New York • London

Published by AltaMira Press
A division of Rowman & Littlefield
A wholly owned subsidary of The Rowman & Littlefield Publishing Group, Inc.
4501 Forbes Boulevard, Suite 200, Lanham, Maryland 20706
www.rowman.com

Unit A, Whitacre Mews, 26-34 Stannary Street, London SE11 4AB, United Kingdom

British Library Cataloguing in Publication Information Available

Library of Congress Cataloging-in-Publication Data

Names: Schensul, Jean J. | LeCompte, Margaret Diane.
Title: Ethnography in action : a mixed methods approach / Jean J. Schensul and Margaret
  D. LeCompte.
Description: Lanham : Rowman & Littlefield, 2016. | Series: Ethnographer's toolkit, second
  edition Book 7 | Includes bibliographical references and index.
Identifiers: LCCN 2015037201| ISBN 9780759122116 (pbk. : alk. paper) | ISBN
  9780759122123 (electronic)
Subjects: LCSH: Ethnology—Methodology. | Ethnology—Research.
Classification: LCC GN345 .S36194 2016 | DDC 305.8001—dc23 LC record available at
  http://lccn.loc.gov/2015037201

∞™ The paper used in this publication meets the minimum requirements of American
National Standard for Information Sciences—Permanence of Paper for Printed Library
Materials, ANSI/NISO Z39.48-1992.

Printed in the United States of America

We dedicate these volumes to three dear friends and colleagues who unfortunately have passed away in the absolute prime of their creative and inspiring lives.

Marlene Berg, who was a partner and muse in the creation and growth of the Institute for Community Research. Marlene never missed an opportunity to act as brilliant and positive social critic; she was the first to jump on a new idea and make it better. As a dedicated educator, researcher, and activist, her passion for social justice and her willingness to fight for so many important causes—housing, employment, children's rights, civil rights, LGTBQ youth of color—and her introduction of the concepts of critical consciousness and collective efficacy in Participatory Action Research and in our own lives inspired us all over more than twenty-five years of collegiality and friendship.

Janette Klingner, a passionate researcher and activist on behalf of second language learners in school and children with disabilities, who entered into her higher education career after many years as a public school teacher, but still earned early career awards and multiple accolades from all the professional associations to which she belonged. Janette was tireless in meeting with both lay people and educators all over the country to promote programs to support children with challenges, even when her own health was failing. More than that, her warmth, caring, brilliant mentoring, enthusiasm, and her glowing smile lit the world for generations of students. We shared so many interests, and her absence remains a daily loss. There just wasn't enough time.

Adrienne Anderson, an environmental activist and consummate community-based researcher and teacher who taught generations of undergraduates and community members how to ferret out corporations that poisoned poor and minority neighborhoods with radioactive and carcinogenic contaminants and then conspired with governmental authorities to hide their actions. With her blonde hair, diminutive stature, and her sweet southern drawl, she disarmed those on whose evildoings she was about to pounce—with lawsuits and Freedom of Information Act demands. No corporation was too large to escape her notice or too nefarious to terrify her. Termed a "water warrior" and the "Karen Silkwood of Colorado" by her supporters, Adrienne earned the enmity of those same corporate and political interests, whose vicious character assassination failed to stop her but ultimately forced her out of the university. She, too, died in mid-career, a probable victim of the very toxins she was trying to keep out of the Colorado water supply.

CONTENTS

LIST OF TABLES AND FIGURES

LIST OF EXAMPLES

ACKNOWLEDGMENTS

We would like to begin by acknowledging each other—and our partnership, We have been writing the first and second editions of the *Ethnographer's Toolkit* for the past twenty years. It has become an intrinsic part of our lives. Throughout, we have traveled to numerous conferences, enjoyed great food and good wine, and shared homes, ideas, life stories, recipes, shopping, friends, and art and most of all, innovative approaches to research methodology. The *Toolkit* has fostered and enriched our friendship, our intellectual growth, our teaching and training capacity, and our ability to negotiate, disagree, and engage in rigorous debate. It has sustained us through family and work-related crises. And we in turn have been sustained throughout this long journey by a number of people whom we would like to acknowledge in this last book of the *Ethnographer's Toolkit*, second edition.

First, we owe a great debt to Stephen Schensul, anthropologist/methodologist/co-author, life partner of Jean Schensul, friend and colleague of Marki LeCompte, and first author of Book 2, for his clear thinking, his radical insights, his methodological rigor, his generous spirit, his endless love for his family, and his continuous support and encouragement that allowed Jean to spend the hundreds and thousands of hours that the *Toolkit* demanded, and for his patience in setting aside the many activities that he and Jean could have shared to make both editions possible, especially the second edition.

We also owe thanks to Margaret Weeks, our friend and colleague at ICR, whose tolerance for "just another book deadline" made it comfortable for Jean to write at home as well as at work and to meet deadline crunches as they appeared on the horizon. We thank her for never deviating from her own commitment to rigorous community-based participatory research with vulnerable women, illicit drug users, and young people who have struggled to deal with the impact of HIV on their lives and their families, for her efforts in ameliorating the root causes of HIV, and for her dedication as its second executive director to sustain and grow the Institute for Community Research.

Perhaps most important, we must acknowledge that these volumes would lose all their vitality without the inclusion of extraordinary work by literally hundreds of our students, friends, and colleagues whose work is described throughout the seven volumes. The books are a tribute to their contributions to ethnography in practice and in action, and we are grateful that they allowed us to include their work in the volumes. We also must acknowledge the vision and commitment of all the editors who believed in the work and encouraged us. Mitch Allen first suggested the idea of a collection of books that he called a "toolkit" and persuaded us to embark on the project. Alan McClare, Wendy Schnaufer, and Leanne Silverman, editors who successively assumed responsibility for our project, were and have been fantastically flexible in adjusting to our own ever-scrambled schedules, and committed to making sure that the books appeared in print. We thank Andrea O. Kendrick and others who worked to market the second edition of the *Toolkit* to the multiple audiences that have come to use it; last but certainly not least we must thank Jehanne Schweitzer for her meticulous oversight of the book's copyediting, design, and production. Jehanne's work is unseen, but without her the *Toolkit*'s complex formatting and clear articulation would not have been possible.

We owe our families a great debt of gratitude for support and for believing in us even when they didn't quite understand what we were up to and why, and why all those many years of work made us happy though they wouldn't make us rich. Appreciation and love to Schensul and Schachter parents who were always proud of our work and took pleasure in showing off the first edition; Schensul sons, Michael and Daniel, now professionals—one a social scientist and the other a public defense lawyer—with growing families, found "other things" to do in the 1990s while the first edition was being written and have been nothing but proud of a recalcitrant mother who loved to write; their partners Meredith Schensul and Nikolin Eyrich, also professionals, and their children, all of whom will be happy to share more dinners and vacations now that the last two books are finished; and Walter Morgan, an engineer father, and Elizabeth Morgan, a counselor and teacher, who encouraged their daughter Marki's intellectual curiosity and risk taking, and who never told her that she couldn't accomplish anything she attempted, and who, with brothers Don and Bill, always displayed entire editions of the *Toolkit* on their respective coffee tables. Michael Lau, Marki's partner who put up with absences and kept reminding her that she had to get back to writing—he kept Marki's nose to the grindstone during the entire second edition; and Justin Lau, a wise and perceptive teenager who kept asking questions at the dinner table about what on earth we were doing, and why it was important. His questions served as a member-check for the validity of our work for young people.

INTRODUCTION TO THE
ETHNOGRAPHER'S TOOLKIT

The *Ethnographer's Toolkit*, a mixed methods approach to ethnography, is a series of seven texts on how to plan, design, carry out, and use the results of applied ethnographic research. While ethnography as an approach to research may be unfamiliar to people accustomed to more traditional forms of research, we believe that ethnography will not only prove congenial but also essential to many researchers and practitioners. Many of the investigative or evaluative questions that arise in the course of answering basic questions about ongoing events in a community or school setting or in the context of program planning and evaluation cannot be answered very well with other approaches to research, such as controlled experiments or the collection of quantifiable data alone. Often there are no data available to quantify or programs whose effectiveness needs to be assessed. Sometimes, indeed, the research problem or issue to be addressed is not yet clearly identified and must be discovered. In such cases, mixed methods ethnographic research provides a valid and important way to find out what *is* happening and to help research-practice or intervention teams plan their activities.

Ethnography is often—and mistakenly—perceived to be a "qualitative" approach to inquiry. We take the position that research questions, whether they ask basic or formative questions or lead directly to action or application, are not driven by methods. Rather, the questions that we ask, and the ways we deconstruct and model them and design our research, are answered through careful choice of a wide variety of qualitative and numerate methods. Thus, we have tried to frame the *Toolkit* as a mixed methods approach. By mixed methods, we refer to the array of options that are available for collection and analysis of data to answer meaningful questions.

Finally, the *Toolkit* responds to the continuing need to develop capacity for systematic approaches to inquiry in students of all ages, education levels, and in all formal and informal educational settings. Too often, students, especially in some of the social and health sciences, are exposed to theory but do not learn how to build theory or operationalize it. Or they learn to conduct experiments but are not exposed to ways of asking questions about how and why things work or do not work. Middle and high school students may learn to do secondary research but don't have the opportunity to think through and collect primary data on questions that matter to them. And community residents and organizations may want to collect their own data to forward their development agendas but don't have the skills or resources to do so, or the research language that enables them to negotiate with university or other research collaborators. We have tried to design the *Toolkit* to be accessible and useful to all of these constituencies.

NEW IN THE SECOND EDITION OF THE *ETHNOGRAPHER'S TOOLKIT*

In this second edition of the *Toolkit*, we have updated many sections of the books and, based on feedback from our colleagues, we have clarified many of the concepts and techniques. Book 1 of the *Ethnographer's Toolkit*, *Designing and Conducting Ethnographic Research: An Introduction*, remains an introduction and primer, but it includes new material on data collection, definition, and analysis as well as new chapters on research partnerships and using ethnography for a variety of applied purposes. In Book 1 we define what ethnographic research is, when it should be used, and how it can be used to identify and solve complex social problems, especially those not readily amenable to traditional quantitative or experimental research methods alone. Book 2, *Initiating Ethnographic Research: A Mixed Methods Approach*, now is devoted to the process of developing a conceptual basis for research studies and to more detailed questions of research design, modeling, and preparing for the field experience. Books 1 through 4 emphasize the fact that ethnography is a peculiarly human endeavor; many of its practitioners have commented that, unlike in other approaches to research, the *researcher* is the primary tool for collecting primary data. Book 3, *Essential Ethnographic Methods: A Mixed Methods Approach*, demonstrates that ethnography's principal database is amassed in the course of human interaction: direct observation, face-to-face interviewing and elicitation, audiovisual recording, and mapping the networks, times, and places in which human interactions occur. Further, the personal characteristics and activities of researchers as human beings and as scientists become salient in ethnography in ways not applicable in research that permits the investigator to maintain a more social and conceptual distance from the persons and phenomena under study. Interpretation of ethnographic research results emerges only from the process of engaging researcher understanding with direct, face-to-face experience.

Book 4, *Specialized Ethnographic Methods: A Mixed Methods Approach*, is a collection of ten individually authored chapters that includes new chapters on cutting-edge approaches to ethnography such as participatory video methods, and cultural artifacts, as well as chapters on hidden populations, using archival and secondary data, cultural consensus analysis, network research, and spatial analysis.

Book 5, *Analysis and Interpretation of Ethnographic Data: A Mixed Methods Approach*, has been updated and linked more closely to the theoretical and conceptual approaches outlined in Books 2 and 3, and it includes new examples.

Book 6, *Ethics in Ethnography: A Mixed Methods Approach*, and Book 7, *Ethnography in Action: A Mixed Methods Approach*, are entirely new to the *Toolkit*. Book 6 provides extensive detail on the burgeoning field of formal and informal research ethics, includes chapters that address the special considerations needed for ethical procedures in team and collaborative research, and examines the way that the environment for research has changed in ways that mandate new procedures for complying with ethical principles. Book 7 is entirely focused on the application of ethnographic mixed methods research to the design, implementation, evaluation, dissemination, and teaching of collaborative and participatory forms of multilevel research in community and university settings to address disparities and contribute to positive changes in local communities in their broader contexts over time.

We have designed the *Toolkit* for educators; service professionals; professors of applied studies in the fields of teaching, social sciences, social and health services, medicine, communications, engineering, the environment, and business; advanced undergraduate and graduate students; and professionals working in applied field settings who are interested in field research and mixed methods ethnographic research. The examples we include throughout the books are drawn from these fields as well as our own research projects and those of our colleagues. We also believe that the *Ethnographer's Toolkit* will be useful to any researcher, whether novice, apprentice, or expert, who desires to learn how to, or more about how to, carry out high-quality ethnographic and mixed methods research.

INTRODUCTION TO BOOK 7

In *Ethnography in Action*, the final volume of the *Ethnographer's Toolkit*, we tackle directly the many issues and considerations in the use of mixed methods ethnography to achieve social, educational, health, and other "practical" goals and outcomes related to improving quality of life in general. More particularly, we advocate its use where communities and groups experience inequality, marginalization, and disparate access to societal benefits. We assume that you, the reader, would not be reading this book unless you had a strong desire to make a positive difference in this world and to use research as part of a broader set of strategies to contribute to social change. Possessing this desire, commitment, and passion is a requisite for addressing a series of questions, considerations, and decisions about how to embark on the process of inducing change. These include:

- What skills, beyond those of research, do we bring to the task at hand?
- What kinds of change are we personally interested in? What values, beliefs, and views inform how we define what constitutes a safer and more just world? Are we interested in transformational change, the goal of which is to reframe structures, policies, and institutions that promote inequitable distribution of resources and opportunities? Or are we interested in initiating the more immediate forms of change that improve the local lives of individuals? Do we begin by investing in long-term relationships? Or do we develop a short-term alliance to solve a specific problem?
- How can we appropriately map our inclinations regarding skills and change onto a situation that calls for intervention?
- What are the settings we choose? They may be communities, schools, or other institutions, government bureaucracies, the military, business enterprises, or even universities. They may be local, global, or both.
- What partners can we identify, and what partnerships can we forge to maximize the probability that our work will be useful?
- How do we actually "do" or conduct participatory or collaborative research?
- What is the "value added" component of integrating collaboration and participation into the definition of research topics, designs, identification of data collection and analysis strategies, development and interpretation of results, and strategies for dissemination and use of research results?
- What approaches to change—what intervention guidelines—might we apply? What "actions" do we want to move toward and with whom? Do we utilize principles and methods of evaluation, behavioral intervention, education, community organizing and advocacy, design expertise, organizational change, social movement theory?
- What innovative ways can we use to share research conducted from an action perspective with the communities and constituencies with whom we work?
- How can we work with our partners to merge both local or everyday and scientific knowledge with research methods in applied partnerships to create desired changes in individuals, groups, and inequitable structures and policies?
- What are some effective ways to teach participatory research and action in the community and in the university, and what infrastructure is required to support them?

In this book we try to answer many of these questions through examples of our own work and those drawn from the work of many other action-oriented mixed methods researchers both inside and outside the university.

It is not possible to cover all of the different domains of practice in one volume, so we have made choices. Following the outline established in chapter 9 of Book 1, we have selected to focus on several specific areas of practice that fall under the rubric of "action." All of them involve partnerships or collaborations of various sorts. Most of them are focused on improving the quality of life in underresourced settings populated by marginalized people or communities and populations undergoing major transitions. Each demonstrates different uses of ethnography as well as other skills.

The areas of practice involving the uses of ethnography that we discussed in Book 1 are the following:

- Informing public audiences by disseminating information to them
- Developing interventions and evaluating them
- Influencing educational practice
- Using Participatory Action Research (PAR) as a form of social transformation
- Using ethnography to contribute to decision making
- Contributing to science

We have chosen to expand the summary in Book 1 using a slightly different and improved organization of chapters. Here, in chapter 1 of Book 7, we begin with definitions, including what the practice of research in action looks like, as well as the meaning of community, context, values, and organizational bases for the conduct of applied ethnography and partnerships. In the second chapter we examine long-term involvements in different "fields," to show how applied ethnography evolves in different and emergent ways over time to enhance action in the form of desired change efforts. In the section called "Building Blocks," subsequent chapters describe and operationalize how the components of such projects are created. Chapter 3 describes methods of building collaborations and partnerships that are based on and enhanced by ethnographic practice. Chapters 4 and 5 show how theory, developed "emically" or locally/indigenously and inductively, intersects with "etically" or externally available social science–based "midrange" theories of action. As we noted in Book 2 and throughout the *Toolkit*, "modeling" or conceptualizing and displaying graphically the main domains or concepts in a research/intervention approach is very important in building the base for further research and in guiding change efforts. It is a way of working with people in an action setting to build local or "indigenous" theory that reflects and explains their meanings and lived experience. Participatory modeling helps research collaborators conceptualize the "system" in which they wish to intervene and how it can change. It can also help to identify desired end states and ways of achieving them. Thus chapter 4 is devoted to ways of engaging in participatory modeling problems and anticipating possible solutions to theorize and drive appropriate interventions along with externally derived theories discussed in chapter 5. Chapter 4 closes by revisiting a methodology described in Book 2, chapters 4, 5, and 8, that considers how to model problems and hypothetical causes and organize community assets and resources related to problems so as to contribute to solving multilevel problems in innovative and locally responsive ways.

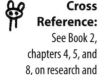

Cross Reference: See Book 2, chapters 4, 5, and 8, on research and intervention modeling

Interdisciplinary, or "etic," theory can be very helpful in both expanding and locating local theory in a broader context. In chapter 5, we consider a variety of theoretical orientations at the individual, group, and community level derived from anthropology, sociology, and psychology that ethnographers and their partners can draw upon in expanding and guiding their locally derived ideas about intervention.

In chapter 6, we review some of the main ways that ethnographers translate research into intervention approaches, through formative exploration in local settings, the creation of content for interventions at different levels, and the development of appropriate evaluation measures and methods. We describe how to collect data and how to adapt data-collection methods to collaborative settings so that partners can join in deciding which methods to use, how to implement them, and how to analyze them as a group. In doing so, we link methods to models. Chapter 7 is devoted to ethnographic evaluation. We introduce the chapter by contrasting typical evaluation designs used in experimental or policy research with the strengths of mixed methods and more qualitative approaches to evaluation of actions or practice. The latter can tell us about *why* and *how* things happen, thus enhancing other approaches that simply measure whether or not they *do* happen.

Dissemination of research results is the focus of chapter 8. One of the complaints directed toward all manner of researchers is that the results of empirical research are not returned to the study community, even when members of the study community are directly involved in the research! In this chapter, we describe key elements required in preparing interactive and engaging experiences with research results that offer opportunities for researchers to share implications of studies with community partners and members. These practices further enhance understanding of the results and increase the likelihood that they will contribute to problem solving.

The next three chapters address ways of teaching ethnography in action to adult community researchers, high school and middle school students, and undergraduate, graduate, and postgraduate-level students. Chapter 9 concentrates on a specific form of applied ethnography—Participatory Action Research (PAR)—which involves teaching youth and adults to become action researchers so that they themselves have command and control over the research and the actions that follow. PAR has a long history in the social sciences; we briefly review some key milestones in that history, describe approaches to youth and adult PAR, and consider its advantage and disadvantages in achieving desired social and transformational change.

In chapter 10 we argue that before college and university students, who are the eventual drivers of PAR in community settings, can be properly trained, universities and departments must have structures in place to make it possible for faculty to establish relationships with local communities and sustain those relationships over time. In chapters 2 and 3 of this book, we describe some long-term efforts to do this from the community perspective. In chapter 10 we provide details on what structures should be in place to help creative faculty to do good collaborative, change-oriented research with community collaborators and partners, so that they can train their students through participation and example. We also suggest how reward structures in higher education must change to encourage such activities.

In chapter 11 we provide examples of how PAR and other forms of collaborative research can be integrated with classroom teaching, practica, and internships to enhance community change efforts while building student experience. Teaching students how to engage in collaborative

Cross Reference: See chapter 2 of this book on long-term relationships and chapter 3 on building partnerships

ethnography in action in classroom settings can be challenging because of time constraints, student reservations about the approach, grading practices, and many other problems. Here we show how committed faculty and researcher trainers have tackled these issues, giving concrete examples of classes and projects implemented at various levels in higher education.

CAVEATS

In this book, we cannot cover the vast array of literature in ethnographic mixed methods or inquiry in action in every important and relevant area. Though much of ethnography suggests or has implications for policy change, we limit our discussion of policy change as a form of action to chapter 8 where we include it as a form of dissemination. Instead, we want to illustrate some additional ways that researchers can systematically use their newly minted or advanced ethnographic skills to bring about direct transformational, structural, social, and substantive forms of improvements in the immediate circumstances that constrain people's lives. We also want to suggest ways of extending these skills to the many opportunities that arise as new sectors and fields of work emerge. Such new sectors require basic social science input to clarify the people, behavior, and contextual factors involved and to use the information to improve desired processes and outcomes.

1 ⬥▬●▬●▬●

DEFINING ETHNOGRAPHY
IN ACTION

INTRODUCTION

In this first chapter, we define what we mean by action and the research/practice/action interface. Next we turn to a discussion of the meaning of community and context and the role of individuals in social change. Culture and its role in ethnography in action, and in all forms of practice including education, health, and development interventions, is the focus of the chapter's next section. We then review the values that define the main types of action or practice in which ethnographers tend to be involved. We assert that all research is value based insofar as researchers make decisions—value judgments—about which research questions are important and why. Nowadays, because so many engaged and public scholarship movements have addressed social justice issues and because of the increasing importance of research to remedy disparities relevant to public needs and priorities, ***applied researchers often no longer have, or even want, the luxury of choosing their research questions for purely theoretical reasons or personal interest. What's important has been laid out already by the community or research partners.*** Nevertheless, when researchers choose to focus on a specific domain of social problems, either because they believe that it needs remediation or because they work for or with specific or communities, companies, or organizations who feel that the issue is

Key point

1

important, they end up making value-based choices. These choices have ethical and practical implications that must be considered in advance of, during, and after the work is completed and even as it continues and transforms into something else.

The ethnographer's organizational base, the funders, and the communities with which ethnographers work also shape and determine the direction of work. These entities have characteristics that may or may not be responsive to action-oriented ethnography. Usually this has to do with the political nature of the topic and the ways in which current resources are shared unequally among stakeholders, since remediation often means—or is perceived to mean—that those more privileged will lose some power or resources. However, it may also have to do with other competing organizational or institutional priorities. These viewpoints and voices count because ethnographic work is usually conducted in community settings, in community-based organizations, and with community people affected by issues that cannot simply be ignored and that research can address. Oftentimes, community voices lead the discussion, especially in Participatory Action Research approaches. This can mean that, at times, the values and viewpoints of ethnographers do not quite match with those of the various stakeholders in applied research projects. In such cases, consensus and agreements must be negotiated, resolved, or otherwise addressed.

Most applied ethnographic efforts require partnerships and collaboration. Without some form of relationship building, no ethnographer can figure out what changes are important in the setting or have success in making crucial changes relevant to it. We have described many ways of building research relationships throughout the *Toolkit*, **Key point** especially in Books 1, 2, and 3. However, *applied partnerships require an additional step beyond what we already have described, insofar as they involve joint efforts to accomplish a goal that is not the ethnographer's alone.* Researchers establish many types of relationships, including contractual agreements with companies that purchase ethnographic services, consultancies, and collaborations that involve shared resources. We are mainly concerned with the kinds of partnerships ethnographers establish with communities to bring about various short- and longer-term changes or transformations that address social, educational, or health problems, gaps, or disparities. Here there is more likely to be a real and equitable exchange of support and knowledge that both adds to a community's capacity to face a health/educational or other need or disparity, and at the same time matches the ethnographer's proclivities, talents, passions, skills, research track record, and research team.

DEFINING THE RESEARCH/PRACTICE INTERFACE

Our definition of ethnography in action is rooted in the history of action research and linked to current collaborative trends in health, the environment, epidemiology, and education as well as community-based participatory research for health and educational action research. Action research initially was defined by its founders in the 1930s and 1940s; these included Kurt Lewin in psychology and Sol Tax in anthropology (Tax 1958). In their terms, action research involves the continuous intersection of research questions and problem solving. Though these towering figures referred to different settings (Lewin, for example, referred to unions, and Tax to Native American tribes), *the elements of the approach remain the same:* **Key point** *linking research and action for social change affecting people who have experienced social, cultural, health, and other forms of injustice. Though neither of these seminal action researchers emphasized the importance of partnerships, both reflected in their writings on the strategic necessity of involving affected groups in determining research-based outcomes.*

The civil rights movement inspired the development of many important action research strands, summarized in several excellent publications and book chapters mainly by sociologists (Greenwood and Levin 1998; Kemmis and McTaggart 2005; Whyte 1991) and a more recent Canadian overview by Catherine Etmanski et al. (Etmanski, Hall, and Dawson 2014). An action research approach has been reiterated in the work of many social action researchers elsewhere—in Brazil though the work of Paulo Freire (Freire

1970; Freire 1981); in other parts of Latin America/Colombia through the work of Fals Borda and colleagues (Fals-Borda 1987; Fals Borda and Rahman 1991); and in the United States through the work of sociologist Philip Nyden (Nyden 2010; Nyden 2012), anthropologists Schensul and Schensul (Schensul 2010; Schensul and Schensul 1992; Schensul and Schensul 1978), psychologist Michelle Fine and colleagues (Stoudt, Brett, Fox, and Fine 2012; Torre, Cahill, and Fox 2015), and feminist sociologist Brydon-Miller (Brydon-Miller 1997; Brydon-Miller, Greenwood, and Maguire 2003). It is also framed in health studies as community-based participatory research (CBPR) in health, as described by Minkler, Wallerstein, Israel, and colleagues and many others who have created the canons for its use in public health (Israel et al. 2012; Minkler and Wallerstein 2010).

Referring to these distinctions, we differentiate between *ethnographic practice*, a term often used to mean the conduct of ethnographic research to increase understanding and produce ethnographic interpretations, and *ethnography in action*—the use of ethnography as a way of learning, knowing, synthesizing, and interpreting directed to the accomplishment of specific action-oriented tasks and desired outcomes. The term *ethnography in action* refers to the many different ways that ethnographers use theory, methodology, and research results together with their community partners—not just to suggest solutions for, but actually to solve economic, environmental, health, educational, and other social and cultural problems. By defining ethnography in action in this way, we directly confront and reject the dichotomization of research and practice in journals with titles such as "practicing anthropology" or "theory into practice" or those approaches that take the position that practice is valuable to scholars mainly because of what it contributes to theory. We appreciate the sentiments of Rylko-Bauer and colleagues, whose statement we have adapted from the original by substituting *ethnography* for *anthropology*. They argue that we should seek a

> meaningful convergence of methodologically sound, critical, reflexive, and engaged ethnography—a convergence that builds on and learns from the extensive

past experiences of putting ethnography to use—
[that] will free us up to focus on differences that
actually do matter in the real world: the compelling
divides that separate those who have from those who
do not, those who are honored from those who are
stigmatized, those wielding disproportionate power
from those with limited agency and voice, and those
who are central from those who are marginalized.
(Rylko-Bauer, Singer, and van Willigen 2006, 187)

The research/action link has been portrayed in different ways by different authors. Lewin, and more recently
Kemmis and McTaggart, view the link as ongoing, referring to action research *cycles* (in earlier work) and more
recently as the action research *spiral* (Kemmis and McTaggart 2005, Lewin 1946). Schensul has referred to the spiral of action/research/action (Schensul 1985). Schensul, Mosher, and others at the Institute for Community
Research (ICR) have created a diagram that consists of
interlocking cycles of design, data collection and analysis, action, and reflection (learning from action) over
time—all leading to a desired end goal. Figure 1.1 makes
it very clear that ethnography in action refers to the ongoing interaction of "research and action," leading toward a
social change or social-improvement goal.

Cross Reference: 🐰
See discussion of reflection in Book 6, chapter 9

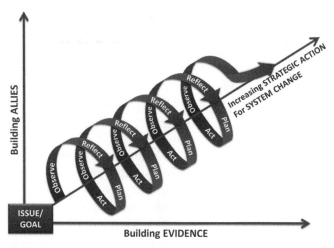

FIGURE 1.1   Participatory Action Research (PAR) spiral. Mosher and Schensul.

DEFINING CONTEXT AND COMMUNITY IN ETHNOGRAPHY IN ACTION

The key elements of ethnography in action (or Participatory Action Research or community-based participatory research) that will guide our discussion are that:

- It is participatory or collaborative.
- It is community or site based.
- It is directional, designed to lead toward social change goals and ends.
- It involves the interaction of research and action or practice.

The Idea of Community

One of the earlier hallmarks of ethnography is the notion of "community" as a place where people, issues, and problems are to be studied and addressed. "Community" in this sense refers to "place based" research and associated action; thus, community can include the locations where people live, work, go to school, interact and communicate, get treated for health problems, play, and get involved in political action.

Prior to World War II, the communities that ethnographers studied were perceived as isolated places, culturally distinct from the mainstream, and not much affected by outside factors. The image of the local rural, farm, or "peasant" community isolated from external dynamics has long since been put to rest. But the speed with which globalized flows and multinational corporations, alliances, and political machinations can affect local lifestyles, social and climatic conditions, and health problems produces complex and constantly changing environments in which new cultural elements, organizations, institutions, and relationships are created and co-created. This ongoing process of change, accommodation, synthesis, adjustment, creativity, and conflict raises many questions about defining boundaries for purposes of intervention and evaluation purposes, about who should or could participate in intervention efforts, about how to determine the acceptability of an innovation and how to think about its sustainability.

However, not all ethnographic work is "place based" in the traditional sense. In fact, most ethnographers think of "community" in multiple ways. For example, not all ethnographers work at the local level; many work in mediating organizations that link larger processes and policies to local situations and international nongovernmental organizations (NGOs) such as Family Health International, Path, the Futures Group, or the Academy for Educational Development, all large international nonprofits that obtain and manage subcontracts with smaller organizations or conduct evaluations of cross-national or other multisite programs. Regardless of vantage point, however, most ethnographers understand and refer to the idea of local "places," localities, or geo-social sites and spaces as the locations where people live and in which many do their work. These sites are connected to the rest of the world through people, communication flows, ideas, economies, and power dynamics. Communities may be thought of as politically bounded, community bounded, bounded by shared identities, bounded by the scope and membership of organizations, and as networks. The latter can mean as well that communities can exist at least partially in cyberspace as networks increasingly form on the Internet and through social media.

Politically Bounded Communities

Politically bounded communities are spaces defined and bounded by governmental regulations. Thus municipalities, cities, towns, and villages can be thought of as "communities." All have recognizable names and identifiable official boundaries and are sites where people live, interact with each other, shop, go to the doctor, go to school, or work and enjoy public parks and other entertainment resources. These "official" communities are likely to consist of many different "subcommunities" or groups of people defined by their place of origin, historical patterns of arrival and settlement or land use, their geography, their socioeconomic status, language, racialized identity, or work affiliations. Such officially designated communities also include policy-making bodies, service institutions of various sorts, community organizations, voluntary organizations, cultural groups with different forms of cultural expression, and so on. Researchers who decide to work in politically bounded entities must make decisions about with whom to work and for what reason, and identify the pros and cons of their alternative options.

Community-Bounded Spaces

The term *community-bounded* refers to social spaces whose boundaries are defined by residents alone or in conjunction with official boundaries.

EXAMPLE 1.1

BOUNDING AND NAMING HARTFORD, CONNECTICUT'S, NEIGHBORHOODS

The boundaries of the thirteen named neighborhoods of Hartford, Connecticut, were constructed in the 1960s by a group of city residents working in conjunction with city planners. This group came together to discuss geo-social differences across the city. They then divided into groups and walked each geographic subarea of the city, talking to residents about their perception of the boundaries of their areas. Using maps, each group specified the geographic boundaries of each of the areas and named them. The boundaries were checked with residents. Thirty years later, in the early 1990s, a participatory demographic study of these same neighborhoods brought together residents of each neighborhood to conduct their own surveys on issues that affected their neighborhood. In doing so, researchers and community organization representatives saw that the neighborhoods still retained social coherence and identity. Oral histories of each of the neighborhoods reinforced this observation (Schensul and Schensul 1992).

EXAMPLE 1.2

IDENTIFYING THE BOUNDARIES OF "SLUM AREA" SUBCOMMUNITIES

Approximately 52 percent of the city of Mumbai consists of designated slums. The term *slum* refers to land that is owned either by the Bombay Municipal Council (BMC) or by private corporations. People, primarily migrants from other areas of the country, have been allowed to settle in these designated and named slum areas but are subject to removal for land redevelopment purposes at any time. Slums may

be very large or quite small in population. For example, the famous Mumbai slum of Dharavi, the location for the film *Slumdog Millionaire*, was known as the largest slum area in south Asia, with more than one million inhabitants. Even the smaller designated-as-slum areas consist of subareas, whose boundaries are only sometimes officially designated for census purposes.

Mandala, a small slum of about 65,000 people in the western suburbs of Mumbai, consisted of named subcommunities, but the boundaries of these subcommunities were not very well defined. The designated subareas had names known to all the residents, but only two of the five within its boundaries were officially listed by name in census listings. Even the official boundaries of Mandala itself were not exactly clear. To obtain the boundaries of Mandala, researchers worked with local political parties and development officers to match maps and arrive at a general consensus regarding size of population and community boundaries. Within Mandala, researchers used social-mapping strategies and walked the community with key informants to come to consensus on the boundaries of the internal subcommunities. These named subcommunities were notably different in their migration history (people came from different parts of the country), language (Marathi or Hindi), time of residents' arrival (communities ranged from ten to thirty years in age) and religion (predominantly Hindu or Muslim).

Like communities that are politically bounded, the composition of resident-bounded neighborhoods and subareas may be quite complex. In some cases, residents may be divided in their views or may have histories of conflict and competition over scarce resources and territory. Some communities or groups within a community may have experienced discrimination, segregation, and political manipulation. For these reasons, in Example 1.1, researcher/facilitators were careful to make sure that all of the residential and organizational constituents in each neighborhood were involved in the bounding process, survey development and use, and compilation of the neighborhood's oral history, in order to avoid exacerbating any sociopolitical divisions that might have existed. In the second instance, researchers also made sure to get to know people in each of the areas, using a methodology that we describe for identifying and building partnerships in chapter 2 of this book.

Communities of Identity

Communities of identity are defined by Israel et al. as "entities in which people have membership," socially created dimensions of identity, created and re-created through social interaction (Israel et al. 2012, 8–9). They may be geo-socially located or dispersed but are linked via recognized common identity, shared cultural commonality, and social interconnectedness. Some communities of identity are easy to find; they may actually seek out researchers to help them address health-related or other injustices. One such community of identity is an asthma advocacy group whose members are knit together by their common concern with environmental factors contributing to high levels of asthma among their children. An LGTBQ group advocating the introduction of a new HIV pre-exposure prophylaxis in the form of a pill called Truvada is another community of identity. Other such groups include ethnic-specific neighborhood development corporations (e.g., La Casa de Puerto Rico, Hartford, Connecticut), racial/ethnic or age-specific advocacy groups (Urban League, Black Panthers, Grey Panthers, etc.), city commissions on adolescent health, anti-obesity alliances, pro-life groups, and advocates for school reform, labor unions, and the Grange, a locally centered national organization serving residents and farmers in agricultural areas. These groups are natural partners for ethnographers wanting to work in the specific topic areas they represent. They make strong claims, have a well-established sense of identity, often have a stable organizational structure, and have a clear sense of the changes that need to be made to serve their mission or goals.

Indian tribes and nations and other indigenous or aboriginal groups (such as the Taino Indians of the Caribbean, Native Hawaiians, First Nations and American Indian/Native Alaskans, Navajo people, Maori or Australian Aborigines, and Vedda people of Sri Lanka) constitute specific forms of community of identity based on a strong sense of ethnic identity and clear experience of marginalization. Such groups have experienced long-standing injustices and have a strong commitment to reestablishing their language, culture, indigenous health, and subsistence practices and to reconstructing their own educational programs.

This is made easier when they retain claim to their traditional lands and have some degree of independence from national governments within which they struggle to survive and flourish, but even groups that have lost their traditional homelands have similar commitments.

Communities of identity may also be geographically dispersed but closely knit through multiple interlocking networks. Tibetans emigrating from India to various locations in the United States remain connected through the Internet and through cultural and mobilization centers (e.g., Tibetan House in New York City and the Tibetan Nuns Project in Seattle, Washington) and activities in larger cities in the United States including New York, San Francisco, and Seattle. Nigerians in Connecticut are linked to friends and relatives from their cities and towns of origin in Germany, Canada, Australia, and many other places. Q'anjoba'l-speaking Maya from Guatemala who have immigrated to the United States similarly remain connected through native-language blogs and Internet connections, as well as through Pastoral Maya, an organization fostering indigenous Maya culture sponsored by the U.S. Catholic bishops. Local groups or "communities" can be thought of as points or nodes in systems of dynamic networks influenced by many factors in multiple ways. For example, working with Nigerians in central Connecticut means understanding the geo-social locations in which they live and how they are connected economically, socially, and politically to other such communities elsewhere in the world, to their country of origin, its history, and to the communities there from which they have emigrated in the recent past.

Organizations as Communities

Organizations are bounded by virtue of both geography and membership. Many ethnographers work in such boundary-defined institutions or groupings of institutions. Some of these institutions extend to communities in the surrounding area or beyond. Researchers who work with building residences, schools, school systems, libraries and library systems, government agencies, large businesses such as General Motors, or arms of the military in their respective countries often consider these entities and their extensions as communities. These ethnographers do "place-based" research and intervention along with those who work directly with communities of residents. As it is with some communities of residents, it may be challenging at times to define the boundaries of certain organizations since they may overlap with, or be embedded in, other organizations or constitute a dispersed network with members that emerge only under certain circumstances (for example, nations participating in G20 meetings). Special efforts need to be made to bound such systems or define them for both collaboration and study.

Communities as Networks

This concept reflects the idea that most individuals are networked together in multiple ways—gay young men who party and socialize together; midlevel professionals linked through leadership training programs as well as their work; art teachers who attend common workshops; and musicians who depend on personal networks for gigs. The concept of community as network is very important, both as a means of tracing relationships and of diffusing information and interventions through the connections among people. Organizations such as those providing HIV prevention services, specialized pediatric care, or afterschool programs for high school youth also may be networked for cross referrals, exchanges of information, and mutual supports. Though these networks may begin initially by being communities of identity, resources, and information, opportunities and risks flow from close, or proximate, to more distant "regions" of the network. Approaches to change that are network based have the potential to reach far beyond those originally exposed.

Drug use networks have been shown to extend to locations outside the geo-local community as a result of residential dislocation or the instability, imprisonment, or illness of key members. They also may be national or international, as in the case of drug-dealing networks, which can stretch across the world. A network approach to defining community is quite consistent with an ethnographic approach, since research and intervention practice often favor a focus on "whole" communities rather than components.

Some communities of identity are forged on the Internet through self-help groups (e.g., people suffering from vertigo, obesity, autism, or MS); substance-use information sites (Erowid, DanceSafe); groups of people who have, or whose relatives have, rare and poorly understood diseases; or mental health and other treatment programs. Other such communities may consist of people who engage in self-harm (anorexics, or teens who self-mutilate or cut themselves), engage in predatory sexual behaviors (pornography or pedophilia), or are self-designated "jihadists" and white supremacists. Though the many participants do not know each other personally, they are linked by their common concerns and attempts to promote or modify their own behavior and that of others. It is possible for savvy ethnographers to study these sites (Keim-Malpass, Steeves, and Kennedy 2014), by identifying themselves, obtaining admission, collecting data, entering into dialogue with participants, and working with those sites with positive or health-oriented goals to develop or extend their intervention approaches based on participant input and feedback.

The citizen science movement offers another networked approach to community. Citizen science is a movement to democratize science and engage the public through crowdsourcing. Crowdsourcing in research refers to an Internet-based open offer to participate in scientific endeavors through providing ideas, solving wicked or complex problems, and collecting data. Citizen-science efforts began with a publication in 1995 that laid out the components of the approach (Baron 2009). Now citizen science is widely used to engage lay researchers in projects that are, for the most part, generated by scientists and seeks involvement of nonscientists in the areas of environmental conservation, astronomy and weather observations, counts of birds and other wildlife, and general exploration of scientific phenomena. People from any walk of life can respond to websites that seek public involvement in scientific inquiry. Slowly, new forms of citizen science are emerging that are led by citizens rather than scientists and are environmental and social justice motivated. Crowdsourcing can also bring global networks together to focus on responding to critical events and crises such as earthquakes, tsunamis, and civil wars, and the decline or resurgence of endangered plant and animal species (Clarke 2013; Wiggins and Crowston 2011). And it can involve local communities in using multiple large data sets to understand what may be happening in terms of climate change, the built environment, local or regional disasters, or other factors (Brown and Allison 2014; Liu 2014; Swain et al. 2015).

One advantage of ethnography is that it provides methods and tools that researchers can use over time to engage with, become immersed in, and learn about the communities where they hope to work. In this section, we have tried to outline the variety of ways that ethnographers can consider, define, and engage with "local communities" on their own terms and on community terms. Next we discuss the central role of culture in shaping the context and content of ethnography-driven social change/intervention efforts.

THE CENTRALITY OF CULTURE AND SOCIAL ORGANIZATION IN COMMUNITY CHANGE EFFORTS

Definition: Community/institutional culture refers to community history, demographic change, cultural and linguistic dynamics, social and political organization, health and educational development, points of friction and conflict, and potential partners, all of which are necessary for furthering appropriate responses to intervention development and social change efforts

Ethnography is central to developing a clear understanding of **community/institutional culture**. The methods and tools of ethnography also provide the means by which researchers can access indigenous knowledge and discover local cultural, social, or historical "hooks" (symbols, rituals, roles) that could shape appropriate socio-culturally situated interventions (Agar 2005; Nastasi et al. 2014; Nastasi and Schensul 2005; Schensul 2009; Schensul et al. 2009; Simonds and Christopher 2013). These community or institutional cultural resources are best discovered in partnership with community knowledge bearers and actors, through ethnography as shared lived experience.

Communities, businesses, and other institutions also are commonly described and defined by their **culture**. Culture is socially constructed; the duration of any specific cultural form can vary from very long to very short. Cultural commonalities do not necessarily map onto ethnic or racial groups, or even to so-called communities of identity (such as African Americans in Boston working on reducing asthma in their communities or families of those with amytrophic lateral sclerosis (ALS) advocating for improved financing of research to discover much needed treatment approaches). And not all members of a community share common norms, conventions, or knowledge. Community experts in Philadelphia's largest Black neighborhood may know a great deal about community history and development, leading them to work against forces of gentrification, but not all residents have similar knowledge, nor do they wish to act accordingly. New teachers in a school may know more about collective processes of teaching science education, while longer-term teachers have embedded knowledge of school culture that impedes their initiating innovation.

Cultural consensus analysis, an approach developed by anthropologists Romney and Weller (Miller et al. 2004; Romney, Batchelder, and Weller 1987; Romney, Weller, and Batchelder 1986), offers a systematic way of identifying the degree of congruity of beliefs or knowledge about a topic in a community or group (e.g., beliefs about HIV and contagion, the medicinal properties of plants, efficacious methods for teaching science and math, or behavior surrounding childbirth) and identifying individuals or groups that vary in distance from the norm (i.e., those who know less, are less closely affiliated, or may even be a distinct group within that community setting). These differences, internal to any group, reflect important differences within a community that should be considered when working toward a community change goal, and could even be used as the basis for dialogue and resultant co-construction of new norms.

Community members are embedded in an often complex cultural environment at the same time that they are connected through relationships and meanings that come from shared history, the effects of media, current economic conditions and forces, and many other factors. They also are familiar with other change efforts and change agents. Community cultural knowledge, sometimes referred to as *tacit* or *everyday* knowledge, is derived from many sectors with differing opinions, knowledge bases, and values and can be transformed through co-constructive processes into new forms of cultural and social capital. These can be harnessed and utilized to transform social systems.

At the same time, communities are complex, characterized by economic, social, and political disparities, which shape cultural differences across class, special interest

Definition: Culture can be defined as conventional or shared beliefs, norms, and knowledge that are expressed in behavior or practices and products or artifacts

Cross Reference: See Book 4, chapter 3 on elicitation techniques for cultural domain analysis

groups, and communities of ethnic/racial or other identities. Thus, ethnographers and community members may find internal structural, social, and cultural conflicts, contradictions, and counter-influences that challenge the task of working toward a desired end. Webs of relationships with different degrees of overlap and connectivity can act as channels through which information, resources, power, novel ideas, and other elements, such as legal and illegal products and disease, are exchanged. Power, influence, and authority differences are typical of these networks and play an important role in affecting intervention success. Understanding the culture of a community setting calls for learning how these networks are structured and how they function to further or prevent specific change efforts.

Learning about the culture of institutions embedded within communities (such as service or voluntary organizations) and organizations is also important in locating sources of power and influence. As British anthropologist Holmes notes, "Not only hospitals, but universities, scientific laboratories, global health charities, and government agencies all have their own cultures, although they might seem less obviously cultural than the kinds of cultures anthropologists traditionally study" (Holmes 2014, 1609). Understanding what these cultures are and how they work can help to avoid reinforcing class or other divisions and promote the creation of alliances to overcome long-standing barriers to change.

In sum, culture is both cognitive (in the mind, or patterns *for* behavior) and behavioral (expressed in actions taken, or patterns *of* behavior) (Jacobs 1987). It is shared, that is understood, but not equally or in the same way, by all members in a bounded community or other setting. Ethnic/racial and other communities of designated or self-designated identity may share some but not all of the cultural norms within a particular group; not all Native Americans participate in pow-wow celebrations, and not all African Americans celebrate the holiday Kwanzaa. Thus, cultural congruity cannot be assumed for any group but must be verified through ethnographic research and cultural consensus analysis. Culture also is heavily influenced by structural factors (economic constraints, political representation, institutional norms and rules, media impact, immigration forces, and policies). Many Navajos now alter the timing of the *kinaalda,* or coming-of-age, ceremonies for young women to accommodate public school schedules. New cultural norms and behaviors are co-constructed by subgroups within, or linked to, the larger group, and it is this process that results in "culture change"—a new understanding of the circumstances that communities want to change and new processes (behaviors) for bringing about desired changes.

DEFINING VALUES IN ACTION

Ethnography directs us to an "emic" approach, meaning that ethnographers hold foremost in their consciousness the requirement that they keep an open mind and learn from others about their values, beliefs, perspectives, and ways of doing things. Ethnographers deduce indigenous "theories" of culture from these modes of learning through immersion in a cultural experience. ***The emic approach, however, assumes neither cultural relativism, nor cultural absolutism. It implies giving value to understanding other perspectives, but gives little guidance to researchers as to when either their own or others' values can or should be questioned.*** Ethnographers have to learn to interrogate their own values and the values of others—a practice which is important in all ethnographic endeavors, as we note in Book 6 of the *Ethnographer's Toolkit* and is especially important in applications of ethnography. Prior to World War II, many applied ethnographers worked in European or American colonial administrations or in agencies of the U.S. government which had authority over indigenous or local populations. Many of these researchers questioned the legitimacy of such authority (Rylko-Bauer, Singer, and van Willigen 2006), but most of the questioners remained in government employment, despite their misgivings about the efficacy and even morality of the policies they promulgated and had to enforce. Now, western governments have changed their administrative policies to some degree, and many anthropologists work within governmental offices to forge policies that protect local populations from envi-

Key point

Cross Reference:
See Book 2, chapter 2, on positionality; and Book 6, chapter 8, on self-reflection

ronmental threats, poverty, dislocation, and the possibility of disease and infection. Many others, however, work in social-justice and social-change environments outside of governmental agencies and university departments, in schools, museums, research and development agencies, and other alternative settings. Regardless of the setting, assessing personal values remains important for all applied work.

In the past decade, ethnographers have faced a number of controversial issues that call for careful searching of personal values and convictions as well as examining the effects of their actions on other professionals in the same field and the disciplines with which they are connected. One such issue is the involvement of social scientists, including anthropologists, in the Human Terrain System Project (HTS).

EXAMPLE 1.3

THE HUMAN TERRAIN SYSTEM PROJECT

The Human Terrain System Project is a program of the United States Army, Training and Doctrine Command (TRADOC) program. It employs personnel from social sciences to "provide military commanders and staff with an understanding of the local population (i.e., the 'human terrain') in the regions in which they are deployed." The objectives have been to use social sciences to provide cultural training, sociocultural studies to improve military understanding of local cultures and settings, and psychological, cultural, and other "human terrain" advisors to the military and lecturers at military institutions. Some social scientists "embedded" with combat troops were to be armed, presumably for self-protection.

Though there was considerable discussion in anthropology as to whether anthropologists should support any military action at all, the primary problematic issue in the case of the Human Terrain System Project was one of protecting the people being studied. American and other anthropologists working in war zones or potentially contested areas with local populations had established relationships of trust over long periods of time. Their research and applied work with these communities depended on their transparency and known relationships with NGOs and government entities that permitted their involvement in the country. Working for the American military, critics believed, would jeopardize the work of the anthropologists and might well place them in a position of harming rather than supporting the communities which had shared their intellectual and cultural resources with them. It also could reveal the identity of people with whom anthropologists worked and endanger them if they were individuals or groups who the military, insurgents, or government forces felt were enemies. Critics claimed that anthropologists or other social scientists who had firm commitments to preserving confidentiality, trust, and minimization of harm for their informants might be in a position to violate the ethical principles of the discipline. Further, local populations, being uncertain of the stance of social scientists approaching them, might refuse to share information. Should an untoward event happen, such as the death of many villagers, the entire discipline might be blamed, even if such tragedies actually had nothing to do with the anthropologist involved (González 2008).

In response, a subcommittee of the American Anthropological Association Executive Board prepared and delivered a statement on the Human Terrain System Project on October 31, 2007. That statement, posted on the AAA website, takes an organizational position against social science involvement in the HTS, especially for anthropologists. The statement is reproduced in the textbox (http://www.aaanet .org/about/Policies/statements/Human-Terrain-System-Statement.cfm).

The U.S. military's HTS project places anthropologists, as contractors with the U.S. military, in settings of war, for the purpose of collecting cultural and social data for use by the U.S. military. The ethical concerns raised by these activities include the following:

1. As military contractors working in settings of war, HTS anthropologists work in situations where it will not always be possible for them to distinguish themselves from military personnel and identify themselves as anthropologists. This places a significant constraint on their ability to fulfill their ethical responsibility as anthropologists to disclose who they are and what they are doing.
2. HTS anthropologists are charged with responsibility for negotiating relations among a number of groups, including both local populations and the U.S. military units that employ them and in which they are embedded. Consequently, HTS anthropologists may have responsibilities to their U.S. military units in war zones that conflict with their obligations to the persons they study or consult, specifically the obligation, stipulated in the AAA Code of Ethics, to do no harm to those they study (section III, A, 1).
3. HTS anthropologists work in a war zone under conditions that make it difficult for those they communicate with to give "informed consent" without coercion, or for this consent to be taken at face value or freely refused. As a result, "voluntary informed consent" (as stipulated by the AAA Code of Ethics, section III, A, 4) is compromised.

4. As members of HTS teams, anthropologists provide information and counsel to U.S. military field commanders. This poses a risk that information provided by HTS anthropologists could be used to make decisions about identifying and selecting specific populations as targets of U.S. military operations either in the short or long term. Any such use of fieldwork-derived information would violate the stipulations in the AAA Code of Ethics that those studied not be harmed (section III A, 1).

In addition to these four points about the activities of anthropologists working in the HTS project itself, the Executive Board has this additional concern:

5. Because HTS identifies anthropology and anthropologists with U.S. military operations, this identification—given the existing range of globally dispersed understandings of U.S. militarism—may create serious difficulties for, including grave risks to the personal safety of, many non-HTS anthropologists and the people they study.

Conclusion

In light of these points, the Executive Board of the American Anthropological Association concludes (i) that the HTS program creates conditions which are likely to place anthropologists in positions in which their work will be in violation of the AAA Code of Ethics and (ii) that its use of anthropologists poses a danger to both other anthropologists and persons other anthropologists study.

Thus the Executive Board expresses its disapproval of the HTS program.

In the context of a war that is widely recognized as a denial of human rights and based on faulty intelligence and undemocratic principles, the Executive Board sees the HTS project as a problematic application of anthropological expertise, most specifically on ethical grounds. We have grave concerns about the involvement of anthropological knowledge and skill in the HTS project. The Executive Board views the HTS project as an unacceptable application of anthropological expertise.

The Executive Board affirms that anthropology can and in fact is obliged to help improve U.S. government policies through the widest possible circulation of anthropological understanding in the public sphere, so as to contribute to a transparent and informed development and implementation of U.S. policy by robustly democratic processes of fact-finding, debate, dialogue, and deliberation. It is in this way, the Executive Board affirms, that anthropology can legitimately and effectively help guide U.S. policy to serve the humane causes of global peace and social justice.

Nonetheless, many social scientists were not completely opposed to working on a variety of tasks and assignments with the U.S. or other militaries. Some social science researchers, including Montgomery McFate and Andrea Jackson, argued in favor of involvement. They claimed that this offered an opportunity for applied anthropologists to be gainfully employed while serving the country, saving soldiers from potentially explosive cross-cultural misunderstandings and helping to avoid unnecessary violence and death because of them. In an often cited paper, they argued for the establishment of a Pentagon office of operational cultural knowledge staffed by social scientists with strong connections to services and soldiers (McFate and Jackson 2005, 20).

Anthropologists and other social scientists remain free to make their own decisions as to how and where and in what ways they preferred to work with the military and whether they wished to work on any aspect of the HTS project. Both of us were invited to train military personnel in the use of ethnographic methods, and, despite initial ambivalence, we decided to avoid doing so because we could not be sure (nor could we ever be sure under any circumstances) how the knowledge might be used.

Working in Communities Experiencing Injustices

Ethnographers often find themselves in positions where their research is conducted with, and has implications for, communities or groups experiencing inequitable treatment. From this standpoint, researchers will want to assess their own stance in relation to such communities. What position do they take when working with a community that is experiencing dislocation and gentrification or one in which people of color experience systematic discrimination and abuse, like Ferguson, Missouri, and Baltimore, Maryland, or a city like Detroit or New Orleans, where many neighborhoods remain in extreme poverty as a result of economic decline or environmental disasters? What stance should researchers take when working with Mexican, Salvadoran, Middle Eastern, or other immigrant communities in the United States whose residents fled their countries of origin to escape poverty, death threats, and persecution? Ethnographers, regardless of whether they are "insiders" (from the community) or "outsiders" (not from the community) or both, must challenge themselves to determine what motivations they have for working with such communities and what they hope to accomplish. The ability of researchers to address issues arising from any of these or other similar challenges rests on how motivated they are to change inequitable conditions, how able they are to listen to, and learn from the perspectives of, those living in the situation, and it rests on the skills and experiences of the researchers and their community partners to bring research and resources to bear on the problem. Researchers should thus ask themselves the following questions:

- What do I hope to achieve for myself and with the group or community?
- What is my motivation for working with this group or community?
- What can I do if my goals and objectives do not coincide with those of the group or community with which I am collaborating, and whose situation we hope can change through our joint work? What tools do I have available to help us negotiate toward a common set of goals, objectives, methods, benchmarks/achievements, and end results? How can these tools add to what the community or group already is mobilizing to bring about change that benefits them?
- What do I do if the tools I have or the community has are not useful? Are there other methods or networks of resources that I can bring to bear on the situation?
- What people or groups ultimately are responsible for what needs to be done in this situation?
- What is the potential for sustainability if I embark with my partners on this venture?

Working for Employers Whose Actions May Undercut an Ethnographer's Efforts

Ethnographers also may find themselves working in situations in which their employer or funder's actions may have direct or indirect negative implications for others. Typical situations include:

a. Involvement in neighborhood development for lower income residents with a housing advocacy group while a university—even the university in which the researcher is working or teaching—is purchasing property in the same neighborhood to gentrify housing for its faculty, actions that squeeze out poorer local residents.

b. Involvement in HIV treatment adherence research with people living with HIV (PLWA) in a neighborhood near a large hospital for which the researcher is working, while that hospital's inpatient facility is known to provide inadequate care for PLWA suffering from opportunistic infections.

c. Performing research for intervention on breast feeding program among Latinos in the United States with funding from a company profiting from the distribution of bottled formula to hospitals in low- and middle-income countries.

d. Working with teachers to conduct empowerment-oriented pedagogical approaches in school systems that systematically discriminate against students of color by suspending them from school without recourse, in the case of fights or altercations.

Each of these common situations involves an obvious inherent contradiction. Resolving the contradiction does not mean rejecting the funding source or leaving an institution with unjust or harmful policies in order to find another base from which to do research. It does involve the following:

■ Assessing the relative contextual risks and benefits of moving toward the desired goal

- Realistically appraising the actual possibility of success
- Evaluating the potential gains and losses to the people affected by the issue if the proposed strategies fail
- Evaluating the potential personal and professional losses to the ethnographer if he or she pursues the desired goal, and it fails
- Considering the ability of the funder or institution to stop, undermine, or support the effort
- Evaluating the relative power and influence, formal or informal, of the researcher both in the institution and beyond
- Assessing the capacity of the researcher and partners to negotiate consensus and success
- Identifying the personal characteristics of all parties (ethnicity, race, age, residence, degree, etc.) that make negotiation toward success more likely

Working in Complex Communities with Multiple Constituencies

Any community or group, even one that is considered a community of "identity," includes among its members considerable diversity of values and opinions which must be understood before attempting to build collaborations or plan for action. Regardless of whether they are from a study community or are entering it for the first time, researchers must figure out how to move beyond their current level of knowledge or skill so as to enhance their ability to implement change goals. To do this, we suggest the following steps:

- Engage with many "gatekeepers" and key informants so as to learn about and understand contemporary community dynamics.
- Read local newspapers diligently for local news, controversies, decision makers, and neighborhood concerns.
- Reach out to and engage with sectors of the community with which researchers are not familiar and which might be difficult to reach (for example, transactional sex workers, youth not in school; homeless

Cross Reference:
See Books 1, 2, and 3 for discussions of research with gatekeepers and key informants

people; CEOs of local businesses that have influence over community political decision making; voluntary organizations advocating community rights that do not appreciate or want the help of "outsiders."

- Identify together with community residents the "assets," experiences, "felt needs," concerns, and cultural bases of local communities or organizations and patients/service seekers.
- Work with and support those groups whose values and goals are widely representative.
- Work with those groups to negotiate with or confront differences of opinion within the community, and if possible, help to resolve them.

Working in Teams

Of necessity, ethnography in practice is usually conducted in teams. Multiple insights and skills are needed to resolve pressing issues. Thus, members of a research team engaging in ethnography in action may come from different backgrounds, including some who live in the location in which the project is to take place. Those local participants also may be experiencing, or being affected directly, by the problem to be solved. They may be trained or lay researchers; they may be highly visible in the study community. They may be vulnerable to job loss, community criticism, conflicting religious principles, or other factors that shape their values. All of these value variations and stances can create challenges within the team and in reference to the project and must be considered and negotiated in an applied ethnographic situation.

EXAMPLE 1.4

WHEN A PROGRAM DIRECTOR'S VALUES DID NOT COINCIDE WITH THOSE OF THE PROGRAM TEAM

A group of community women requested that the Institute for Community Research work with them to create a drug abuse prevention program for young teenage girls and their mothers or other caregivers. The Center for Substance Abuse funded a five-year prevention program to focus on preventing drug use by improving communication between girls and their mothers. The design called for parallel action research programs in which girls and their mothers met separately to identify and reflect on risks and opportunities in their lives and the quality of their mutual communication. The approach was based on an earlier PAR program for women in which participants engaged in self-reflection, power analysis, identification of an issue, research, and action together (Schensul, Berg, and Williamson 2008) and an earlier PAR program for teens that included prevention education and a PAR project (Schensul 1998). The project also obtained an additional AIDS-prevention supplement focused on reducing sex risk. Working with the program required talking about the sensitive issues of drug exposure, drug use, boyfriends, and sex. The project also included the possibility of discussing sexual identity.

The program hired a director who was well known in the community, had an education background, had worked with ICR in the past, and was an emerging artist, an important qualification for a program that planned to use a variety of research and art forms to explore identity and promote communication and community action. As the team was building the curriculum, which included the AIDS-prevention supplement, it became clear that the director was not comfortable with including a module on sexuality and HIV protection unless it focused only on abstinence. From our prior work with young teens, we were fairly sure that at least some of them were likely to have boyfriends and to have been involved at least occasionally in some form of penetrative sex. We also know that evaluations of abstinence-only programs showed clearly that they were unsuccessful, especially once teens were already sexually active. Nonetheless, the director did not believe that girls of thirteen to sixteen should be sexually active and thought that the best way to deal with it was to deny that any sex was taking place and to support an abstinence-only policy. The rest of the research team supported the idea of offering abstinence as an option while, at the same time, addressing personal protection and relational intimacy. Though she understood the team's stance, this position was not one that the director could accept so she resigned from the program and found other ways of working with teens. She did remain connected to ICR in other ways for some time. Thus, this difference in values had a happy ending (Nastasi and Berg 1999).

Defining values is a continuous process that engages researchers and their collaborators on an ongoing basis throughout the life of a project. Values permeate the initiation of a partnership; its continuation through the conduct of data collection, data analysis, and interpretation; and its engagement in using the data in multiple ways to bring about any form of change. At each stage in the life of the project, and often in between, value differences may emerge and will require negotiation. Often—in fact, usually—such value conflicts are resolvable, but sometimes they are not. Researchers and constituencies in a partnership project should ask themselves the following questions about these considerations at the start of a project.

- What is this partnership trying to accomplish? Do I agree with it? Do I agree with all of its implications?
- What is my personal/professional interest in this partnership and project?
- Given the partners, the stakeholders, the resources and the larger context, do I think there is a reasonable possibility of accomplishing the partnership goals? My goals?
- How do my own values and goals map onto those of others in the alliance, group, or consortium?
- If there are apparent conflicts from the outset, how serious are they?
- Am I convinced that all parties that are part of the project will be heard and will have an equal place at the table?
- Is the structure of the project equitable?
- Do I trust the leader or facilitator? And if I am to be the leader, do I have the skills, motivation, and time to do the work?
- What is the history of such efforts in the past?
- If the responses to the above are negative now, or will be in the future, will I be able to leave the project without negative repercussions?

It is never the case that all values, goals, and desired outcomes are apparent and completely transparent from the outset. It sometimes requires months and even years for significant differences in beliefs, values, goals, and desired changes to emerge. Sometimes the signs of difference and conflict are visible initially, but are ignored. At other times, they evolve, or emerge as the context changes. Thus, constant monitoring is required.

EXAMPLE 1.5

EMERGENT DIFFERENCES OF OPINION IN PROCESSES AND DESIRED OUTCOMES WHEN
THE CONTEXT CHANGES

In 2008, the Institute for Community Research embarked on a program, funded by
a national foundation, to engage community residents in an action research project.
The foundation wanted community residents to use a large bank of secondary data
as part of their theory of development. ICR argued that without actually collecting
important data themselves, community residents would not know how to approach
or to query the data. Participatory Action Research (PAR) was chosen as the way
to form a group to take on, study, and act on a significant issue in a ten-year community development model focusing on building social capital. Ten years of foundation funding offered good potential for knowledge co-construction, leadership
development, and informed use of the secondary databases for which the foundation was providing funding to improve ease of access. Three cycles of PAR teams
worked on issues of importance to African American and Puerto Rican families in
the two target neighborhoods of Hartford. Over time, leadership began to emerge
and to speak to politicians, educators, and others about their concerns, based on
their newly acquired knowledge.

In the fourth year of the program, the foundation decided to hand over its
declining resources to a cross-city professional group representing the neighborhoods. At the same time, the national foundation began to question whether the
PAR approach was really producing "leaders." It became apparent that the local
PAR groups, the cross-city project committee, and the national foundation each
had a different definition of the concept of "leadership." Eventually, the local PAR
groups' notion of leadership prevailed, given the transfer of funds from the foundation to the local project committee. The definition of leadership espoused by
the city project committee was based on ability to speak in public, but the extent
to which the speaker could speak from both acquired knowledge and experience
was not important. As the context changed, the purpose of the project shifted
from improving the ability of residents to obtain information on a topic *in order
to be able to speak with authority*, to simple public-speaking ability. Further, the
definition of leadership shifted from engaging in informed criticism to providing
public endorsements. Finally, a program designed to develop authentic neighborhood leaders with a strong sense of identity, ties to the neighborhood, and a good
knowledge base was defunded.

Were there warning signs in this case? There were several. First the foundation
was uncertain about whether and when to turn funding over to local interests. Second, initial lack of clarity existed as to whether all twenty-two cities in the program
would continue through the decade. And third, ICR had had prior negative outcome
experiences in organizing community advocates through PAR in a city dominated

by downtown and business interests. Nevertheless, there was enough ambiguity to support ICR participation, despite ongoing concerns about whether PAR as the leadership development approach would be challenged or allowed to evolve.

In this example, there was sufficient congruency of values purpose and vision at the outset for ICR to agree to participate in the program. After considerable advocacy and explanation of what was essentially a simple idea — people who develop and implement projects that require numerical data are much more likely to understand and use the numerical data of others—the national foundation agreed. As long as the national foundation protected the model of PAR for leadership development in community settings, the effort could survive. However, once a decision was made to turn resources over to local stakeholders who had other agendas, the context changed and the program intent was undermined. It ended suddenly when the foundation decided to terminate funding in the fifth year.

 **EXAMPLE 1.6**

TERMINATING AN ETHNOGRAPHY IN ACTION PROJECT IN A SCHOOL DISTRICT WHEN THE SUPERINTENDENT REPUDIATED THE PROJECT'S PHILOSOPHY

The Navajo superintendent of the Pinnacle school district, located in the Navajo Nation, invited an anthropologist knowledgeable about school reform initiatives to consult with and help the school district to develop a curriculum that would boost the achievement of the district's students. As a way to improve student attendance and interest in school, the anthropologist suggested developing a set of instructional methods and curricular content that reflected Navajo ways of teaching and learning, as well as emphasizing Navajo cultural content and language. The superintendent was enthusiastic about this approach, so the anthropologist assembled teams of teachers and, with the help of the high school librarian, began to develop the needed materials. She also linked the teacher teams up with other anthropologists and scholars who had conducted similar interventions. The anthropologist also initiated a program to increase the number of Native American teachers in the district by helping teacher aides who had had some college actually obtain a college degree and teacher licensure, and by creating a Future Teachers Club for local high school students. One of the anthropologist's graduate students was an experienced career counselor who had worked in the admissions office of her university; this graduate

student evaluated the transcripts of all interested teacher aides in the district, help-ing them to identify the most expeditious way to turn what often was a hodge-podge of unrelated courses, taken simply because they were offered near to Pinnacle, into coherent degree plans leading to graduation, certification, and ultimately, to teach-ing jobs with the Pinnacle district. The graduate student also recruited a teacher sponsor for the Future Teachers Club and began recruiting club members. The project continued for four years and was beginning to have some success in build-ing interesting Navajo content into the curriculum and rendering both interactions between teachers and students and instructional methods more culturally compat-ible. A Navajo-English dual-language program also was initiated in the elementary school. One day in the middle of the winter semester, the anthropologist was called by the superintendent, who informed her that he had had a change of heart about culturally relevant curricula; rather, he felt that the district should pursue the same curriculum and use the same instructional methods as white schools did. "Indian kids have to pass those state tests, so they need to learn what white kids know." The superintendent had heard of a core curriculum program in Ohio called "The Mod-ern Red Schoolhouse" (Kilgore 2010), which he wanted to adopt entirely, abandon-ing all the prior efforts toward culturally relevant and compatible schooling.

Modern Red Schoolhouse (www.mrsh.org) is a comprehensive school reform project developed in 1992 by the Hudson Institute, a conservative public policy organization in Indianapolis. It was one of eleven such projects funded by the New American Schools project, a public/private initiate, which the first Bush administra-tion advocated as a way to overhaul American public education. That and Eurocen-tric core curriculum ideas fostered by then-Secretary of Education William Ben-nett constituted the ideas that the superintendent wanted to implement in Pinnacle (Datnow, Hubbard, and Mehan 2002; Kilgore 2010).

By choosing this program, he would replace the existing culturally embedded program and curriculum with a program that devalued Indian culture and encour-aged an assimilationist approach. Unable to persuade the superintendent that high achievement and test scores were compatible with support of Native American knowledge and practices, the anthropologist told the superintendent that she could not help him implement the Modern Red Schoolhouse because she did not believe in its approach to educational reform or in the philosophies its supporters espoused. And she left the project.

EXAMPLE 1.7

BREAKING A CONTRACT BECAUSE OF ASSESSED LACK OF COMPATIBILITY WITH INTERVENTION GOALS AND OBJECTIVES

The Institute for Community Research forged a contractual relationship with an organization involved in housing development and family supports. The contract

was to implement a local arm of a program for birth mothers, step-, pseudo-, or fictive mothers, and their daughters, by providing it with space, equipment, and staff. The goal was to improve relationships between mothers and daughters, to keep girls from running away, and to make sure they had support around sensitive issues such as sex, pregnancy, STI exposure, and HIV. ICR had worked with the organization in prior years and had a compatible relationship with its staff. Once the program was funded, ICR initiated a dialogue to begin the program by hiring staff and defining space. It became clear fairly quickly that the principles and agreements that were mutually decided upon when the project was in the development stages did not reflect reality on the ground. The organization's priority was housing and neighborhood development, not improving the relationships among family members, and the local meeting space that was to have been available no longer existed. Consequently, with help from board members on both sides, the organizations agreed to break the contract for collaborative work, without ending their overall relationship.

ORGANIZATIONAL BASES AND TRAINING FOR ETHNOGRAPHY IN ACTION

Ethnography in practice can be implemented from many different organizational bases and with different degrees of experiences. Organizational bases include university academic departments and centers, national and international nongovernmental organizations, and independent research centers as well as government offices. They also can include other locations where anthropologists or those with training in anthropology use their ethnographic experience to help them manage their work better. Experience and training do make a difference. People who have had undergraduate degree training in anthropology will use their experiences in ways that are quite different from those who have had no such training, and the latter will differ markedly from those with advanced training in methods, field experiences, project development, and thesis presentations. Each level of formal training confers specific skills and advantage in terms of "making a difference."

THE IMPORTANCE OF COLLABORATIONS AND PARTNERSHIPS

Throughout this chapter and elsewhere in the *Toolkit*, we have emphasized the importance of partnerships in ensuring that ethnography can be conducted well. We have described in detail why the multiple skills, resources, and networks subsumed in partnerships are central to using ethnography to improve the lives of people in communities or beyond. Here we describe the formation of collaborations that are focused on research and action to combat a specific (or a general) social ill. Table 1.1 describes different types of research partnerships.

In ethnography in action, a research partnership is one that includes ethnographers, other researchers, community or citizen researchers, and others, who act on the belief that research can improve new or ongoing efforts to solve a problem, eliminate structural inequities, build new and alternative institutions, and otherwise contribute to social-change efforts. These issues are complex, embedded in the structure of the communities themselves and in the broader political and social context within which communities are always situated. No researcher can address them alone; communities include within their boundaries knowledge, experience, assets, and resources that can be drawn upon to do better research and to create, build or rebuild, and advocate for specific organizations, problem solutions, and goals. Institutions external to bounded communities should not be ignored—they too may also offer resources and potential solutions. Finally, complex problems call for transdisciplinary research—research that combines and integrates the perspectives and methodology of different disciplines into new and innovative approaches. And they call for intersectoral action—the pooled capacities and resources of institutions working in the fields of education, health, economic and community development, agriculture, culture and tourism, environmental issues, architecture, and the built environment. Some combination of all may be required to address intransigent issues such as diabetes, water quality in urban areas, or elevated school dropout rates.

TABLE 1.1 Dimensions of difference in types of research partnerships

Dimensions of Difference in Types of Research Partnerships	Ethnographic Research Teams	Interdisciplinary Research Teams	Action/Applied Research Teams
Purpose/Goals	To conduct team ethnography in local or multiple sites simultaneously.	To conduct interdisciplinary research with ethnography as one element in the study.	To conduct ethnographic research with community partners to solve pressing community problems.
Membership	—Ethnographers (may also include students).	—Ethnographers; —researchers from other different social science research traditions.	—Ethnographers; —other researchers; —non-researchers committed to social change based on research knowledge.
Types of Data Collected	—Text data from in-depth and semistructured interviews; —elicitation data; —mapping and network data; —ethnographic survey data; —audiovisual data.	—Text data; —elicitation data; —mapping and network data; —audiovisual data; —survey data (ethnographic and non-ethnographic); —psychological, sociometric, epidemiologic data; —biological data (laboratory assays), etc.	Participatory: —text data; —elicitation data; —mapping and network data; —service use data; —survey data; —process evaluation data; —outcome data; —cost/benefit data.
Intervention?	Not usually	Not usually but may include a theory-guided intervention, often derived from a non-ethnographically informed discipline.	Always some form of intervention at multiple levels. May include: —formative or exploratory research; —problem identification; —intervention/ action —reflection/ evaluation.

(continued)

TABLE 1.1 *Continued*

Dimensions of Difference in Types of Research Partnerships	Ethnographic Research Teams	Interdisciplinary Research Teams	Action/Applied Research Teams
Challenges	—Overcoming the individualism of traditional ethnographic research; —developing comparable cross-site coding categories; —sharing information; —maintaining confidentiality; —maintaining continuing information exchange across project sites and staff; —deciding on protocols for shared authorship.	—Integrating ethnographic and other approaches to research; —triangulating ethnographic and quantitative data; —ensuring equity of ethnographic data and results in informing the study; —developing an interdisciplinary study team language; —maintaining communication across disciplines and project components.	—Ensuring equal engagement of all relevant partners; —avoiding domination of research over practice; —negotiating a common action research agenda in the face of multiple interests; —maintaining partner participation; —managing conflicts among partners; —ensuring partner participation in all aspects of the research; —making sure that research results influence action. On a continuous basis.
Reasons for Choice	—Desire for cross-site problem exploration; —desire for research partners; —enjoy dialogue and exchange; —need stimulation to publish.	—Enjoy interdisciplinary thinking; —see social problems as interdisciplinary; —have interdisciplinary background; —believe that different approaches to research are complementary.	—Desire to use research for social change; —believe that research and action are improved with community and stakeholder involvement/ transformational purposes; —commitment to community or organizational improvement and equity;

(continued)

TABLE 1.1 *Continued*

Dimensions of Difference in Types of Research Partnerships	Ethnographic Research Teams	Interdisciplinary Research Teams	Action/Applied Research Teams
			—desire to build and test theory in action; —believe non-researchers can learn to conduct and use research for their own benefit; —like challenge of negotiating appropriate research tools for the setting.

SUMMARY

In this overview of Book 7, we have covered several main issues that apply to programs and projects using ethnography in action. We have provided definitions for the research practice interface, arguing that research and practice are not separate realms of activity but are intertwined in different ways and may even take place simultaneously. We have suggested that most ethnography takes place in local communities and have broadly defined communities to include local settings; community-based institutions such as schools, residential buildings, and clinics; and networks of people, both local and global, including Internet communities. We have, however, emphasized that most ethnography takes place through the collection of data obtained directly from persons in community settings, and is focused on their views and interpretations. We have raised the question of values in ethnography in practice, emphasizing that researchers should be aware of their motivations in entering into any social-change process or program, as well as the skills and abilities they bring to it. Further, we've raised the question of what to do when values—those of the researcher and the community of concern or those within the project team—clash and suggested ways of addressing values-based conflicts. Finally, we have pointed out why partnerships of different kinds are essential to the enterprise of ethnography in action, a topic we come back to in chapter 3. In the next chapter we will discuss in greater detail different approaches to ethnography in action in community settings. Chapter 2 describes a number of long-term development efforts that include many separate research-in-action projects, as well as several shorter examples. It sets the stage for describing the building blocks for conducting ethnography in action in the rest of the book.

2

USING ETHNOGRAPHY IN ACTION TO CHANGE SYSTEMS

INTRODUCTION

Ethnography in action involves initiating long-term and, ideally, sustainable interventions together with people in local communities. In this chapter, we place in context the steps that we recommend in the development of ethnography in action—participatory and collaborative research with communities for social change—by providing readers with examples of different longer- and shorter-term approaches to action research change strategies and approaches guided by and embedded in ethnography that resulted in changes at the individual, group, and community level. First we introduce some longer-term community health and educational development efforts in the United States and elsewhere so that readers can see how different ethnographic research approaches and action/practice interfaced and evolved over time. Then we turn to some examples of short-term projects that may be more realistic to operationalize for researchers and researchers in training who want to be involved in transformative action but are not in a position to make long-term commitments to a single community, organization, or other site. Our goal in the chapter is to show how prolonged and/or dedicated commitment in a local (or networked) field setting provides the history, the context, and the relationships out of which can grow a number of interrelated research and action efforts. We show how theory development and mixed methods ethnography intersect at different points with people, places, partnerships, and situations to initiate, continue, sustain, and expand research and action processes.

To begin, we return to the concept of community discussed in chapter 1. Many social scientists are now interested in "community level" interventions. At different times, researchers in different fields have come to the recognition that tackling social, health, environmental, and educational problems often requires a "whole community approach." Anthropology, sociology, cultural geography, community psychology, social work, education, nursing, and public health are among those fields that locate their work in the context of local communities. As we said in chapter 1, the terms *community based* and *community-based participatory research* refer to investigations and subsequent actions that arise from communities and are carried out in local settings and with local partners.

Grounded Communities

 Key point

By community, we mean a bounded socio-geographic unit that may be defined by official bodies such as municipalities, by censuses, or by the residents or occupants themselves. These types of communities, which are elsewhere referred to as "grounded" communities, are locatable on the face of the earth (Schensul 2009, 242) and generally are "named" or have an identity recognized by others. They may be cities, towns, or villages, neighborhoods, or even parts of neighborhoods that have specific characteristics that are widely recognized. They include a wide variety of people and groups—residents, community and civic organizations, service centers, political actors, and regulatory bodies. Though appearing stable at one moment in time, they are actually dynamic systems, changing over time in response to internal and external circumstances and responding to political and other influences (Chaskin 2001; MacQueen et al. 2001; Shediac-Rizkallah and Bone 1998). They include resources and opportunity structures

(Kretzman and McKnight 1993), various forms of cultural and social capital, liabilities, and risks, and unequal distributions of power and resources. All of these aspects of "community" must be considered in both shorter and long-term change efforts.

Communities That Are Partially or Not At All Located in Physical Space

Other kinds of communities may be formed in cyberspace by individuals who are joined by common interests, ideologies, training, or disciplines and who communicate via the Internet, social media, letters, telephones, or online face-to-face forms of communication. Like grounded communities, they are "named" or have an identity recognized by others, possess cultural and social capital, and common practices and customs. Though appearing stable at one moment in time, they, too, actually are dynamic systems with many of the same unequal power relationships as those possessed by grounded communities. We described some of these in chapter 1, including terrorist organizations, networks of citizen scientists, individuals suffering from rare diseases, professionals in many fields, collectors of rare plants or books, and disciplinary researchers around the world.

Key point

Ethnography as a Means of Understanding and Working with Communities

Ethnography is a critical tool for understanding local community structures, culture, history, and sociopolitical organization, especially when conducted with knowledgeable community partners. *Ethnographic methods provide the best means for understanding local community and indigenous knowledge, meanings, and behaviors. They allow us to identify those critical cultural elements that can form the basis for culturally based interventions.* These sometimes are referred to as "cultural hooks" for identifying who must be approached (intervention gatekeepers), which people are likely to be partners (allies) that can make success possible, and which ones are likely

Key point

to present obstacles to intervention or who would be likely to undermine efforts toward a desired goal or undo a project once completed. The *language* we have used above to describe communities is very general and politically neutral. However, the *application* of ethnography in action, though systematic, is not at all neutral, especially since it focuses on communities that may be:

- experiencing historical social, economic, and educational injustices;
- undergoing social and cultural marginalization;
- fighting to reintroduce and revitalize elements of traditional culture in the face of loss;
- facing cultural and linguistic stigma and discrimination;
- experiencing environmental degradation and the loss of natural resources such as farmland or fishing rights;
- dealing with identified inequities and gaps in educational and other forms of service delivery;
- trying to address various forms of addiction;
- experiencing the effects of poor food quality on their health.

Ethnography in action may address:

- design improvements in services and technology that equalize access and improve health;
- systems improvements in health delivery to vulnerable populations;
- supply challenges in the distribution of essential medicines to rural or otherwise underserved people;
- Discriminatory, inappropriate, or illegal forms of product marketing;
- Policies that result in unjust imbalances in public/private support for essential services such as transportation, communication, banking, education, and health care;
- Inequitable representation of diverse cultural producers to the public, including minority artists, performers, and traditional folk artists and craftspeople.

In other words, ethnography in action is concerned with creating places and spaces that ensure the equitable and effective representation of ordinary people in the communities and institutions where they experience injustices to enhance their ability to transform those institutions. Thus, many of the issues that we discuss in Books 1, 2, 3, and 6 with respect to positionality, insider/outsider status, and methodology apply to ethnography in action, especially when it is put into service for social problem solving to improve quality of life for those who are not fairly represented in the places where policies are generated and decisions are made and carried out that affect their lives. Such unjust actions inevitably create conflicts and controversies. In assessing the possibility of participating in or even initiating efforts to change or transform conditions in communities or other settings, ethnographers and their partners should consider sources of power and resource imbalance, as well as other factors that may constitute obstacles to communication between themselves and potential community partners in their projects. These may include:

Cross Reference: See Book 1, chapter 1; Book 2, chapter 2; Book 3, chapters 2 and 3; Book 6

- Gender
- Relative age
- Family, tribal, clan, or caste affiliations and connections
- Ethnicity/country of origin
- Linguistic preferences
- Ideological or religious affiliations
- Social class
- Sexual preference and gender orientation
- Perceived roles and responsibilities in the community
- Institutional "baggage" (e.g., the community's prior experience with the researcher's institution or type of research—or any research—being proposed)
- Perceived roles, responsibilities, and skills needed for the partnership
- Personal appearance and style

It is important to remember that the execution of ethnography in action is not the same as traditional ethno-

Key point

graphic research. ***The search for partners in community-change efforts differs from the search for partners as key informants in traditional ethnography.*** Key informants in ethnographic research are those with special expertise in some aspect of community life who remain close to ethnographers throughout the life of a study. Partners in a change effort may still be key informants, but they also will be activists or potential activists committed, as individuals or through their organizations, to improving and transforming conditions in their own communities (Allen et al. 2013; Davis and Reid 1999; Schensuls et al.

Key point

2009; Schensul 1979). **Activist partners also can be critical in helping researchers to shape appropriate intervention strategies, avoiding the exacerbation of existing fractures and conflicts in the community, and engaging in the multiple tasks of mixed methods ethnographic research and collective analysis.**

INTERVENTIONS: A DEFINITION

Interventions in the social sciences at times have been thought of as "social engineering," that is, technocrats making decisions and taking action with respect to what they believe will improve the health and well-being of a population without considering their wishes. Thus, the term *intervention* has both "neutral" and nonneutral meanings. Differences among these meanings shed light on why "interventions" may be perceived negatively by some scholars in the social sciences, including anthropologists. The following are some meanings of the term *intervene* (http://www.merriam-webster.com/dictionary/intervene):

- To come between points of time or events
- To enter as an intrusion on ordinary circumstances
- To enter so as to modify or hinder (as in the case of a fight)
- To interfere with an outcome or condition so as to improve it
- To interfere with another nation's internal affairs to compel an action

Nonneutral meanings are those that involve power differentials between the so-called architects of the intervention (the interveners) and those who receive it (the recipients). Some of these definitions of the term *intervention* imply that those with greater medical, socioeconomic, political, cultural, or strategic power have a legitimate *right* to intervene in or interfere with the behaviors and actions of others with less power, including nations, groups, or people with specific behavioral or medical problems. Those rights claimed by interveners can supersede the rights of people upon whom interventions are imposed, even to the extent of causing them harm. In these instances, interventions cannot be thought of as participatory; in fact, they are just the opposite. They may be designed to further the goals of the interventionists instead of the recipients.

We adhere to closer readings of the more "neutral" sense of the term, those readings that suggest both a "coming between" and an act taken to improve a negative situation. In other words, contrary to the earlier view, we believe that interventions should be actions taken to make things better—to reduce conflicts, to bring people together, to change environments, and to improve the quality of life. Unfortunately, neither the nonneutral reading of "intervention" nor its neutral reading includes the ideas of equality and participation between those who implement an intervention and those who are subject to it, and neither is specific about ethics of treatment for the target of the interventions. Most references to intervention in the health and mental health fields have to do with providers whose role is to remedy unhealthy situations, often at the individual level. They are devoid of the concern shared by ethnographers in action for disparities of power and participation between researchers and others—without which ethical and just research cannot be assured. Fortunately, this individualistic and hierarchical orientation is slowly changing because both research and testimony on service provision are showing that "patient" participation or partnership in various forms of treatment or prevention produces better outcomes. This finding is so important that a new institute for funding it has recently come into being: The Patient-

Cross Reference: See Example 2.5 in Book 6, which describes the "rights" psychiatrist Ewan Cameron claimed over the mental, emotional, and even physical state of his patients

Centered Outcomes Research Institute or PCORI (http://www.pcori.org/). PCORI supports many different participatory research-based approaches to improving treatment, access, and services, all of which include patients as active and equal partners.

But what might "intervention" in community settings look like? First, as we have said, communities—including schools, hospitals, and their settings—are ongoing and dynamic systems in which indigenous or local "interventions" to solve local problems are occurring all the time in the form of campaigns, special events, programs, and community development efforts introduced by community members, local government, political activists, and politicians. Most communities have considerable assets and capacity for problem solving, decision making, and action (Kretzman and McKnight 1993); without these resources and capacities, they would be unlikely to survive. But these resources must be recognized and activated to have utility. While some local or indigenous interventions may involve dialogue and partnership and community mobilizing, others have none. And, most important, many indigenous or local change efforts have little or no involvement with research.

By contrast, when social scientists become involved in "interventions," they generally introduce research into the picture. Often they bring theories and approaches derived from their respective disciplines and want to assess or test them—even when the researchers themselves are from the affected community. The challenge for researchers is how to integrate "external," science-based, or "etic" research and theory with the ongoing local "theorizing" and active problem-solving activities of the community in question. This must be done without stifling local energy and activism and in ways that further community goals and directions

 Key point for change. *Such social science/ethnography-based interventions can be thought of as systematically partnered, planned, conducted, and evaluated social science–based cultural products that engage with the lives of people and institutions to result in outcomes that are hoped for by community members as well as researchers.* They occur in the context of multiple additional factors, events, and processes—which also can be thought of as interventions—that may have the effect of speeding, slowing, reducing, or otherwise affecting the rate of change toward a desired outcome (Hawe, Shiell, and Riley 2009). For example, efforts to implement a language-instruction intervention designed to help immigrant students learn English more quickly can have the concomitant and unanticipated effect of creating a perceived threat to the immigrant parents' native language and culture. The hostility created by the former efforts, in turn, can mobilize parents to create Saturday or after-school classes where their own language and culture is taught. A serious rift in the community between ethnic groups can only be avoided if community members' and researchers' schools can convince all sides that focusing on both English acquisition *and* support for natal language and cultures is an effective means to improve student achievement overall; they do not have to compete with one another.

The process of ethnography requires researchers first to get involved in the life of the setting, and then to learn through the eyes of the people and together with them what is important to them and how to think about change. This is a crucial requirement whose necessity has emerged from the experiences of generations of applied researchers and the communities with which they have worked. Ethnography also requires researchers to see communities as "whole," complex, multilayered, and interactive entities and the interventions introduced as intersecting with other ongoing processes. Learning with local residents about a complex community problem and assessing together with them different strategies for addressing it can produce multiple different ways of tackling a problem. These approaches may emerge all at once, or at different points in time. If attended to, researchers and community members can anticipate that the emerging approaches will facilitate forging synergistic links that move communities toward desired change (Schensul and Trickett 2009, 242).

Since improving the circumstances of community members' lives is the central focus of ethnography in action, involving residents and local organizations as partners in research and intervention is the most effective way to accomplish this mission. Doing so:

Cross Reference: See Book 1, chapter 1; Book 2, chapters 1–3; and Book 3, chapter 1

- ensures the presence of and enhances local voices;
- creates solutions that make sense;
- generates a foundation for more meaningful, culturally and situationally driven, locally owned solutions to local problems;
- supports intervention strategies that potentially are more sustainable;
- contributes to sounder evaluation and problem solving.

 Key point

Authentic partnerships democratize science and bring tacit, everyday or unspoken knowledge and lived experience to bear on a common community problem. They counter technocratic and governmental hegemonies and contribute to enhanced community advocacy (Schensul 2002). It's important to keep in mind that the ethnographic approach to intervention combines external knowledge, theory, and experience with in-community intervention and the lived experiences and perspectives of those in the change setting. ***In an ethnographic approach, opportunities and strategies for change emerge from the setting rather than being imposed on it.*** Thus, researchers often have to "wait for a break" or hope for a "hook"— that moment when a problem emerges or a culturally embedded solution presents itself.

EXAMPLE 2.1

FINDING THE PROBLEM: OTITIS MEDIA (MIDDLE EAR INFECTIONS) IN PUERTO RICAN CHILDREN

When Lisa Allen, a medical anthropologist, was reviewing medical records in a Hartford-based community clinic that had been established with the support of anthropologists at the University of Connecticut, she noticed that ear infections appeared frequently among Puerto Rican children. She began to ask the medical providers and mothers why that might be the case. Many of the mothers she spoke to told her that otitis media was a big problem for them because children did not improve with medication. They were chronically sick, in pain, and crying and their illness interrupted family life in small apartments. This discovery produced further questions about why the children did not improve. It resulted in a two-year project to work with the health center and a pediatric clinic at a local hospital using mixed methods to examine how doctors treated young Puerto Rican children and how mothers were managing medications. That research showed that

doctors at the local hospital outpatient clinic were not seeing the same patients repeatedly. Because they were residents, they rotated so that children seldom saw the same physician on return visits. Further, the residents were not reviewing charts thoroughly. Faced with too many patients and not enough staff, they skipped over charts and repeatedly prescribed amoxicillin (the pink medicine), not realizing that children had been prescribed the same medication over and over again in the previous months. At the same time, parents did not realize that they should complete the prescription; instead, they were administering the medication until the child's symptoms (but not the infection) disappeared. When the infection reappeared, they repeated the same pattern. These data provided the basis for a two-part intervention with mothers/caregivers on how to administer medication for ear infections, and with physicians and other clinic providers to improve chart reading, to learn to ask questions about patterns of infection and past medication, and to prescribe different antibiotics according to need.

Researchers often use an ecological or a systems model to help them conceptualize emergent intervention approaches that can be applied at the level of individuals, families, groups, communities (for school and after-school use, in churches and on playgrounds, in clinics, social service agencies, and buildings as small communities and through networks), the media (through small print, social media, cell phones, television, and radio), and policy (testimony, or advocacy with policy makers, community organizing, and meshwork). Community leaders, residents, and organizational administrators often think in terms of systems as well. They may be all too well aware that the reasons for poor results are "systemic," that is, they lie beyond the control of individuals. Some examples of systemic causes are ineffective school administration, poor training and monitoring systems in local police departments, limited and expensive transportation systems, understaffed social service and medical facilities, and gaps in the delivery of essential drugs to local pharmacies or outlets. Working together to sift through and conceptualize these issues takes some time and much research. Thus, some change efforts may extend over years and generate multiple components, while others could be of short duration and limited scope.

Cross Reference: See Book 1, chapter 3; Book 2, chapters 4 and 5; and chapter 5 in this book

Local communities and other partners can make strong commitments to interventions when those interventions are rooted in community culture, have local meaning, and address significant challenges. In the next sections of this chapter, we discuss several different collaborative approaches to interventions that required long-term investments in community development in health, economy, jobs, and culture. Subsequently, we also describe some shorter-term, project-specific interventions with many of the same characteristics but lacking the sustainability of longer-term efforts.

INVESTMENTS IN COMMUNITY HEALTH AND EDUCATION

One of the best ways to see how research and related interventions/actions can be integrated is to explore the history of some longer-term efforts by researchers and local communities to remedy health, educational, and other disparities. These usually involved entering and coming to understand the setting, building partnerships, finding links between research and action, developing culturally responsive institutions, and supporting the development of a sense of community as well as student human resources. Several good examples are

- The West Side Chicano Development Project: community action research and development program to build community service and activist institutions in Chicago (1969 to present) (Gaviria, Stern, and Schensul 1982; Schensul 1978; Schensul 1980; Schensul 1979);
- the Hartford, Connecticut, experience: developing community based research organizations to promote and cultivate transformative change in health and mental health (1976 to present) (Schensul et al. 1987, Schensul and Schensul 1992, Schensul et al. 1982, Schensul and Schensul 1982, Singer and Weeks 2005);
- the Memphis experience: addressing racism and environmental inequities (1970s to present) (Hyland and Bennett 2013; Hyland and Maurette 2010; Hyland and Owens 2005);

- the Alaska experience: building Native Alaskan education and health programs from the ground up (Barnhardt 1999, Barnhardt 2002; Barnhardt 2005; Barnhardt 2008; Barnhardt and Kawagley 2005; Barnhardt, Kawagley, and Hill 2000; Rasmus 2014; Rasmus, Charles, and Mohatt 2014);
- the Detroit experience: building an urban health research program (Doan et al. 2012; Farquhar et al. 2005; Israel et al. 2001; Parker et al. 2003; Schulz et al. 2000).

We introduce these programs using a framework that includes exploring the setting, seeking, and finding partners, building culturally reinforcing institutions and programs, introducing research funding sources, and maintaining sustainability. Throughout, we highlight important concepts introduced earlier or referred to later in this book.

EXAMPLE 2.2

THE CHICANO COMMUNITY DEVELOPMENT PROGRAM

The Setting

The late 1960s, the period marked by the great civil rights movements of the twentieth century, offered ample opportunity for innovations in the application of ethnography to social justice issues (Schensul and Schensul 1978). In a well-documented case study, ethnographer Stephen Schensul and his colleagues, together with Chicano community activists in Chicago, entered into a long-term process of community development. During the first phase, as a recently graduated PhD, Schensul took a position with the Community Mental Health Program of the West Side Medical Complex, in Chicago. This program had the resources to develop a community research team. Schensul quickly discovered that the team was unsuccessful in its efforts to use survey and ethnographic data to persuade predominantly white middle-European-American mental health service providers to expand their capacity to serve the rapidly growing and diverse bilingual Mexican population in the neighborhood. He then made the strategic decision to *take the research team to the community*. At that point, he had no idea that the work he was about to begin would result in a large-scale integrated action research effort with multiple projects, including embedded studies, student training, and community institution building—all addressing issues facing the Mexican community.

Finding Partners

To find partners, Schensul initially connected with a group of basketball-playing, male gang workers in a local settlement house. They were inspired by the national civil rights scene and were ready to take on larger roles as activists in their own community. Open to both teaching and learning, they knew their community and were ready to participate in research for activist/community-change purposes. They joined the research team, bringing their local knowledge and their understanding of which approaches to research could be both acceptable and successful in the highly politicized neighborhood environment. Development of the project was an emergent process, in which one idea or event led to another as perceived needs arose and available resources were identified.

Finding the Connection—Linking Research and Action

An early activity illustrating the potential of research to change policy through action involved a community-initiated rapid assessment of the quality of English as a Second Language (ESL) programs for Mexican American children in local schools. Parents were very dissatisfied with the quality of education in these programs because children were not learning English. A group of community activists and parents joined forces with the research team to devise a way of gathering rapid assessment information from local classrooms. Because parents had the right to enter classrooms, it was possible to organize teams of observant parents, activists, and researchers to visit a number of ESL classrooms simultaneously, using an observational schedule that they had worked out jointly. They observed instruction in a sample of classrooms hours, met afterward to combine and interpret their data, and used the data to show that children were not speaking English in class. The community team presented results to school board members, with one result being a bilingual consent decree and the introduction of real bilingual education in the Chicago Public Schools. This project illustrated the power of community research to achieve policy change through informed advocacy. It was central in consolidating a broad consortium of people and organizations which came together for a variety of different purposes but were all interested in community development (action) through research (Schensul 1978).

Building Culturally Reinforcing Institutions

In the early 1970s, federal resources were becoming available for a wide variety of service opportunities. Building institutions that could respond to the historical, cultural, educational, and material/health needs of the growing Chicano/Mexican American population was a priority for neighborhood activists in Chicago. Conceptualizing and developing these institutions grew from the interaction of ***anthro-***

pologists who understood systems and culture, neighbor-   **Key point**
hood activists who could draw on their cultural repertoires
and social capital, researchers who could use ethnography to
understand the changing neighborhood and its subpopulations, and links between
those activists, anthropologists, politicians and federal funding sources. The development of a drug treatment program for Mexican Americans was an excellent
illustration of this fusion of skills and capacities. Schensul and his anthropologist
colleagues, in discussion with former drug user/organizers and youth activists recognized that injection drug use was a problem in the community, especially for men.
The group was aware that there were three groups of drug users in the neighborhood, those coming from the southwest United States, those coming directly from
Mexico, and those who had lived in Chicago for generations. Ethnography provided
background on drug patterns and needs for all three populations, sufficient to provide the material for a federal grant to initiate a drug treatment program BASTA
(Brotherhood Against Slavery to Drugs, or "Enough!/Stop!" in Spanish).

A second example emerged from the federal government's initiative to address
gaps in trained personnel needed to work in emerging immigrant communities with
different cultural backgrounds. The Department of Health and Human Services
(HHS), then the Department of Health, Education and Welfare (then HEW) made
funding available for the training of paraprofessionals. A subgroup of the research/
activist informal coalition that included the director of a local community mental health center serving Chicanos came together to develop a strategy for training
paraprofessionals based on an emerging literature on Mexican American mental
health issues and indigenous concepts. The resulting Chicano Mental Health Training Program, trained several cycles of paraprofessionals from the neighborhood to
assist mental health professionals in providing improved bilingual-bicultural services to families and children.

While neighborhood men were organizing around men's issues, women were
also gaining visibility as activists, participating in national marches and meetings
and promoting the development of programs and organizations at home. Women
leaders, in conversation with other women in the community, realized that while
some young mothers fared well after pregnancy, others lacked support and did more
poorly. The women wondered what accounted for the difference. Seeking a cultural
explanation, they identified the demise of the "*cuarentena*," the forty-day post-birth
period during which women traditionally were sequestered and supported by family
members. Among women who had lived in Chicago for a generation or more, that
practice had been diminishing in importance and often was not carried out. The
women leaders, working with mental health professionals and researchers, decided
that a study of women's supports during pregnancy and post-birth would be important as the basis for re-introducing the cuarentena in a form suitable for the Chicago
context (Gaviria, Stern, and Schensul 1982).

Introducing NIH and Other Funding Sources

Chicano colleagues at the National Institute of Mental Health (NIMH), a major research funder in mental health, recognized that activities in Chicago had national significance and could produce good community-initiated, community-based research. They made a visit to Chicago to encourage the alliance to apply for a research grant from NIMH. In short order, a grant application was submitted by Stephen Schensul, Moises Gaviria, and Gwen Stern, with the Chicano mental health center as the base. The proposal was funded to do a study of variation in perinatal support and mental health status post-birth among women with different migration histories. Community women were the researchers. The study showed that women who had more perinatal support had better mental health; and it paved the way for the development of an intervention, *Dar a Luz*, to support pregnant mothers during the pre- and postnatal period. As far as we know, this marked the first instance in which an NIH grant including *indirect or administrative costs* to support research infrastructure was awarded directly to a community organization.

Sustainability

Stephen and Jean Schensul and their baby lived in the west side of Chicago community became part of community life with other young families, and engaged in many activities with community activists to further the visibility and the economic, cultural, and political development of the 18th and 26th Streets Chicano neighborhoods. This joint approach merged local knowledge and the tools of ethnographic research to build a neighborhood social, cultural, health, and mental health infrastructure created and administered by neighborhood-based professionals (Schensul 1980; Schensul 1974). The work of these early Chicano leaders, bolstered by formative research and program development, resulted in a new generation of activists that has included a number of elected public officials,

　　　　The "Chicago" model emerged in the context of a politically and financially favorable environment in which young minority activists were claiming a legitimate role in American life. They needed research data to make their case and administrative guidance to develop alternative, culturally oriented institutions that could more effectively serve their communities. The problem was that though the social scientists knew that a "community of emerging identity" existed, which included representative activists with whom to partner, no alternative community institutions existed that could appropriately serve them. A heady mix of ethnographic mixed-methods research, creativity, and activism enabled Schensul's social-justice-oriented community research team to join forces with a local community and organizers. Drawing on a combination of ethnographic research and their lived experiences together and over time, they created the new cultural, health, mental health, and social service organizations required to serve the newly arrived population of children, adults, and women from different parts of Mexico and the American Southwest. The funding generated by the creation of these organizations also supported an activist infrastructure that first sent both men and women to national conferences on Chicano rights and, later, to political positions in city and state government and participation on foundation and industrial boards. The Schensuls remained in the Pilsen neighborhood until 1974, but even after they left, they have returned regularly to catch up with developments. Stephen Schensul is still called upon for help with proposals or other development activities. Some members of the activist network moved to Texas; others, including Juan Velazquez, Maria Mangual, and Albert Vazquez have passed away, but a number of the original people remain in the neighborhood. The "elder activists," including Felipe Ayala and anthropologist Gwen Stern, mentor new research activists with advanced degrees who want to make a difference in addressing the continuing problems of poverty, gang violence, and the never-ending land grabs that mark neighborhoods undergoing continuing gentrification.

In the next case study we focus on forty years of experience using applied research for social transformation in the industrial capital of Connecticut. This example of ethnography for health development began with links between the Department of Community Medicine and the University of Connecticut anthropology program first established by medical anthropologist and methodologist Pertti Pelto. By 1976, the university had hired Stephen Schensul to extend these links into the community through relationships with community activists in low-income neighborhoods, a large public housing project, and Puerto Rican community organizations promoting greater equity for Latinos in health, education, housing, and economic development.

EXAMPLE 2.3

THE HARTFORD EXPERIENCE—BUILDING COMMUNITY-BASED RESEARCH INFRASTRUCTURE FOR HEALTH WITH THE LATINO COMMUNITY

The Setting

Forty years ago, the city of Hartford, Connecticut, was one of the most impoverished small cities in the country. It remains so today. Once a wealthy industrial and insurance capital, by the 1960s, the factories had closed or moved to the nonunionized southern United Sates, and in the early 1980s, the financial sector shrank and insurance companies started to shift their headquarters to Philadelphia, Boston, and New York. The people who stayed, including Puerto Ricans and West Indians who had arrived via contracts for work in the tobacco fields, and African Americans, who had come as part of the great industrial migration north during the 1930s, experienced an economy in decline, schools in disrepair, and health facilities geared toward middle-class white suburbanites. A city which had been a residentially and economically diverse and flourishing center became intentionally geographically segregated. The civil rights movement of the 1960s had resulted in marches, protests, and violence. The white establishment responded by using a variety of devious strategies including harassment of African American businesses that were located throughout the city, which caused owners to move to the safer, newly Black, north end of the city. This, in turn, shifted Latinos to neighborhoods near the city center, thus acting as a bridge between the white ethnic south end of the city and the Black north end. It led to two seventh–eighth grade middle schools, one geographically located convenient to Latino areas and mainly Latino, and the second close to the north end and mainly Black. White parents advocated successfully for K–8 neighborhood schools and thus had the option of sending their children to schools within walking distance. Although *de facto* segregation is declining over time, the city, which is arrayed north-south along the Connecticut River, remains predominantly white in the southern neighborhoods, with Latino/as in the central neighborhoods, and African American/Caribbean in the northern neighborhoods.

As in the previous example, the city's institutions were unprepared for a large influx of people from diverse ethnic/racial, linguistic, and cultural backgrounds, with limited incomes, and significant social, economic, health, and mental health needs. This situation offered the new medical anthropology program at the University of Connecticut opportunities to participate in the socioeconomic and cultural development of communities experiencing injustices while making a contribution through research by training and involving students in applied research.

Finding Partners

In 1976, Pertti Pelto, a medical anthropologist at the University of Connecticut, Storrs, was seeking placements for graduate students in field experiences in the Hartford urban area. He invited Stephen Schensul to assist in the creation of field school settings in applied health research using mixed-methods approaches in community settings. While Pertti Pelto was leading research seminars in applied anthropology, Stephen Schensul established two field settings upon becoming a member of the Department of Community Medicine. One was the Charter Oak Rice Heights housing project (known as "Charter Oak"), the most impoverished and largest of the area's public housing projects and home to several well-known and outspoken Black community health activists, and the other was La Casa de Puerto Rico, known as "La Casa." La Casa, a Puerto Rican advocacy organization, was one of the first community-based organizations (CBOs) in the United States committed to conducting research as the basis for advocacy and community action in health, housing, economic development, and education.

Making the Research-Action Connection

In Charter Oak Terrace/Rice Heights, Schensul convinced Mattie Bell, the leading activist in that public housing project, that research conducted by community residents could enhance their ability to advocate for improved services and infrastructure in the face of an unresponsive white city sanitation office. They initiated a program to train community residents as health researchers; several new medical anthropology students were involved. The committee's first study focused on proving to unconvinced and racist city administrators that garbage was strewn about on the housing project grounds, not because of the residents' sloppy habits but because of inadequate city garbage control and pickup. The residents used timed observations and photographs to show that garbage Dumpsters were filled to overflowing because they were not emptied regularly and that Dumpster floors were filled with holes, allowing rats to enter. Thus, they were able to show convincingly that garbage overflow and rat infestations resulted from city mismanagement rather than resident irresponsibility in the all-Black-and-Latino housing project. To emphasize their point that the ubiquitous rats in the neighborhood were the result of inadequate garbage control, they trapped a rat and left it, dead, in the city manager's car along with the outcomes of their study. They got the results they demanded—improved sanitation control. Feeling empowered, the resident group of community research advocates conducted a second study with the help of Schensul and medical anthropology and medical students—a survey to document perceived needs in the community. The results of this survey convinced residents that the community badly needed a local community health center; several years later, they were able to argue for a clinic to be funded, first by the city of Hartford, and later with federal community health center funds.

At the same time, at La Casa, Schensul and Pelto convinced the La Casa health committee and its chair, health advocate Maria Borrero, to conduct a series of disease-specific (asthma, schistosomiasis) and generic health assessments with local and external funding sources. La Casa also had a well-functioning education committee that had brought suit against the board of education, resulting in a bilingual consent decree. Jean Schensul's interest in activist educational research brought her to the education committee to propose a Participatory Action Research training program in education. The committee decided on a three-year project to train adults to monitor and evaluate the bilingual consent decree.

Building Culturally Reinforcing Institutions

When building a community-responsive health clinic at Charter Oak Terrace/Rice Heights emerged as the top priority in the public housing project, a community-wide committee was formed to develop it and to forge the infrastructure to qualify for federal funding. The committee included medical anthropology faculty and students who were learning to do good research in an action setting—in this case, the creation of a new community-responsive health clinic, with a resident board of directors and a politically motivated multiethnic staff of health professionals. The clinic was funded as a Federally Qualified Community Health Center (FQCHC) and given a location in several contiguous apartments in one of the project buildings. The center remained there for more than ten years, fighting for its right to exist in that location until it was forcibly relocated under HOPE VI, a federal program to dismantle public housing (Chedekel 1998).

> A community health center Hartford's Charter Oak Terrace housing project will remain open as bulldozers start chewing up the remaining buildings in the complex this month. The Hartford Housing Authority has backed off trying to force the Charter Oak Terrace/Rice Heights Health Center to vacate its Overlook Terrace building—at least for the next three months, during the first phase of demolishing the complex's "ABC" side, and possibly longer.

Eventually the center was compelled to move to another neighborhood nearby, losing its community base. With a stakeholder rather than community board, it now occupies two locations central to Hartford's Latino community, in the midsouth section of the city, and includes approximately thirty ethnically diverse bilingual health and dental providers. The center serves thousands of Hartford patients each month.

Meanwhile, while working with the health committee, Stephen Schensul and health advocate Maria Borrero invented the idea of an organization founded to do health research with federal funding. Thus was born the Hispanic Health Council (HHC), a community-based research organization like La Casa, but focused on health. Borrero and Schensul's vision was to develop an independent organization that could conduct health research among Latinos and advocate for changes in the health care system that would benefit the larger Latino community.

Identifying Funding

With the experience of drawing NIH funding into community settings behind him, Schensul, together with Borrero and Jean Schensul, began to construct larger multiyear NIH grants, one for a mental health cultural epidemiology survey and the second for a Puerto Rican mental health training program for staff at local mental health agencies. In 1978, the National Institutes of Mental Health awarded them a grant to assess barriers to mental health care (NIMH, Schensul S, principal investigator (PI), M. Borrero, co-PI). In the next year, an additional five-year NIMH training grant to train mental health professionals in cultural aspects of Latino mental health also began (NIMH, investigators Stephen and Jean Schensul and Marie Borrero). In 1979, with National Institute of Education funding, they initiated a training program for community residents in educational action research for advocacy (NIE, Schensul J., PI). A local foundation provided overhead and a director's salary. With these sources of funding, Maria Borrero became the founding director of the Hispanic Health Council (HHC) and Jean Schensul joined as research director to develop a broad research agenda.

The mental health study provided the HHC with formative data including maps of the Latino neighborhoods in the city, narratives of health and mental health help-seeking behavior, and a good picture of problems in accessing health care. The funded program for training of mental health providers utilized information generated by the first study to create training manuals and procedures to be used by mental/behavioral health clinics. Then, with multiyear funding for one of the first Area Health Education Centers in the country, Stephen Schensul was able to support the founding of a unique organization that bridged the University of Connecticut and Hartford's Black and Latino communities, placing researchers in departments and community organizations interested in community-based health research for social transformation, and building health educational and research infrastructure capacity in organizations such as the HHC and the Black Coalition for Health Issues.

At around the same time, Jean Schensul and Borrero headed a third NIMH grant to develop and evaluate a culturally specific bilingual approach to mental health crisis management for the police department. It was designed to avoid

acceleration of household problems. When called in to intervene in household conflicts, the police often failed to respond appropriately to the dangers facing women
in domestic disputes, which left them exposed to greater potential for violence. The
approach involved training the police and accompanying them as brokers/inter-
preters on household visits on a 24/7 basis. The study improved police interaction
with the Puerto Rican community and produced a deeper understanding of different types of mental health crises (Schensul, Nieves, and Martinez 1982). Additional
funding from a local foundation for a library and many other specific basic and
intervention studies in Latino health and mental health followed, including research
to prevent smoking among adolescents (McGraw et al. 1991) and child abuse and on
alcohol use (Singer, Davison, and Yalin 1987).

In the mid-1980s, in a broader experiment with research-alliance building, the
HHC facilitated links with other agencies to address HIV—a citywide threat resulting in the first community-based consortium to do research on HIV knowledge and
attitudes in the country and in public housing. The alliance first forged through
this study, the AIDS Community Research Group, grew into a larger coalition of
organizations and expanded into a long-term city wide program of HIV-prevention
research (Schensul et al. 1989). Many other HIV prevention studies followed under
the joint leadership of Merrill Singer and Margaret Weeks (Dushay et al. 2001; Himmelgreen and Singer 1998; Needle et al. 2003; Romero-Daza, Weeks, and Singer
2003; Singer et al. 2001; Stopka et al. 2003; Weeks et al. 1998). Since then, with the
involvement of Merrill Singer and others, HHC funding has drawn upon multiple
sources of funding—federal, state, private, and donor based—to sustain its research,
health promotion, and advocacy work.

More than fifteen years ago, nutritionist Rafael Pérez-Escamilla (University of
Connecticut/Yale) approached the HHC to develop a long-term partnership around
nutrition and related health problems. Since then he and Grace Damio (HHC) have
partnered in an NIH-funded health disparities center focused on diabetes prevention and nutrition. The center sponsored more than seven years of community dialogues, focus groups, and other formative research to develop peer-based
intervention to promote breast feeding, exercise, and dietary changes (Chapman
and Pérez-Escamilla 2013; Dharod et al. 2004; Pérez-Escamilla et al. 2015; Pérez-
Escamilla, Garcia, and Song 2010). Other grants have supported training in cultural
competence for medical and other health professions.

Training Students

These housing project and HHC sites and projects offered graduate students and a
number of well-known anthropologists and medical students from different backgrounds opportunities to conduct community-driven research for their MA and
PhD programs while working directly in support of community development and

health in local neighborhoods, clinics, and community-based organizations. Among these researchers were Jan Hogle (University of Wisconsin, Madison), Peter Guarnaccia (Rutgers University), Jeffrey Backstrand (Rutgers University), Joel Gittelsohn (Johns Hopkins University), Susan Meswick (City University of New York, Queens), Merrill Eisenberg (University of Arizona), Claudia Santelices (Northeastern University), Nancy Romero-Daza (University of South Florida), and David Himmelgreen (University of South Florida).

Sustainability

As part of its mission, the HHC supported the development of many other Latino art- and health-related organizations in the city, helping to build much-needed social and health infrastructure. The HHC also gave research a positive face in urban communities and organizations that had been used, misused, or ignored by researchers in the past. Its ability to bridge communities and cultures helped to build new interagency networks and heretofore nonexistent links to mainstream institutions and organizations, including hospitals and health clinics that had not served Latinos well in the past. Relationships with university faculty and students from many schools were helpful in generating these successes and have continued to the present. In the ensuing years, the HHC has become a statewide umbrella organization for Hispanic health prevention, case management, training, and education. Recently, it celebrated its thirty-fifth anniversary. It continues to provide informational, case management, nutritional, and maternal and child health programs in Latino communities throughout Connecticut.

Adding to the activities in Hartford has been The Institute for Community Research, another long-standing action research institution founded in 1988.

 **EXAMPLE 2.4**

BUILDING BRIDGES TO HEALTHIER COMMUNITIES: THE INSTITUTE FOR COMMUNITY RESEARCH

The Setting

In 1987, Jean Schensul shifted from the Hispanic Health Council, taking lessons learned from a decade of research and development there as research director, to form the Institute for Community Research (ICR), a new organization that bridged action and research, communities and groups in Hartford, elsewhere in the United States and internationally. The impetus for formation of the ICR was that, despite its five universities, no research centers existed either in Hartford or elsewhere in the state that were conducting community-based research for community development and social justice across the diversity spectrum. The period preceding ICR's founding saw the evolution of community engagement centers and programs and disparities centers that emerged in large part in response to the HIV/AIDs crisis and the call for citizen involvement in research and research agendas. Further, with immigration from other areas of the world—Latin America, East and West Africa, the Middle East, Asia, and Eastern Europe—and the globalization of health problems such as HIV and various forms of influenza, a clear need existed for a community-oriented research center that took a global perspective. Finally, Connecticut was the only remaining state in the United States that did not have a folk arts program supported by the National Endowment for the Arts folk arts program. Developing a program that could reach beyond the boundaries of the state's primarily white mainstream arts interests was an important way to merge ethnography with material and performance culture for health while highlighting emerging artists and communities. With the support of other ethnographers, health activists, and artists, Jean Schensul and colleagues created a community-based research organization (CBRO) based on principles of collaboration, cultural representation, transformative interventions, and Participatory Action Research (www.incommunityresearch.org) and funded with substantial amounts of federal funding from the National Institutes for Health (NIH), the Substance Abuse and Mental Health Services Administration (SAMHSA) the federal Department of Education, the National Endowment for the Arts, and a variety of other national and local foundations and other funders. The mission of the organization was and remains the conduct of research with community partners to further justice and equity in a multicultural, multiethnic world. During its nearly thirty years of operation, ICR has:

- fostered a twenty-five-year history of prevention research in HIV as described below;
- founded and supported the Connecticut State Folk Arts Program, known as the Connecticut Cultural Heritage Arts Program (referred to as CHAP), promoting healthy communities through the culture and art of many invisible and underserved national and cultural groups in the northeast region of the country;
- developed, with the Connecticut Commission on the Arts, the NEA, and the State of Connecticut, a statewide training and capacity building program for underserved urban artists and presenting organizations representing diverse disciplines, communities, and ethnic/cultural groups that has changed the cultural landscape of Connecticut (the Inner City Cultural Development Project/Urban Artists Initiative);
- developed nearly fifteen years of continuous research on youth culture and substance use, including many different approaches to involving youth and

young adults in prevention programs and their own creation of large-scale interventions based on youth culture and performance;

- developed a twenty-year program of continuous research and development with older adult senior centers and senior housing buildings, focused on resident/member involvement, building public health campaigns, and involving residents in the development of interventions they want to improve their health;
- built a long-standing program of ethical conduct of community-based partnership and participatory research and embodied it in the regular meetings and operations of the Institute for Community Research IRB;
- founded and supported a number of new organizations through cost sharing and other forms of alliance, focused on health, culture, and education.

Cross Reference: See chapters 3–5 in this book

These long-term programs of research and action are ongoing at ICR (www .incommunityresearch.org) and are described in more detail in several publications (Schensul 2005; Schensul 2010; Schensul 2015; Schensul and Schensul 1992).

The ICR conceptual model is represented in Figure 2.1. Here, to illustrate the way ICR as a community-based research organization operates, we focus primarily on work in HIV/AIDS prevention.

ICR Intervention Model

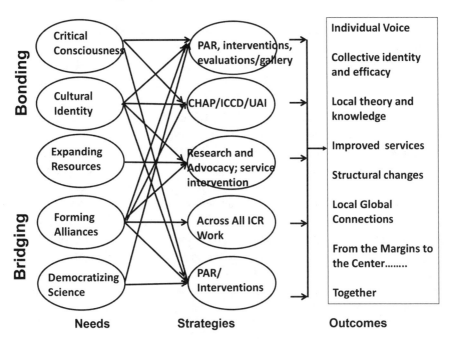

FIGURE 2.1   ICR intervention model.

Identifying Partners

In its early years, the organization established a blueprint for action, first exploring the idea of partnership research for community development and the reduction of disparities through discussions with many different sectors of the community, from political leaders to organizations, and with community residents
directly. These dialogues resulted in a loose network of associations and individuals, all supportive of the action-research concept and ready to join together
to work on specific issues. For example, the HIV-related work initiated at the
Hispanic Health Council formed the basis for the ICR-based AIDS Community
Research Alliance. The first step in moving forward that multiethnic cross-agency
alliance (HHC, ICR, Urban League, Hartford Health Department, Latinos/as Contra Sida, Hartford Dispensary, AIDS Project Hartford) was to apply for National
Institute on Drug Abuse (NIDA) funds to do prevention research, bolstered by the
ICR's initial neighborhood study that identified general needs and gaps in HIV
knowledge. The first two NIDA-funded HIV-prevention studies compared culturally based brief prevention interventions with drug users, the main population to
be affected by HIV, to a standard informational intervention, and shorter (four-
session) to longer (two-session) interventions (Weeks et al. 1996).

Building Culturally Based Institutions

Based in ethnic-specific community organizations, the culturally based approaches
drew on main cultural themes identified by HIV preventionists in the two "ethnic"
organizations. The Urban League (African Americans), focused on community survival, civil rights, and freedom to choose, and Latinos/as Contra Sida (LCS, now
Latino Community Services), the Latino/a site, focused on family (familia), dignity
(dignidad), responsibility (responsabilidad), and respect (respeto). Both approaches
proved to be more effective than the standard intervention.

These early programs helped to build the health department of the Urban
League and to forge independence for the LCS site, which had formerly been the
"Latino arm" of a local AIDS organization. LCS, now Latino/a Community Services, has continued to flourish, expanding into other areas of service. The alliance
continued its work with a program of education to adolescents, a case management program, and the formation of an alliance of women against substance abuse,
again with federal funding. Over the past twenty-five years, this core network of
organizations has partnered in different ways to respond to emerging needs in HIV
prevention and treatment. One thread has been prevention in high-risk locations,
identified through ethnography and network analysis, and evaluated with network
analysis (Weeks et al. 2002; Weeks et al. 2001). A second has been women-controlled
protection methods, with work on female condom use, and pre-infection prophy-

laxis (Weeks et al. 2010). A third, more recent direction initiated by Margaret Weeks, has been on testing and treatment, with ethnographic and network research on gaps in treatment, the use of pre-infection prophylaxis, and the identification of factors contributing to the "treatment cascade," the multiple points at which people drop out of treatment.

Guided by experienced social scientists, programs of research and development with youth, older adults, women, drug users, and cultural groups evolved all over the state. These programs forged networks of organizations that have continued to work in "living alliances" over several decades, moving from one area of need to another. For example, the infrastructure built during the initial phases of HIV-related work on culturally targeted intervention studies with injection drug users led to case management and AIDS-education programs—from male users to women and addiction and from what women needed, to women-controlled protection methods, including pre-infection prophylaxis and HIV adherence and the treatment cascade. These programs combined ethnographic qualitative work, surveys, network research, spatial analysis, and culturally based interventions with equitable cost sharing arrangements, different partnership configurations, and the involvement of affected people—women at risk, injection drug users, heterosexual young adults—in research and intervention.

Other similar long-term programs as noted earlier, have focused on different aspects of aging (Robison et al. 2009; Schensul J. et al. 2009; Schensul, Levy, and Disch 2003; Ward et al. 2004), youth and substance use, the engagement of artists with researchers (Schensul et al. 2012; Schensul and Dalglish 2015; Williamson et al. 1999), and Participatory Action Research (Berg 2004; Berg, Coman, and Schensul 2009; Berg and Schensul 2004; Schensul, Berg, and Williamson 2008).

Students

Over time, and across projects, high school, undergraduate, graduate, and postdoctoral students who have sought placements at ICR have been involved in a variety of activities—helping with data collection, cleaning, and analysis; introducing new methods and approaches; conducting their own substudies; and forging links to new community partners. Lwendo Moonzwe, a sociology PhD and MPH student, joined a study of ecstasy use among young adults to lead the recruitment effort in downtown clubs, an environment where she had personal connections. Elicia Flemming, a post-BA student entering graduate school, took leadership in a pilot study of flavored cigar use among young adults, making connections with ICR partner organizations working with youth to locate candidates for interviewing and for data sharing. Mark Romano came to ICR as an undergraduate anthropology student attending a state school and stayed for two years to conduct outreach and intervention with injection drug users. In summer field schools funded by the National Institute of Drug Abuse, many high school and college students of color have been able to work on small projects affiliated with ICR's larger studies. One team of high school students developed the prototype activities and marketing tools for an ICR performance-based intervention to prevent urban youth from initiating alcohol and marijuana use, the CDC-funded program known as "Xperience." Another group helped a team of club-drug researchers to develop a series of animated panels with quotations derived from in-depth interviews and photographs of local scenes. Jose Garcia, an MSW student at the University of Connecticut, received a minority supplement to a NIDA grant to study the exchange between the informal and the formal drug economy on a street that was home to a local drug market. He now does economic policy analysis for a policy research center in New York. Nitza Dias joined ICR as a graduate from Holyoke College to do a needs assessment of youth in the ICR neighborhood and stayed to become the coordinator of a foundation-funded study of Puerto Rican children's activity levels. She now works as an educational consultant.

Teaching action-oriented ethnography to lay researchers from local communities, and to university and high school students for their own action research projects, is an important part of ICR's use of ethnography for change. ICR has functioned as a field school for teens during many years of summer youth research institutes, and for young scholars of diverse backgrounds wanting to learn community-based participatory research methods. Approaches to instruction in communities and university settings are described in chapters 10 and 11 of this book with examples drawn from around the country and the globe.

Cross Reference: See chapters 10 and 11 in this book for approaches to instruction in communities and university settings

Funding and Sustainability

ICR's funding strategy from the start involved two integrated approaches: a) foundation funding, and b) funding from state and federal public institutions (e.g., HHS Office of Women's Health, Office of Maternal and Child Health; NIH institutes including the National Institute on Mental Health, National Institute on Alcohol Abuse and Alcoholism, National Institute on Aging, National Institute on Dental/Cranial Research, National Institute on Education, National Endowment for the Arts). Total funding from NIH and other federal sources alone amounted to more than $42 million from 1989 to 2015. However, continued funding diversification is required to support independent organizations such as ICR and HHC, an ongoing challenge especially in an increasingly resource-constrained environment. Relationships with supportive university faculty and other research centers have been beneficial in combining resources to seek funding in funding-constrained environments.

ICR remains a hub of research for community research and action in the areas of HIV, substance use prevention, aging, Participatory Action Research, education, the arts, and oral health. Though the topics may change with the researchers and the need, the overall mission of the organization does not. And its alliances, forged and honed over many years, continue to work together to address critical health and cultural issues that affect diverse communities in Connecticut and beyond, as they arise. ICR now sustains a number of research alliances through its links with regional universities to broaden the role that research can play in addressing health and social justice issues.

The Hartford experience highlights several important processes. As in the Chicago case study, politically motivated researchers with sound research skills were able to link with advocates and advocacy-oriented community organizations interested in conducting research to transform service institutions and prevent the growth and acceleration of community health problems. Unlike in Chicago, however, most of the Hartford researchers were working from a community-based research organization, rather than from a university base. They did this with a clear understanding of the constraints of the economic and discriminatory political infrastructure in the city at the time. As in Chicago, the initial partnerships led to the development of new community organizations to fill a gap in meeting health needs. Similarly, external funding sources were willing to fund research partnerships, and researchers and their community partners learned how to envision and write competitive research and intervention grants. Both the Hispanic Health Council and the Institute for Community Research are planned interventions in already ongoing and substantially inequitable systems; they took similar steps separately and together to work with sympathetic allies over time to create new programs of research, cross-agency linkages, and connections with local universities that continue to address health, education, and cultural representation disparities.

Though much remains to be accomplished in the areas of employment, housing, and cultural reasearch development after almost three decades of work, researchers in Hartford can point to significant health-related changes— reduced rates of HIV infection, improved diabetes prevention programs, better older-adult health, and better access to health care via better informed and substantially diverse health personnel and advocacy for the Affordable Care Act. And, as important, there are many more alliances and a much higher degree of trust among organizations willing to work together for health equity in central Connecticut.

EXAMPLE 2.5

MEMPHIS: UNIVERSITY-COMMUNITY ACTION AGAINST POVERTY REFORM IN THE MISSISSIPPI DELTA

The Setting

The Lower Mississippi River Delta, spread across six states, continues to be the poorest economic region in the United States (Farney 1989; Gnuschke et al. 2008; Hyland 2008; Hyland and Maurette 2010; Hyland and Timberlake 1993). Memphis, the socioeconomic hub of the region, is the poorest city in the United States. Slavery and caste/class divisions constituted structural barriers that still limit African Americans in their pursuit of economic and social mobility. At the same time, the Memphis region has created and maintained an extensive cultural heritage as well as a long history of advocacy and activism.

For the last forty years, social scientists, mainly anthropologists, have been involved in efforts to support development, both in the Mississippi Delta and in Memphis as its urban center. As Hyland and Maurette note,

> The longitudinal commitment presents the opportunity to see micro and macro changes through time as a non-lineal, complex process that involves academics (applied ethnographers) . . . , community residents and partners in multiple types of engagement around social justice issues affecting the region, and to explore how the top-down and bottom-up approaches to poverty reform struggle to find a common working arrangement. (Hyland and Maurette 2010, 216)

African Americans and poor whites, a sizable minority, have been voiceless as the area has suffered from a century of social and economic neglect. Even after the civil rights movement of the 1960s, they continued to experience the ill effects of paternalistic and oppressive economic and political structures and a dual economy in which minorities struggle for survival and the white power structure fares well. The situation is typical of colonial domination everywhere. While residents do expect support from the government, they are, at the same time, reticent about raising their voices to advocate for their needs. Further, a shameful lack of basic education and literacy skills marks the Delta area population, creating continuing challenges for voting and community-organizing efforts. With high rates of migration of rural poor people to Memphis, an underdeveloped economy focused on low-level wage labor coupled with the marginalization of Blacks and poor whites by the white power structure, has reinforced generations of dependency and racial divisiveness.

The Partners

Anthropologists have worked in this area for the past forty years, "building a knowledge base around advocacy design and implementation of alternative development approaches within the context of the paternalistic political tradition of Southern Progessivism, while charting a path for a more comprehensive engaged anthropology" (Hyland and Maurette 2010). This long-term effort has engaged community residents, academics, researchers outside the academy, and others in a variety of approaches to social-justice issues. Hyland and Maurette define this form of long-term engaged scholarship as "promoting agency among the marginalized . . . practically transformative and academically germane."

In 1969, as similar processes were unfolding in Chicago (noted earlier in this chapter) several community-directed agencies were created in Memphis, with federal funds from the U.S. Department of Health, Education and Welfare (HEW). These agencies built on the spirit of the civil rights movement, and the passion of local Black activists, and supported research on community needs in small-, and then larger-scale, community-development projects. From his University of Illinois base, Dimitri Shimkin, a civil rights scholar activist and anthropologist, led early collaborative research efforts and provided opportunities for community collaborators and researchers to focus on health issues such as hypertension and to train community participants in research skills.

Students

In the late 1970s, the University of Memphis created an MA in applied anthropology. The Department of Anthropology was trying to come to terms with the impact of a 1968 strike by local sanitation workers seeking equitable compensation and better working conditions, the assassination of Martin Luther King Jr. in the same year, and multiple other social injustices. The department was guided by the work of the then department chair, Thomas Collins, who focused on the voices of workers, seeking to explain the dual economy through core-periphery theory. That theory held that white economic and political interests benefitted greatly from the production of low-paid Black and white workers—and at their expense. Collins's work on educational tracking and desegregation, plant dislocation, and other structural factors that concentrated disadvantage in the Black community of Memphis laid the basis for the activist stance of the new applied anthropology program. Its focus became the building of regional alternatives to traditional approaches to poverty in Memphis. The curriculum focused on documenting emerging cultures, offering field experiences in local organizations, working with stakeholders in government and other academic institutions to identify problems, and creating new knowledge to make information and problem-solving approaches available to youth and the general public.

Linking Research and Action

Over the years, the program used a number of innovative strategies to bring community residents, faculty, and students together in joint-research and community-development activities, including:

- co-constructing documentation of history, accomplishments, and struggles (Hyland 1979), including jointly constructed "historical monographs" and videos;
- development-oriented conferences such as the first Neighborhood Revitalization Conference in Memphis;
- connections to job conferences and other city-planning efforts;
- collaborative research and resulting action to document problems between service programs and companies and local Black and low-income communities, as well as building new approaches to education, small business development, and summer jobs;
- recruitment of students, especially local students, into internships where they were guided in the conduct of field research that emphasized local community voices and contributed to local development;
- linking local research to national policy initiatives through programs such as Free the Children;
- participation in strategic development and cultural heritage plans;
- engaging residents, faculty, teachers, and students in mapping neighborhood assets for neighborhood planning using GIS data (Hyland and Owens 2005a);
- contributing research and resident voices to the rehabilitation of deteriorated public housing through federally funded HOPE VI federal housing and community rehabilitation programs;
- participating in linking organizational, employment, and service resources to provide various forms of support to residents moving toward full employment;

- working with local foundations to build the capacity of local groups to revitalize neighborhoods by providing small grants to build university-community partnerships and strengthen local organizational capacity; and
- supporting community organizations and other entities to generate additional federal and state sources of funding for various forms of community development.

Sustainability

The Memphis approach continues to expand as its network of former students, 50 percent of whom remain in the area to work on environment and development problems, continues to connect research with action and to join forces with the university on longer-term efforts.

The Memphis case example illustrates the variety of ways that surveys, interviews, mapping, documentaries, use of secondary data, and interdisciplinary collaborations can contribute over time to the emergence of new and empowering approaches to community development. It shows how a handful of dedicated researchers based at a university, and committed to an action/research approach, can build multiple collaborations over a long period of time in attempts to counter the effects of long-term community disinvestment and disempowerment. As in the earlier examples, Memphis community-development efforts overall have not fully solved the intransigent problems of long-term economic and political marginalization and racism, but they have made inroads in ensuring that the voices of residents and local leaders are heard in policy-related decision making. By basing action research for community development in a university, community leaders and researchers have provided a solid grounding for continuing and expanding local efforts, maintaining close links with community organizations, rallying stakeholders, and training students, together with communities to conduct research for development purposes in many different ways.

EXAMPLE 2.6

CHANGING EDUCATION IN NATIVE ALASKA

The Setting

Alaska demonstrates an inspiring illustration of the ways in which researchers and educational activists joined forces with Native Alaskans to develop multilevel approaches to changing the system, content, and structure of educational delivery and training for Native Alaskan children and youth. Educational anthropologists at the University of Alaska, Fairbanks, have been working with Native Alaskans for the past thirty years to take advantage of the opportunities presented by the Alaska Native Claims Settlement Act, passed in 1971 (Barnhardt and Kawagley 2005). The act provided the basis for a vastly expanded and newly organized Native Alaskan education system at multiple levels, based on research on indigenous knowledge systems (Barnhardt and Kawagley 2005; Barnhardt, Kawagley, and Hill 2000). An early response to the act was a mandate to develop secondary schools in the network of 125 Native communities that were isolated and at long distances from Alaska's large cities.

Partnerships

Under the direction of Ray Barnhardt, a professor of anthropology at the University of Alaska, Fairbanks, field researchers such as Barbara Harrison visited communities to engage with local village corporations to define and describe the nature of what these new high schools would be and to tutor students (Harrison 2001). From this action-research effort grew the realization that standardized curricula imposed from the "outside" were not culturally congruent with Native educational concerns and would not encourage youth to stay in school.

Strengthening Cultural Institutions

The University of Alaska, Fairbanks, responded by developing the Native Teacher Education Program, designed to train university faculty, both Native and non-Native, to prepare Native teachers in their own communities. This allowed them to integrate effective instructional concepts with local beliefs and practices (Barnhardt 1999; Barnhardt 2002; Barnhardt and Kawagley 2010). In a reflective article written in 1977, Barnhardt, who was the long-term academic coordinator of the program, describes the development of this rural teacher training program and raises critical questions about what it means to train Native teachers. These questions still are relevant in any effort to build research and education programs based on local cultural knowledge, language, and identity (Barnhardt 1977). First, Barnhardt argued that it was important to train Native teachers because they were more familiar with indigenous ways of learning and knowing, could relate more effectively to Native children, could act as positive role models, and constituted a good investment because they would remain within the state. Barnhardt and his colleagues determined that universities, however well intentioned, were unable to recruit Native people to higher education or keep them in school once they were enrolled. Among the most important reasons for this was the existence of a significant disjuncture between the motivations, cultural expectations, and needs of university programs and those of Native Alaskan students, many of whom had responsibilities to their families and communities that made moving to Fairbanks unfeasible, even if a more supportive environment for them had been created on the campus. Thus, the best way to train teachers was in their own communities.

Barnhardt and his colleagues also realized that the Western notions regarding the role of "school," "teacher," and "student" were foreign to native communities, as were mainstream methods of instruction. In effect, despite the distinct cultural differences between European Americans and Native Alaskans, actual schooling in rural Alaska differed very little from schooling in any mainstream urban area in the United States. To be successful, the researchers would need to find ways to protect and nurture the intrinsic cultural qualities that the native students brought with them and help them to fuse traditional-cultural knowledge with more mainstream ways of knowing and teaching. At the same time, they needed to help the native teacher education students maintain the essence of their identity and unique ways of relating to children. Their goal was to build on the resources of Native culture and knowledge while avoiding the trap of viewing native culture as a deficit to be overcome rather than an asset upon which to build.

To address these challenges, the three primary faculty and eight undergraduates—mainly Native—and eleven locally identified team leaders—built learning teams in each of eleven field sites. Here, the undergraduates and local trainees, all student teachers, participated as partners in the development of the curriculum. The teams remained in the community as participant ethnographers, and each teacher training team was taught the tools of ethnography, including mapping, observation, interviewing, surveys, and visual documentation. Together they learned much about the aspects of education, teaching, learning, socialization, and child development in their community using mapping, observation, interviewing, surveys, and visual documentation. They produced a community study that served as the basis for developing their own instructional programs. The students were able to support each other in their program while working in their own communities, and they could rely on elders for support while their instructors were back in Fairbanks.

Sustainability

The joint engagement of University of Alaska faculty and students with Native student educators in the field has continued to the present. A significant component of this training program involves experience living and working in Native communities (Barnhardt 1999). Barnhardt noted in 2002 that over a twenty-five-year period, more than thirty faculty members had become part of community life, learning from Native peoples and integrating their experiences and knowledge into their teacher-training activities. In the process, they have become more open, flexible, and able to problem solve—qualities that he considers essential for success in a field faculty role (Barnhardt 2002).

The university also has changed in response to Native educational needs. Indigenous cultural knowledge has been incorporated into public education programs, and indigenous schools and programs of education have been created (Barnhardt 2005, Barnhardt and Kawagley 2010). In the mid-1990s, with funding from the National Science Foundation and the Annenberg Rural Challenge, the Alaska Federation of Natives, together with the University of Alaska, teamed up to implement the Alaska Rural Sytemic Initiative (AKRSI). The purpose of the program, called "Native Pathways to Education" was to bring people together throughout the state to implement a five-year series of initiatives to systematically document the indigenous knowledge systems of Native Alaskan people. They then developed educational policies and practices that effectively integrated indigenous and Western knowledge through a renewed educational system. This project, as well as the earlier groundbreaking work in Native educational instructional development, has contributed to a uniquely culturally framed set of state educational standards, responsive to all subjects and instructional processes involved in public education in Alaska. The Alaskan Native approach to cultural conservation and comprehensive education is framed by and available to the public through the programs and products of the Alaskan Native Knowledge Network (ANKA) (http://www.ankn.uaf.edu/index .html), a regularly updated website that includes publications, educational resources and curricula, training programs with the University of Alaska, Fairbanks, and other materials useful to educators, students, Native communities and the public at large.

The Fairbanks/Native Alaskan experience, like others that support the development of indigenous and decolonized public educational approaches in Hawaii, New Zealand, Cambodia, the Navaho Nation of the United States, and communities in Latin America, arises from a set of important antecedent conditions. These include:

- widespread concern about the negative experiences of indigenous or Native students in school and high rates of school dropout;

- citizen advocacy promoting the passing of legislation supporting indigenous rights;
- advocacy-oriented social scientists and educators— sometimes from these same communities—who are intent on creating new culturally rooted educational institutions;
- fully collaborative relationships between local communities and researchers; and
- a vision of culturally driven education programs and institutions and the processes that permit them to emerge and thrive.

Resources such as these often evolve, as Barnhardt notes, in a somewhat chaotic or dynamic and interactive manner. Their goals are loosely envisioned, and their pursuit follows multiple paths, causing research to intersect with action— that is, interventions, policy change, education, use of media, curriculum development, and advocacy—over time. Finally, the impetus to act in all of the above listed examples appears to come from the directed energy of one or two key people, in part because they have written the articles describing the work. However, in each instance there clearly are many other actors and participants who have shared the same convictions and offered their skills, resources, and reflexivity to the overall success of the endeavors, each in their own way.

EXAMPLE 2.7

THE DETROIT URBAN RESEARCH CENTER

The Setting and Funding

The Detroit Community-Academic Urban Research Center is an urban consortium that includes various schools of the University of Michigan and a variety of other organizations and institutes that serve the greater Detroit area (http://detroitcenter .umich.edu/projects/detroit-community-academic-urban-research-center). It developed from an earlier collaboration between the university, the Detroit Health department, and community organizations funded by the Kellogg Foundation. That collaboration helped to develop guidelines for later work. When the Centers for Disease Control (CDC) offered funding for cooperative agreements for the development of urban research centers (URCs), the University of Michigan consortium applied for and received one of four grants awarded nationally.

The Partners

With these and later project-based funds, the consortium has grown to include more university schools and departments (nursing and social work, as well as the Institute of Popular Health), the Detroit Department of Health and Wellness Promotion, eight community-based organizations (Community Health and Social Services Center [CHASS], Communities in Schools, Detroiters Working for Environmental Justice, Detroit Hispanic Development Corporation, Friends of Parkside, Latino Family Services, the Neighborhood Service Organization, the Detroit Neighborhood Partnership East, Inc./Warren-Conner Development Coalition), and the Henry Ford Health System. Other organizations have joined as members of the steering committees of specific URC related projects (www.detroiturc.org).

Linking Research and Action

The Detroit URC has focused on the identification of structural and social determinants of health outcomes and the development of community-based interventions to address them in the east, southwest, and northwest sides of Detroit. The Detroit URC

> promotes and conducts interdisciplinary, community-based participatory research which recognizes, builds upon and enhances the resources and strengths in the communities involved. The research and interventions conducted contribute to the understanding of the relationship between social determinants, the built environment, protective factors, intermediate outcomes, and long-term health outcomes specific to urban environments. The knowledge gained contributes to the design of appropriate public health interventions, programs and policies aimed at promoting health equity (http://detroitcenter.umich.edu/projects/detroit-community-academic-urban-research-center).

The work of the URC and its associated projects is participatory, collaborative, and intended to have both short- and long-term outcomes. In its early years, the consortium developed procedures guiding partnership research similar to those outlined in chapter 3 of this book. It also refined a list of problems affecting the communities of concern. The methodology used was simple and effective: devise an initial list of problems, determine whether other agencies were working in the same areas, reduce the list to a shorter one focusing on key areas of concern, determine whether these areas were suitable for URC attention, and narrow the list to three. The final priorities were health care access and quality, housing quality and health, and violence (Israel et al. 2001, 8). The CDC grant included project funds which focused on the development of a village health worker partnership in east Detroit and the creation of consortium infrastructure, a complex task requiring the establishment of norms and rules for community-based research partnerships, balancing task orientation with a process focus, selecting priorities, negotiating the complexities of both university/community relationships and intra-community relationships, finding and distributing financial resources equally, and evaluation and self-reflection—among others.

Since 1995, the Detroit URC has focused on a number of longer and shorter range projects that constitute a blend of research and intervention. The research is led by investigators at the University of Michigan and conducted in partnership with various communities and organizations concerned with specific problems. Community Action against Asthma (CAAA) is a good example of a long-term program of research and intervention to address the significant problem of environmentally exacerbated asthma in Detroit. CAAA is a research partnership, formed in 1998 with funding from the National Institute on Environmental Health Sciences (NIEHS) to the University of Michigan. Funding for different aspects of the program has continued with grants from NIEHS and the American Psychological Association. Members of the two-city consortium include community-based organizations in east and southwest Detroit and Dearborn, health and human service agencies in the city of Detroit, and university representatives. "CAAA is involved in both intervention and epidemiological research focusing on environmental triggers for asthma" (http://sitemaker.umich.edu/caaa/who_we_are) (Parker et al. 2003). The consortium has produced a substantial number of scientific publications on a variety of approaches to research and structural interventions to reduce asthma in Detroit, including formative research on factors contributing to high levels of indoor particulate matter (Doan et al. 2012; Parker, Batterman, et al. 2011; Parker, Robins, et al. 2011) and interventions including the introduction of free standing air filters and air conditioners (Batterman et al. 2013; Du et al. 2011) and studying and reducing diesel exhaust (Robins et al. 2010).

The Detroit URC is a good example of a "living alliance"—a core group of representatives of organizations concerned with quality of life in a specific environment that initiates, endorses, and takes on new members to support projects related to its mission (Radda and Schensul, 2011). As in other cases, this long-term effort to chip away at intransigent, structurally and situationally rooted health problems takes time. It also requires continuous infusions of new sources of revenue, most of which are obtained by investigators at the University of Michigan. Like the University of Memphis, the School of Public Health of the University of Michigan pays close attention to training and mentoring doctoral and postdoctoral researchers who value and are skilled at interdisciplinary community-based participatory research and practice. Postdoctoral trainees in the CBPR approach have dispersed all over the United States and help to promote community-engaged, social-change-oriented health research in their universities and with community partners.

The long-term development efforts described here are not unusual in the fields of sociology, public health, anthropology, and more recently geography and psychology. They depend on committed and politicized researchers, a stable base with continuous funding, specific communities of reference—namely, those experiencing clear problems and issues that need to be addressed. These efforts identify internal and external resources, the resources, assets, and capacities needed to address problems or issues, and enough time to participate in organizing efforts on behalf of their constituencies. Political circumstances, funding policies, national and state/regional norms and values, and other factors also are critical in shaping both the circumstances that communities wish to change—which may shift over time—and the resources available with which to address them.

We have used these cases as exemplars of the many longer-term social change efforts carried out by researchers and their alliances, spread across different disciplines in locations across the United States and Canada. These researchers have worked together over time with whole communities, neighborhoods, cities, and networks of rural communities to change social, structural, and individual factors that result in significant health, social, educational, and environmental disparities. Such efforts can be found in most countries. Wherever they exist, new researchers, including students, can engage with them and find ways of using their skills to contribute to local improvements. They can learn how to work with local communities and broader settings, and make contributions to science at the same time. In her book *Collaborative Programs in Indigenous Communities*, Barbara Harrison describes how she did just that when she was a graduate student, when she joined the Rural High Schools Program initiated by the University of Alaska, Fairbanks (Harrison 2001). She goes on to talk about many other such efforts involving "collaborative fieldworkers." For her, the collaborative fieldworker is not the charismatic and persistent leader who works from a university or even a community base to build large-scale alliances. The fieldworker is the student, or new faculty member, or researcher with limited potential for generating resources (at least initially), who wants to build relationships that enable people in local communities to use research to improve their conditions. Graduate schools with long-term links with local communities can make it easier for such students and new faculty to integrate into ongoing research and change efforts.

EXAMPLES OF SHORTER-TERM COMMUNITY-BASED RESEARCH PARTNERSHIPS FOR CHANGE

There are many very good examples of shorter-term or single-intervention studies that constitute collaborations with local communities that have high potential to bring about important changes in health and education but are not linked specifically to larger development efforts. Many of them take place in the context of broader historical and structural changes that create enabling circumstances and alliances, collaborations, or other structures that have arisen to respond to such issues. Programs of intervention research to prevent the spread of HIV offer an excellent example of such efforts. Since the mid-1980s when HIV was first recognized as a national/international issue affecting large numbers of people involved in risky transmission behavior, representatives from HIV advocacy organizations have argued forcefully in support of directing more laboratory and behavioral science resources to prevention, testing, treatment, and service coordination. As a consequence, many millions of dollars have been dedicated to addressing the multiple faces of HIV, and many researchers have been involved in research on all aspects of HIV at multiple levels.

Early psychology-driven intervention studies by necessity involved partnerships with local sites and people affected by HIV or at risk of contracting it. One such partnership was the well-known peer opinion leader approach created by Jeffrey Kelly in collaboration with gay men in bars. In this study, researchers identified peer leaders through a nomination process, trained them in HIV prevention, and asked them to deliver the intervention to their networks. The effort had a significant impact on young gay men (Kelly et al. 1990). Working in partnership with a local Black activist, psychologist Roberta Paikoff and her colleagues in the West Side community of Chicago developed an early multilevel intervention that linked parents, schools, and community in a sex and HIV-prevention education program with young teens (McKay et al. 2004). Tom Coates, a psychologist, and Ron Stall, an anthropologist/epidemiologist, and their colleagues at the University of California, San Francisco (UCSF), worked with NIMH funding to counter HIV in the deeply affected San Francisco gay community and beyond (Catania et al. 1992, Kegeles, Hays, and Coates 1996). With funding from local foundations for interventions, they helped to build a number of collaborative interventions and evaluate them (Schensul 1999). Many community-based community-researcher partnership approaches to preventing HIV among drug users were funded by the National Institute on Drug Abuse. These projects used innovative approaches, including mixed methods, network research, and rapid assessment, to motivate organizations and alliances of stakeholders to address HIV in their communities.

Most of these ventures were spearheaded by universities that worked with communities to obtain the funding for their intervention studies, and they engaged many students in the process. Some of them transferred skills to the participating communities as did Paikoff and her colleague in Chicago, and Kegeles and colleagues working with gay men through the Manpower project (Kegeles, Hays, and Coates 1996). However, in most cases these efforts, important as they were in developing innovative ways of countering a serious and rapidly moving epidemic, came to an end when the funding stopped, despite significant efforts to institutionalize them locally. That is not to say that this work is not important in producing good results for science which could be scaled up for use in other communities. However, it does not have *local* sustainability unless it is embedded in local

community efforts and has the promise of being continued with community resources after the immediate source of funding has disappeared (Schensul et al. 2005).

EXAMPLE 2.8

ADDRESSING HIV IN MUMBAI—THREE INTERVENTIONS

A good case in point is the innovative approach to preventing HIV in Mumbai undertaken by a consortium of international institutions including the University of Connecticut, the Institute for Community Research, Hartford Connecticut, the International Institute for Population Sciences, the International Center for Research on Women, Population Council Delhi Office, a teaching hospital in Mumbai, the Mumbai Municipal Council, the National Institute of Medical Statistics, and the National AIDS Control Organization. The team, led by Stephen Schensul, an anthropologist, and Ravi Verma, a community psychologist, consisted of anthropologists, psychologists, demographers, local nontraditional Ayurvedic, homeopathic, and other alternative health providers (known by the acronym AYUSH), an epidemiologist, and physicians. This consortium, a living alliance with slightly changing membership depending on the mobility of key researchers and the nature of the intervention study, has developed three large-scale five-year community-based participatory research (CBPR) intervention studies, all with community partners.

The first project worked with medically trained physicians and local AYUSH providers, using the notion of sexual dysfunction/men's sexual problems (*gupt rog*) to address sexual health and other issues brought by married men (Schensul et al., 2004). The study's primary hypothesis was that reducing concern about sexual function in marriage would prevent men from seeking extramarital relationships, which could reduce the likelihood of transmitting HIV. The design involved comparing a onetime intervention delivered by more than sixty AYUSH providers in one study community of about 200,000 people to the same intervention delivered by allopathic (Western medicine) physicians in a male-health clinic established by the partner hospital. The intervention was based on ethnographic research showing that *gupt rog* was a significant problem related to masculinity that sent men to the doctor. Using a narrative approach, the providers elicited stories that explained the presenting symptoms and then helped the patients to devise a culturally situated explanation of the problem linked to improvements in communication with their spouses. The intervention was very successful—the results showed significantly reduced sexual risk seeking and alcohol consumption. The study results and manual were disseminated nationally, and the study team made efforts to institutionalize the men's health clinic, but staffing it became a problem and it did not survive. The specific efforts came to an end with the funding, though the ideas and relationships in the field continued.

While in the field, researchers identified women's sexual health concerns, manifested in an idiom of distress known as *safed pani* or white discharge. Presence of this nonmedical condition was associated with marital conflicts and gender power differences in marriage that led men to seek other relationships. A second five-year intervention study was implemented with most of the same institutional partners, who received funding to address this problem and worked to do so with local partners, including mosques, a community health clinic where the program initiated a *women*'s health clinic, and a network of NGOs concerned with women's health and gender issues. Women reporting *safed pani* were randomized to a counseling-only intervention arm, a couples' intervention arm, and a standard treatment arm. Women (or couples) attended up to six counseling sessions to address culturally based issues related to marital relationships and conflict. At the same time, to change community norms, Imams delivered gender equity messages which they developed with the intervention team to their followers in sermons at Friday prayers. Community based service organizations (CBOs) and women's organizations also intermittently delivered gender equity messages through marches, banners, and health fairs.

The effects of the intervention, both at the community and the individual level, showed that the intervention dramatically improved marital relationships and gender equitable norms. However, the program as a whole could not be locally institutionalized. Though Imams continued to deliver messages on a regular basis, efforts to integrate the counseling program into a local degree-granting institution, to be delivered via monitored student interns, were not successful. Neither could the women's health clinic be sustained for financial reasons. Nevertheless, the study has been widely recognized in India and hailed as a national model (Schensul et al., 2009).

The third study, guided by the focus of HIV research on treatment, is a site-based intervention study taking place in collaboration with antiretroviral treatment (ART) centers at large hospitals throughout the greater Mumbai area. Funded by the U.S. National Institute for Alcohol Abuse and Alcoholism, it is a multilevel intervention with individual, group, and community components, conducted in collaboration with key service organizations and the government's AIDS control program. It is designed to be integrated into the national program of treatment for people with HIV. However, unlike the prior studies, this study includes three U.S.-based institutions, two international India-based NGOs, the government AIDS Control Organization and the ART centers. It is integrated into the Indian AIDS policy, program, and service delivery system. The research team anticipates that there will be as many constraints as there are facilitators, both to implementation and institutionalization; as the government changes, treatment guidelines change, and the caseload of PLWA (people living with AIDS) increases. Though it is based on prior intervention experience with men and on research on drinking among men in Maharashtra, both the formative research and the interventions have to be newly created for HIV-positive men and their circumstances. Thus, the study began with in-depth interviews with drinking men, a screener to iden-

tify the prevalence of drinking among HIV-positive men, and a 361-person survey to evaluate new scales and assess drinking and adherence measures. These data will provide local input into the formulation of individual interventions that counselors can use with drinking men, group interventions with small groups of HIV-positive men, and a community-level intervention to address HIV-related stigma, which is persistent and has a chronic effect on the identity, confidence, and emotional stability of seropositive men. With strong government support, there is some considerable hope that this multi-intervention approach will have longer-term effects and can be scaled up.

In this long-term program of "short-term" intervention research projects, involving sequential studies in different communities and settings with similar partners and related outcomes, more than twenty graduate students and as many twenty faculty members from participating institutions in India, as well as several from the United States, have contributed in different ways to the research efforts. Five-year program cycles and other shorter-term programs of funded intervention research involving multiple stakeholders, including community partners, offer many opportunities for faculty, students, other researchers, and HIV activists to become involved for short periods of time. Interested learners can enter at any point, and with guidance from PIs and program staff, can conduct research of benefit to the programs and to the local community. Another strength of this type of effort is that the Indian organizations and investigators involved have been part of the research program from the start, and they are in positions to continue to obtain funding for specific projects from multiple sources as long as HIV research remains relevant in India.

Finally, a number of universities and schools have long histories of training graduate students to become involved in their own short Participatory Action Research projects, among them the University of South Florida (anthropology), Cornell (rural sociology), and City University of New York Graduate School (psychology). These brief studies, often a semester or a year in duration, usually involve students who work with local groups on local problems using a participatory approach. Sometimes, these local programs have given way to larger, more sustainable efforts led by university faculty with partners, funded by local or national foundations and based on the work of large-scale alliances, as in the case of the PAR program started by Cornell's rural sociology program. The medical anthropology program at the University of Connecticut, the Social Science and Development Program at the University of Kentucky, and the applied anthropology at Teachers' College, Columbia, all began in the 1960s and 1970s with the formation of alliances or funded projects in which students were placed, often in centers dedicated to specific development activities. In contrast to individual student efforts, these larger development efforts have greater sustainability and offer students better examples of faculty-student-community collaborations and a longer history of ways in which research facilitates actions. Students and new faculty who want to learn how to conduct research and intervention studies are advised to seek out longer-term programs such as these and discover both what they can contribute and what they can learn from their participation.

SUMMARY

In this chapter, we have set out to describe a number of longer- and shorter-term programs in which research and various forms of action intersect over time to lead toward transformational change in local communities. We have seen that, regardless of duration, these efforts have somewhat similar characteristics. They call for a creative and impassioned mix of skilled researchers and community partners or alliances willing to take on entrenched power structures, racist and otherwise discriminatory policies, and long histories of economic, social, and cultural marginalization. Finding or establishing a well-run alliance is required for long-term development since neither researchers nor activist community individuals or organizations are strong enough by themselves to transform hierarchies of local (or at times national) power. Such alliances are sufficiently well organized to be able to take on and finish projects and tasks, and sufficiently flexible to undertake new issues as they arise.

All of the initiatives we have described use a broad mixture of research methods, including observation, interviews, mapping, elicitation techniques, photography and video, network research, rapid assessment, surveys, and analysis of secondary data, to move their work forward. Sometimes the research is conducted by the researchers alone; at other times, it is carried out by partnerships under CBPR guidelines; and occasionally technology transfer takes place as in the case of Memphis and Hartford, where local communities were trained to do research.

In each case, the specific interventions are theoretically driven. Many use a general ecological approach, with multiple intervention components introduced at the same time. Others, such as Memphis, began with historical research and shifted toward alliances and more targeted efforts directed toward groups and policy makers. The intervention theories are appropriate to level (individual, group, community, etc.), always consider the input of those most directly affected, and are often culturally and always situationally appropriate (i.e., feasible and acceptable).

Successful structural change, continuity of development efforts, and sustainability of process and effect are persistent issues in longer- and shorter-term intervention programs. All of the efforts we have described involve multiple sources of relatively long-term funding. The work of development, whether in health, education, housing, or the improvement of fisheries stock cannot persist without duration and without adequate funding. For this reason, all such efforts are vulnerable to the vagaries of government policies and funding decisions. Thus, mobilizers must be open to constantly searching for and finding new funding and development opportunities and must be creative in accessing them, while at the same time not undermining their missions.

In this chapter we have not paid attention to the ways in which theories guiding social change/intervention efforts are developed by stakeholder groups and participating communities. Instead, we have concentrated on providing the larger picture of the many ways in which research and action are intertwined in longer and shorter programs of research. In the next chapter we begin a review of the building blocks of ethnography in action: building research collaborations and partnerships that make the long-term process of social change, social action, and social justice possible.

3 ━◆━◆━◆━

BUILDING PARTNERSHIPS AND COLLABORATIONS FOR ETHNOGRAPHY IN ACTION

INTRODUCTION

In the previous chapter we examined long- and short-term ethnographically based action research efforts in education, community development, and health. In all of the examples, partnerships among researchers, community leaders and residents, and community-serving organizations were central in starting the work, and they also were central in continuing, expanding, and sustaining it. In this chapter, we focus on the process of forming and sustaining ethnographically based research partnerships. Their mission is to establish relationships that create opportunities to use research to remedy social, economic, historical, educational, and other socially constructed problems, inequities, disparities, and injustices. Partnerships and alliances can support short-term/one-time projects, and they can and do expand and change over time as new activities and programs emerge and new people and organizations are required. We begin with a caveat: not all situations lend themselves to problem solving, even over time; and not all situations offer opportunities for research, even if it is to move toward an important cause. Nevertheless, the only way to know whether research and cause can join forces is through building relationships out of which the marriage might emerge. Thus we begin by describing different types of research partnerships or alliances involving ethnographers, other researchers, community partners, and stakeholders of different types.

A **research partnership** involves an equitable collaboration among ethnographers, researchers from other disciplines, and nonresearchers who want to study a pressing problem together in order to transform it. We focus on the relationships between ethnographers and other researchers and the communities and groups with which they work to learn about pressing social, political, health, educational, or other problems in order to solve them. An **ethnography in action research partnership** links researchers and communities in the conduct of research to solve pressing social and other problems.

In the first section of this chapter, we review the different perspectives on action or applied research partnerships, situating them in the world of research, intervention, transformation and social justice. Next, we outline some of the circumstances that favor participatory and collaborative approaches over other approaches to improving health, education, equity, and social welfare. Then we turn to how ethnographic research can help identify good partners and allies. Finally, we review some principles guiding effective research partnerships for change and discuss a range of partnership models, describing what makes them good and how to maintain and sustain them.

Definition: A research partnership involves an equitable collaboration among ethnographers, researchers from other disciplines, and nonresearchers who want to study a problem together in order to transform it

Definition: An ethnography in action research partnership links researchers and communities in the conduct of research to solve pressing social and other problems

CONTEXTUAL FACTORS THAT FAVOR ETHNOGRAPHIC COLLABORATIONS FOR CHANGE

A number of changes in the contexts and environments for research over the past thirty years have helped to create a more favorable atmosphere for developing collaborative partnerships designed to solve community problems. Throughout, many researchers, community and public sector advocates, businesses, and health professionals have argued that partnerships are critical to good problem-solving social science research.

- Stakeholders now realize that complex social problems require input from all sectors.
- Collaboration among scientists is increasingly common and often required.
- Research technology has become more user friendly.
- Communities recognize their right to have influence over research directions, designs, and results representation.
- Researchers and providers now recognize that participant input into research and service programs increases effectiveness.
- The boundaries of what constitutes good evidence for assessing medical, educational, and other outcomes and program impacts are expanding.
- Constraints on public/private resources call for consistent evaluation to increase accountability.
- Communications technology increases the rapidity and reach of interventions, advocacy, and results.
- Funders, including foundations and the National Institutes of Health and their affiliates, realize that collaborative research with affected communities can produce better science, especially with respect to reducing health disparities.

What all the foregoing means is that, first and foremost, most social, educational, and health problems are complex. They include multiple components, interacting and sometimes unknown causes, and positive and negative feedback loops, and they do not respond well when approached with single or simple solutions that fail to consider all the multiple constituencies and forces that created them. For example, stopping the "school to prison" pipeline is a complex social problem. This concept, the "pipeline," refers to school policies that facilitate school dropout and subsequent student behavior that violates the law. The pipeline is initiated by school policies that suspend or expel students who often have been marginalized because of their poverty, race or ethnicity, or sexual orientation. Such students then may

begin illegal or anti-social activities that result in imprisonment. This has produced prisons flooded with low-income
African American and Latino young men, largely because
they are most likely to be targeted for harsh treatment in
school (Peak 2015; Porter 2015; Wilson 2014).

Another complex problem is the "treatment
cascade"(Mugavero et al. 2013). The term *treatment cascade*
refers to the process by which people who have been diagnosed as HIV positive drop out of HIV testing, then treatment, and finally medication adherence at different points
in the very complex and often poorly coordinated health
care system through which they are supposed to receive
treatment. The idea of a treatment cascade was developed
when it became possible to measure the level of the HIV
virus in individuals and in populations. Once it became
clear that effective treatment could reduce the viral load in
individuals' blood to undetectable levels, thereby preventing transmission from person to person, the HIV research
and treatment community shifted its primary focus from
community prevention strategies (education focused on
avoiding multiple sex partners, using protection, and avoiding injecting with unclean needles and syringes) to prevention through treatment. Proper treatment, it was argued,
could result in virtual elimination of transmission in a
population if every infected person took medication as prescribed. However, treatment as prevention of transmission
could be effective only if every person at risk was identified,
screened, diagnosed, enrolled in treatment, able to obtain
and willing to take medication consistently, and capable of
obtaining the supportive services needed to ensure treatment continuity. This idea can apply to any public health
problem that calls for continuous treatment to avoid infect-
ing others; it has long been used for tuberculosis and now
is recommended for hepatitis C. Superficially, the problem looks simple. Once an effective treatment has been
developed, get people diagnosed, into treatment, and on
medication. However, more than 30 percent of the people
diagnosed never achieve sustained medication adherence.
The problem is complex because the American health care
system is fragmented, patients can move from one service
provider to another, tracking systems for following patients

do not exist, organizations do not cross-refer patients to different or more effective providers, case managers are ineffective, providers go out of business, and patients are vulnerable to life crises and difficulties stemming from their social, cultural, economic, and other circumstances.

Other examples of complex problems include managing the impact of climate change, preventing malaria, improving the quality of local food supplies in low-income neighborhoods, and controlling the spread of flavored tobaccos. Trying to treat these problems by implementing a single solution, such as simply handing out free bed nets for malaria, importing water to dry overcrowded urban areas, or banning flavored cigarettes is ineffective because there may be many contributors to the problem not addressed by the single solution. Partial responses such as those above will be ineffective at least, or may even lead to worse results.

Recognizing and addressing complex problems require the use of complex, trans-disciplinary, multi-sectoral and community-engaged approaches, holistic mixed methods ethnography, and ongoing engagement with the multiple systems that have been identified as contributors to both the causes of and the solutions to human problems. Devising new contextually and culturally tailored approaches to learning problems in children, for instance, may require psycho-social understandings of how learning occurs, ethnographic observations to compare how different kinds of children learn in different social and cultural contexts, formal assessment by school psychologists using culturally appropriate tools, the services of physicians to determine the potential impact of clinical problems on learning, as well as architects, pedagogical experts, parents and local community representatives, and new ways of changing environments to accommodate different learning styles.

Still another complex problem is asthma management. Effective asthma management requires that people with asthma be able to access and use health care that connects them to skilled and responsive providers on an ongoing basis. They must have insurance that permits them to purchase the right medications at the right time; they may need help to find ways to overcome cultural or personal factors that interfere with medication administration. This is complicated by the fact that asthma often results from exposure to environmental causes that require the removal of toxins, pollutants, and insects from home and community—a process that may be well-nigh impossible. Working on these complex human problems can't be done without the active participation of the communities or institutions affected by them and the involvement of scientists and interventionists from different disciplines and traditions.

A second catalyst for change has been the growth of movements fighting against the exclusion or misrepresentation of the realities faced by communities and indigenous populations that are underrepresented in the power structure, including African Americans, Latinos, the LGTBQ population, undocumented residents, Native Americans, people with disabilities or stigmatized health conditions, immigrants, or other potentially marginalized groups. Such groups now rightfully demand to be involved in improvement of services that affect them, by becoming informed about their own communities, engaging in the political process and research based advocacy, and joining in various forms of participatory research. These movements, which began in the 1970s and came to the fore in the mid-1980s, have grown very significantly as more members of underrepresented groups have gained advanced educational degrees or have become partners in research programs. In addition, several important national networks have worked to promote citizen involvement in science. In the 1990s the LOKA Institute, now based in Washington, DC, and working worldwide, was founded to bring ordinary citizens into science decision making, which also served to bring together other kinds of organizations involved in community-based research. The idea of these organizations was to frame a national community research agenda for community development and environmental research. The Community Research Network (CRN) now is "a trans-national network of research and grassroots organizations conducting community-based research for social change." Its mission is to create a system through which grassroots, worker, and public-interest organizations, together with local governments, can find solutions to social and environmental problems and participate more effectively in public policy by establishing the agenda and controlling the results of research (Mugavero et al. 2013). The CRN is based in the European organization Living Knowledge, the International Science Shop Network (http://www.livingknowledge.org/livingknowledge/), which furthers science and societal relationships and science in the public interest.

The Community Network for Research Equity and Impact (CNREI), sponsored by Community Campus Partnerships for Health (CCPH), a national organization committed to fostering productive community-engaged research in health, is another example of a community-based research network (https://ccph.memberclicks.net/network-for-research-equity). In 2006, CNREI was formed as the Partners Forum to advocate for the equitable involvement of widely diverse community organizations in community-based research projects that partner with universities. Many of the 450 organizations that belong to CNREI also conduct their own research. Key to formation of the network was the discomfort that community organizations felt with the unequal balance of power between themselves and the universities that were approaching them to participate in research partnerships. As a condition of federal financial support, universities were required to enroll minority participants into federally funded studies and to disseminate the results of research into local communities. They appealed to local organizations to help them find such participants. However, that recruitment caused hostilities within the communities, whose organizations commonly complained that universities were asking them to refer patients to studies without properly compensating them for their recruitment time or not compensating them at all. Communities also charged that they were not invited to be involved in studies affecting their constituencies and that researchers rarely, if ever, delivered research results back to the communities from which their participants or patients had come. The CNREI has met nationally on a yearly basis and in smaller regional groups to share perspectives and devise ways of advocating for more and more equitable, community-based research and partnerships. At the same time, members support each other in demanding that universities share resources, time, and results with their community partners and include them as authentic investigators in the research. The widespread recognition of how scientists have misused and taken advantage of local communities, combined with larger social movements focused on community activated science, has led to community awareness that research can and should directly benefit the people and organizations affected and that the best way for this to happen is through equitable partnerships.

In the mid-1980s, the Environmental Protection Agency (EPA) developed a program of involving stakeholders in research to address service and health aspects of environmental problems. This Participatory Action Research model helped to guide the programs of the National Institute for Environmental Health and Safety (NIEHS), which made funding conditional on involving local stakeholders in research on environmental health issues. Now the EPA promotes collaborative problem solving (CPS). Collaborative problem solving involves information collection at multiple points in the process from all stakeholders.

> CPS involves proactive, strategic, and visionary community-based processes that bring together multiple parties from various stakeholder groups (e.g., community groups, all levels of government, industry, and academia) to develop solutions to local environmental and/or public health issues. Partnerships and negotiations are required to achieve such solutions. Partnerships refer to arrangements through which different stakeholders work together to achieve a common goal. (http://www.epa.gov/sustainability/analytics/collps.htm)

The Agency for Health Care Quality (AHRQ), a federal funding institution dedicated to producing and disseminating evidence to improve health care (http://www.ahrq.gov/) wrote the first public statement about patient involvement in health research and care in 2004 (Viswanathan et al. 2004). Since that time, the National Institute of Health, new public health research funders like the Patient

Centered Outcomes Research Institute (PCORI), and the translational science movement have all called for greater community engagement in improving public health programs and the quality of patient care, and in reducing unacceptable health disparities. In the world of activist scholarship, public health researchers such as Barbara Israel (Israel, Krieger, et al. 2006; Israel et al. 2001; Israel, Schulz, et al. 2006), Meredith Minkler and Nina Wallerstein (Minkler and Wallerstein 2010; Minkler, Wallerstein, and Wilson 1997), and their colleagues have worked hard to produce a public health movement that focuses research on equitable social-justice-oriented university-community partnerships to reduce health disparities. The same movement toward collaborative research for social change can be seen in community psychology, reflected in the critical approach of Nelson and Prilleltensky (2010) and publications such as the *American Journal of Community Psychology*.

In anthropology, collaboration was evident in the early work of Sol Tax, who coined the term *action anthropology*. In the 1980s, collections by Eddy and Partridge (1987), Schensul and Eddy (1985), Schensul and Stern (1985), and Stull and Schensul (1987) summarized examples of collaborative or team ethnographic and interdisciplinary research experiences in the United States and elsewhere. And there are newer publications by Reason and Bradbury (2008), Whyte (1991), Scrimshaw and Gleason (1992), Schensul and colleagues (Berg and Schensul 2004; Schensul et al. 2006; Schensul and Schensul 1992), and Bartunek and Louis (1996). More recently, discussions of community engagement (Low and Merry 2010), advocacy research (Schensul and Schensul 1978; Schensul et al. 2014), and public anthropology (Beck and Maida 2015; Borofsky 2011) have been prominent in the literature. Several journals including *Practicing Anthropology* and *Human Organization*, an interdisciplinary applied publication, discuss collaborative and participatory research. *Collaborative Anthropologies*, a journal devoted to collaborative approaches in anthropology, was initiated by Eric Lassiter, whose perspective on collaboration in ethnographic research begins with the stance that all ethnography is by definition collaborative (Lassiter 2005). It includes many articles on joint ethnographic writing, action research, and participatory research with social movements.

Applied fields such as education also have been using ethnographic research to evaluate innovative programs since the 1970s. Often funded as part of federal program-development activities, ethnography itself has become an accepted part of the educational researcher's repertory (Fetterman 1984; Gitlin 1994). Ethnography in action increasingly is being used as a means to identify disparities in educational services, to develop remediation for such disparities, and to improve the overall quality of the educational experience for children. In addition, collaborative projects involve partnering teachers and researchers in ongoing programs to design, test out, evaluate, revise, and re-administer innovative programs, especially in science, reading and mathematics (Penuel and Fishman 2012).

Another important catalyst for change that is *not* favorable to collaborative, Participatory Action Research and social-justice-oriented change stems from neoliberal ideological efforts in the United States and elsewhere to downsize government and reduce funding for public services and research. The movement to shrink government began in the United States with the Republican administrations of the 1960s and 1980s. It is based on the ideological premise that "the best government is the least government," and the conviction that social services and infrastructures of all kinds should be provided by individuals, not governments. The idea is that these services, when government funded, promote the proliferation of unnecessary public bureaucracy and should be allowed to wither away. This movement has significantly reduced public funding for any kinds of agencies promoting social services, including those in health and mental health, education at all levels, social services, transportation, housing, food services, police, fire, consumer and environmental protection, and physical infrastructure. The process of public sector "shrinkage" reached its zenith with the U.S. government's decision to institute a process known as *sequestration* in 2011, when the U.S. Congress could not agree on a federal budget acceptable to fiscal conservatives and neoliberals. As defined by the Congressional Research Service, sequestration "entails the permanent cancellation of budgetary resources by a uniform percentage. Moreover, this uniform percent reduction is applied to all programs, projects and activities within a budget account" (http://uspolitics.about.com/od/thefederalbudget/a/What-Is-Sequestration.htm). Sequestration is initiated as an across-the-board percentage cut in the budget when the budget deficit exceeds a legislatively established allowable amount, and Congress itself cannot make decisions on where and how to make cuts. Sequestration practices have fallen particularly hard on programs serving those most in need, including food stamps, WIC, and housing for the poor, and also on Native Americans and federally funded tribal support programs. Even though those payments to tribal members are mandated by long-standing treaties between the U.S. government and Native American nations, they have not been exempted from sequestration cuts. The reductions have halted tribal construction projects for schools, housing, and health facilities; reduced money available to tribal people for health care and food; and eliminated a whole range of infrastructure improvements which are sorely needed to keep the United States safe. Neither private nor corporate funding nor philanthropy has been able to substitute for these losses in revenue.

These fiscal policies have had an overall deleterious impact on all forms of programs for low-income, non-mainstream, marginalized, and otherwise challenged populations. Declines in federal support for social welfare programs over time have promoted a scramble among nonprofit and governmental social service agencies for increasingly scarce resources and, as well, led to increased emphasis on fiscal accountability and intervention efficacy. This, in turn, has led to implementation of less effective, but cheaper, solutions to social problems. It also increased scrutiny for possible fraudulent use of public and non-profit funding. As many once-public social services and educational institutions have been privatized or come to rely on philanthropy or business partnerships for funding, they have been pushed to institute cost-saving measures that obviate the kind of attention to unpacking complex social problems that has been the hallmark of ethnography in action. As the overall pot of money available for all forms of services gets drastically smaller, nonprofit service and other organizations have been forced into competition with one another for scarce resources. Some of these organizations have tried to develop cheaper and readily accessible program evaluation measures that service organizations can use easily but that poorly assess the real impact of innovations. Ultimately, many have tried to develop ways to collaborate, instead of competing, for service funding. However, the overall effect is to discourage collaboration and community participation, and to place emphasis only on innovations that can be implemented in a short period and evaluated cheaply and easily.

These processes can be seen quite dramatically in education, where the effects of the No Child Left Behind Act (NCLB)—as the re-authorization of the Elementary and Secondary Education Act in the United States has come to be known, and its successor, "Race to the Top"—now are becoming obvious. No Child Left Behind reforms focused on testing the achievement of children and teachers rather than on creating innovative ways to improve teaching and learning. Performance is narrowly measured by tests in the basic skills of reading, writing, and math, and rewards in education are pegged to test performance. Children cannot be promoted, teachers do not receive merit pay, and schools have their overall funding reduced unless they achieve at a certain standard, set by each state. Since all rewards are determined by student performance on standardized tests, practice in public education has been reduced to "teaching to the test." Standardized and "high stakes" testing also has reduced evaluation of educational programs and assessment and measurement of student achievement and teacher effectiveness from broad-based measures of educational effectiveness and student/teacher growth to the use of norm-referenced standardized tests and randomized controlled trials (RCTs) using only quantitative standardized tests, even though it is widely recognized that RCTs are very difficult to implement ethically in public education. They also focus only on "effect size," or mean overall results, to measure success, rather than examining the variations in impact which are crucial to tailoring education to individual and group needs.

Increasingly, efforts sponsored under NCLB have come under close scrutiny. They have had little impact on student achievement and have been rejected in a majority of states, in particular because they are seen to be punitive to students most in need. They pay little attention to educational processes, context, and program implementation, which educators know are as important as outcomes in shaping educational programs. Further, excessive time in classrooms is spent preparing to take tests, rather than teaching the curriculum. Teachers, parents, and students alike are beginning to boycott the frequent high-stakes standardized tests mandated in most K–12 grades. *Increasingly, educators are hoping to turn more heavily to partnerships in education and ethnographic/mixed methods approaches to evaluation, including participatory forms of assessment, which facilitate more complex approaches to understanding the complicated and multiple factors that influence educational achievement.*

Key point

A parallel dialogue about research methodology in health has shifted the conversation away from RCTs and toward other innovative designs that utilize different forms of comparison for different purposes (West, Duan, and Pequegnat 2008). One approach developed by Linda Collins, a methodologist at Pennsylvania State University, and her colleagues identifies multiple predictors (intervention components) of best practice outcomes in drug and tobacco prevention or cessation programs, and compares them against each other (Chakraborty et al. 2009). Comparative effectiveness research (CER) compares across existing forms of medical prevention, diagnosis, treatment, or monitoring approaches already known to be effective to determine "which work best for which patients and which pose the greatest benefits and least harms. The core question of comparative effectiveness research is which treatment works best, for whom, and under what circumstances" (http://en.wikipedia.org/wiki/Comparative_effectiveness _research). Pragmatic trials used in CER measure effectiveness, or the benefit one treatment produces in relation to another in routine clinical practice. By contrast, RCTs measure only whether interventions work or not by comparing the new treatment or intervention against an unrelated program or standard practice (Roland and Torgerson 1998).

These designs, which open the door to various forms of collaboration and community involvement, have emerged to some extent from the translational research movement (Anderson and Shattuck 2012; Cobb et al. 2003; Green and Glasgow 2006). **Translational science and design experiments movements are designed to shift health, education, and social science interventions from controlled environments in clinic, laboratory, and other controlled settings to the real world of schools, communities, and other organizations.** *Translational science or design experimentation requires research partnerships and real world designs that bring partners into the research process,* and many large universities include significant community partnership components in their translational research centers.

Successfully accessing research sites and partners, such as neighborhoods, clinics, schools, and residential buildings, depends on how well researchers demonstrate the utility of their research. An important component in demonstrating utility is involving potential critics and users in the research process. *If research is a powerful tool for influencing policy and public opinion, then communities should have influence over what research is conducted with them, and whether the tools of research used in each setting are appropriate.*

Across fields from folklore to sociology, anthropology, political science, archaeology, psychology, geography, and history, there have been continuing discussions regarding representation, or who has the right to describe the culture or lifestyle of the group in question and in what ways that culture should be portrayed. In the past, ethnographers' views and descriptions were rarely challenged, either by colleagues, key informants, or members of the study community. Only occasionally did ethnographers enter the same field as another similarly oriented researcher to investigate the same phenomenon. When they did, it was usually at two different time points, making it impossible to disaggregate the effects of time and

Definition:
Translational science and design experiments movements are designed to shift health, education, and social science interventions from controlled environments in clinic, laboratory, and other controlled settings to the real world of schools, communities, and other organizations

Key point

Key point

Cross Reference:
The issue of representation is discussed in greater detail in Book 1, chapter 3; Book 2, chapter 2; and Book 6

history from the separate interpretations of the ethnographers themselves. We already have referred to the restudy of Tepoztlan, a Mexican "peasant" community first studied by ethnographer Robert Redfield in the 1930s. By the time Oscar Lewis, another well-known ethnographer, revisited it, it had changed considerably, but it was difficult to assess how much of the change was "real" and how much of it represented differences in experience, data sources, and the different perspectives of the two researchers (Lewis 1951; Redfield 1930). In another highly publicized case, the New Zealand anthropologist Derek Freeman returned to Micronesia to study adolescence, seeking to repeat earlier work by Margaret Mead (Mead 1928). His interpretation of the life circumstances of adolescents, released after Margaret Mead's death, differed from Mead's, initiating global controversy (Freeman 1983). Though he was misled in his analysis, some of the changes he observed and reported on could have been attributed to differences in his sources of information, the fact that he was male and Mead was female, increasing Western influence on youth culture and experience over a forty-year period, and the influence of Christianity on sexual expression. Most anthropologists writing about this controversy have since discredited Freeman's reports (cf. Shankman 2009).

Today, however, research participants have much to say about how best to carry out research in their communities since they know their constituents better than the researchers do, and they have a clear sense of how they want themselves to be represented. Including them in the research process requires mutual collaboration and bi-directional learning and communication. The Internet offers communities from one end of the globe to the other the never-before-available power of instant communication and access to information. It is not surprising then, that while ethnographers seek research partners, community constituents also seek researchers to help them answer pressing questions about how to improve their quality of life or their ability to advocate for themselves and for others. They also want a central role in interpreting, communicating, and using the results of research about them.

ADVANTAGES OF ETHNOGRAPHY AND INNOVATIONS THAT FACILITATE COLLABORATIVE PRACTICE

New research technologies make it easier for researchers and local or nonlocal community partners to collaborate. Ethnography offers a common language and set of methods for defining research questions and for sampling, collecting, coding, analyzing, and writing up qualitative data. Many free tools for collecting data are available for group use on the Internet; they offer access to surveys, elicitation tools, and sorting exercises. Internet-facilitated face-to-face interviews can be collected by screen capture video programs to be screened, shared and discussed, coded, and analyzed later on. Computer-based data management packages can be shared across sites and are user friendly and accessible to community residents and young people who can help with the tedious process of coding, managing, and analyzing large bodies of ethnographic text data, including field observations of behavior or social settings and conversations with informants (Habib et al. 2012; Junker 2012; Miles and Huberman 1994). These technological tools require ethnographers to define and operationalize their variables clearly and early on in the data-collection process in order to communicate with one another and with the software designed to help them do so. Computer programs make it easier for teams of researchers and their partners from different backgrounds to define commonalities across settings and sites and to analyze their data together. All of these technological advances enhance the potential for high-quality and sustained research partnerships.

Cross Reference: See Book 5, chapter 8, on managing qualitative and quantitative data with computers

In the current sophisticated digital environment, it is no longer necessary to depend solely on telephone calls, fax machines, public mail services, text-based communications, or radio and TV messaging to reach wide audiences. Internet-based data collection tools such as SurveyMonkey, batch "E-mail"; network sites such as Facebook, ResearchGate, LinkedIn, Tumblr, Twitter; and audiovisual sharing sites such as YouTube, make it possible to communicate research results, obtain survey responses, share publications, initiate dialogue threads, and diffuse intervention messages to populations all over the world.

ETHNOGRAPHY IS CRITICAL TO IDENTIFYING GOOD PARTNERS

As we have said throughout the *Ethnographer's Toolkit*, ethnography is a face-to-face, immersion methodology. It both compels and assists researchers to enter the "field," build relationships, and learn from others' daily experiences what it means to live and work in that setting, what is important, and what needs to be changed from the point of view of the "inhabitants." Ethnographers enter a setting because they believe that aspects of that context are important in understanding human behavior. Believing that context matters, ethnographers want to make as many observations as possible about aspects of the setting and context that could have implications for people's lifestyles, interactions, transmission of information, and quality of life. For example, we can learn from residents of senior-housing buildings how they describe their interactions with other residents. But when researchers are actually spending time in their building (the "field setting"), they can *see* how people interact and with whom; they can observe the nature and quality of residents' interaction, and they can use continuous comparisons over time and place to note how patterns of interaction change throughout the day, in hallways, meeting rooms, and in informal gathering places. Most importantly for partnership purposes, over time researchers can see for themselves who is likely to be a good key informant, key actor, and key partner in the setting. Familiarity with ongoing social life in that building thus helps to build needed relationships for further work and to develop more insightful in-depth interviews and survey questions. Equally important, residents can see and interact with researchers on their own "turf" and learn to trust each other.

Entering a larger community setting for purposes of exploring partnerships for change usually requires steps similar to the conduct of ethnography for non-applied purposes. In the early stages it calls for identifying key organizations, individuals, social groupings and networks, cultural resources, inequities and their actual and perceived causes, and other dimensions of community cul-

ture and social life. As we noted in the previous chapters, *the search for partners in community-change efforts differs from the search for partners as key informants.* Key informants in ethnographic *research* are those with special expertise in some aspect of their community's life who share their knowledge often on an ongoing basis. While partners in a *change effort* may be key informants, at the same time they also are activists committed to improvement in their own communities.

Key point

Once directionality or purpose has been achieved for an ethnography in action project, ethnographers must engage in strategic identification of individuals, organizations, and institutions that play key roles in the community, learn about them, come to know their membership, attend their meetings, visit their homes and organizations, and eventually forge relationships with them to build trust and make progress toward a common purpose. The more researchers come to know people in the setting, the more likely they are to be accurate in both their observations and interpretations because they have been taught both to see and to question reality by experienced local people who may become their research partners. Such field experience both delimits and manages researcher bias and forges strong relationships over time.

EXAMPLE 3.1

ENTERING THE ARENA OF HOMELESSNESS ACTIVISM IN CONNECTICUT

When community psychologist Heather Mosher left Oregon to work in Hartford in 2012, she brought with her a firm commitment to continue her participatory action research with people whose housing situations were unstable. However, she knew nothing about the dynamics of homelessness in Connecticut. Over a three-year period, she started learning from the ground up, first by interviewing homeless drug users and other unstably housed people to find out about their circumstances, and then by learning about the temporary shelter network in Hartford. After some time, she began to reach out to organizations working to prevent homelessness in the state. She first contacted the Connecticut Coalition to End Homelessness and then other organizations working with or providing services to different groups of homeless people, including youth. She was able to join existing networks, observe them by attending meetings, interview key people, analyze the results, and select as partners those organizations working with unstably housed youth (youth living with friends, relatives, or in temporary unsafe places)—a topic she wanted to explore. In 2015, she and her allies received a grant for a pilot study to involve unstably housed youth in creating and investigating different strategies for finding people like themselves who were disconnected, who were not being reached by existing agencies, and who had good reasons to remain hidden. It took Mosher three years of ethnographic work and alliance building, as well as identification of multilevel sets of connections and resources—state and private organizations, shelters and homeless people themselves—to put together a participatory project that could contribute to improvements in the lives of homeless and unstably housed vulnerable young people.

EXAMPLE 3.2

ETHNOGRAPHY HELPS TO IDENTIFY PARTNERS FOR A MULTILEVEL INTERVENTION IN A MUMBAI COMMUNITY

During the years 2006–2011, an interdisciplinary Indo-U.S. research team consisting of anthropologists Schensul and Schensul, psychologists Bonnie Nastasi and Ravi Verma, statistician Niranjan Saggurti, and professor of social work Shubhada Maitra, along with an experienced field team of Indian HIV-prevention researchers developed the framework for a multilevel program to prevent HIV among married couples in India. The project was based on more than ten years of prior research and intervention and the good relationship researchers had created with a health center in a large urban low-income community which was home to many migrants from north India. Seventy percent of the community was Muslim, and there were many mosques throughout the study area, as well as organizations providing services and working for women's empowerment.

The research was set in the context of widespread gender inequality in India (https://en.wikipedia.org/wiki/Gender_inequality_in_India) and based on prior studies showing that women experienced multiple stresses and tension (tenshun) in their lives, which they expressed in an idiom of distress (Nichter 1981) referred to as *safed pani*, or white vaginal discharge (a noninfectious condition treated symptomatically with antibiotics). Gender inequitable norms and practices were the foundation of their distress. The goal of the project—a commitment of all of the partners—was to change gender norms at multiple levels by working with married women (the individual level), couples in a group setting (the group level), and entities in the community (the community level). Achieving better spousal relationships and reducing restrictive gendered expectations for women's behavior was anticipated to reduce *safed pani*, improve sexual and emotional health, and reduce the risk of sexually transmitted diseases incurred when men sought alternative relationships outside the house rather than working to solve their marital problems.

The individual and couples interventions were based at the community health center. But the community level intervention was to be introduced later in the study, and it was not at all clear with whom the project could collaborate in what could be a sensitive intervention. An ethnographic assessment of organizational resources in the study community conducted through mapping and in-depth interviews with key informants in nongovernmental organizations, voluntary women's networks, and mosques suggested that representatives from these three entities could become partners in the intervention. The formative research showed that the mosques had the capacity to reach many men through Friday prayer and sermons (*takrir*) and that the CBOs and women's organizations could reach women. Further investigation revealed that the Imams were open to the development of more gender-equitable messages that they could deliver through *takrir* on a regular basis. The CBOs were less flexible, because of funder constraints, but were open to generating and delivering messages to women through regular service programs. The voluntary women's organizations (*mahila mandals*), however, were not sufficiently stably organized to serve as a focus for intervention. The study team thus made the decision to work most closely with the mosque sector to develop and deliver messages to men, and to assist the CBOs to deliver gender equitable messages from a women's perspective as part of their routine annual fairs, marches, and other activities recognizing women, which were part of their ongoing mission.

The private sector requires a slightly different approach. Ethnographer Maryann Abbott conducted research with private dentists' offices treating pregnant women on Medicaid. It is very difficult to access these offices because most of them are smaller, their margin of profit is relatively low, they are very busy, and they are historically reluctant to participate in research. Responses to surveys, for example, are very low, usually below 15 percent. Her first step was to identify a range of offices that differed in size and the degree to which they were delivering recommended services to pregnant women, based on a list provided by the state funder. She then chose a sample of offices to represent maximum diversity and approached more than twenty of them, inviting them to participate in a brief treatment risk assessment. While doing so, she was able to talk with receptionists, observe in waiting rooms, speak with dental service providers, and obtain initial information about the ways in which these offices related to their female clients. After initial data collection and analysis were completed, the next step was to speak to dentists' associations about the potential for an intervention that would move offices toward equal provision of recommended treatments (screenings, cleaning, fillings, emergency care, x-rays, etc.) to low-income, pregnant women clients. This example illustrates the variety of ways that the approach and the research tools that ethnography provides can help to identify people and institutions in a setting who are interested in research or a research problem, and are ready to partner in an action-oriented study. The next step is to develop a structure and set of principles and procedures for partnership. This involves meetings with sympathetic dentists serving pregnant women and young mothers.

PRINCIPLES OF PARTNERSHIP RESEARCH FOR SOCIAL AND TRANSFORMATIONAL CHANGE

Given the dramatic rise in the importance of partnerships that link communities with needs to researchers, many documents have been created that enumerate principles of good research partnership. Most of these documents describe participatory forms of research that involve communities, however defined, and researchers, wherever they are based. We add our own experiences to the principles in these documents. First, we outline the principles of collaboration that guide our own conduct in participatory research with communities, and we then provide examples of other such documents as well as Internet sites for readers' further review. Our own guiding principles for ethnography in action are the following:

- The research should be important and relevant to the community involved and should address pressing issues and disparities.
- The research should address inequities or structural causes of the problem at multiple levels, rather than focusing only on individual-level change.
- The partnership should be based on common interests and desired outcomes.

- The partnership should be representative of the diversity of the community where the work is to be done.
- Diversity principles also should govern selection of university-trained researchers as well as research partners.
- All members of the partnership should have equal power and influence over the research process, including selection and focus of topic, research theory, design and methods, analysis procedures, interpretation and representation, and feedback to wider community audiences.
- Resources should be negotiated openly and allocated equitably across the partnership.
- The wider community should have an opportunity to discuss the research at key points and contribute to it.
- Learning should be bi-directional; even if they are from the study community, researchers should learn from residents and organizations serving them, and residents should learn from the researchers.
- The study should be culturally congruent with the study community in terms of language, content, means of communication, study design, and representation practices.
- Procedures should be in place for addressing differences of opinion and conflicts—should they arise.
- The research should contribute to partner organization and wider community well-being, above and beyond the process and results, through capacity building, networking, and resource sharing.
- Ways should be found to sustain the research effort after the project is completed.

Below are some examples of these and similar principles in use.

EXAMPLE 3.3

PRINCIPLES OF COLLABORATION GUIDING THE ROCKY MOUNTAIN PREVENTION RESEARCH CENTER COMMUNITY ADVISORY BOARD (CAB)

Since the program was authorized by Congress in 1984, prevention research centers have been funded by the Centers for Disease Control to organize prevention and wellness efforts for chronic diseases. The funding is available to schools of medicine and public health that are mandated to establish partnerships and networks that collaborate to develop prevention/wellness strategies. The University of Colorado, Denver, is one such institution, funded to support the Rocky Mountain Prevention Research Center (RMPRC). "The mission of the RMPRC is to advance healthy lifestyles and prevent chronic disease among residents and communities in the Rocky Mountain region by conducting, disseminating, and serving as a resource for community-based research and policy. The RMPRC is committed to the principle of participatory research, a collaborative research approach involving our community partners in the research process" (http://www.ucdenver.edu/academics/colleges/PublicHealth/research/centers/RMPRC/about/Pages/Mission.aspx). The RMPRC relies on community members, including its Community Advisory Board (CAB) in the San Luis Valley (SLV), to inform decisions about the direction and scope of its research projects in the SLV. See Table 3.1 for the guiding principles of the CAB.

TABLE 3.1   Guiding principles of the Rocky Mountain Prevention Research Center

Principle	Operational Definition
Health equity	Promote health equity and reduce racial and socioeconomic health disparities
Collaboration Diverse partners	Collaborate with multiple organizations, groups, and individuals Seek out partners that represent the diversity in our communities
Community driven	Seek out and be responsive to community-identified needs Incorporate community input into intervention strategies
Participation	Utilize participatory methods throughout all phases of research, translation, and dissemination
Empowerment	Be a catalyst to communities for the improvement of their health
Rigorous and useful	Conduct rigorous and useful research
Sustainable and transferable	Develop programs that are sustainable and transferable Work with individuals with different areas of expertise
Interdisciplinary	Bring multiple disciplines to bear on understanding and acting on a problem
Resource sharing	Make resources go further through strategic interdisciplinary partnerships

A similar set of principles guides the work of CBPR.

 **EXAMPLE 3.4**

COMMUNITY-BASED PARTICIPATORY RESEARCH (CBPR) FROM A PUBLIC HEALTH PERSPECTIVE

CBPR as an approach is rooted in the action research models of the 1970s and 1980s and applied to communities experiencing health disparities. CBPR methods are based on the following principles as specified by a team of leading CBPR methodologists (Israel et al. 1998, 178–80; Israel et al. 2012). Community-based participatory research:

- recognizes community as a unit of identity;
- builds on strengths and resources within the community;
- facilitates collaborative partnerships in all phases of the research;
- integrates knowledge and action for mutual benefit of all partners;
- promotes a co-learning and empowering process that attends to social inequalities;
- involves a cyclical and iterative process;
- addresses research topics from both positive and ecological perspectives;
- disseminates findings and knowledge gained to all partners;
- involves a long-term commitment by all partners.

Community organizations also can develop their own set of principles, often quite similar to those created by professional organizations.

 **EXAMPLE 3.5**

MOTHERS ON THE MOVE

Mothers on the Move is a grassroots organization in New York City committed to fighting for social justice. Their website states:

> Mothers on the Move / Madres en Movimiento (MOM) is a member-led community organization which was founded in 1992 as a vehicle for low-income people of color to take strategic leadership in campaigns to transform ourselves and our communities. MOM envisions a society where resources and benefits are equally shared, and where people play a role in community decision-making in proportion to the degree they are affected. We are fighting for a South Bronx where future generations have clean air,

well-resourced & community-controlled schools, safe streets, green space, good jobs and more control over the wealth that their labor creates. (http://mothersonthemove.org/mission.html)

Though they do not specifically include research as part of their mission or their principles, as a group of young mothers in school themselves, they were very concerned with the low performance and high dropout rate of students in the Bronx. These parents linked with staff of New York University's Institute for Education and Social Policy to compile disaggregated standardized test score data by school and neighborhood to demonstrate that they fully understood how the achievement gap affected their children's and grandchildren's education. The data revealed abysmal test scores from the southern part of the district, where more poor and working-class African Americans and Latinos lived, and above-average performance of students in the northern, wealthier, and whiter neighborhoods. After visiting schools in the southern part of the district and witnessing firsthand the harsh treatment of students and deplorable learning environments there, parents organized more than a decade ago to close the academic achievement gap within District 8 by forming Mothers on the Move/Madres en Movimiento (MOM).

Working with Michelle Fine at City University of New York, MOM designed a Participatory Action Research (PAR) project to explore how young people, their parents, and community members have mobilized for improved educational resources, opportunities, and the fulfillment of their dreams. Their principles, listed below, reflect the goals of a grassroots advocacy organization working with others of like mind. Though the principles do not mention participatory research specifically, PAR has been one way of mounting advocacy movements toward educational equity in the south Bronx.

- We are organizing to build a just society where there is equal economic, social, and political opportunity for all.
- We work collectively, based on our love for our children, our families, our community, and humanity.
- We have faith in each other, that together we will create a better society.
- We believe in respect, dignity, and equality for everyone, regardless of ability, age, culture, gender, sexual orientation, or any other defining characteristic.
- We celebrate the power of our diversity.
- We invite people to join us and share in the struggle to reach our goals.

These principles reflect the social-justice orientation of the organization and are entirely consistent with the PAR/CBPR approach MOM employed in its efforts to transform educational structures in the south Bronx.

EXAMPLE 3.6

PARTNERSHIP RESEARCH AND EVALUATION AT THE CDC

In the 1990s, under the leadership of Lawrence Green, a public health epidemiologist at the Centers for Disease Control, the CDC developed a program of research and evaluation emphasizing community-based partnership research for health. The program began by announcing the development of urban health centers and associated alliances, and then offering open opportunities to apply for project specific health research partnerships addressing health disparities. This was later followed by the incorporation of community-based research approaches into CDC-funded prevention centers. In the process, reviewers from different sectors were trained to evaluate the proposed approaches, utilizing a set of guidelines that could be used as a checklist for anyone considering a community-based participatory research project (http://www.lgreen.net/guidelines.html).

These partnership principles and guidelines for review are fairly typical of most guidelines for participatory or collaborative research for social change. Like others, they focus on social-justice issues; equitable relationships based on trust, resource allocation, mutual goals, and anticipated outcomes among all research partners; and equal value attributed to both science-based and local knowledge. The principles could serve as a general blueprint for the formation of new alliances and collaborations as they are established.

The next example describes the formation of a community research alliance, and the approach that the Community Research Alliance, described in the next example, used to formulate its own guidelines.

EXAMPLE 3.7

A NEW ALLIANCE FORGES COMMUNITY RESEARCH PARTNERSHIP GUIDELINES

In 2011, the Institute for Community Research, with funding from a local center for clinical and translational science at the University of Connecticut Health

Center, formed a small pilot alliance of organizations to build a community engagement arm. The goal of the pilot work was to permit the alliance to learn about community-based research (CPR) and clinical trials and to prepare partner organizations for community-university partnership research and ethical recruitment of diverse populations into clinical trials. During the first several years, a group of six organizations met to create curriculum and to train staff in these areas. In 2012–2013, the alliance expanded to include twenty-two organizations, only some of which were experienced at collaborative research, including NIH-funded research. The alliance was charged with developing a set of guidelines for community-based partnership research that could be supported by both community organizations and university faculty.

In 2013–2014, alliance members met to review the nature of their organization and to break into subgroups, one of which focused on partnerships and the second on ethical recruitment practices. The ICR staff team reviewed literature on these two topics and presented the reviews and citations to each of the working groups and to the committee of the whole. The literature review provided some background for discussion in the subgroups, but the organizations also had their own experiences and perspectives to share.

Both of the subgroups met three times to develop principles and guidelines with explanations; they then met in whole-group sessions to review several drafts of the integrated document. Once the entire alliance was satisfied with the document, it decided to share the materials with experienced University of Connecticut Health Center faculty members sympathetic to participatory research approaches. This meeting produced a number of positive changes to the document and an executive summary. In addition, based on the community/faculty interaction, a plan was devised to share the guidelines with groups of faculty at the University of Connecticut Health Center and on the University of Connecticut's Storrs Campus. The goals were to obtain feedback and buy-in and to solicit engagement in possible CBPR partnerships. See Table 3.2 for the executive summary of the guidelines.

TABLE 3.2   Principles for Effective Community Partnership Research

---

The Institute for Community Research, the Community Research Alliance and CICATS

This document summarizes guidelines to facilitate collaborative community research involving university or other institutionally-based researchers and community organizations and community service providers. Members of these research collaborations will be referred to hereafter as "research partners." It is designed to support a collaborative framework for the research partnership. This Synopsis should be used in conjunction with the longer version of the same, entitled Executive Summary and/or the full Guidelines for Community Partnership Research which provides additional details, definitions, examples of successful and challenging collaborations, and a list of additional resources.

(continued)

TABLE 3.2 *Continued*

I. Involvement of all partners in the research process
- Research partnerships should be collaborative. Collaboration should involve joint negotiation of study topics, designs and approaches, analyses and interpretations; investigators and staff reflecting the ethnic, racial and other characteristics of the study population(s); mutually agreed upon policies regarding joint ownership of data and dissemination of research results including to the community in which the study takes place; and commitment to resolve any disagreements or conflicts that might ensue.

II. Respect for and commitment to the community where research takes place
- The study community(ies) should be clearly identified. The research partners should demonstrate an interest in and commitment to working with the study community(ies); members of the study community(ies) should agree to the study and its importance; the research partners and the identified community(ies) should demonstrate mutual understanding and respect; and all research partners should ensure that information and knowledge about the community is incorporated and applied in all phases of the research process (planning, implementation, evaluation, analysis and dissemination).

III. Relevance and benefit of the research
- All research partners should agree on the relevance and benefits of the research and identify ways to link the research to community needs and interests in an authentic way.

IV. Effective communication among research partners
- Communication and input should flow in both directions between researchers and community partners. The research partners should work together to ensure the creation and implementation of policies and infrastructure that facilitate financial and decision-making equity in the research process.

V. The ethical conduct of research
- All research must be conducted in compliance with the Office of Human Research Protections. Local community advocates and university faculty familiar with community-based research should be included on the Institutional Review Board. Attention should be paid to the risks and benefits of the study for individual participants and the community as a whole.

VI. Recruitment in community settings
- Community based/clinical trial recruitment efforts should engage research partners to improve recruitment efficiency, quality and ethical practices. Recruitment partnerships may require sufficient financial support to be viable.
- Communications to the community should include information about the project, its utility to the community, and plans regarding follow-up communications.

VII. Capacity-building, resource sharing, and sustainability
- The research partnership should promote co-learning and capacity-building among all partners to include, but not limited to, funding, grant writing, improving organizational credibility, and increasing knowledge about research and about the community.
- Research partners should negotiate agreements on resource sharing across the partnership initially and re-negotiate as needed over time.

FORMING A RESEARCH PARTNERSHIP

Some key steps must be followed when forming a research partnership, regardless of the initiator's base in a community, school, clinic, or research center/university environment. The first is getting to know the community setting well enough to build trusting relationships with organizations, key informants, residents, and others. This means investing initial time and resources in the community, building rapport, exploring the many different sectors, interest groups, organizations, and assets of the community, as well as some of the main problems it faces. In earlier books, we have discussed many ways in which ethnographers can become immersed in community life and gain access to organizations, families, important events and rituals, and other activities. In this instance however, we are not exploring a community purely from the perspective of an investigative ethnographer searching for a topic; we are seeking to identify potential "communities of identity" —organizations or groups that have already identified an issue that they want to confront; key informants who have power and influence over people, money, actions, and policymaking; and people who are ready to take action to improve the quality of life in their setting. This process has been described in Schensul (1985) and integrates ethnography with principles of community organizing—identifying issues, information, allies, and resources. It transpires over time and is ongoing. As Arcury notes:

Cross Reference: See Book 2, chapters 2 and 3; Book 3, chapter 2

> Successful projects take the time to explore or map the structure and resources that exist in the community. Such an exploration discloses the different groups in the community, community leaders, and the resources and skills available in the community. It also delineates how other communities share social space with a specific community. Understanding community structure is an ongoing process as communities are dynamic and change over the life of a collaboration. ... Academic organizations also are dynamic social units (e.g., deans leave, presidents change, department chairs resign). Individual investigators and com-

munity organizations must continue to be aware of
this part of the structure with which they must deal.
(O'Fallon, Tyson, and Dearry 2000, 44)

EXAMPLE 3.8

IDENTIFYING KEY PARTNERS IN A STUDY OF WOMEN'S EXPOSURE TO HIV IN ZAMBIA

Ethnographer Lwendo Moonzwe, a Zambian, returned to her home city of Lusaka to
conduct a study of women's exposure to HIV in one of the largest urban settlements
in the country. Though she was from Zambia, she had lived in the United States for
some time and was unfamiliar with the structure of this particular urban settlement
and the organizations that served it. Through her contacts in the very extensive religious sector in Lusaka, she was able to identify the organizations involved in HIV
services and prevention in the community in which she wanted to work, and to solicit
their help. They formed an advisory board to her study. In addition, she entered the
community, a municipality, through its formal political structure. In this way, she was
able to identify local politicians and health workers who were very much involved with
the well-being of the community and especially concerned about women's health.
They joined the study as informal partners, providing advice in research design and
information on community history and development. These two groups joined her in
the dissemination of study results and were able to use those results for the creation
of more economic opportunities for women whose impoverishment moved them
toward transactional sex, thus placing them at risk for HIV.

Some research partnerships are small initially and then
grow much larger over time. Peggy Shephard, the executive
director of WE ACT, an environmental advocacy organization based in West Harlem, New York, described the history
and evolution of the partnerships WE ACT formed to confront significant environmental hazards affecting asthma
and respiratory disease.

EXAMPLE 3.9

THE EVOLUTION OF PARTNERSHIPS FOR ADVOCACY AND ENVIRONMENTAL ACTION IN
NORTHERN MANHATTAN/HARLEM

In 1988, in its early years, WE ACT sought advice from Dr. Jean Ford at Harlem
Hospital for data on asthma in Harlem. The identification of excessively high rates

resulted in Dr. Ford's linking WE ACT to others at the Harlem Health Promotion Center to discuss diesel particulates and their impact on asthma. Later, Columbia University's Environmental Health Center granted funds to carry out a pilot study in Harlem on the effects of diesel particulates in school-age adolescents. Though the school board granted permission for the study after much discussion, the principal of the target school refused to participate, and the study was conducted with another partner, a private junior high school. The study, which appeared in WE ACT's *Uptown Eye* newspaper two years ago (2012), was published in the June 1999 publication of the *American Journal of Public Health*. Through the Environmental Health Center, WE ACT youth and adults performed car, truck, bus, and pedestrian counts at key intersections in four neighborhoods where the EPA was already monitoring for small paticulate matter (2.5 parts per million). A figure of 2.5 PM or more is considered hazardous to health as these tiny particulates can penetrate cells and be stored in bodies, affecting overall health as well as respiratory problems. In addition, the youth wore personal air monitors to gauge their personal exposures. They found that at four key intersections, the level of PM 2.5 measured 200 percent above the EPA's new contested standards for small diesel particles. These data have been helpful in getting the EPA to fund community-based monitoring in the State Department of Conservation's air monitoring network. WE ACT disseminated the results to the community and published them in *Environmental Health Perspectives*. WE ACT also initiates studies with foundation grants and subcontracts to faculty at Columbia.

WE ACT's path led from the community to a local hospital, and from there to faculty at Columbia's NIEHS-funded center; this bi-directional collaboration has continued to the present.

Another partnership that began modestly and grew much larger over time was the AIDS Community Research Group. This Hartford, Connecticut, community–based AIDS research group began with a citywide multiethnic consortium that included the Hispanic Health Council, the Institute for Community Research, the Urban League, Latinos Contra Sida (now Latino/a Community Services), and the Hartford Health Department. It developed into a broader intervention research network of agencies, and grew yet again with the addition of case management and education programs. Unlike the previous example, this partnership did not include a university. The way in which it developed and changed over time was described in greater detail in Example 2.2 of this book.

PARTNERSHIP CHARACTERISTICS, STRUCTURES, AND OPERATING PRINCIPLES

What are the characteristics of a good community research partner? When selecting and bringing together community partners, both experience and the literature suggest considering some or all of the following characteristics:

- Demonstrated commitment to the issue through a history of involvement in research, advocacy, education, or other activities related to the issue
- Recognition of the value of community research and evaluation
- A relatively stable financial base and the ability to provide or receive subcontracts
- Low staff turnover
- The ability to commit at least one staff person to the partnership
- Regular attendance and good input into project planning meetings prior to receipt of funds
- Availability of space required for the project
- Human, cultural, financial, or other resources to bring to the project
- A clear decision-making structure and personnel policies

As described in Example 3.9, universities usually are involved in community research partnerships because most researchers are based in universities. Far fewer are housed in hospitals, clinics, and applied research centers and fewer still in nongovernmental organizations (NGOs) such as museums, libraries, or other community-based organizations. Finding good university partners can be a challenging task, though recently it has been made easier by emergence of the CBPR movement in public health and by similar movements in education, sociology, environmental studies, nursing, and social work. It has also been supported by the funding of community engagement cores in clinical and translational research centers. These centers around the United States are encouraged by their NIH funding sources to promote translational research in community settings, and a number of them are committed to making sure that faculty are familiar with the principles of community-based participatory research and ready and willing to move in that direction.

What are the characteristics of a good *university faculty partner*? Among them are:

- A passionate commitment to remedying disparities by addressing the social and structural factors that contribute to them
- Willingness to do research outside the walls of the university
- Willingness to meet in a community setting on a regular basis
- Readiness to participate in a variety of community activities as part of getting to know and be known in the community
- Willingness to take the viewpoints of community partners seriously in planning the research
- Appreciation for community knowledge and culture
- Readiness to share the data, results, and author-ships on papers and presentations with community partners
- The use of language that recognizes the joint nature of the work ("we" rather than "I," "ours" rather than "mine").

In chapters 10 and 11 of this book, we describe for students and faculty and illustrate, with examples, training approaches that are designed to prepare them for authentic community research partnerships.

Sometimes, it is necessary to take a risk and leap into a partnership without being sure that each and every partner is the right or best choice. One such example involved a study of exposure to HIV of older adults in senior housing. Anthropologist Jean Schensul of the Institute for Community Research approached sociologist Judith Levy of the University of Illinois School of Public Health. Neither researcher knew each other well—in fact they had only just met at a conference hosted by the National Institute on Drug Abuse. Both had backgrounds in community-based HIV-related intervention research and aging research; both were marginally involved in network studies, and both had been funded by the National Institute for Drug Addiction (NIDA). Levy, however, had published on older-adult sexuality, a topic which was central to the study application since most older adults who are exposed to HIV risk are exposed through sexual transmission. When Schensul approached Levy, they both agreed to take a chance on collaborating, and their proposal to NIDA for one of the first studies nationally on older adults and HIV exposure was funded shortly thereafter.

Other situations do not work out quite as well, such as the case of Greta Gibson, whose interpretation of research data was not congruent with her partner's (Gibson 1985) or Schensul's choice of partners in a substance abuse prevention program, where the partner organization did not offer physical environments suitable for working with young teens and the contract with that organization had to be retracted.

A **research partnership** includes one or more people who see themselves as researchers, regardless of their base of operations, and at least one community organization, group, or institution affected by an important health, education, or other problem that will be addressed through a combination of research and action. Below are descriptions of several types of partnership structures with different roles in the research/action mix. Readers should keep in mind that these partnerships can be overlapping, and one form of partnership can morph into another over time. Furthermore, there is no logical sequence to the development of different types of partnerships, although, in line with our overall approach to ethnography, we suggest that *it is unwise to form a research partnership without sufficient involvement in the community to be able to identify the proper partners needed to move the work forward.*

Definition:
A research partnership includes one or more people who see themselves as researchers, regardless of their base of operations, and at least one community organization, group, or institution affected by an important health, education, or other problem that will be addressed through a combination of research and action

Key point

Contractual Partnerships and Agreements

One way to make more certain that all parties to a partnership understand the goals of the project and what each expects from the other is to enshrine those understandings in a contract. A contractual partnership is one in which financial or other resources are shared toward a common end through a formal and legally binding contractual arrangement. The resources involved can include:

- Project directors' salaries
- Project staff salaries
- Supplies to accomplish project goals
- Local transportation and travel expenses for conferences
- Incentives for participants for recruitment and time devoted to data collection
- Space and infrastructural costs (computers, software, communications, furniture)

Formal contractual arrangements usually involve financial transactions and designated roles, responsibilities, and benchmarks. They also describe conditions under which the contract may be broken. The best contractual partnerships are those involving trust, collaboration, information sharing, and full-scale participation in the study. Contractual relationships in a community-based participatory project that does not pay attention to these important elements are not likely to work out very well.

Some partnerships do not include transfers of funds. Instead, they specify agreements among partners about responsibilities or contributions that involve informal sharing of resources such as time, space, and other in-kind contributions. In ongoing action research with older adults in senior residences in central Connecticut, for example, some of the participating residential buildings wanted memoranda of agreements from the study, to ensure adherence to the commitment to bring programs to the buildings. By contrast, researchers wanted to confirm the provision of such things as private space, a community room, privacy for oral health screenings, and so on.

Alliances

Other partnerships consist of formal or informal alliances. The Detroit Urban Health Alliance grew out of Centers for Disease Control (CDC) funding to develop urban health centers. The alliance consists of more than thirty community organizations and stakeholders that meet regularly, host programs, support projects, review and help to develop grants, and function in other ways. The alliance has not incorporated as a 501C3 nonprofit organization, but prefers to remain a flexible network of organizations that convene as a group regularly but also work in smaller groups on specific issues. The central Connecticut HIV/AIDS Pre-exposure Prophylaxis (PrEP) alliance consists of physicians and health service providers, community service providers, and advocacy organizations working with populations at risk of HIV infection, including people who are lesbian, gay, transgender, bisexual, or queer or questioning (LGTBQ), women in transactional sex work, and drug users. The group is working together in another loose alliance to understand responses to HIV prophylaxis through pre-infection medication such as Truvada and to address gaps in service to HIV positive people. The Vaccinate for Influenza Prevention Alliance in Connecticut was a loose vertical alliance including stakeholders from state, city, private-provider, and public-sector services and communities affected by limited vaccine acceptance. Members of the alliance provided access to vaccines, educational materials, and financial resources for those without insurance and input into research design and instrumentation (Schensul et al. 2009). Other constructed alliances or partnerships involving Participatory Action Research with youth and adults who may or may not be affiliated with any organization, alliance, or informal group will be the focus of attention in chapter 9 of this book.

WHAT MAINTAINS AND SUSTAINS ETHNOGRAPHIC RESEARCH/ACTION PARTNERSHIPS?

When partners come together to solve intransigent social, health, or educational problems, they face a number of challenges and barriers. Their missions, principles, and policies may be different. Their personnel policies (vacation days, daily schedules and time monitoring, salary levels, and fringe benefits) and the way they manage their personnel also will differ, creating the potential for conflict among employees working together across organizations. University salaries for the same work may be twice as high as, or significantly lower than, those in the NGO sector. The financial resources organizations can command and their financial stability vary. Thus, some organizations may be unable to contribute to partnership social events or grant-writing marathons. The speed with which different organizations can make decisions varies considerably, depending on their degree of bureaucracy; high levels of bureaucracy can create frustrating waits for contractors to obtain required signatures. Some organizations have institutional review or institutional ethics boards whose approvals must be obtained while others do not. Employees in organizations without institutional review boards (IRBs) may not be familiar with the important duties of IRBs and might not understand why IRB reviews are mandatory. They may resist calls for changes in organizational functioning required to comply with research ethics guidelines. Some community organizations are familiar with the language and culture of universities, having worked with them in the past, while others have little or no experience with faculty or university administrative requirements and constraints or teaching/tenure requirements. Some organizations have prior experience in the conduct of research, but the research approaches with which they are familiar are very different from the theory-guided, experimental designs that are the currency of much intervention research in social, public health, and education settings. The main mission of one organization may be to provide service to one client at a time, while another's may be advocacy with public-policy makers, addressing the needs of many. One organization may be hierarchical, maintaining strict monitoring and control over staff, while another prefers to maintain a "flat" authority structure where staff members are freer to make their own decisions and keep their own schedule.

Cross Reference: See Book 1, chapter 10, and Book 6, chapters 3 and 4

The cultures of organizations also differ. Some tolerate "gossip" or talk among employees about each other but others don't; some have diverse staffs but others do not. Some allow flexibility in scheduling but others cannot be because of their service delivery program. Some have policies that don't allow for involvement in certain types of research. In the early days of the AIDS epidemic, some AIDS organizations only supported anonymous testing for the disease, but involvement in research studies that called for testing required confidential, but not anonymous, testing so that blood samples could be linked to participants. Organizations that could not agree to confidential testing could not participate in federally funded AIDS research. Meshing or integrating all of these differences in a research partnership can be overwhelming.

The experience of many research partnerships suggests some principles to follow in anticipating and addressing the potential controversies and conflicts that can arise throughout the life of a research partnership. These principles include:

- A clear and agreed-upon problem or set of problems should be accepted by all.
- An additional set of agreements should be established for cases where the initial problem must be modified in light of field conditions or other considerations.
- All parties should identify in advance their resource assets, strengths, and constraints.
- Cross-partnership infrastructure should be equitable. Representatives from each partner organization should become members of an administrative or steering committee, and each partner should have an equal voice in decision making. Project directors should be responsible for making sure that this is the case and facilitate decision-making equity throughout the life of the project.
- Equity includes equal representation of all ethnic/racial, linguistic, and other groups representative of the organizations and the study population in decision-making structures. Whistleblowers who point

out the existence of unequal distributions should be encouraged to help find solutions and should never be punished.

- If at all possible, financial resources should be allocated equally or equitably throughout a partnership consortium according to criteria laid out in advance.
- Organizations should play to their strengths in an action research/intervention project. An organization that is supposed to provide services should be able to do so. An organization that already offers administrative support and coordination and the services of an IRB should be assigned that responsibility.
- The research design should be understood and supported by all members of the partnership. Whether or not a study involves an active intervention, each and every member should follow the requirements of the study protocol. This may be challenging for service organizations that tend to place service to clients before everything else.
- Organizations should state clearly their interest in various components of a study. Some organizations in a partnership may be interested in all aspects of the research, from the study model to intervention and instrument design. Others may only want to be involved in the design, administration of assessment measures, and decisions about how to present the results.
- Changes will occur and flexibility is required. Organizations that may take one position at the outset may change their position. Often, especially in the NGO sector, there is considerable staff turnover among lower-level staff, who are exactly the staff who are likely to have the closest relationships with people in the community. The latter eventuality should be anticipated and planned for.
- Organizations should find ways of accommodating differences in personnel management. Behavior tolerated in one organization may be unacceptable in another. When necessary, these differences should be dealt with in ways that hold the organization, not

individuals, responsible, and strategies for encouraging behavior change at the organizational level should be developed.

- The partnership should have in place mechanisms for resolving cross-partnership conflicts or issues that arise in the community that affect all members of the consortium. These could include reporting systems and structures, regular sessions to discuss problems in project work, formal grievance structures across all organizations, and agreements about communications among organizational administrations about problems that occur in one organization that affect the others.
- The partnership should have established performance criteria for all members and clear protocols for dealing with failures to comply with contractual agreements.
- When all else fails, an external "arbitrator" should be available to help to negotiate intractable problems.

All of the foregoing means that dialogue, trust, relationships, negotiation, and positivity are all required to maintain and sustain a partnership.

ADVANTAGES AND CHALLENGES OF RESEARCH PARTNERSHIPS

Almost anyone who has worked in a partnership involving research and action for change, transformational or otherwise, has both expressed enthusiasm and complained bitterly about the experience. Usually such comments are personal, based on whether the partner member is having a good day or not. Research partnerships, like the problems they are designed to attack, are complex for all the reasons mentioned above. The larger the network, the greater the likelihood that one or more differences in policy or practice will become intolerable to someone, who will then complain to someone else in his or her project network or even to others outside the project. The complaints will eventually arrive at the door of a designated project director who will try to figure out what to do about them. Or an incident will occur in the community that calls for a partnership-wide huddle. These events are routine and should be expected.

Notwithstanding, there are many advantages of partnerships.

- More resources can be brought to bear on the solution of complex problems.
- Community voices can be more readily engaged in thinking through relevant research-related issues that have immediate and long-term implications for their own well-being.
- Methodology, including data collection approaches and survey instruments, is improved if those affected, who know their own communities, provide input.
- Community involvement can produce theoretical and design innovations.
- Community members and organizational partners can use research results immediately.
- All research team members can grow together.

Research partnerships that cut across the fractured landscapes of local communities and disciplines that have been isolated by specialized interests and unequal power structures can bring otherwise separated people together and further conversations that by themselves may be sufficient to move the community change agenda forward. At the same time, partnerships can help to shrink the university/community divide through shared intellectual and cultural capital, resources, job development, and capacity building. Finally, by drawing on the creative capacity and advocacy of partner membership, research partnerships can generate more funding and broader advocacy for much-needed community change, especially with respect to structural inequities and their health, mental health, economic, social, and cultural consequences.

At the same time, partnerships bring many challenges. Some that we have mentioned above are inherent in the differences across organizations. Partnership development for community change takes time, a resource that new, especially minority university-based, researchers do not have if they expect to obtain tenure. Key leaders may move, retire, or die. Other researchers may depart for other jobs, such that their initial partnerships must search for replacements, sometimes without success. Organizational members of research partnerships are not always stable—there can be considerable leadership staff turnover and financial instability over a multiyear period. Partnerships need to be flexible in order to be able to respond to changes in funding streams, community dynamics, needs, and leadership, as well as political and other shifting factors in the larger social context. Single-purpose partnerships may not have much flexibility to reframe themselves when a project is over. All in all, however, the benefits of a creative partnership far outweigh the disadvantages in building organizational and community capacity, strengthening relationships across age/ethnic/racial and other boundaries, improving research quality, and creating more possibility for solving intransigent, complex, and multifaceted social, educational, and health problems.

SUMMARY

Chapters 1–3 of *Ethnography in Action* have built the conceptual and structural basis for doing ethnographic research to promote social change. Chapter 1 provided basic definitions; chapter 2 described longer- and shorter-term efforts to bring about transformative community change at multiple levels. Chapter 3 lays the base for solving complex problems by providing a blueprint for forging the partnerships that are central to reducing social, health, and educational inequities. In chapter 4, we turn to ways that ethnographer/collaborator teams can work together to build inductive and indigenous theory, based on local knowledge. Chapter 5 shows the connections between these local theories and social and systems-science-based theories of intervention. Our argument is that everyone can build their own theories of how things work and how they can be changed and, if they wish, link them to discipline-based theories of change.

Cross Reference: See Book 1, chapter 5, and Book 2, chapters 4 and 5

4

DEVELOPING LOCAL THEORY: PARTICIPATORY MODELING AND INTERVENTION DESIGNS

INTRODUCTION

In chapter 2, we described a number of sustained long-term "interventions" in systems, with many interrelated projects and programs of research over time. We laid the foundation for considering the building blocks of applied ethnography in action:

- building relationships,
- establishing ongoing projects and activities,
- considering sustainability.

The critical process of building research teams and partnerships to accomplish the shorter- and longer-range goals identified in the chapter 2 case studies is described in chapter 3. In this chapter we focus on the local development of applied or action theories. These local theories evolve from the experiences of people living in a setting and affected by a problem. As theories of change, they are "causal," suggesting multiple factors that produce social problems and injustices, and creating directions for change that draw upon community resources at the individual, group, and community levels, and beyond.

Ethnographers collect information and generate locally valid explanatory theories of "how things work." As we have said in Book 5, inductive generation and testing of "micro-hypotheses," or hunches about how things relate in the field, build over a period of time to form a pattern that can be explained in local terms, but that also may be linked to midrange theories and to larger paradigms or lenses. In Book 2, we discussed the importance of theory in ethnography and why initial or formative models are useful in guiding further research. We suggested that it is rare that ethnographers enter the "field" or a study site without any knowledge of the culture, topic to be studied, or people with whom links would be important. It is no longer feasible or practical for ethnographers simply to be plopped into a study setting without any prior preparation, a reality that explodes the mythical ideal of the lone ethnographer, minus preconceptions, paddling her canoe up to the beach of "her" unstudied island (Galman 2007, 14). And in the case of international research or research involving schools, hospitals, or other institutions which are private or semiprivate, it is not possible. Prior preparation is necessary that involves visiting the study site, building relationships with organizations that could support the study, and learning something about research topics that will enhance the research direction. Prior preparation also involves creating formative models or initial theories that provide initial guidance for ways to approach investigations in the first stages of the research. In Book 2 of the *Toolkit*, we described the steps that ethnographers could take in the construction of these initial models.

Since it would be difficult, if not impossible, for any ethnographer to develop a formative local theory without the involvement of people from the study site, ethnographers who are interested in research, but not necessarily research in action, create their initial models using local information and local informants. But they do not seek partnerships with the people who are affected by problems, conflicts, or issues in the community and who would like

Cross Reference:
See Book 5

Cross Reference:
See Book 2, chapters 3 and 4

Key point

to take action to resolve them. Ethnographers *as researchers* are not acting as ethnographers *in action*. **In this chapter our focus is on developing local theories of change with people who want to alter a situation in their community or their work setting and then creating links between them and strategies for action.** We focus explicitly on the development of *actionable theoretical models developed together with partners or collaborators that lead toward local change*

Key point

strategies. However, **even research in action begins with thorough prior ethnographic preparation.** Without it, any actions proposed or taken will be ill informed or naïve at best, and even harmful at worst.

CREATING PARTICIPATORY THEORIES OF ACTION OR CHANGE

Development of participatory change theory is guided by a series of assumptions.

- Everyone can create theories of how things work and how they change.
- Everyone can think of ways in which the quality of their lives can be improved.
- Theories of change should be developed together with those who are defining and experiencing the problem and want to see a difference in their lives.
- Theories of change are critical in nature; they are the products of analyses of conditions that produce undesirable effects and additional analyses of conditions that could produce desired remediation.
- Local theories of change can lead to novel discoveries that contribute to social transformations.
- Local theories of change can be adapted to other places, situations, and times (e.g., they can contribute to science and community development simultaneously).

Everyone old enough to do research can and does generate theories about "how the world works" and what "actions" can bring about desired changes and why. Children make assumptions about how things work even before they learn language. The process of learning culture requires a series of small tests over time, from which children—and ethnographers—learn. Through engagement and experimentation, they become cultural experts in linguistic and behavioral performance. Ethnographer Fred Erickson used the term "jiggle the system" to describe how teachers identified instructional gaps in their classrooms, introduced small innovations to correct them, and then observed the consequences. These teachers were theorizing change processes or "mechanism" and testing their theories by devising new actions they thought would work (i.e., produce the desired results). Theorizing and hypothesis testing (linking concepts) through action is an inherently human activity that we have elsewhere called "playing with ideas" (LeCompte, Judith, and Tesch 1993). While it can seem to be a playful, even a trial-and-error process, human activity and learning cannot take place without it.

In chapter 3, we've shown why partnerships and collaborations are important to creating any kind of social change. Based on their lived experience and their traditional cultural practices and beliefs, people living in a setting have many ideas about what needs to be changed and why. They have collective experience in anticipating what the direction of change needs to be and what resources are available in their own communities to make them. They may have important experiences and stories to share that illustrate why certain proposed directions will not work, or what change efforts have been successful in the past. Outsiders or insider/outsiders can bring important insights to a problem but will never know as much as those who have experienced it. People in a setting, a community, a school, or a health care system, have "indigenous ways of knowing" (De Leeuw, Cameron, and Greenwood 2012; Simonds and Christopher 2013; Tuck 2009). This term refers both to insider knowledge and to long-established cultural traditions embodied in everyday experience. It also refers to the right of indigenous peoples to build their own research agendas and select their own approaches to knowing, validating, and verifying the subjects that are of most concern to them (Chilisa 2012; Grayshield and Mihecoby 2010; Smith 2012). Building theories of change that are intended as blueprints for action is useful only when it builds on local or indigenous knowledge and involves the participation of knowledgeable local people (Agar 2005; Vanderbroek et al. 2011).

As we noted above, change theory is inherently critical. It questions the legitimacy of current practice, questions what keeps a desired outcome from happening, and asks what might enhance the probability of it happening. This requires some thoughtful preparation through initial activities that encourage people to observe their environments closely; discuss them using a critical structural, disparities, or gap analysis; and ponder what they find useful and desirable. Critical change theory especially questions more closely the existing political, economic, and other structures that justify or contribute to undesirable or unjust situations, particularly as experienced by segments of the population who do not hold power. After all, people who occupy the apex of the social structure often are quite happy with the quality of their lives and see no reason to change their circumstances, even though their privileged existence is created at the expense of others. As Example 4.1 illustrates, even children are very capable of analyzing, understanding, and acting on injustices.

EXAMPLE 4.1

THEORIZING AND TACKLING BULLYING IN AN ELEMENTARY SCHOOL

Connecticut fourth-grade girls identified harassment (bullying) as a big problem in their school. They first defined what they meant by harassment. They identified where harassment occurred in their schools, what types of harassment existed, who perpetrated it, and why it was not observed by responsible adults. The girls mapped the areas where harassment was occurring and who was responsible for it. From this analysis, they found that boys were harassing girls in hidden places (in closets, under stairwells, or in locker rooms) where teachers could not see it happening. They also discussed what assets or supports were available to help students avoid harassment. From this analysis, they created their own gendered socio-spatial theory of harassment, collected data to illustrate their theory, and used the results to advocate that teachers and administrators prevent it from happening through peer-based anti-harassment education, avoidance of risky

locations, and spatial monitoring. Their theory was far more accurate in both predicting and targeting harassment than typical generic approaches to preventing bullying that offer general education sessions in health or social development classes or individualized or group counseling interventions to eliminate bullying behaviors among girls and boys who were identified as bullies.

Most groups generate at least some theoretical assumptions that have already been described in the literature and some concepts that may already be associated with established measures or methods of observation. However, they also are very likely to generate new concepts that are locally meaningful and potentially generalizable to other similar groups. Developing novel concepts, theoretical assumptions, and hypotheses is critical to creating culturally congruent and meaningful interventions. It also is an underreported way of noting how communities and local partners can contribute to science in CBPR/PAR.

EXAMPLE 4.2

DEVELOPING LOCAL THEORIES OF MOTHER-DAUGHTER CONFLICT

A group of African American mothers in a local New England organization were concerned about their relationships with their early teenaged daughters. They began to discuss with ethnographer Marlene Berg what their concerns were and why. They felt that their daughters were not planning sufficiently for their futures, because they were not thinking about doing well in school and what careers they might choose. Several of the mothers said that by getting pregnant early, their daughters had justified dropping out of school and "putting their lives on hold." By this the mothers meant that early pregnancy had set them on a path that made it difficult for them to go back to school, complete their high school education and get decent-paying jobs, and that the financial constraints that they experienced because of their lack of education limited their options as adults. In stories about their own lives, they identified lack of information about career options, the "social currency" of pregnancy, the emotional nature of their relationships with boyfriends, and the potential advantages of having a child for financial stability (eligibility for government reimbursement) and living independently as some of the reasons for getting pregnant. They regretted putting their own lives on hold, and saw their daughters traveling down what was to them the same undesirable path. However, by pressing their daughters to avoid pregnancy and do well in school, they created conflict with their daughters. They wanted to develop a program that would encourage their daughters to take career risks and seek alternative female role models. They also felt that as mothers, they needed the opportunity to learn new ways of communicating with their daughters that would reduce conflict. In their stories, they identified the primary source of conflict between themselves and their daughters to be their inability to counter prevailing and continuing pressure toward early pregnancy. Their theory of change involved the development of a program that would change peer norms and offer their daughters options while supporting mothers when they reflected on their own life lessons and tried to understand the life situations of their daughters. They also wanted to be able to communicate more positively with their girls.

Puerto Rican mothers also were experiencing conflict with their teenaged daughters. They too wanted to protect their daughters from early sexuality and premature pregnancy, but their concerns came from a different source. These mothers were primarily Spanish speaking; they felt vulnerable in an English-speaking environment, which they did not understand very well. In addition, in a power and role reversal, their daughters spoke English and often were the translators for their parents. In the New England environment, the protections traditionally available in Puerto Rico were missing—neighbors and relatives who looked out for girls' welfare, a godmother or aunt with whom the daughter could discuss problems, and social pressure to avoid sex without avoiding intimacy. With none of these supports available, and limited ability to ask questions about their daughters' school and social environments, mothers told stories about perceived unsafe school environments, intruders entering school bathrooms, stalkers on city streets, and unchaperoned parties. These mothers constructed narratives that reflected their own sense of vulnerability and their inability to protect their daughters from external forces beyond their control. Efforts to protect daughters by keeping them at home were having the opposite effect—girls were arguing and running away from home, sometimes with their boyfriends and in doing so, exposing themselves to *more* risk. They thought that a program that would help them to understand better the environment their daughters were living in and, at the same time, help the girls to minimize their risks of exposure to sexual abuse, violence, and unwanted pregnancies would be helpful. Working with both groups, the facilitators were able to help the women to draw out two different primary "causal models" for their concerns and their ideas of how to address them. Discussions with both groups showed the commonalities and differences in each of these explanatory narratives and resulted in a culturally tailored bilingual program for mothers and daughters separately, as well as a process for assisting them to share their perspectives and resolve their differences.

Getting to Local Theories of Action

Storytelling is one favored way of getting to local theories of action, but there are other ways that help to illuminate and expand on a problem and illustrate factors contributing to it. ***Theories of change, by their nature, have historical depth.*** Through reflections, stories, and other means, people think critically about their experiences over time and emerge with patterned explanations for their current situation. In considering alternative futures (theories of change), it is necessary to consider what can bring about a desired change, how long it might take, and whether there are short- and long-term goals and outcomes for change. To consider the past, personal or communal timelines are a useful tool. We have described these timelines as a means of collecting ethnographic data in Book 3. When working in a group setting, personal and communal timelines are important for helping individual group members to see how "their story" fits into a common, collectively constructed historical narrative. That narrative then can be used to discuss how the current situation came about. As Evelyn notes, "Narrative form allows for the expression of individual, personal stories, as well as the knowledge that individual stories also represent shared elements of collective experience, which in turn interact with and modify our individual and collective knowledge" (Evelyn 2004). Identifying commonalities in immigration history, coming to terms with struggling with a new living environment, determining how a community faced a disaster like a hurricane or historic flood, facing challenges in getting access to good day care, dealing with unresponsive health care facilities—all help a group to come together, share experiences, and define institutional challenges and policies that need to be changed. The past provides reason and a foundation for imagining alternative futures. Considering alternative futures involves also imagining changes within both individual and group timelines—short, intermediate, and long term—and how to get there (e.g., http://www.elon.edu/docs/e-web/predictions/Futures%20Thinking%20Wkshp.pdf). Thus, the individual and collective timeline is a useful

Key point

Cross Reference: See Book 3, chapter 5 for additional methods for collecting qualitative data

way of revisiting the conditions leading to the present and imagining possible alternative and more desirable futures.

Artistic approaches such as photography and video, prose/poetry, theater, and collection and display of artifacts are additional useful tools for personal and group reflection on lived experience and desired futures. Guided photography, for example, can help a group in a neighborhood undergoing disinvestment to look critically at images of housing, highways, parks, and other features of built environment that they might not otherwise notice—deteriorating porches, garbage under highways or in streets, the condition of a swimming pool or tennis court in a local park, cracks in sidewalks. Many researchers use reflexive writing or word images to invite individuals and groups to reflect on injustices (Cahnmann-Taylor et al. 2014; Evelyn 2004).

When developing local participatory theory and models, it is very important to stay close to local language. Local language is more accurate in the conveyance of nuanced meanings; it is important to avoid trying too soon to translate such concepts into the language of already-developed theories or constructs. *Nervios,* an idiom of distress (Nichter 1981) associated with long-term or acute situational anxiety, as in "*ataque de los nervios*" among Puerto Ricans (Guarnaccia, Lewis-Fernández, and Marano 2003; Guarnaccia et al. 2010; Lopez et al. 2011), maps to some degree onto the psychiatric notion of "neurosis." But the overlap is not complete, and neurosis has no present reference in lay Spanish (or lay English). When working with a group to build explanatory theory, a good facilitator would not leap immediately to the idea of "neurosis" or another psychiatric diagnosis, but would work with the group to explore the concept of "*nervios*" by itself, its causes and solutions, and then turn with the group to the literature on the topic of "*nervios*." Only after so doing might they—with caution— link it to other, nonindigenous or "etic" terms for related phenomena from social and health sciences disciplines. Finally, the facilitator would move the group to explore and identify indigenous and other valued resources for coping with "*nervios*," which might or might not include either spiritual healers or counseling.

The term "local" or "emic" theory refers to the theory itself. The process of generating it is situationally specific. First, theoretical concepts are situated in the cultural context and setting in which theorizing is taking place. The use of local linguistic terms, local concerns, and indigenous or locally generated connections among them produces situationally specific theories. At the same time, the process of generating these theories also is situationally specific. Facilitators who assist in building theoretical frameworks, links, and hypotheses should be familiar enough with the setting to ask questions that will help the participants make connections. Thus, while it is possible to develop a general "script" for generating group models, that script also must be adapted for local circumstances.

Characteristics of a Good Participatory Research Facilitator

By now it must be clear that participatory theory development through group modeling requires a good facilitator in order to ensure that locally generated theory is as sound, socially and culturally valid, and complex as possible in relation to the problem. By *facilitation*, we mean the instructional pedagogy and the teaching techniques that facilitators use with a group of research partners to engage them with the problem under consideration, to help them identify the multiple factors that contribute to a problem, and to determine why these actually are contributing factors, as well as what existing assets and resources could help address the problem, and in what ways. A good theoretical explanation depends both on the developmental level, experience, and contextual understandings of those involved and on the instructional sophistication and contextual understanding of the facilitator(s).

A **participatory research facilitator** is an interactive instructor whose goal is to enable members of a group to engage in a dialogue. The dialogue draws on their own knowledge and experiences, to identify key issues and goals/outcomes, make causal explanatory links between hypothesized causes and results, select processes for

Definition: A participatory research facilitator is an interactive instructor whose goal is to enable members of a group to engage in a dialogue that draws on their own knowledge and experiences, to identify key issues and goals/outcomes, make causal explanatory links between hypothesized causes and results, select processes for understanding the situation in greater depth, analyze and interpret the results, and choose steps for action

understanding the situation in greater depth, analyze and interpret the results, and choose steps for action. What is required to be a good facilitator?

- Ethnographic understanding of the setting, including prior cultural exposure
- Ideally, the ability to speak the local language, or the availability of a skilled and trained local language facilitator, or facilitation partner/translator
- The ability to elicit local knowledge and local concepts without reframing them in "scientific" terms (e.g., to stay close to the local language)
- Familiarity with ways of conceptualizing complex social phenomena by using an ecological approach or other complex system metaphors (e,g., root cause analysis, ecological maps, complex linear diagrams)
- Enough familiarity with the setting to assist the participants in filling in one or another or all of these systems diagrams
- Familiarity with or ability to obtain generic social scientific literature on issues and concepts that emerge in theory-building discussions
- Capacity to reflect and recognize the dimensions of difference and similarity in the facilitator-participant researcher relationship
- Critical consciousness of structural factors leading to the disparities that participants invariably identify
- Ability to envision change opportunities and strategies in the setting that are congruent with participants and partners
- Readiness to partner as a change agent

In addition to these characteristics, first and foremost a good facilitator should be able to empathize with people and to sense when things are or are not going well for a group member or the group as a whole. As with other forms of researcher/partner relationships or relationships between ethnographers and collaborators, power and other status differentials are always present; their impact must be considered on an ongoing basis. In addition, facilitators have biases, especially with respect to their own perceptions of a complex problem and its possible solutions. Suspending biases and predilections and preferences for causal links and alternative actions is a challenge that good facilitators face during each moment of facilitation sessions. In the next section of this chapter, we turn to a discussion of how to model change, and metaphors for doing so.

MENTAL MODELS: ECOLOGICAL MODELS, ROOT CAUSE MODELS, ECOMAPS

The world is a complex place. Models simplify our understanding of the world and our ability to predict or anticipate what will happen in it, by selecting what we believe to be the most important components of a social or cognitive/social system and then developing hunches or hypotheses that explain their connection. Thus, models are mental or cognitive representations of reality that reflect the interaction of individual/personal characteristics, experience, and beliefs with interpretations of what is going on in the world (Dalle Molle, Kuipers, and Edgar 1988). These mental or cognitive representations could be called "maps of perceived reality." As such, they are profoundly affected by the positionality of those who create them. Managers will have quite different understandings of the causes of unproductivity from those of workers who work long hours for little pay under difficult working conditions. We also described earlier how preteens had quite different ideas about where and how harassment was occurring in their schools from teachers and could clearly represent them, though their teachers could not.

See Books 1, 2, and 6 for discussions of positionality and its impact in ethnography

Models also can also be group or collective representations. Regardless of how many people create them together, models nonetheless are incomplete representations of reality, and all models therefore are "wrong" (Sterman 2002). What that means is that they are incomplete or best guesses. Nevertheless, we all use models to anticipate, predict, and explain outcomes. When they don't quite fit, we try to change and improve them.

Individuals who live and work together often show a high degree of similarity in their mental models of cultural domains (Borgatti and Halgin 2011; D'Andrade 1992;

Holland and Quinn 1987). Culture itself is constituted or constructed based on negotiated and shared cognitive models of the way the world works in multiple domains and subdomains (Romney et al. 1996). These commonalities and differences among individuals who occupy the same place and time, experiencing similar issues and challenges, create the dialogue that renders group modeling exercises such an exciting and rich enterprise.

To understand and bring about change in complicated or complex systems such as communities, hospitals, or health care delivery mechanisms, ethnographers identify as many variable domains and subsystems, processes, and interruptions as possible, then explore their associations insofar as they are known. They then narrow the scope to what seem to be the best contributors to a problem and to its possible solution (Schensul, Schensul, and LeCompte 2012), and explain why these solutions were chosen. The social science perspective that deconstructs situations into constituent components is not always immediately translatable into settings in which people think in metaphors or holistically through stories and cases. But stories, narratives, performance, and other means generally make it possible to create visual representations of explanations for things, and to anticipate alternative desired futures. Book 2 provides examples of what these representations look like and how they can be created.

Cross Reference: See Book 2, chapters 4 and 5 for examples of models

Shared cognitive representations of systems or components of systems constitute definitions of culture. We can use consensus modeling as a means of defining culture as *measurably shared cognitive models* (mental models, mental or cognitive maps) that link concepts, processes and cultural domains (D'Andrade 1992; Romney, Weller, and Batchelder 1986). Consensus modeling is the basis for arguing that group modeling exercises with a wide representation of people from a cultural setting can produce reasonably accurate systems models (Borgatti and Halgin 2011). We have found in years of practice that creating models collectively produces better and more realistic approximations of reality with which to start the process of generating participatory or collaborative approaches to change. Hovmand and colleagues have actually been able to demonstrate that the more stakeholders involved in mental modeling of complex dynamic systems, the more accurate the model is likely to be in representing change over time (Hovmand, Brennan, and Chalise 2011). In the next section of this chapter, we show how facilitated group dialogue can produce collective representations of mental models that are culturally situated and move communities toward research and intervention for individual, social and structural change/transformation.

Models are metaphors for research in action. As we have mentioned in Book 2, chapter 4, there are different types of models that facilitators and research groups can use to begin the process of exploration. Many models are linear or interactive. A *linear model* leads logically from input to process to outcome. Constructing a linear model requires being able to think and speak about cause and effects. Linear models focus on changes in a dependent variable (an effect or outcome) that occur because variations occur in an independent variable (a cause or predictor). The units of interaction that link predictor to outcome variables are standardized (one specified unit of measurement of an independent variable X leads to a specific kind of change in a dependent variable, Y). Longitudinal complex linear models take contextual factors at multiple levels into consideration and examine how multiple variables at different levels intersect and change over time. Linear models are often quantified, but they are equally useful as research/action tools when they are *not* quantified. They help people assess more clearly what their problem is and what might be causing it, even if it is complex.

A simple example is represented in Figure 4.1. It shows a digital camera that has taken a photograph (INPUT). The camera with the photograph is connected to a computer. The photograph is transferred to the computer, which is linked to a printer. Once the photo has been transferred to the computer, with the proper command (PROCESS), it can be printed (OUTPUT). This looks like a simple system—camera to computer to printer. There are two requirements to produce this result: technological subsystems (digital camera, computer, and printer) and their links (the right connectors). Human processes also are required—pressing the command

Cross Reference: 🐰
See Book 2, chapters 4 and 5, on modeling

INPUT   **PROCESS**   **OUTPUT**

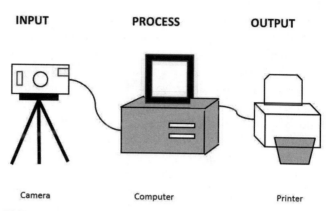

Camera   Computer   Printer

FIGURE 4.1   A simple linear input-output model.

that transfers the photo to the computer and placing the cursor on the print command, which prints the photo. Other considerations include: the camera must have batteries; the computer must have storage space; the computer must have a printer device file that allows it to connect to that specific printer; the printer must be plugged in or run on functioning batteries; and the printer must have color printing capacity to print a color photo. Someone must make sure that all this happens, and then remember to click on the print command! And finally, to complicate matters, if the situation requires multiple outputs—that is, multiple color photos, it may be very inefficient since it often takes a long time, depending on the printer, to print even one photograph.

Further, other circumstances at any given point can affect whether the output is achieved. For example, a passerby could walk directly in front of the camera, blocking the photograph, or the computer might have been dropped just before setup, as its owner tripped over a loose piece of cement at the entrance to the building. This might create a disconnected screen, resulting in inability to check the storage drive and find the photo and print it; or someone might have mistaken a black and white printer for the color printer, thereby making it impossible to print the desired output—a color photograph. Or, at the last minute, a storm could cause a loss of electricity just as the computer was about to run out of battery power and therefore prevent storage and printing.

There are several lessons here. First, even a simple input-output model is not as simple as it seems. Second, trying to think first about all the possible things that could go wrong and prevent the desired photograph from being printed is more efficient when carried out in a group. Third, determining how to avoid a negative outcome, or even how to generate more desirable outcomes, is also more readily and efficiently done by a group. Fourth, some things are within our control (making sure the technology works, is connected, and the right buttons are pressed), but others, such as storms, tripping, and unanticipated behavior of others are beyond our control. We can only create models based on what we can think of that we perceive to be real, no matter how simple or complex they are.

A cultural model might look something like that in Figure 4.2.

FIGURE 4.2   A simple linear cultural model.

In this model, Indian married men concerned about their sexuality, an important component of their masculine identity, express their concern through "*gupt rog*," a form of sexual dysfunction which leads them to pursue other women outside their marriage and have sex without a condom.

These linear (left to right) models (Figures 4.1 and 4.2) stop at the output. Linear models don't take into consideration feedback loops or reverse connections among the components or subsystems of the model. And they do not take into consideration change over time. However, if the printer had a connection to the computer that instructed the computer to stop the printing should the colored ink run out, the system would include a **feedback loop**. The feedback loop can be seen in the diagram in Figure 4.3 or in Figure 4.4.

Definition: Feedback loops are causal connections that occur when an output to a process within a system feeds back to an input in the same system

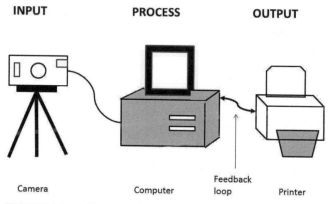

FIGURE 4.3   A linear model with feedback loop.

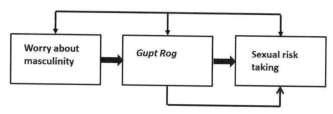

FIGURE 4.4   A cultural model with feedback loop.

We will use these concepts in our modeling exercises.

Now we turn to generic metaphors that help to identify ways of thinking about context and the ways that context shapes the way people behave in groups. Metaphors also can help create new strategies for change. These "model metaphors" are themselves theoretically based, but are quite flexible in their use. In the pages that follow, we describe the *ecological metaphor*, the *root causes metaphor* and the *eco-mapping metaphor,* and show how, through proper facilitation, they can help groups to work together to identify the complex causes of sometimes equally complex problems.

1. The Ecological Metaphor

We mentioned ecological approaches earlier in this chapter and in Books 1 and 2. Here we revisit the concept, looking at different approaches to ecological framing of social (and environmental) context. Ecological metaphors divide the world into "sectors" that help us to think collectively about what affects a situation and where we can intervene to change or improve it. They are always represented as oval or circular "bull's-eyes" with either "the individual" or another central or important entity in the center. An example (and there are many) of an ecological metaphor is found in Figure 4.5.

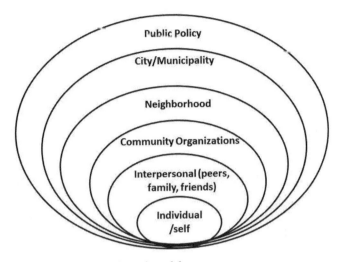

FIGURE 4.5 An ecological model.

As the figure shows, the diagrams are arrayed so that the individual (person) or the "intrapsychic" (internal to the person) is situated centrally, and the radiating concentric circles or ovals represent different social "levels" that show the "social subsystems" that affect the individual. These subsystems are often viewed as arrayed at degrees of social distance from the individual, a convention established by Urie Bronfenbrenner in his presentations of ecologically framed impacts of social organizations and institutions at different degrees of impact, indirect and direct, in relation to the individual (Bronfenbrenner 1989). The "outside" circle, in other words, has less direct impact on the center than the concentric circle embracing the center, but it affects all of the circles in some, often unmeasured, way.

When most people think of a significant issue that affects them directly, they place themselves at the core of the ecological metaphor. They often stop right there, placing responsibility for the problem on "the individual."

The ecological metaphor pushes them to consider factors beyond themselves that account for social problems, health disparities, and cultural gaps or denials. We can use work with mothers of preschool children as they prepare them for life as an example to script questions that promote broader systems thinking.

EXAMPLE 4.3

SCRIPT TO EXTEND EXPLANATIONS OF "CAUSALITY" BEYOND THE INDIVIDUAL

Q. What is causing your child to perform badly in preschool?

A. My child has a bad temper.

Q. But your child does not have a bad temper at home, and the teachers don't say that he has a bad temper.

A. My child doesn't know his letters. When the teacher asks him, he runs around or jumps up and down.

Q. Why doesn't he know his letters?

A. I could not teach him because I myself cannot read.

Q. But why does the teacher not know that your child doesn't know his letters?

A. The teacher doesn't ask. He just wants the children to repeat the letters.

Q. Why do you think the teacher doesn't ask?

A. The teacher has too many children in his class, and he doesn't have time.

Q. But the teacher could have asked you about your child.

A. Yes, but this happens during parent-teacher meetings in November, and we are only in October.

Q. Why don't you ask for a meeting with the teacher?

A. The teacher doesn't speak Spanish.

Q. Why isn't there a teacher that speaks Spanish when so many of the children and parents do, as their first language?

A. I don't know—there should be more.

This sequence probes the reasons for perceived failure to perform at the preschool level, from the perspective of a nonliterate, Spanish-speaking mother who does not recognize initially that a number of contextual/systemic factors are contributing to why her child is perceived as underperforming. However, she comes to understand them at the end. The facilitator must have some familiarity with broader contextual issues in order to ask these questions. The ecological metaphor guides the questions to the parent, family, school, and teacher and to cover a broader number of factors at different sociopolitical levels.

Respondents who come to understand that there are broader contextual factors may identify them and, using the ecological metaphor, place them in concentric rings around the individual. A script is the following:

EXAMPLE 4.4

SCRIPT TO DEVELOP ECOLOGICAL "LEVELS" FROM THOSE HAVING THE LEAST TO THE MOST INFLUENCE ON A PERSON

- What are the names of the (blank) concentric rings in a diagram? For example, you can think about what might cause obesity in teens. Probes, what about their food choices? (SELF) What about what their family cooks or family pattern of eating (FAMILY)? What do they have available to eat and drink at school (SCHOOL)? What do they buy after school (COMMUNITY)? What do their friends eat (PEERS)? What about the way the media portray food (MEDIA)? The restaurants they pass on their way home from school (COMMUNITY-LICENSING)?
- So what would you call these? For example, mother's cooking/family preferences might be "family"; what your friends eat might be "peers"; what your mother can purchase at corner stores could be "community"; what you see on television could be "media."
- Now that we have named most of the levels, let's arrange them so that they have greatest to least influence on a person. For example, what influences a person more? Mother's cooking or what peers eat? Do you think that the media has more influence on you than peers, or your mother's cooking, or your own personal preferences?

This debate continues until the group agrees on the sequencing of the concentric rings.

The next step in the process involves using the "named" rings or contextual "levels" as the basis for identifying the factors that promote the undesired behavior or end point. Participants discuss what it is about "family" that might contribute to obesity in a family member, using the rubric "list, explain, compare, contrast" and generating hypotheses as follows:

- Listing (brainstorming) all the things that the group believes could contribute.
- Explaining each item so that all of the members of the group understand it.
- Comparing/contrasting each, and discussing and comparing (analyzing) each one.
- Linking each logically to the outcome by explaining its connection (generating hypotheses).

The group might agree that the use of too much cooking fat at each meal contributes to teen obesity. Once there is agreement on family-level contributors, the next step is to repeat with other domains. Thus, the group might agree that stopping at McDonald's on the way home from school contributes to teen obesity, or that the availability of sugary drinks in school vending machines contributes to obesity, and so on. This ecological analysis of "causes," once complete, can be readily converted into a linear model.

In ecological modeling, it is very important to remember that the concentric rings do not have to be arrayed around the well-being of individuals (egos). They can just as readily be arrayed around a structural or organizational problem, such as lack of access to clinical care. If participants were working on this problem, the dialogue would focus on what accounts for difficulty in accessing clinical care. The script would be the following:

- Defining the focus (the central circle). That is, what does *lack of access* mean?
- Identifying the predictors leading to the focus—lack of access. What makes it difficult for people to access clinical care? (Probes might include transportation, staffing, hours, attitudes of provider personnel, language differences, wait times.)
- Locating the responses in concentric circles.

The discussion should focus on those factors that are institutional in nature, not those that have to do with patient lack of information or resistance or fear.

Involving a group in ecological modeling has a number of benefits.

- It requires that participants move beyond locating responsibility for a problem within the individual only, rather than including larger systemic issues.

> *This can be difficult, as much research in social science* **Key point**
> *and in the Western world is predicated upon a single*
> *individual, capable of providing a response or being*
> *a unit of analysis. Thinking beyond the individual can seem like thinking*
> *"outside the box" for many people.*

- It requires that all participants discover, discuss and define context as consisting of multiple "levels," sectors, or other locally or culturally appropriate ways of subdividing the environment for analysis.
- It calls upon members of the group to utilize targeted analytic skills (listing, comparing, contrasting, listening, exchanging ideas, negotiating, analyzing, and hypothesizing). Group members may have little experience in such activities and will need to be provided with examples and trained.
- It results in a common initial perspective on the issue.

Once having gone through this exercise, participants can then speculate about what can be done to remediate the problem at one or all of the levels included in the model.

●━━●━●━━●

2. Root Causes Metaphor

The root causes metaphor is useful in seeking non-obvious and non-superficial explanations for a problem, especially in the context of disparities and injustices. Root cause analysis is a form of linear causal chain analysis that looks for the origins of a problem by pushing causal analysis back as far as possible. The process involves asking *why* at each step. If there is obesity, why? If it is because there are too many fast foods, why? If there are too many fast food restaurants, why? If there is poor regulation, why? If there are payoffs, why? If the group is satisfied with the answer to the last question, then the root cause of the problem has been approximated. The advantage of the metaphor is that it pushes the participants to move beyond the obvious and toward more structural explanations for a problem. At the same time, there usually is not a single root cause for a complex social problem. Thus, root cause analysts have to be careful to remember that at any step in the logical causal sequence, there may be multiple other factors that play a significant role. For example, as we showed in the complex linear model, one reason for obesity may be lack of opportunity for exercise. Thus, if the primary or only focus is on increasing licensing restrictions to avoid clustering of fast food restaurants, the problem is unlikely to be solved. The solution must include safe and pleasant places to exercise and programs to encourage people who are not accustomed to exercising to do so.

3. The Ecomap Metaphor

The ecomap metaphor locates people (groups, networks, and even individuals) in social space. It provides a more intimate means of examining an entire community through the lens of social groupings. Traditionally used in social and therapeutic practice, the ecomap is a way of working collaboratively with a family or group to explore familial or social network relationships in interaction with their environment. We present it here as a form of social mapping in which groups (families, informal groups, or even focus groups) identify families and other social groups and their interconnections and locate them and the locations they relate to on a map, which they draw. Similar to the other metaphors, an ecomap begins with an issue. Facilitators/researchers first identify a group that is willing to discuss the issue. The facilitator then interrogates the group about the issue in the following way.

Q. Tell me about which groups you know might be affected by or somehow involved in this issue. Do they have a place where they gather? Can you show the places where they gather on this blank map? You don't have to be accurate.
Q. So now that you have placed these three groups on the map, are there any others?
Q. Tell me, who is in these groups?
Q. How and why do these groups relate to each other?
Q. Can you tell me, on this map that you have drawn, where each of these groups usually goes? Why do they go there? What is near where they go? Does it matter?

Q. Do any of the groups or their members engage with other groups in these places? Or are they segregated?

Q. Are there places where any of these groups are involved in (legal) or (illegal) activities. Do you know why they are involved and what they are involved in? Why in that spot?

By working with local informants over time, the researcher can determine which groups (or so-called gangs) are involved in specific activities, and which of these activities help to avoid the scrutiny of local police or their surrogates.

Drawing an ecomap with a family or group offers the following benefits:

- It introduces a geographic component to ecological modeling.
- It helps to understand the relationship between people as groups and the groups (and individuals) they relate to in a community.
- It helps to understand what potential danger individuals might incur as a result of a larger, more regional study.
- It provides the opportunity to engage local trustworthy people in intervention discussions.
- It can produce discussions of the locations/sites where intervention/action activities of various sorts could take place.

PARTICIPATORY SCRIPTS FOR CONSTRUCTING LINEAR MODELS

Once participants have understood the broader context of the issue under consideration, they can turn to a more analytic model very easily. The above example helps us to see how a simple and a complex linear model can be constructed. Following is a script and design for a simple model on obesity. It is best to create the model collectively by working on a blackboard or whiteboard with erasable markers, or on a table top with paper circles, squares, and connectors, and small index cards. Glue-backed "sticky notes" also are useful.

1. Create a square and place it to the left on a board or sheet of paper.
2. Place the concept of concern (obesity) inside or below the square.
3. Take the elements in each of the concentric circles, and place them in circles connected to the square.
4. Draw lines connecting the circles and reconstruct the hypotheses that connect the circles, to make sure they represent the views of the group.

Every model tells a story. The initial story told by the group that created this model is the following: "There are four main things that influence obesity in teens. All of them are somehow related to obesity. But if we read from the left-hand circle, the model says that fast food availability is connected to mother's cooking and friends' food preferences. These are linked directly to obesity, but they are also linked through buyers' available resources. (See Figure 4.6B, bottom left part of model.) So, if buyers have less money, no matter what their friends' food preferences are, they will purchase less fast food and eat more mother's cooking, thus avoiding obesity."

Describing these connections makes intuitive sense but not "scientific sense." So the group must discuss why they think each of these circles relates to the others; they must articulate the chain of logic that links the circles in Figure 4.6B. The group goes on to explain, "If greasy, high-calorie, tasty, and cheap fast food is available at fast food restaurants, and if friends like fast foods and go to such restaurants often, then people will eat these foods when out with their friends. If they like these foods better than the food they eat at home, they will put pressure on their mothers or others in the household who cook to make food more like fast food restaurant food—fried chicken, hamburgers with cheese and mayonnaise, french fries with ketchup, macaroni and cheese, and pizza with triple cheese. The combination of high-calorie, high-fat fast food, friends who eat it and apply pressure on their peers to join, and comparable food cooked at home results in consuming too many calories and people get fat." In this linear model, participants read from left to right; the circles represent different domains of influence affecting individual behavior (eating habits), which result in obesity.

Someone in the group may say that the issue is not simply overconsumption of calories, but underexercising. The group will then have to consider lack of exercise as a contributing factor to obesity and repeat the process by asking why insufficient exercise occurs. The answers from group members may be that girls do not exercise as much as boys (giving cultural explanations such as gendered differences in activity levels or activity choices or not wanting to get sweaty and grubby because boys don't like girls who aren't clean and tidy); that there is no convenient or safe space to exercise (a community-level explanation); that there is not enough time during the day to exercise because of other responsibilities (the fault of work or school). Each of these explanations needs further interrogation to arrive at the social and structural factors that produce it in the first place. With this broader understanding, the types of interventions and the points at which they can be introduced will become clearer. Most groups will produce multilevel, complex explanations for a problem they are facing.

It is possible to build a linear model to explain an organizational-level or structural problem. If, in the case of the above model, the group decides that a significant problem is the clustering of fast food restaurants in particular locations, then it becomes important to know not only how such restaurants contribute to overeating, but what "produces" the clustering. (See Figure 4.6B, upper left part of model.) This launches researchers (and the group) into a discussion of the factors that result in clustering of fast food restaurants in specific neighborhoods, in many of which there are substantial numbers of unduly heavy people. In this case, the outcome to change, or the "dependent variable" (the square), is clustering of fast food restaurants. The group then discusses the reasons why such clustering might take place and emerges with structural explanations: less local political resistance, fewer zoning and licensing restrictions, higher density of population making the location more attractive to businesses.

If the group wants to consider multiple causes more clearly, it can construct a new and more complex model, one that links the "organizational" or structural domain and the "population" or individual/family/peer domain, each with

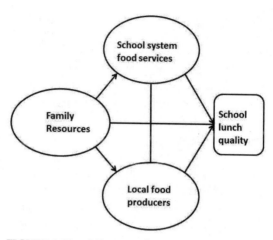

FIGURE 4.6A   A linear model with a single problem.

their separate but potentially interconnected links. Figures 4.6A and 4.6B portray the models the group constructed to make these connections. The first model, 4.6A, suggests that all three predictive domains (school system, local food producers, and family resources) have roughly the same effect on the outcome and do not privilege any one of them. Model

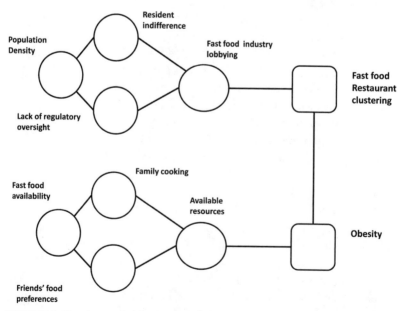

FIGURE 4.6B   A complicated linear model with two interconnected dependent variables.

4.6B highlights the importance of the structural-dependent variable (clustering of fast food outlets) by treating it separately and linking it directly to obesity. A research or intervention model based on 4.6B would be required to reduce clustering (along with other factors) to reduce obesity.

In this more complex model, it becomes readily apparent to the group that it is not possible to address obesity without considering multiple interventions at different social and structural points or levels. What those interventions are, how to conceptualize and operationalize them, how to see them as interconnected, and how to measure them are the next set of challenges.

At this stage, the linear model is preliminary. It provides the basis for several possible next steps. If not enough is known about the domains or if the team is uncertain about whether the domains are exhaustive, further research is required. If there is no time for further research and immediate action is required, steps can be taken to develop interventions by guesstimating or hypothesizing what is required to bring about a transformation in the issue or problem that is being addressed.

FURTHER RESEARCH TO ENHANCE MODELS

Almost always, the theoretical model requires further breakdown in the form of unpacking the main domains. This involves vertical modeling. **Vertical modeling** deconstructs a large concept of domain into its constituent components. Thus, the example "family food preparation" might consist of the following components: disposable income for purchasing food, locations for purchasing food, food preferences, content of food preparation, family members' ability to cook. A Mumbai team doing research on the contributory role of alcohol in HIV risk might break the concept down as follows: alcohol type, alcohol cost, alcohol containers, alcohol drinking frequency, drinking amount, drinking partners, places where drinking occurs. All of these concepts must be disaggregated into their component parts so that they can be described or measured. For example, *alcohol type* would involve listing all the different types of alcohol known to

Cross Reference: See Book 2, chapter 4 for a more detailed discussion of vertical modeling

Definition: Vertical modeling is a way of deconstructing a large concept or domain into its constituent components

the group that might be used in the community. The process is both more educative and more efficient when it is participatory since researchers alone would not necessarily know what types (or brands) of alcohol are available, which are preferred, and which are actually drunk.

EXAMPLE 4.5　　　　

BUILDING A COMPLEX MODEL EXPLORING QUALITY OF SCHOOL LUNCHES: INDUCING HORIZONTAL, VERTICAL, AND MULTILEVEL MODELING SIMULTANEOUSLY

A capacity-building program was funded at the Institute for Community Research (ICR) to assist food-justice organizations in Connecticut with youth programs to embed Participatory Action Research in their community organizing activities. ICR was interested in trying to shape their action direction and wanted to assess where research was required and for what purpose. One group was anxious to involve youth in research but did not know toward what end. To clarify, ICR arranged a three-hour workshop, to which two youth coordinators from the community, two older teens, and one young adult came. To begin the discussion, we first talked for some time about the goals the youth wanted to pursue, including access to high-quality, cost-effective, environmentally sound, and healthy lunchtime food products. We proposed the development of a complex model that explored the factors contributing to lack of improvement in school lunches in their urban public high school. They were interested in exploring both what contributed to lack of improvement and what might need to be done to bring about transformative changes in the overall "school lunch system." However, other than mobilizing students to advocate for improvements in the lunch system, they had no other plans in mind by which to achieve their goals.

They began with the idea of *poor quality* school lunches. First they discussed the meaning of poor quality. A listing and discussion produced taste, smell, appearance, freshness, presentation, amount, and a number of other dimensions—all of which were further defined:

- taste—not enough seasoning, overcooked;
- smell—not differentiated, steamy, unappealing;
- freshness—wilted fresh foods, meat in gravy dry around the edges;
- presentation—no decoration, dregs remain, all the same color;
- amount—not enough to satisfy appetite.

The question, "Who eats school lunches?" resulted in a discussion of five types of students: those who brought their own, those who received school lunch free or at a reduced prepaid rate, those who did both, those who ordered their lunch from else-where to be brought into the school, those who did not eat lunch. The group real-ized that students might not fall readily into one group or another, based on their observations. They also observed that though the prepaid lunch consisted of one set of food products, students also could choose from others. Thus, they observed that some students who were on the prepaid lunch program chose to pay for other foods and did not eat their prepaid lunches. The potential complexity of student behaviors in relation to lunches suggested that they could not assume the presence of a group of students who were so discontented with the quality of lunches that they would be willing to mobilize to advocacy for improvements. Further, they did not know enough about how students were making choices. Thus, they decided they needed more information on the demographics, decision-making behavior, food prefer-ences, and overall culture of school lunch behavior.

These dedicated young activists were interested in pursuing change strategies. They began to discuss who could make decisions about school lunch quality. One member of the group pointed to a woman in charge of school lunches—"the big boss." Another member of the group said that she only executed contracts for food services that were decided on by the board of education. This led to a discussion of what the woman could and could not control and to the political context of food services to public schools. While different members of the group had bits of information about contract bids, quality oversight, and food storage, the group rec-ognized that they needed far more information about the way that food arrived at the school cafeteria. One participant mentioned that 10 percent of the school food budget was undesignated and could be spent on local products. This resulted in a discussion of what farmers were producing local high-quality foods and were able to produce them in sufficient quantity for use in the school system. This observation raised the question of the relationship of local food producers and manufactur-ers to the school system and whether students could do anything to enhance these relationships. The discussion ended with a review of where in the emergent system decisions could be made that might affect food quality.

From this discussion emerged the rudimentary model in Figure 4.7, with darker outlined circles or squares identifying which domains required much more infor-mation collection to determine whether (and which) actions, if any, could feasibly be taken. Without having a clearer understanding of how the components of the system functioned, how they related to each other, who were allies, who had power to make decisions, where decisions would actually have an effect, and what the vari-ation was among students, any actions this group might have undertaken could easily have resulted in lack of results, or even pushback in an undesired direction.

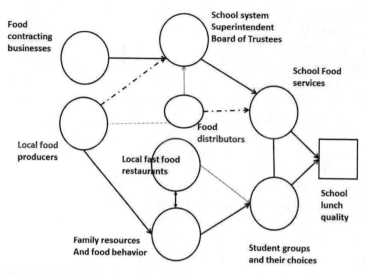

FIGURE 4.7   A complicated model showing factors related to school lunch quality.

This model provided guidelines for a plan to do the following:

- interview the food services coordinator to understand what she controlled, how food contracts with the board were established; and which part of the school lunch budget was unrestricted;
- interview students, followed by a survey to learn more about their food preferences, family food habits, and their level of dissatisfaction with school lunches, a measure of readiness for mobilization;
- list and investigate local food producers to see if any were selling to the board of education, or would, and what products were available in sufficient quantity;
- geographically locate fast food restaurants near schools.

We discuss the ways in which collaborative researchers can choose among various ways of collecting data and deciding on intervention designs in joint projects in chapter 6.

SYSTEM DYNAMICS MODELING

The above discussion on food quality in school lunches produced a rudimentary system dynamics model. **System**

dynamic models try to account for causality in complex systems by examining the nonlinear and changing interaction of key variables in a defined "system" *over time* and to predict longer-term outcomes. Complex systems are defined as having three primary characteristics—they consist of *subsystems* that *interact* with each other to produce unanticipated interactions and *consequences* with nonlinear (curved or fluctuating) patterns of change in outcomes over time. Subsystems are connected by interacting feedback loops that either enhance the direction of the system overall or a component of it, or balance or stabilize it. For example, the continuous production of greenhouse gases and the emergence of developing countries into high levels of production of greenhouse gases results in ever-expanding indicators of global warming. Constraints on the production of greenhouse gases in a large country like the United States or China would have a balancing or slowing effect, though not likely one sufficient to completely stop the rise in sea water or the melting of glaciers. However, it might reduce the forward motion. Over time, with enough regulatory action, or with a global recession reducing manufacturing and oil consumption for transportation and other purposes, or both, the level of greenhouse gases might go down. These oscillations in the level of greenhouse gases might continue for some time unless very significant efforts were made globally to reduce them, thereby stopping production, and eventually slowing indicators of global climate change. System dynamics approaches identify the primary domains and processes that intersect in *nonlinear* ways over time. As noted, the rates of change in the processes may vary over time, may vary for different processes, and may be influenced by reinforcing (maintenance) and balancing (oppositional) feedback loops which can be considered positive or negative, depending on the desired direction of change (Weidlich 2005; Wilby 2005).

Those interested in complex dynamic systems can choose among (a) network modeling (flowing information through networks), (b) agent-based modeling (examining how differential rates of change in key contextual factors influence the interactive and emergent behaviors of units in the model, based on their interaction with contextual factors), or (c) system dynamics models that utilize causal

Definition: System dynamics models try to account for causality in complex systems over time and to predict longer-term outcomes by examining the interaction of key variables in a defined "system"

loop and stock and flow diagrams to illustrate multiple variables interacting at different rates over time (Luke and Stamatakis 2012). A **causal loop diagram** is a schema for describing positive and negative feedback loops in a system without defining the "dependent variable" or the outcome that is to be projected over time. A **stock and flow diagram** is a simplified version of a causal loop diagram that shows when and how the most important feedback loops influence the curve of the dependent variable over time. While all three forms of modeling are useful, an advantage of system dynamics modeling is that it focuses more on structural and social, and less on individual, factors as drivers of desirable or undesirable social and health processes. Second, it allows for interaction of multiple variable domains in relation to each other over time to predict long-range patterns. And third, it allows modelers to vary the degree of interaction among specific variables to see the effect on outcome, thus providing guidance for choosing intervention alternatives. System dynamics modeling is very consistent with the way in which social science system thinkers view the world.

System dynamics (SD) modeling requires the following elements:

1. Defining the boundaries of the system (which subsystems and processes are part of it and which are not, even though they may have an effect upon it)
2. Identifying main variables and reinforcing and balancing causal feedback loops (causal loop diagrams)
3. Determining how the feedback loops reduce or increase rates of change in key study variables.
4. Estimating logjams and time delays (or time accelerations) in the model (which things slow processes down or cause delays, bunch-ups, or speed-ups at times).

History (multiple time points) time delays or accelerations and feedback loops that intersect to produce different rates of change in a specific phenomenon are the key factors that differentiate a nonlinear system dynamic model from a linear model.

Our dynamic systems model identified subsystems that influenced school lunch quality over time. We bounded the system initially by including in it school food production and marketing, local and national factors, availability of local prepared food (fast food restaurants), the local school system, high school teens in the community, and their families. The first two subsystems were external to the geographic community and the others internal to it. Bounding the system involved including the institutions whose actions affected directly the quality of lunches and which could be influenced by change agents. The poor quality of lunches had persisted over time but appeared to be worsening. This required examining changes in the subsystems that might account for this dynamic. Feedback loops began to emerge in some of the subsystems. Among students, some were indifferent, some liked school lunches (possible reinforcing feedback loop), and some opposed them in favor of alternatives (possible balancing feedback loop). Within the board of education, reinforcing feedback loops included local food providers' approval of current food contracts as part of their own contractual agreements, pressure on board members to choose specific food contractors, and indifference on the part of food-system personnel. Balancing feedback loops included parental groups campaigning for better food, local food producers advocating for a bigger percentage of the food contract budget, and some support within food services offices for improving food quality.

Figure 4.8 tells part of the story outlined above. It suggests that if parents and students work together to promote provision of higher quality foods, it will have a positive impact on the board of education, which will modify its contractual arrangements, thereby improving school food service commitment. These advocacy efforts will also directly affect the quality of food for school lunches. At the same time, indifferent students will reinforce the negativity of food services personnel, who will pay less attention to food quality. The relationship of local food suppliers to the board of education is unknown, and the relationship of external food suppliers to the board of education is unspecified. All of the

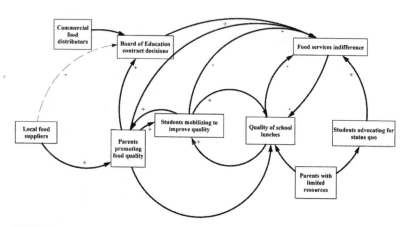

FIGURE 4.8 A causal loop diagram showing feedback loops facilitating and impeding progress toward school lunch quality improvement.

foregoing means that the model is incomplete. It does show, however, the forces in several subsystems that make a difference in the quality of school lunches. Further breakdowns will show multiple feedback loops, which interact with each other. Researcher/activists will have to determine where, and in which components of the system, they can make a difference, and what the effects will be on the rest of the system and the nonlinear changes in the quality of school lunches. One of the advantages of a system dynamics model is that the interactions among all the subsystem variables can be quantified and projections made about changes in the outcomes over time. In addition, introducing changes to the system, including new elements or new actions of subsystems, can be estimated or calculated, so research partners can actually estimate the efficacy of their interventions without actually implementing them, and then test their guesstimates against real-time change efforts.

✦ Definition:
Domains are conceptual areas/topics/things that need to be changed and their associated possible predictors and consequences

WAYS OF IDENTIFYING INTERVENTION APPROACHES FROM A MODEL

Whether before or after collecting data related to their model, if the group decides that they would like to generate an approach to intervention, it is best to use a "domain approach." **Domains** are conceptual areas/topics/things that need to be changed and their associated possible predictors and consequences as in the models above. One script for doing so is the following:

Cross Reference: See Book 1, chapter 4; Book 2, chapters 4 and 5

- Examine carefully and discuss as a group the meaning of each of the domains in the model.
- Decide which ones require more information in order to determine importance in influencing the outcome, which ones cannot be influenced with the resources at hand, and thus must be eliminated even if they might be important to address, and which ones must and can be addressed.
- Consider how each of the causal and dependent domains might be changed. This could involve:

  - *reversing the pattern* in the domain—for example, if peers are influential in unhealthy attitudes toward food and eating habits, change their attitudes to become more positive;
  - *creating a pattern replacement*—for example, creating new peer networks. If peer influence is important, introduce those who are or might be obese to cooking clubs (where they could learn better cooking, where to purchase good inexpensive food, and where they could meet others interested in the same things;
  - *promoting alternative options* —for example, promote the sale of non–fried products or limit use of mayonnaise in fast food restaurants with site specific discretion;
  - *creating new structures*—for example, alternative entrepreneurial activities for food trucks selling fresher fast food products with fewer calories, less salt and fat.

These efforts require collective work and cannot be carried out by individual researchers or activists.

In the next section of this chapter, we explore a more complicated process of linear modeling for developing interventions and assessing resources for doing so by working together with local communities. This methodology is outlined in Book 2 and we repeat it here, in the context

Cross Reference: See Book 2, chapter 9

of collective intervention/action planning around school lunch quality and obesity prevention. The transformation process involves starting with the notions of *organization* and *population*. We can refer to the ecological model to better understand this difference. Here, *population* refers to those levels that are situated at the center of the ecological bull's-eye—individual, family, peer, partner, and so on. *Organization* refers to structural, social, and systemic factors that affect a problem or issue at the contextual level; organizational components of a system are found in the concentric outer rings or levels of the ecological model—schools/churches, service organizations, community, media, policy, policy makers, and so on. In the model below, fast food restaurant clustering is an organizational-level domain and obesity is a population-level domain. At the *organizational* level, we can identify the following independent variables (or variable domains) as listed:

- Fast foods industry lobbying. We can define this as lobbyists promoting *more relaxed licensing*.
- Lack of regulatory oversight. We can define this as *insufficient personnel* to review the locations of all outlets requesting licensing.
- Resident indifference. We can define this as *residents' inactivity in promoting better quality food facilities in their neighborhoods*.
- Population density. We can define this as *high number of people per geo-social unit* (census tract, block).

At the population level, we can define additional variable domains:

- Family cooking: as preparation of food similar to fast food preparation (frying, use of batters on food, use of mayonnaise, high salt content, soft white bread buns).
- Friends' food preferences: peers prefer to socialize while eating in fast food restaurants.
- Family resources: families like to eat out but can't afford more costly restaurants.

■ Fast food availability: people live near fast food outlets.

The first step in the exercise is to decide on one or more desirable outcomes that could result from changes in the "independent variable domains." This is very important because a desirable outcome may not be simply the reversal of the model outcome or dependent variable. It might be something else altogether. The next step is to fill in these issues in the population row of the square in Table 4.1. The resource column is left blank. The variables or variable domains identified in the far right-hand column are those that need to be changed or transformed.

TABLE 4.1 Causes and factors needing change at the organization and population levels

	Resources	Independent (IV) Domains	Variables That Need to Be Changed in Each Domain
Organization		• Fast food industry lobbying • Lack of regulatory oversight • Resident indifference • Population density	• Fast food outlet density • Insufficient personnel • Few politicized food advocates • High density of residency per square block
Population		• Family cooking • Family resources • Friends' food preferences • Fast food availability	• Preparation of fried foods • Families' preferences for eating out inexpensively • Friends socialize in fast food restaurants • Too many fast food restaurants close to home

The next step is to identify local *resources or assets* available to the group that might be useful in addressing the gaps identified in the right-hand column, which we have labeled "independent domains." Resources and assets at the organizational level are various types of organizations (libraries, schools, service organizations, religious institutions), cultural resources (history, language, rituals), parks and recreational areas, social networks, natural resources (rivers, lakes, hiking trails, wilderness), and so on. There are a number of useful sources that can provide guidance in identifying resources or sociocultural, linguistic, biological, and political/economic capital, and others on cultural capital (Kretzman and McKnight 1993; Yosso 2005). Local resources and assets at the population level are named "youth," "adult," and "voluntary" groups, including church groups, kinship and family groups, peer networks, mentorships, and community helping resources (spiritual leaders, informal leaders, politicians, community advocates). Identifying these resources requires the involvement of local people who know their communities or settings well and is a group activity.

TABLE 4.2   Resources available to change factors requiring transformation

	Resources	Independent *Domains*	Independent Variables That Need to Be Changed
Organization	• Local food justice organizations • City/town council reps. • National food advocates • Public housing developers	• Fast food industry lobbying • Lack of regulatory oversight • Resident indifference • Population density	• Fast food outlet density • Insufficient personnel • Few politicized food advocates • High density of residency per square block
Population	• Culinary programs • Food sharing clubs • Recreation centers/ sports groups • Media personalities	• Family cooking • Family resources • Friends' food preferences • Fast food availability	• Preparation of fried foods • Families' preferences for eating out inexpensively • Friends socialize in fast food restaurants • Too many fast food restaurants close to home

The next step assumes that the outcomes or dependent variables (fast food clustering at the organizational level and obesity at the population level) can be changed if the independent variables are modified. It also assumes that the change will occur faster if the independent variables all can be modified. Finally, it assumes that links can be made between the resources available and the independent variables at both the organizational and population levels to bring about change.

The next step requires two things:

- Deciding what kind of change should take place in the independent variables at each level.
- Deciding how the available resources might make a difference at that level.

First, links can be made at the organizational level (linking (a) and (b) in Figure 4.9). To begin, we could ask the following questions:

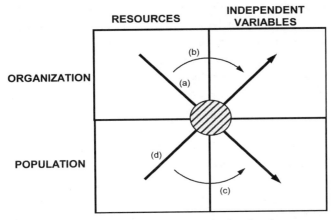

FIGURE 4.9   Relationships among organizational and population resources and gaps.

- How can food justice organizations prevent lobbyists from successful promotion of the value of fast food restaurant density?
- How can city council representatives address the lack of personnel to ensure proper surveillance of fast food restaurant licensing?
- How can national food-justice advocates increase the awareness and political activity of local residence by convincing them of the importance of controlling the numbers fast food outlets in their neighborhoods?
- Can public housing developers affect the density of lower income populations in this neighborhood, to reduce its attractiveness to fast food industry lobbyists?

The next question concerns the population level: How can resources identified at the population level be utilized to affect population-level independent variables (linking (c) and (d) in Figure 4.9)?

Subsequent question sets ask what organizational resources can address population needs (linking (a) and (d) the typical intervention question), and what population resources can address organizational needs—That is, are there ways that members of communities and population sectors can assist organizations to do outreach, conduct education, organize services, and become partners in the efforts of the organization to address health problems? And conversely, what population resources can address organizational needs (linking (c) and (b)).

The answers to these questions begin the process of framing the intervention model. The mission, goals, and objectives for the example of obesity can be described in the following way:

MISSION (derived from the population dependent variable): To reduce obesity in our city

GOALS (derived from the selected population and organization independent variables):

Organization

- To reduce the density of fast food outlets
- To improve surveillance over fast food outlet licensing
- To improve the quality of snacks availability at fast food outlets and corner stores
- To increase the number of critical food advocates in neighborhoods where there are clusters of fast food outlets
- To join forces with advocates of lower density mixed-income housing
- To create more urban farms and community gardens

Population

- To teach family cooks how to reduce fat, salt, and sugar content in preferred foods

- To develop recreational and sports programs with youth groups
- To involve youth in urban farming

Resources at the organization and population level can then be applied to any or all of these objectives to achieve the desired short-range (change of dietary intake and cooking behavior) and long-range (reduction in obesity) mission.

This approach can be used with simple single-level and multilevel models, with complicated models, and with system dynamic models when assessing how to modify feedback loops or introduce new ones into an oscillating or progressively declining system.

SUMMARY

In this chapter, we have described a variety of approaches to ethnographically based modeling for social change based on "emic" or indigenous/local approaches to creating locally meaningful change theory. We have made the assumption, tested through years of experience, that anyone, including young children, can generate theories of how things work or don't work, through modeling processes we have described and scripted. We have offered some practical metaphors for thinking about how systems work and how they can be changed and provided some modeling exercises and scripts for use in facilitating group discussion based on local knowledge and newly acquired ethnographic information preparatory to modeling. Though the metaphors for these approaches are somewhat different, the net result is the same—identifying through a combination of storytelling and disaggregation/description the complex of factors that produce a negative or undesired situation, and strategies for considering how to bring about change in the situation. The strategies sometime involve reversals in the independent variables or identification of new independent variables. They require analysis and application of the resources available to address the problems defined in the predictor or independent variables.

These participatory modeling exercises are the basis for developing and shaping strategies for change that are embedded in the experiences, meanings, rituals and language of community residents and other stakeholders. The exercises offer researchers tools for building upon community and resident knowledge, working with them to assess community assets and resources to address known community problems. They are designed to enhance and extend local evaluation and problem solving capacity and can be integrated with community organizing activities, and campaigns of various types.

In the next chapter we consider the "etic" or science-based theories that can map onto and help to guide operationalization of the locally developed interventions. In the language of the social sciences, these theories help to specify and to measure the processes and means through which an intervention is supposed to work. While resources identified for use in an intervention which we have described in this chapter tell us what people have to work with in a local system, they do not tell us exactly *how* to work with the resources or *why* we would expect applying them would actually work. Etic theories, especially those that are congruent with local ways of knowing and changing, can help to guide the development of these interventions and explain why they should work.

5 ●━◆━●━◆━●━◆━●

LINKING LOCAL AND SOCIAL SCIENCE THEORIES

INTRODUCTION

In the last chapter, we reviewed different approaches to local, emic, or indigenous, theories of change and illustrated ways to elicit them with specific interview scripts. Using these techniques, ethnographers working with community teams can produce one or more simple or complex local change models. Using the "conversion" script at the end of the chapter as well as accompanying ethnographic methods, these teams can identify the availability of community and other external resources to apply to complex problems with multiple theorized contributing factors. The local cultural, social, and institutional resources identified by the research/action team can be operationalized in the form of approaches to intervention in the same way that the models themselves are developed—by figuring out how they can be transformed into specific actions and activities directed toward the desired change.

At the same time, higher level theoretical paradigms and midrange "etic" or social science discipline-based theories, from which there are many to choose, can offer guidelines and additional inputs in shaping interventions. They also can link emergent local theories and action steps to broader processes and literatures. In this chapter, we review families of social science theories at different levels (e.g., organization, population, individual, ecological,

Cross Reference: 🐰
See Book 1, chapter 3 on research paradigms

169

system theories) to understand how they can connect to local theory and can become useful in operationalizing the approaches to change that local theory suggests. All such midrange theoretical approaches are abstractions from concrete events and data; in that sense, they are "generic," rather than being embedded in a specific context. However, these midrange discipline-based "etic" approaches can be used with locally derived theories derived from multiple disciplines to inform what appears in local settings and help to explain what also appears in other, similar settings. All "emic," or discipline-based, approaches benefit when researchers use standard ethnographic methods to engage in formative research that sharpens the content and make it relevant to local settings. Below we provide examples from multiple disciplines to show how midrange theories have been utilized in conjunction with ethnographically based locally derived theories. We have tried to select those that move research/activist teams toward critical, empowering, and transformative action.

DEFINING "EXTERNAL" OR "ETIC" THEORY IN ETHNOGRAPHY IN ACTION: REVISITING THEORETICAL PARADIGMS

Earlier, in Books 1 and 2 of the *Toolkit* series, we have discussed various approaches to theory and theory development. In both books, we refer to the major orienting paradigms that social scientists often use to guide their work, in particular, critical, empirical, interpretive, and ecological or systems theories. We call these approaches *paradigms* or *epistemologies* because they represent ways of viewing, interacting with, and "knowing" the world. As such, they provide blueprints for investigation or for guiding the direction of research. Below we review the major epistemologies shaping social science research and approaches to practice.

Cross Reference: See Book 1, chapter 3, on theoretical paradigms

Positivism

Positivist approaches argue that reality is external, observable, and understandable and that research conducted with adequate procedural rigor and proper controls for bias can generate replicable and generalizable results. Similar replicable and generalizable results can be obtained if the same standards of rigor and control are applied to applications or interventions. Some would argue that the ideal intervention should be constructed so that it can be replicated in similar settings, and that the conditions under which it is administered or applied should rule out external influences by means of careful research design and standardization of the environment. Ethnographic research in general and "experimentation" in real-life settings in communities and schools has shown conclusively that most interventions that are carried out in community settings are only partially controllable, and that controlled interventions do not generalize well to other settings (Green and Glasgow 2006). In addition, positivist approaches to problem-oriented research are usually driven by scientists, not by communities or others trying to address the issues that are affecting them, from their own perspectives. However, positivism reminds all researchers and science-based activists that scientific rigor is a requirement assuring the quality of all investigations, including ethnography in action.

We have tried to argue throughout the *Ethnographer's Toolkit* and elsewhere that while ethnographers are working increasingly hard to make apparent just how rigorous their work is (cf: Bernard and Gravlee 2014; LeCompte, Judith, and Tesch 1993; Pelto and Pelto 1978), positivist approaches also are now moving toward greater understanding of the variety of ways in which context, human resource differences, and other factors must be considered in attempting to carry out cultural, cognitive, and behavioral interventions in real-life settings. In fact, a whole new realm of science referred to as "dissemination and implementation" science is evolving, one that is trying to understand how real-world conditions affect the ability of researchers to conduct intervention approaches in "uncontrolled" "real-world" situations. Implementation science involves local organizations and people trying to bring about a change in defining and studying the conditions under which that change can happen and whether and how an existing approach, even one that has been shown to be useful elsewhere, would be relevant in a new and different setting (Demiris et al. 2014; Gaglio, Shoup, and Glasgow 2013). This movement is reflected in the so-called new public health approach that recognizes that decision making in health fields (substitute "education," "environmental," or any other fields) is neither always rational, nor are interventions always based on known risks that scientists see and try to control. Rigg and others point out that ethnographic and participatory approaches can get closer to the more authentic ways that people make choices in their own specific contexts (Rigg, Cook, and Murphy 2014).

Taking a positivist approach when engaging in ethnography in action should not be construed as constraining or disregarding the possibility of generating locally meaningful theory or precluding collaborating with others. It surely does not mean using only instruments or measures that have been "validated" in similar settings. It does mean considering that an approach developed in one place might be appropriate for another *if* that second place is culturally and situationally similar to the first. This approach has been called "comparability," and it is an analog to canons for external validity and replicability (LeCompte and Goetz 1981). It also means that content, format, delivery, and observation/evaluation measures must be adjusted to reflect the new intervention situation. Finally, it argues for the importance of developing local explanatory theories of change systematically, together with local collaborators, and together testing its congruity with and linkages to "etic" theory. In this way, the best possible theoretical framework for an ethnographically based intervention or action study can be ensured.

One allegation often leveled at positivistic approaches is that, in attempting to preserve objectivity, positivism attempts to separate and distance the researchers from the setting and the people in it. This has resulted in the work of ethnographers, and especially ethnographers engaged in advocacy-oriented action to be labeled erroneously as "nonobjective." Some novices have even interpreted the demands for objectivity to mean that they cannot interact with, or even like and enjoy the company of, people in the community they are studying without being accused of bias. However, such disengagement not only is impossible—especially for ethnography in practice, which consists of a partnership between researchers and local communities and other settings—but is poor research practice. In fact, *what positivism requires is not conceptual distance from the people or the setting, but from the outcomes of the research.* This canon exists to prevent researchers and others from ignoring findings that are contrary to their hypotheses or hopes, or from manipulating data or representing results in ways that support their biases but that contradict actual findings. While ethnographers involved in action research or other interventions do certainly have hopes for specific outcomes, as do their partners, the interventions in which they engage should never be based on prior research and other studies that contradict facts on the ground. And the facts on the ground should never be ignored if they contradict the researcher's and community's hopes. For example, in the obesity study mentioned in chapter 4 of this book, members of the action/research team could ignore the wide range of other contributing factors in designing an intervention, which could leave them well open to accusations of bias or lack of objectivity. As we have argued elsewhere in the *Toolkit*, good research and interventions require understanding ourselves, and our own biases, as well as our collaborators' perspectives and what is important to them and *their* biases. At the same time it is necessary to discuss and reflect together on our mutual biases, as well as other contextual sources of interference in our research and our actions. It is these processes, along with careful and systematic data collection, that open the door to positivist dialogue and render ethnographic methods both rigorous and "replicable."

Key point

Cross Reference:
See Book 2, chapter 2, and Book 6, chapter 9, for a discussion of the role of positionality and reflection in research

Critical Theory

Critical theory, as described in Book 1, chapter 3, guides us to the generation of knowledge through the analysis of relationships of power and sociocultural and structural asymmetry. This paradigm argues that the "known" (received knowledge) is what those in power wish to be known. Critical theorists explore how the political economy of a state or

Cross Reference:
See Book 1, chapter 3

other political body exerts domination over citizen sources of information, knowledge, and action and, in particular, how unequal distribution of power affects the lives and rights of minoritized groups. These theorists are interested in uncovering and describing relationships of power, and they recognize that hegemonic forces such as instutionalized regulations, hierarchies, norms, and practices can be taken for granted in ways that make them invisible to the very people who suffer from them. They must be rendered visible and interrogated if inequities in these relationships and the variety of health, cultural, education, political, and environmental disparities that arise as a result are to be changed. The application of critical theory in ethnography in action is important, both in generating local theory and in examining the contextual and structural factors that must be transformed if equitable outcomes are to be achieved.

Critical theorists encourage us to recognize that the processes of knowledge generation, sharing, and use should be available to everyone, especially people affected by untenable, inequitable, or socially unjust situations over which they would like to exert more control. Further, since knowledge is power, knowledge itself should be equitably distributed (Schensul 2002). A collaborative or participatory approach to critical ethnography in action involves working collectively with people living in structurally and socially inequitable circumstances to analyze gaps in the distribution of power and resources—hence gaps in knowledge—that affect their lives, to identify assets such as cultural capital available to counter these inequities, and to take action to distribute them more equitably in order to remedy the specific circumstances.

Freire refers to this process as developing and acting upon critical consciousness (Freire 1970; Freire 1981). **Critical consciousness**, according to Freire, is the awareness of discrimination and the oppressive structures that cause it. An elaborated view of critical consciousness deconstructs the term into constituent elements, each of which has important implication for interventions. They include:

Definition: Critical consciousness, according to Freire, is the awareness of discrimination and the oppressive structures that cause it

- "the awareness of inequity, oppression and liberation" (Watts, Griffith, and Abdul-Adil 1999);

- an understanding of the social, structural, and political-economic antecedents of oppression;
- a set of skills to "help individuals to deconstruct experiences of oppression as they occur" (Isom 2003);
- the ability to understand others' perspectives or thoughts about experiences of oppression or its consequences (Quintana and Segura-Herrera 2003)

Critical consciousness is important in understanding and acting upon structures of oppression; at the same time, it recognizes the importance of self-reflection in understanding how those structures are embodied and why they must be eliminated (Thomas et al. 2014). Freire would suggest that while consciousness or critical awareness of a problem is crucial to any transformative action, alone they are not sufficient to solve problems. Applying critical theory and critical consciousness throughout the process of ethnography in action is essential to generate the evidentiary data base upon which effective action strategies and plans depend, and to ensure both equitable collaborations and long-term attention to remediative actions rather than simply perpetuating social injustices.

Constructivist/Interpretivist Approach

The constructivist/interpretivist paradigm holds that reality, or what people know to be true about the world, is socially constructed by people as they interact with each other in specific settings. For interpretivists, the existence of multiple perspectives on reality, in which different people have different understandings and perspectives about the same events, is normal. This is why the very wealthy can feel that a $125 ticket to a sports or cultural event is a bargain, while it is completely out of range for working-class or poor people. Interpretivists are concerned with how people make meaning of their situations and their lives and communicate that meaning to others. A constructivist approach is central to the development of local or emic theories of change, and to the ethnography and other activities that lead to active implementation and evaluation of change strategies. Because an interpretivist perspective on culture and social change would argue that both the concepts "culture" and "social change" are "socially constructed," a constructivist approach based on interpretive principles provides a way to understand how collaborative efforts can socially construct varying analyses of power relationships, identify structural barriers to achieving desired outcomes and devise agreed-upon strategies and approaches

 **Key point**   to cultural and structural change. ***Constructivist principles underlie all collaborative research approaches that support the idea that people working together across different disciplinary, professional, class, and cultural boundaries can co-construct new approaches and generate new knowledge together based on their negotiated lived experiences and shared inquiry.*** Participatory Action Research (PAR) approaches combine critical and constructivist approaches with empirical methods of data collection. Interpretive, positivist, and critical approaches thus are complementary, not mutually exclusive, in applied social-justice/social-action research (Lin Chih 1998; Roth and Mehta 2002).

Ecological and System Theories

Ecological, system dynamics, and network paradigms consider how different sectors or subsystems within a larger system interact in a dynamic manner to affect a situation. Ecological models are usually applied to real-time situations (Goodman et al. 1996; Mohatt 2014; Trickett et al. 2011). As proposed by Bronfenbrenner (1989), ecological theory suggests that systems have social organizational "levels" based on whether their influence on individuals is direct or indirect. Bronfenbrenner's work focused on the micro-, meso-, and macro-level social organizational influences on children and adolescents. More generic approaches help us to understand that there are sectors that can be conceptualized as levels, including media, political institutions, community organizations, religious institutions, social programs, peer networks, and families, that extend beyond the individual and that intersect to result in a complex set of factors that influence individual interaction. The ecological approach also suggests that any entity or problem within a "level" is a concern for all levels because of its potential influence on other sectors and on individual behaviors within the system. And, in the same way, making changes in any level has implications for other levels and the desired outcomes.

Systems approaches help us to visualize what happens over time and project it into the future. Network studies can be modeled to show how information or diseases flow through personal networks that are connected to others, over time and under specific conditions, and how network structures and flows can be changed to result in individual, group, and system change (Weeks et al. 2009). Agent-based modeling systems show how individuals, who act in designated ways, combine their actions under specific circumstances to result in both anticipated and unanticipated or emergent results (Abraham 2014; Ghorbani, Dijkema, and Schrauwen 2015; Lin Chih 1998; Roth and Mehta 2002). System dynamics (SD) approaches are useful because they help to identify the positive and negative feedback loops that intersect along with gaps and time lags to further or impede progress towards a goal over time. As Hovmand shows (Hovmand 2014), SD models can be generated very effectively with stakeholders in the change process, helping them to understand how a system in motion generates actions over time, whether desired or undesired, and how modifications to the system can "bend the trends" to produce a variety of better outcomes. When participant led, rather than researcher led, SD modeling becomes a radical approach to changing systems.

These ecological or systems approaches help us to focus on the ways in which subsystems and the people who live and work in relation to them are interconnected—and how well. They also focus on how information and resources may flow through a system. In chapter 4 of this book, we have illustrated several approaches to "emic," or indigenous, modeling that rest on the identification of social/ organizational levels. In complicated or complex systems such as communities or schools, deciding on the levels to be addressed for both research and intervention is central. For these decisions, an understanding of theoretical levels is imperative.

MIDRANGE MULTI-LEVEL PRACTICAL THEORIES THAT GUIDE ETHNOGRAPHY IN ACTION INTERVENTIONS

Cross Reference:
See Book 2, chapter 4

In Book 2 and elsewhere (LeCompte, Judith, and Tesch 1993; Pelto and Pelto 1978; Schensul et al. 2014; Trotter, Schensul, and Kostick 2014), we have referred to midrange or substantive theories. In terms of their level of abstraction, midrange or substantive theories lie between emic, locally, or indigenously generated explanations for circumstances that are deeply embedded in specific conditions and the paradigmatic or grand theories we have outlined early in this chapter. Midrange theories are generalizable predictions that connect patterns of beliefs, norms, and behaviors observed or generated locally in the specific study setting with classes of more general theories that help to explain, measure, and link them to general, even more abstract paradigms listed above. In applied work, we create local theories through collaboration with partners. Here, we consider some of the midrange, substantive, or practical "etic" theories drawn from multiple social science disciplines that can relate to, help to explain, and then extend what is found in the field. They can thus serve as an additional guide to ethnographic interventions. It is important to draw on these potentially useful publically available social science–based theories when going through the iterative process of developing local or indigenous theories so as to help define, explain, refine, or reject elements, components or steps in an intervention; checking their utility against what midrange theory holds to be accurate in similar or related settings can help avoid adopting unworkable approaches.

We take a very broad and eclectic view of theory, drawing on interdisciplinary theory whenever we find it useful. Using an ecological or systems approach allows us to group several families of theories at the individual, group, and community level, and then at all levels simultaneously (multilevel or social contextual level). All are amenable to sharing with partners from different disciplines and community; they can be explained in lay language, are intuitively understandable, can be integrated with capacity building, empowerment, and advocacy efforts, and have been demonstrated to be useful with communities, other stakeholders, or partners. Indeed, oftentimes, community researchers and partners have "invented" indigenous theories which closely replicate the basic tenets of "etic" theories!

Individual-Level Intervention Theories

Individual-level theories explain what is going on within the individual. They help to explain the decision-making or affective processes through which individuals learn, think, interact with the world, and change their own behavior. In individual-level interventions, even if individuals are considered within a group setting, anything external to the individual—for example, the kinds of people conducting an intervention, the setting, and the group members—is not very relevant to interventions themselves. The individual level focuses on the individual's mental processing of pathways toward change, decision making, and the behavior which is intended to follow. For individual-level interventions, social scientists draw most frequently on theories informing three different classes of behavior. This grouping is based on theories about the sometimes linear and sometimes congruent or interactive processes by which people make decisions. Usually, these theories assume rationality. The most common are those that assume that factors such as knowledge, beliefs, values, intentions, motivations, and feelings of control or efficacy act alone or interact to influence behavioral decision making. Sometimes, norms, or cultural-level beliefs and common practices, are central to these theories. Some theories depend on intentionality, arguing that if people *want* to change, and *intend* to change, they are more likely to do so. Others add a behavioral-skills component, based on the idea that the road to hell (or at least the wrong direction) is paved with good intentions. That is, intentions alone are insufficient to produce desirable practices, and people actually have to *do* or perform their practices routinely as part of the intervention. Actually, it is widely understood that cognitive factors such as knowledge, beliefs, and intentions must be associated with skills development or "practice" in order to be useful. Fishbein's Integrated Model of Behavioral Prediction is one example. It is built on extensive empirical evidence

TABLE 5.1 Examples of families of theories by level with associated concepts

Level	Family Type	Example	Similar Theories	Concepts	Delivery
Individual level	Cognitive-behavioral	Integrated Model of Behavioral Prediction	Theory of Reasoned Action, Theory of Planned Behavior, Information, Motivation, and Behavior (IMB) model	Beliefs, Attitudes, Knowledge, Perceived norms, Perceived risk, Intentions, Behavioral skills	Motivational interviewing, Adapted motivational interviewing, Solution focused counseling, General counseling, Education
		Narrative Intervention Model (NIM)	Narrative therapy		Co-construct, Deconstruct, Reconstruct
	Social learning/social context theories	Social influence/persuasion	Social contagion	Social proximity/shared learning, Perceived pressure	Role model, Peer to peer face-to-face/media
		Education/knowledge enhancement		Substantive knowledge/Comparison or perceived to real	Group delivery of information, Didactic, dialogic
		Social norms	Social construction of group norms	Perceived norms, Behavioral norms	Modeling, Explication, Scaffolding, Reflecting, Querying, Cooperative education, Instructional techniques
	Emotional theories	Affect	Framing theory	Positive-negative emotion	Experiments, games, problem solving

Level	Theory/Model				
Group level	Social learning	Co-construction of knowledge/action	Co-creation; Situated learning	Social construction of knowledge	Cooperative learning (individual, small group, large group techniques); Group modeling group data collection and analysis
	Self-help	Stigma reduction/social support	Social problem solving	Mutual interdependence	Interpersonal sharing, narratives, resource exchange, helping "practice"
	Social action	Social advocacy	Civic engagement; Campaigns	Collective efficacy; Collaborative action; Social cohesion	Skills through practice in social action
Community level	Ecological	Multilevel approach to interventions simultaneously			Multiple activities moving toward same or similar end
	Social network	Social influence through social contacts	Diffusion of innovation	Network centrality, between-ness, multiplicity of interactions, density of network, clusters	Devising messages and materials; Sharing messages through peers or role models
	Agent-based modeling	Interaction of "agents" produces emergent phenomena	Emergent causality	Agent, environment, interaction characteristics	Requires ethnography to determine agents, features of the environment, and how they interact
	System dynamics	Non-linear interactive components of system changing designated outcome over time		Positive and negative feedback loops; Time lags; Gaps; Bottlenecks	Requires ethnography to identify system components; group model development; estimation; secondary data collection to develop projections for dependent and other key variables
Broader reach	Social movements	Groups coalescing on the ground or on Internet to take up a local or global cause	Community organizing	Goals, strategies, tactics, negotiation, confrontation, campaigns	Problem identification, persuasive communication, vibrant messaging, use of network capacities of Internet

supporting the ability of the Theory of Reasoned Action and the Theory of Planned Behavior to explain and predict health behaviors. The model includes background and environmental factors, behavioral beliefs, outcome expectancies, normative beliefs, internal and external control beliefs, self-efficacy, and intentionality. Intentionality is composed of *attitudes* about performing the behavior, *perceived norms* (subjective and injunctive—that is, approved/disapproved) and *self-efficacy*, or one's belief in being able to perform the behavior. Fishbein notes that the relative importance of these psychosocial variables will vary and that developing effective interventions requires understanding the culture of the population, as well as the behaviors and barriers to intentionality (Fishbein 2008). Other related rational decision-making models include Fisher's Information, Motivation and Behavior (IMB) model (Fisher and Fisher 2000), which is based on the notion that correct information will motivate people to change their behavior and that for the behavioral change to be durable, the behavior itself must be practiced; the Narrative Intervention Model (NIM) suggests the same, as described in Example 5.2 below.

All of these interrelated theories *depend on local interpretations of the concepts.* For this, ethnography and elicitation of cultural beliefs, values, and knowledge is required. Ethnography, for example, can determine what "information" or knowledge is needed to help people understand why bed nets protect against malaria. (See example 5.1.) Ethnography is also required to understand why people may be unmotivated to use bed nets in the recommended manner; and finally, even if there is motivation, economic and other factors may intervene to shape what interventionists may call people's inappropriate use of bed nets. Ethnography is required to identify those other factors and help to develop better and more comprehensive approaches to address them. A case in point follows.

EXAMPLE 5.1

MAKING DECISIONS ABOUT THE USE OF BED NETS

Bangweulu Wetlands, Zambia—Out here on the endless swamps, a harsh truth has been passed down from generation to generation: there is no fear but the fear of hunger.

With that always weighing on his mind, Mwewa Ndefi gets up at dawn, just as the first orange rays of sun are beginning to spear through the papyrus reeds, and starts to unclump a mosquito net. Nets like his are widely considered a magic bullet against malaria—one of the cheapest and most effective ways to stop a disease that kills at least half a million Africans each year. But Mr. Ndefi and countless others are not using their mosquito nets as global health experts have intended. Nobody in his hut, including his seven children, sleeps under a net at night. Instead, Mr. Ndefi has taken his family's supply of anti-malaria nets and sewn them together into a gigantic sieve that he uses to drag the bottom of the swamp ponds, sweeping up all sorts of life: baby catfish, banded tilapia, tiny mouthbrooders, orange fish eggs, water bugs, and the occasional green frog. All of these creatures can slake hunger (Gettleman 2015).

This example poignantly illustrates how the best individual- or household-level intervention, demonstrated to be effective when evaluated using scientific methods, is creatively diverted in the interests of survival if people are engaged in rational decision making in a resource-limited environment.

Evaluated interventions that are associated with these theories can help to shape how we think and operate on the individual level and on the cultural level. When they inform efforts to change social norms, either perceived or practiced, they can be incorporated into messages delivered in a variety of culturally, developmentally, and contextually relevant ways, and they can influence public activities that reinforce the cognitive and practice elements of the chosen theory. These means of delivering the contents of an intervention are best identified by working together with people affected by the problem. Their concerns and local knowledge can inform limitations on efforts to change individual behaviors. And those affected can partner in developing various approaches to face-to-face communication—such as counseling, education, practice—that are more likely to work. Local residents, armed with this knowledge base, are also central to delivering locally and culturally framed approaches to individual-level change, in local language, with a conversational manner, and congruent with the ways in which people talk to one another about important issues in the cultural setting.

Individual-level interventions often include interviewing-based approaches designed to draw the participant into a conversation or dialogue. Motivational interviewing, adapted motivational interviewing (Burke 2011; Chariyeva et al. 2013; Rubak et al. 2005), and more standard counseling approaches are all theoretically underpinned by cognitive behavioral theories (Gruber 2012; Hays and Iwamasa 2014; McFall, Treat, and Viken 1997; Kazantzis, Reinecke, and Freeman 2010), theories of adult learning (Knowles 1980), empowerment theory (Perkins and Zimmerman 1995), and solution-focused positive psychology theory (Warner 2013). They are generally based on interactions with the participant that elicit the problem, provide feedback, inquire as to the individual's intentions and plans to change, offer suggestions for change, build on previously successful solutions to the problem, assess the individual's need for resources and support to follow the plan, and consolidate the plan with a formalized agreement. Such counseling-based approaches are culturally tailored because the content is derived from the participant's perspective on the problem, and the plan of action emerges from the participant's own analysis of what is realistic for him or her and available in the environment. Ideally the "counselor" or interventionist should be from the setting, speak the participant's language, and be familiar with the participant's lifestyle.

EXAMPLE 5.2

USING A NARRATIVE INTERVENTION MODEL APPROACH TO PREVENTING SEXUAL RISK BEHAVIOR AMONG MARRIED MEN IN MUMBAI

The Narrative Intervention Model uses an adapted motivational interviewing approach and is sufficiently scripted so that counselors, including lay counselors, can be sure to cover all of the necessary topics. This is especially important when multiple factors may contribute to a negative situation that the participant would like to remedy. Recently, a successful intervention was mounted to prevent HIV risk exposure among uninfected married men in Mumbai. The partners were the University of Connecticut, ICR, Tulane University, the International Institute for Population Sciences, the International Institute for Research on Women, a local hospital with a public health clinic, and the AYUSH (Ayurvedic, Unani, homeopathic and other alternative medical traditions) providers in several large slum areas. The intervention, offered by AYUSH providers, was based on a formative ethnographic study that identified sexual dysfunction (*gupt rog*) as a reason for seeking health care from these providers, and the association of *gupt rog* with having unprotected sex with non-spousal partners. Among the predictors of *gupt rog* were the use of alcohol, marital conflict, hyper-masculinity, work-related problems, poor household conditions, lack of privacy, and insufficient household income (Schensul, Verma, and Nastasi 2004). The Narrative Intervention Model (NIM) combines narrative therapy and social constructivism into an approach in which the provider and patient co-construct the patient's story through elicitations that include identifying the desired endpoint (co-construction). The facilitator discusses discrepancies between the participant's story and his desired "'narrative" (deconstruction), and then facilitator and the patient construct an alternative narrative that leads to risk reduction (reconstruction). The elements of the story that the provider focuses on are those identified in prior mixed methods ethnographic research as leading to sex risk reduction; the reconstruction phase enables the patient to revise the story to introduce alternative behaviors that both agree will reduce his risk behavior (Nastasi et al. 2014). This individual-level intervention is thus deeply embedded in the culture of the community; training helped the providers to understand that a problem that initially presented itself as physiological (sexual dysfunction) actually was a cultural expression of distress with psychosocial contributors. It showed them how to shift from their didactic and prescriptive approach to a more interactive one that empowered patients to take their well-being into their own hands. The outcomes of the study demonstrated that married men who participated reduced their risky sexual behavior, improved their communication with their spouses, and reduced or quit their drinking (Saggurti et al. 2013).

EXAMPLE 5.3

A CULTURALLY BASED COGNITIVE BEHAVIORAL INTERVENTION WITH OLDER ADULTS IN CONNECTICUT

Another set of studies to improve oral health in older adults conducted by a community research team from the Institute for Community Research and the University of Connecticut School of Dental Medicine, led by Jean Schensul and Susan Reisine with partners in senior housing, began with formative research with older adults. The purpose was to identify older adults' worries and fears about oral health and hygiene and problems with physical inability to handle toothbrushes and dental floss. The results of the research (worries and fears) were integrated into Fishbein's Integrative Model (IM) (Fishbein and Ajzen 2010), an "integrated" cognitive behavioral model drawing from several CBT traditions that included norms, beliefs, knowledge, perceived risk, self-efficacy, and locus of control. Scales linked to the IM model to the domains uncovered in the formative work—worries and fears about oral health—were identified or, in the case of worries and fears about oral health, newly constructed—and the research team worked with older adults to evaluate these measures for acceptability, feasibility, and relevance. The domains were then measured in a baseline survey and used as the basis for tailoring a face-to-face intervention based on the specific domains on which participants scored below a predetermined satisfactory cutoff point. The intervention had a skills/practice component. In addition, it included visual feedback of the results of a dental assessment of the condition of their teeth and gums. Participants created a plan for their own future behavior (their intentions) based on their self-assessment of their needs. Three months later, a repeat dental assessment showed that the oral health of the group that had participated in the intervention had improved significantly.

Two interesting aspects of this intervention were indigenous scale development for intervention use and the involvement of residents delivering a health campaign to their peers in linking messages they themselves developed to the overall intervention theoretical framework. The scale evolved from the field-based identification of oral health self-management worries and fears that were a key component in avoiding oral hygiene. Residents identified the key elements of their worries and fears; these became the items in a reliable scale that was used in the intervention to relieve participants of their concerns and worries. The researchers learned it had good predictive value! The second was the active participation of residents in developing oral hygiene messages to deliver to their peers. These messages emerged out of their own consideration of oral health and good self-management practices plus materials other residents had created for use in building-based health education. Residents were introduced in lay language to the conceptual framework for the study. They discussed it and were able to crosscheck their messages with the theoretical domains in the study model and make sure that all domains were effectively covered.

Social Learning Theories

For many years, interventions were conducted based on the idea that people would be persuaded to change their behavior through information delivered by experts (local or professional) in individual or group settings. In general, however, research shows that most learning occurs through engagement with others in both formal (Rogoff 2003; Wertsch 1985) and informal or community settings (Lave 1985). Various models of social and social/contextual learning theories have been shown to be useful for ethnographic interventions at the individual level. Social persuasion models suggest that youth or adults influence each other directly through instruction or encouragement, or indirectly through modeling. Social persuasion can be a form of engaged situational learning, often in a naturalistic setting. Peer-to-peer interventions, which are very common, operate on the basis of modeling, social persuasion, and social support for behavior change; they often occur in a group setting. Educational approaches are similar; they utilize group settings to deliver information that is intended to change behavior. Usually, educational approaches are necessary but not sufficient in sustaining any form of normative, cognitive, or behavioral change—even if the materials are culturally congruent with the audience and delivered in a culturally and linguistically appropriate way. They must be supplemented with other individual, group, or normative community change strategies.

Theories of Affect or Emotion

More recently, theories of emotion or affect have been integrated with approaches based on reason, suggesting that many decisions are based on "intuition" or "feelings" in the moment. Most theories that address emotion or affect derive from the work of Peter Salovey and colleagues on *emotional* intelligence (Goleman 2011; Salovey and Mayer 1989), which they theorize, describe, measure, and define as a legitimate form of intelligence. Emotions and emotional intelligence are viewed as having influence on health and mental health (Schutte et al. 2007) and as intervening in and overriding rational decision making, which often results in less than ideal outcomes (Xie et al. 2011) Intervention approaches are based on the idea that if individuals can become more aware of their emotions, they can manage them better in the context of their decision making (Greco and Stenner 2013, Greenspan 2014).

Group-Level Theories

Group-level intervention theories generally are based on several interlocking sets of ideas related to the social nature of learning and group processes. From an intervention standpoint, as noted above, most formal and informal learning occurs through engagement with others. Thus,

Key point *any activity that takes place with two or more people and is geared toward a specific end can be called a group-level intervention.* Group interventions can be classified as three main types:

- *educational interventions* in which information is delivered in a group setting;
- *skill-building groups* in which group members work together to build their skills collectively. Skills may be cognitive, communication based or specific health, education, or other behaviors. In a group intervention designed to encourage members to help each other with the assistance of a teacher who models and embodies the skills that are desired, individual assistance is generally not offered;
- *process-oriented interventions* in which intervention is designed to encourage group members to learn together, provide feedback and mutual support to each other, share information, and develop a common platform for learning and action. These processes are of greatest interest in and of themselves and in shaping the outcomes of the group and the individuals in it. Process-oriented group interventions require a trained facilitator and provide a strong basis for the development of new, group co-constructed norms and practices.

Specific theories guide what actually happens in the process-oriented group (Combs 1999). Constructivist theory is a helpful guide in shaping group process because it is congruent with theories of cultural construction, creation of social norms, and promotion of culture change. Group processes that lead to cultural construction and reconstruction/deconstruction can be designed, documented ethnographically, and measured quantitatively. Group-process theories suggest that individual thoughts and beliefs depend on interpersonal exchanges, just as does the evolution and transmission of culture (Berger 1990; Rogoff 2003; Wertsch 1985). In social learning situations, more experienced

individuals or facilitators model and mediate the person-environment interaction (a form of mediated learning) for novices. With repeated exchanges in similar contexts, new ideas and behavior become internalized. Interpersonal relationships provide the context for reinforcing shared beliefs and behaviors, thus enhancing perceptions of competence.

Using this framework, it is clear that interpersonal relationships provide the context for creating and reinforcing shared beliefs and behaviors, enhancing perceptions of competence, and encouraging persistence in enacting these behaviors. Furthermore, the social validation provided by peers who value the same beliefs and competencies can serve to enhance a sense of acceptance, efficacy, and self-worth. This, in turn, influences mental health and social-behavioral adjustment. At the same time, constructivist processes create new group norms which are reinforced by group members. An intervention study conducted by anthropologists, psychologists, and educators illustrates how a group-norms intervention based on constructivist theory can be developed.

EXAMPLE 5.4

BUILDING GROUP NORMS IN MIDDLE SCHOOL CLASSROOMS

For fifteen years, a school district in a small city in the northeastern United States had been using a curriculum on improving individual self-management and problem solving to prevent teen violence and improve social decision making. It needed revision. A team of researchers from ICR, including Jean Schensul (PI) and Bonnie Nastasi, and psychiatrists and physicians from a nearby university, worked collaboratively with educators and teachers in the school system to develop and implement a curriculum based on the construction of group prevention norms in the fifth through seventh grades. The goals were to update the curriculum, engage teachers in learning how to facilitate group learning rather than teaching didactically or with scripted curricula, and engage the students in problem solving based on their shared experiences. The teachers in five of the ten schools participated in several days of training and continuous coaching as they tried out the curriculum in their classes. All of the activities in the curriculum were based on principles of cooperative learning. The others were part of the comparison group. Teachers introduced learning exercises and provided instructions to the students. The students worked sometimes individually and sometimes in small groups to do the exercises, discussed the results at their table, and presented them to the class as a whole. The curriculum provided questions and posed dilemmas based on real-life situations and asked the students to introduce their own questions and situations; this deepened the curriculum's cultural relevance. At times, the curriculum required students to create their own individual, and then combined, theories related to specific behavioral outcomes (such as factors contributing to under-age drinking). The groups were expected to come to agreement on what they had learned, and on what decisions were called for in the exercises that posed social dilemmas—what to do at a party where alcohol was served, how to handle a bullying situation, and what to do if there was a conflict with a policeman. They then presented their conclusions to the class. The class discussed the conclusions and came to consensus on the approach. Teachers needed considerable skill to listen carefully, identify common patterns throughout the discussion, and summarize the results so as to bring the group to consensus and closure.

Most students in sixth and seventh grades were exposed to the yearlong curriculum over a two-year period. At the eighth-grade measurement point, survey results showed that students were comfortable in negotiating differences of opinion and in coming to consensus around many issues related to managing risk in their lives. The intervention was found to be more popular among girls than boys; boys needed more instruction in dialogue, debate, and negotiation to consensus. This project demonstrated that, overall, group problem solving through cooperative-learning techniques and sound teacher coaching has the potential to enable both children and adults to discuss and share their opinions and experiences, obtain more information, and build a common platform for changing values, beliefs, and behavior.

When people with a common commitment to change norms, behaviors, and institutions work together to analyze the causes of their situation, they can be guided by constructivist theory to gather and use their information to construct new and shared ideas about social and structural arrangements, as well as ways of bringing about such transformations. In other words, group interventions can build on participants' skills and lived experience, invite them to generate causal models explaining social norms and possibilities for social change—and even, as we describe in chapter 9 of this book—involve them in their own data collection. When this process is undergirded with theories of group integration, social influence, and group learning, interventions with high potential for success can be generated. Of all of the group approaches, this one has the greatest potential for empowerment, both at the individual and the group level, and for the generation of transformative action, especially when based on critical analysis of the structural or social origins of selected inequalities.

Community/Cultural-Level Theories

Many specific interventions, as well as longer-range programs of social change, are directed toward community/cultural-level transformations. Most of the examples in chapter 2 are efforts to transform neighborhoods or larger social entities over time.

Community Development Approaches

The community development literature in anthropology and sociology generally focuses on whole-community approaches. The process of changing and transforming communities draws on a number of different theoretical approaches while at the same time integrating individual- and group-level approaches as required. These approaches begin with the following premises:

- Communities have assets and resources (Kretzman and McKnight 1993).
- Communities can and do solve their own problems using those assets and resources or advocating new ones (Van Willigen 2005).
- Communities have specific needs for research to increase their capacity to advocate, to revitalize themselves in new settings, to argue for social justice and civil rights, to gain political visibility and technological advantage, and to conserve their cultural heritage (Schensul 2005).

Transforming or Creating New Community Institutions

In the formative phase, community-based participatory or partnership research may point out that existing community institutions (museums, schools, health services, social services, libraries) are not providing needed services and programs. In such cases one of two approaches can be useful:

a. attempting to work with existing organizations to extend or expand their capacities (new staff, new programs, new board members, etc.);
b. working to develop new or replacement institutions more closely aligned to the partner community's need, such as community-based research organizations or new service and advocacy organizations.

Formalized community alliances, research, advocacy, and consultation are required to ensure the success of either or both of these approaches. In chapter 2, the Chicago and Hartford experiences highlight the advantages of developing new organizations to further community advancement. The Detroit experience highlights the utility of broad-based community alliances to advocate for and develop a variety of responses, together with communities affected by health and other disparities. Critical approaches to transformation may inform the development of alternative institutional structures. They also inform efforts to change policy and to formulate, justify, initiate, and sustain social movements designed to bring about radical changes in government structures, policies affecting distributed inequalities, needed infrastructure, and health care and other barriers to social, cultural, and mental health/ health well-being.

Communications Approaches to Community Change

Communications approaches are widely used across the social sciences and business to influence norms and change behavior. Sometimes referred to as "social marketing," they apply marketing concepts to the "analysis, planning, execution and evaluation of programs" intended to change individual behavior at the group or aggregate level (Andreasen 2006; Kotler 1989). Social marketing concepts include *product, place, price,* and *promotion.* The notion of *product* refers to the delivery of materials, messages, and processes that appeal to core values and promise tangible benefits for recipients. *Promotion* involves incentives and other means that improve awareness of issues and the need for behavior change. *Price* refers to social, psychological, financial, and other human resource costs of engaging in the behavior. Finally, *place* refers to distribution channels for delivering the behavior to humans, nonhumans, and venues. The concept of unique populations, as used in the context of social marketing, refers to groups that either have not yet been targeted or have been marginalized from the primary means of communicating with the general population. *Segmenting* the market refers to the identification of subgroups whose views and needs must be taken into consideration if the messages are to be effective in changing cognition and behavior. Social marketing segments the market, developing specific marketing mixes tailored to specific subcomponents of a larger market or target audience. Social marketing has been applied with varying degrees of success to the reduction of smoking (Hastings and McLean 2006), addressing sexually transmitted infections and HIV (Pedrana et al. 2014), and dietary behavior and cardiovascular health (Carrete and Arroyo 2014; Jørgensen et al. 2013) by changing social norms related to negative health and other behaviors.

If used strategically, social marketing added as a complement to individual and social interventions can target the structural inequities related to race, ethnicity, class, and power as well as social and cultural norms. Social marketing is empowering when it involves affected people directly in the formulation of appropriate messages, media modeling, and face-to-face communication. Messages can critique received knowledge, norms, and marketing strategies and promote behavior change at both the individual and structural levels, thus reinforcing the potential for change. Social marketing can affect social influence through direct modeling of the behavior and its consequences, communicating approval or disapproval of the behavior, providing opportunities to perform or avoid the behavior, or using coercive strategies to force a person to engage in a behavior or not (Slater, Snyder, and Hayes 2006). Communications theories can be linked with group and individual-level theories in the conduct of multilevel interventions; when bolstered

with a critical theoretical approach, they can result in transformative changes at the individual, social, and cultural levels (Grier and Bryant 2005).

Dynamic Social Impact Theory (DSIT) (Fink 1996;
Latané 1996; Lavine and Latané 1996; Nowak, Szamrej, and
Latané 1990) complements social marketing by suggesting
three central characteristics which increase the likelihood of
acceptance of new ideas: *strength*, or the relative *power* people have in face-to-face situations or via the media to influence others through similarity or homophily or other characteristics, such as wealth, or strength; *immediacy*, defined
as the physical or social space between influencing agents
and those being influenced; and *number*, or the number of
people communicating the new message to the individual.
An environment that is *saturated* with consistent messages
and appropriate options conveyed through *many different
forms* of communication (media, print, and face-to-face),
by effective communicators with powerful messages who
are like, or who appeal to, the public (i.e., homophily) in a
culturally appropriate place in a face-to-face manner will
provide more effective support for individual-level decision
making and social persuasion.

Two brief examples can make these ideas clearer. An
intervention to reduce risk of transmitting HIV among
injection and other drug users invited peers to become peer
health advocates (PHAs) with researchers. These PHAs
developed their own messages and conveyed them, often
in multiple locations, to other drug users in the community, using a variety of different tools. The long-term effect
was significant reduction in risk behavior among the peers
of the PHAs. In the second example, a CDC-funded intervention study to prevent acceleration of alcohol and marijuana use among teens in Hartford called "Xperience: For
Those Who Choose Not to Use," a group of young artists
developed their own drug- and alcohol-prevention messages using their lived experience and a cognitive behavioral framework focused on peer norms and perceived risks.
They transformed the messages into original works of art
and performed before larger and smaller audiences of their
peers and their families, handing out CDs with their music
and spoken words (Diamond et al. 2009).

DSIT explains how messages, including behaviors, are shared and transmitted among members of a social network, and how they diffuse from one part of a community to another through social networks of interconnected people. Network analysis can then identify whether homophily (similarity of messenger to recipient), social proximity, and centrality of the messengers in their networks, separately or together, make a difference in diffusing messages throughout a community.

A generic approach to DSIT is based on the idea that change occurs through social persuasion or even "social contagion" in networks (Crandall 1988; Ejima, Aihara, and Nishiura 2013; Scherer and Cho 2003). This approach uses an implicit or explicit network framework, arguing that all networks or groups/clusters/cliques include people who are more persuasive, some of them positively and others less so. Desired results can be produced by discovering through formative research who the positive persuaders (sometimes called "peer leaders," or "opinion leaders") are and working with them and their networks to develop capacity to influence their "peers" or other network members in positive ways. This approach also can be very beneficial with people who are advocating negative behaviors (such as selling drugs), if they can be convinced that they can play a more positive role in their communities by changing roles. Some researchers have shown that in such cases, negative peer leaders are transformed into very positive forces for change, and in the process, leave their risk behaviors behind.

Using Consensus Theories and Cultural Models in Interventions and Evaluations

Cultural and consensus models theories are based on a view of culture as a set of widely shared or modal cultural beliefs and norms (Romney, Weller, and Batchelder 1986). These theories lead to methods designed to discover degrees of consensus and variation among individual members of a group and to identify to what degree an individual's knowledge of a cultural domain is different from or similar to that of the rest of the group (Weller and Romney 1988). A chapter by Borgatti and Halgin in Book 4 of the

Cross Reference: See Book 4, chapter 3

Toolkit provides a deeper explanation of cultural consensus theory and how to measure degrees of cultural consensus and variations or outliers who might either be different or members of another group. Some researchers use consensus theory to identify core versus peripheral values and may use this distinction to identify emergent differences in a population. Applied researchers have examined differences in health beliefs between providers and patients and used the information to remove cognitive and even patient-specific barriers to heath care (Chavez, Hubbell, and McMullin 1995; Garro and Mattingly 2000). Others have used communications theory to change social norms, and they have measured the changes using cultural consensus modeling (Kostick et al. 2011). Cultural consensus models can also be used to promote narratives or storytelling as part of a narrative intervention approach. By reading the groupings of "clusters" of concepts left to right, lay or professional researchers can construct a story that makes sense and influences discussion and debate that can change thinking, norms, and even behavior.

Community Organizing and Social Movements

Activist ethnographic researchers hold that a community-organizing approach underlies community-level interventions and connects them to social movements. In the previous section, we discussed community-level interventions. These lead logically to efforts to organize communities and other broader networks for social action. Community organizing is often thought of as community "mobilization." In fact, community organizing is a compilation of theoretical approaches that range from critical analysis to confrontational tactics. Here we briefly outline several theoretically driven approaches to community organizing that serve as resources for researcher/activist teams who want to conceptualize and mobilize their constituencies for action-oriented efforts.

In the field of community organizing there are several main approaches, all of which can be integrated into ethnographic mixed methods research:

1. *Transformative or social action organizing.* In trans-
    formative organizing, the scope of concern is the
    inequitable distribution of power and resources in
    a specific setting or population. Theories of change
    using this approach include conflict theory and
    confrontational approaches. This approach sug-
    gests that "winning" small battles or actions will
    lead to social change on a larger level and that, in
    order to achieve these small successes, it is impor-
    tant to build an active citizenry. These approaches
    to change involve mobilization for action, con-
    frontation, persuasion of critical stakeholders, and
    targeting of powerful individuals for change.
2. *Feminist organizing.* This approach recognizes
    inequality and oppression at the societal level and
    systemic structures of power and privilege through
    a gender lens. The approach argues that power
    structures preserve structural forms of oppres-
    sion based on sexism and racism and that those
    who are affected must combat power structures
    to win social change, not by direct confrontation
    but by building divergent structures and alterna-
    tive relationships in society. The approach involves
    addressing practices that uphold power and domi-
    nance: hierarchy, sexism, competition, and calls
    for modeling desired change at multiple levels.
    The approaches to change involve self-help and
    social-organizing groups, coalition building, and
    emphasizing learning communities where people
    can develop and grow politically.
3. *Community building/community development
    approach.* This approach calls for measuring and
    assessing community capacity focused on the "local
    group" (Hartford's east side, Detroit, Harlem, and
    others). Theories of change emphasize consensus,
    asset assessment, promoting recognition that the
    community has all the assets it needs to induce
    change, promotion of community integration to
    oppose *anomie*, or alienation, of individuals or

groups, and contradicting beliefs that change cannot occur because the community lacks social capital as well as the sense that a belief that the combination of social capital and assets recognition will be sufficient for change. These approaches involve collaboration, civic engagement, task groups, and striving for consensus.

4. *Social planning/policy.* This approach focuses on social problems and policy planning. It is primarily driven by technocrats, not by communities, and it assumes policies automatically will change if social and cultural factors change. This approach to change is rational, involving problem solving, data collection, lobbying, developing strategic alliances with political and business interests, exercising power that sways policy, and forming action groups with nonprofits. This approach gives token recognition to the voices of community participants.

(Barrette 2015)

LINKING THEORETICAL LEVELS

System theories offer another approach to thinking about "community level" approaches to change. Two midrange systems approaches are useful for social change purposes: scripting theory and system dynamics theory. The first, scripting theory, links levels (individual, group, and community), and the second, system dynamics theory, offers a strategy for considering how complex systems function over time, and where to intervene to change them.

Scripting Theory and Interventions

Scripting theory creates a link between contextual, cultural, interpersonal, and intrapersonal or cognitive explanations for behavior. Scripting theories assume that patterns of behavior are locally derived and socially learned and change over time. Scripts are patterned cognitive representations of events and event sequences applied to cultural domains (Abelson 1981; Quinn 2005; Schank and Abelson 1977). They represent summaries of larger shared sets of cultural assumptions, beliefs, and understandings about behaviors, events, and their explanations; they are retained for use in specific settings. Scripts are shared by substantial components of a population or community and are developed and given meaning through repeated experience and social engagement (D'Andrade 1995; Vygotsky 1978; Wertsch 1985). Scripting theory has been explored in marketing and applied mainly to questions of sexuality and sexual decision making. In studies of sexuality, scripting theory integrates cultural meanings and rules for sexual behavior (Gilmore, DeLamater, and Wagstaff 1996) with constructed notions of sexuality, perceived sexual opportunities, and actual responses and internalized beliefs and attitudes about sex, sexual identity, and sexual meaning (Thompson 1995).

Simon and Gagnon (Simon and Gagnon 1984; Simon and Gagnon 1987) have described scripts as consisting of three components: cultural scenarios, interpersonal scripts, and intrapsychic or cognitive scripts. **Cultural scenarios** are guidelines for engagement in interactions. They include spatial, situational, social, and behavioral cues leading to defined ends: for example, types of sexual or other activity that can be drawn upon to guide behavior in actual situations. The presence or absence of certain behaviors, such as condom use, in these cultural-level scripts is a salient clue suggesting that these behaviors are not part of the cultural repertoire for sexual encounters (Edgar and Fitzpatrick 1993). Cultural scenarios can be obtained through secondary textual narratives (such as print media), films and videos, and focus groups discussing situations involving sexual relationships, sexual acts, and drug use (Frith and Kitzinger 1997).

Interpersonal scripts involve the combination by individuals of scenarios or components of scenarios to help interpret and shape their behavioral sequences and their sexual or other actions. Settings, partners, friends, power, substance use, and other contextual factors offer cues and opportunities that may shape which cultural scenario is chosen as the model for action and how it is scripted or

Definition: Cultural scenarios are guidelines for engagement in interactions

Definition: Interpersonal scripts involve the combination by individuals of scenarios or components of scenarios to help interpret and shape their behavioral sequences and their sexual or other actions operationalized at any given point in time (Hynie et al. 1998; Simon and Gagnon 1984; Simon and Gagnon 1986). The concept of the interpersonal script incorporates the notion of agency, that is, the idea that individuals are in active engagement with their environment and exert either active or passive choices, regardless of situational limitations. Interpersonal scripts are obtained through detailed recording of actual events and event sequences in which individuals describe what they do, with whom, where, and for what reasons.

Variations in operationalization of scenarios or cultural norms may indicate changing social norms or alternative pathways to similar ends, and deviations from the norm could be related to social risk. The interaction of scenario, context, and agency produces the alternatives and innovations that, when shared, repeated, and internalized, result in development of new scenarios or cultural options for action. Thus, scripting offers an alternative approach to constructivism, in that it records the co-creation of new cultural elements and behaviors, in other words, an intervention.

Definition: Intrapsychic scripts or internalized cultural meanings and patterned practices represent the internalization of repeated engagements with scenarios and enactments of interpersonal scripts through which individual sexual beliefs, attitudes, identities, and strategies are shaped (Holland 1998; Vygotsky 1978). They are generated and reinforced through the media and in specific settings, and enacted, reenacted, and reinforced in the context of partner relationships, social networks, and social settings.

Scripting theory provides a framework for bridging the distinction between cultural or structural determinism and situated decision making. Cultural beliefs, values, and norms shape and determine cultural practices, but actual practice varies because it is determined by the individual's interpretation or definition of the situation. *Agency* can be defined as the individual's ability to "read" the environment, assign intersubjective meaning, create responses, and enact them in ways that may replicate, interpret, or resist norms-based cultural practice (Bucholtz 2002; Raby 2005). Individuals analyze cultural forms and improvise their response to them in the context of changing social and material conditions (Lehmann 2004). In the context of substance use and sexuality or other behaviors, the concept of agency provides the basis for framing how individuals create logics behind how they actively engage with and manage risk by integrating cultural repertoires (components of scenarios) and contextual opportunities and constraints so as to construct sequences of activities leading to expected or unexpected ends. (Mayock 2005; Mclure and Sotelo 2004). Scripts are socially negotiated through networks or groups. Often, a combination of social marketing (societal level), DSIT, or other theories that characterize the flow of information theory through a system and its impact on individuals *and* cognitive behavioral interventions at the individual or group dyad level are necessary to bring about desired changes in cultural scripting at the community level.

System Dynamics Theory for Predicting Change and "Bending the Trends"

System Dynamics Theory (SD) is an approach applied to problems arising in complex social, managerial, economic, or ecological systems characterized by interdependence, mutual interaction, information feedback, and circular causality (Sterman 2002). Based on the early work of Forrester (Forrester 1968; Forrester and Senge 1980), SD is particularly useful in understanding problems that seem to be intransigent, even in response to new policies, regulations, and other efforts to intervene. SD modeling elucidates feedback loops and nonlinear interactions that lead to unintended consequences in the behavior of the system. Feedback loops are causal connections that occur when an output to a process within a system feeds back to an input in the same system. While *reinforcing feedback loops* amplify change, *balancing feedback loops* tend to counteract change, leading to outcomes that often are counterintuitive or different from expectations (Douglas and Wildavsky 1982; Forrester 2007a; Forrester 2007b; Gigerenzer and Gaissmaier 2011; Sterman 2000). Dynamic models try to account for causality in complex systems. SD models consider the simultaneous and nonlinear interactions of multiple forces on nonlinear rates of change (flow) in outcomes of interest by identifying the primary domains and processes that intersect in *nonlinear* ways over time. SD builds on mixed methods, stakeholder engagement, secondary data collection and analysis, and epidemiology to develop computer models and simulations (Forrester and Senge 1980; Luna-Reyes and Andersen 2003) and offers an alternative to ecological approaches to community-based interventions and population health (Hirsch et al. 2012; Leischow and Milstein 2006; Milstein, Homer, and Hirsch 2010; Schensul 2009).

Systems researchers may choose among network modeling, in which information flows through networks; agent-based modeling, which examines how differential rates of change in key contextual factors influence the interactive and emergent behaviors of units based on their interaction with contextual factors; and SD models that utilize diagrams models to illustrate, quantify, and simulate multiple variables interacting at different rates over time (Luke and Stamatakis 2012).

To model local complex problems, some SD researchers (Ford and Sterman 1998; Hovmand et al. 2012) have used group model building (GMB), a form of Participatory Action Research/CBPR, to increase the quality of models and likelihood of stakeholders' implementation of results (Richardson 2013; Rouwette, Vennix, and Mullekom 2002; Vennix et al. 1992). Group model building in SD, like group model building described in chapter 4 of this book, involves experienced and lay stakeholders in the process of conceptualizing, formulating, and analyzing models for problem solving (Richardson 2013; Rouwette, Vennix, and Mullekom 2002; Vennix et al. 1992). Quantification and calibration of SD models typically draws on both quantitative (e.g., survey, epidemiologic) and qualitative data (e.g., stakeholder/key informant interviews) with a specific focus on dynamics, that is, the changes over time. Confidence in SD models is established through a series of mathematical tests to discover programming faults, as well as stakeholder reviews, semantic reviews of main variables (Barlas 1996), and social validation by community and other stakeholders (Latuszynska and Lemke 2013). These procedures establish whether historical patterns can be replicated through behavior-reproduction tests and, more stringently, the ability to predict the impact of policy changes prospectively through policy-assessment tests. Participatory SD modeling is a form of participatory research that is highly empowering because it enables community residents to work together to identify the structure of stagnant situations that sustain inequities, such as those tackled by the Memphis example in chapter 2. There, the community identified forces that intersected to maintain and to counter inequities and those interventions, based on local resources, that residents could draw on to tip the equation in the direction of alternative outcomes.

Ethnographers think in terms of systems as broad-based and interconnected institutional components and sociocultural and political forces, and mental or cognitive models. Shared cognitive representations of systems or components of systems constitute definitions of culture. Social scientists use consensus modeling as a means of defining culture in terms of measurably *shared* cognitive models (mental models, mental or cognitive maps) that link concepts, processes, and cultural domains (D'Andrade 1992). Consensus modeling provides a basis for arguing that group modeling exercises with a wide representation of people from a cultural setting can produce reasonably accurate systems models (Borgatti and Halgin 2011). Ethnographies as complex case analyses have much in common with, but are not quite representations of, dynamic systems (Agar 2004), however, because for the most part they are more concerned with how factors "fit together" and are less concerned with how those factors interact in predicted and unpredicted ways to produce nonlinear trends or outcomes over time. Thus, it remains a challenge to shift conceptually from the linear or systemic models typical of ethnographic (or other social science thinking) to systems dynamic forms of modeling.

Critical Theories and Intervention Approaches

Midlevel critical theories offer guidance for effective attempts to transform imbalances and inequities in the structure and distribution of desired resources and assets, whether financial, social, political, cultural, linguistic, or natural. These theories can be found under community-organizing rubrics. (See pages 197–98.) Most of these theories suggest that important components of the social order must be transformed or eliminated in order to achieve equity. Approaches include:

- the development of critical consciousness and analytic skills, linked to popular education (Christens, Collura, and Tahir 2013; Escueta and Butterwick 2012; Nkoane 2010; Watts, Diemer, and Voight 2011);
- feminist perspectives linking power and gender and taking on ways of transforming both social norms and structures that perpetrate gender-based inequities across the class/race/ethnicity and age spectrums through media, writing, mobilizing, and popular education (Stall and Stoecker 1998);
- confrontational perspectives calling for the mobilization of individuals face-to-face and using social media to hold power holders—including politicians and CEOs—accountable for misuse of resources, fraud, and poor decisions. They also call for reallocation of resources, especially in cases of environmental or health disasters or gross misuse of public, and often private, funds. These approaches tend to mix confrontation via mobilization of large masses of people with attempts at negotiation (Bretherton 2012; Engel 2002; Goldblatt 2005; Mackie 2009).

SUMMARY

In this chapter, we have tried to show that there are families of theories that can be useful at the individual, group, or community level or at multiple levels. These theories can be useful in linking and translating the local theories discussed in chapter 4 into a larger, more general and globalized language of social change interventions. The theories we have chosen to highlight are readily explained in lay language. More often than not, local theorists develop their own ways of thinking about the world, conceptualizing and making links, or generating hypotheses that connect in some way to one or more of these practical midrange theories. There are at times no standard ways to measure the concepts and constructs associated with these theories, or, rather, there are many equally appropriate and effective ways. And these families of theories allow for generating local measures. They also interface with ethnographic methods to discover whether there are, and in what ways there might be, connections between local theories and more widely used "science based" theories. In the next chapter, we turn to issues of methodology for generating local conceptual, formative, or scoping theories for both basic and intervention/application research.

6

DESIGNING AND DEVELOPING INTERVENTION APPROACHES

INTRODUCTION

In chapters 1 and 3, we discussed the importance of building partnerships and trust in community and other settings where researchers hope to become involved in transformational change efforts. We've also begun to address the many issues that can arise in collaborations in which assumptions about relationships differ and members may have different cultures or ways of operating that must be negotiated. Since collaborations go on over a period of time, the relationships, infrastructure, and policies for decision making, publishing, and communicating must continually be examined and modified.

In chapter 2, we described some longer-term transformative efforts involving researchers and multiple partners who worked consistently to build joint capacity in order to move forward a social/health equity and social-justice agenda in or across multiple communities with common interests and with collaborating organizations and alliances. In chapters 4 and 5, we suggested ways of generating local theory that builds on the lived experience, knowledge, and understanding that partners, activists, and actors bring to the problem at hand; we also discussed some guiding paradigms and orienting midrange or "etic" theories that can help researchers and their partners to situate their work and compare it with others.

The field of intervention development is emerging, and there is still little summative literature that illustrates the links between theoretical frameworks, whether indigenous or science based, and steps in the conceptualization and development of real-life actions that can be taken with people to change their lives and circumstances (Glanz and Bishop 2010). In this chapter, we examine more closely the ways in which interventions (action or social change strategies) build on local and discipline-based "midrange" theory and the steps that teams can take in operationalizing them. In describing the process involved, we will show where and how ethnographic data collection methods, both quantitative and qualitative, that are carried out by ethnographers in partnership with community teams enhance the integration of interventions into community culture, social organization, and transformation. Visualizing change levels as a target with concentric circles, we will follow *ecological* logic, moving from developing interventions that make a difference at the individual level (what we will call the innermost ring or "bull's-eye" of a set of concentric circles) through those that affect policy (the outermost concentric ring), keeping in mind that systems change or transformation requires intervention in multiple ways and at multiple levels. We provide examples of how to extend this idea in the last section of this chapter. Decisions regarding interventions are made at any point in a new or ongoing relationship. *The decisions, outlined in the next section, and the action steps to be taken are necessary, no matter whether the action relationship is new or ongoing.*

Key point

DECIDING ON AN APPROACH

The first step in conceptualizing an intervention is for the team to develop a preliminary model together, following

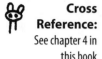

Cross Reference: See chapter 4 in this book

guidelines in chapter 4. This results in a local theory of change. The process should end with an assessment of resources that can be organized to transform the dependent variable. The next step is to make some decisions about the intervention approach, such as:

- Identifying core cultural concepts. Work closely together to identify one or more core concepts or acronym that anchors the intervention and make it meaningful and attractive to the communities affected by the problem. Examples of core cultural concepts are "*comadrona*" (a traditional birth attendant in Latin America); *gupt rog* (diseases of men in India).

- Developing *critical consciousness* among participants. Introduce questions concerned with how to remedy power imbalances, disparities, and injustices associated with the project.

- Identifying intervention level. Will the approach be at individual-, group-, community-, or policy-level intervention? Or is it an intervention that is planned for two or more levels simultaneously? If so, why? Or is it part of a social movement?

- Deciding on the theories guiding the intervention. Determine which additional indigenous and social science theories are helpful, how they can justify the actions to be taken, and the resources applied to those actions.

- Reviewing community assets and resources that can be applied to the approaches.

- Identifying goals and objectives for the intervention based on the formative model and the resources to be brought to bear on changing the "variables" and their relationship to one another.

- Deciding which stakeholders should be involved in creating the intervention. Should it include multiple stakeholders or only those people affected directly by the problem? Why?

- Identifying the "mechanisms" of the intervention. How will it link to the model and intervention resources described in the previous two chapters?

How will it be delivered and by whom, what strategies will it use, and what materials and content will it draw from?

- Deciding on what kinds of involvement the people affected by the situation should have. Should they drive it or play key roles in the conceptualization and creation of the intervention/action, implementing it, and evaluating it, or both?
- Planning for evaluation. How should the planned change strategy(ies) be evaluated? How can the team know if they are proceeding according to plan and whether the plan is working? What if the "plan" is emergent and the outcomes change over time? What instruments/measures, including observations and filming, can be used? Is the design viable, cost-effective, and believable? Will it show success? The best outcomes?
- Determining dissemination strategies. How should the intervention be disseminated in the community and to whom? What about others who should hear about the results?
- Planning for sustainability. Which elements of the intervention are sustainable and in what ways? How can communities and other institutions take up an intervention and make sure it stays and grows over time?

CORE CULTURAL CONCEPTS

What differentiates ethnography in action-driven interventions from other kinds of interventions is that they are based in and extend from local culture and from collaborations between researchers and local actors. From the intersection of both emerge ideas for change that constitute the core culturally meaningful concepts around which an intervention approach can be organized. Some call this the "cultural hook"; other terms refer to interventions that are culturally appropriate, culturally guided, or culturally organized around the meaning systems of local or indigenous people. The strength of these cultural concepts or "hooks" is that they rally people around an intervention because it is meaningful and makes sense to them. Some examples of cultural "hooks" or guiding cultural elements or concepts are:

- *Dais and other Traditional Birth Attendants.* Traditional birth attendants (TBAs) in Africa and Latin America and dais in India, who carry centuries of knowledge regarding supports for pregnant and lactating mothers, have long been identified as the basis for health care interventions in underserved communities (WHO/UNFPA/UNICEF 1992).

- *Comadrona.* In Latin American countries, the *comadrona* is an important figure in supporting women during the perinatal period. The *comadrona* visits women before birth of a child, is present at the birth, consults on any issues that arise after the birth, and helps to rally the family to support the woman during the postnatal period (Wilson et al. 2011). This concept served as the rallying call for the Comadrona Program, a perinatal support program of the Hispanic Health Council in Hartford, Connecticut. It is staffed by trained women from the community and has continued for more than twenty years.

- *Gupt rog.* A Hindi term described earlier that refers to men's sexual health problems. Cultural and structural factors lead to expressions of *gupt rog*; it is an "idiom of distress" that is a marker of marital conflict stemming from gender inequities that prevent men and women from communicating with each other, especially about sexual concerns. It also involves men's inability to fulfill all of their responsibilities as household head, including earning enough money to support the family. The existence of *gupt rog* provided the basis for a brief counseling intervention addressing psychosocial and structural problems, carried out by alternative health care providers (Ayurvedic, Unani, Homeopathic, and partially certified), with whom they were comfortable, as well as physicians trained to address *gupt rog* as a psychosocial problem rather than as an illness (Nastasi et al. 2014).

- *Safed Pani*, meaning *white discharge*, is an idiom of distress among Indian women reflecting unresolved conflict with their spouses, abusive relationships, economic hardship, and worries about children. Women reported *safed pani* as a health problem and were treated for it symptomatically with prescribed antibiotics, in accordance with Indian and World Health Organization guidelines. A situational mental health problem linked to tension, and not an infection, *safed pani* became a marker for selection for a counseling intervention for women and couples to improve communication, and for joint solution of household problems (Kostick et al. 2010).
- *Nervios.* Depending on the severity of its expression, *nervios* is an expression of situational or long-term anxiety among Caribbean Americans, especially women. It is a marker for either situationally appropriate counseling or longer-term counseling including the use of medication or possible acute care (Guarnaccia, Lewis-Fernández, and Marano 2003).
- *Youth Culture.* Youth culture is a cover term for clothing, club/party lifestyle, music, and visual and performing arts preferred by cosmopolitan young people. Popular elements of global youth culture tend to emerge from marginalized and working-class youth who use creative expression as a form of coping and resistance; these elements then spread to other youth. Elements of youth culture have been integrated into many interventions with great success, especially if youth are involved in creating them (Epstein 1998).
- *The "Circle of Life" Medicine Wheel.* The wheel is a "cultural symbol among many indigenous people. It is divided into four equal parts, encompassing spiritual, emotional, physical, and mental wellness as the four essential aspects of health and well-being. . . . It embodies a cultural theory of learning based on centuries of community epistemologies that form the foundation for cognitive and behavioral instruction" (LaFrance and Nichols 2009). The concept of the Medicine Wheel formed the foundation of a sexual risk prevention curriculum for Alaskan Indi-

ans. All parts of the wheel work together to provide cognitive guides to decision making (Kaufman et al. 2012, 142). In the curriculum, the four parts of the medicine wheel touch each other, so that each influences the others; strength to make healthy choices is derived from balance and harmony. When symbolized by a tipi, the wheel also provided the basis for a holistic approach to achieving researcher/ Native Community Advisory Board understanding of Native women's narratives about their encounters with the health care system (Simonds et al. 2011 Figure 1, 840, Simonds and Christopher 2013).

■ *Rite of Passage*. Rites of passage have been well recognized in cross-cultural literature as community events that mark the transition of individuals, often in groups, into a new stage in their lives. While the concept has been applied to any ritualized transition (e.g., transitioning from a shelter to a permanent residence, running away from home to achieve independence), here we refer to ceremonies with greater historical and cultural depth, such as those that mark the transition to manhood or womanhood (e.g., African "bush schools"; the Mexican *quinceañera*, or celebration for fifteen-year-old girls to mark transition to womanhood; the bar/bat mitzvah that marks transition to adulthood in the Jewish tradition; or even the candlelight ceremony that MESA, a program to serve victims of sexual abuse in Boulder, Colorado, holds for volunteers who have completed their forty-day training period, along with the beads they are given after each long-term encounter with a client, etc.). The concept of the traditional rite of passage has been reintroduced in a variety of interventions to reinforce ethnic/community identity (Abusharaf 2006; Beresford 1996; Gennep 1960; Toba 1992).

These metaphors and meanings and others like them provide an orientation to broader intervention approaches that communities and educators can use to guide their work. They are useful and necessary but still not sufficient for comprehensive intervention development.

Effective comprehensive interventions still require answers to questions such as:

- How will the intervention address power differentials throughout?
- At what level will the intervention occur?
- When will it take place?
- Where will it occur?
- How will it be implemented?
- With what intensity?
- Who should implement it?
- Who will be the participants?

Tables 6.1a and b provide a general rubric for organizing decisions about where to situate activity. It's easiest to begin with the unit of impact. Is the intervention expected to affect individuals or groups, entities within a community, or the community as a whole? Policy makers? Structural factors? The built environment? Or all of the above? The answer to these questions should come from the group-generated local model.

TABLE 6.1A   Deciding on intervention level

Intervention Level	Activity Level	Outcome Measure (Unit of Impact)
Individual	Individual	Individual
Group (including couple and peer to peer)	Individual	Individual
	Group	Individual
	Group	Group
Community	Group(s)	Community (of individuals)
	Organization	Organization/organization networks
	Community	Networks/individuals
	Media	Individual
	Policy(ies)	Individual/organizational/ community/media/regulation
Multi-level	Individual/group	Individual and individual/group
	Individual/community	Individual and individual/community
	Group/community	Any combination
	Individual/group/ community	Any combination

Having made decisions about what the intervention is supposed to accomplish and what contributes to both the problem and the desired outcome, it is useful to decide at what level the intervention is expected to have the greatest impact. Is it focused on individual behavioral change, on transforming groups, on changing community policies, or on institutions that wield power or at multiple levels simultaneously? Next, the intervention team should decide exactly *on whom* and *on what* the intervention will have an effect. Is the objective of the intervention to reduce cigar smoking among youth who smoke more than twice a week? Or more than once a month? This is an individual-level outcome. Is the intervention designed to develop exercise groups among young adults who are prediabetic—also an individual-level outcome? Or will the intervention develop youth advocacy groups hoping to prevent cigar advertising in Black communities known to be targeted by tobacco manufacturers—a policy-level outcome? Will it be a program to correct misunderstandings and change behaviors that risk exposure to Ebola, dengue, and other hemorrhagic fevers in communities with low levels of literacy—a community-level outcome? Or is it aimed at development of research capacity in service organizations—an organizational-level outcome?

Next, how will the intervention be implemented, and by whom, to achieve the desired impact? Will it be implemented by individuals or groups? By "insider," or peer teams, or by teams that include a researcher and community member or by individuals in the community? By organizations or networks? By large organized advocacy groups? By media, policy makers, or all of the above? How long will it last? These general decisions are based on the study model and the estimation of resources available to implement the desired changes.

Making these decisions in advance will help to shape the next set of decisions about *how* to actually intervene. In the next section we address most of these issues with examples of interventions at the individual-, group-, community-, and multilevel interventions.

TABLE 6.1B Unit delivering the intervention as related to unit of impact

Intervention Level	Unit of Impact/Outcome	Unit Delivering the Intervention
Individual	Individual	Individual
Group (including couple and peer to peer)	Individual	Individual
	Individual	Group
	Group	Group
Community	Community (of individuals)	Group(s)
	Organization/Organization networks	Organization
	Networks/individuals	Community
	Individual	Media
	Individual/organizational/ community/media	Policy(ies)
Multi-level	Individual and individual/ group	Individual/group
	Individual and individual/ community	Individual/community
	Any combination	Group/community
	Any combination	Individual/group/community

IDENTIFYING INTERVENTION LEVELS

The exercise at the end of chapter 4, which links resources, goals, and objectives to the independent or "causal" domains (see Figure 4.9), helps actors to make decisions about identification of intervention levels while, at the same time, introducing important cultural and other resources elements that are part of the cultural capital of any group (Yosso 2005). Some groups may hypothesize that individuals have the primary responsibility for shaping their behavior. Thus, they will choose to focus on what might bring about change in the way such individuals think about their own behaviors and their beliefs about their ability to act.

Individual Interventions

EXAMPLE 6.1

DEVELOPING A SMOKING CESSATION PROGRAM WITH THE MENOMINEE TRIBE

In 2005 the Menominee Tribe and researchers from the University of Wisconsin, Madison, joined forces to work toward addressing smoking rates that were twice as high as other groups in the state, with associated chronic health problems. During the first three years of the effort, researchers worked with members of the tribe on a culturally tailored research program. The formative phase involved discussions between researchers, American Indian outreach personnel associated with a National Cancer Institute center on cancer prevention, and members of the Menominee tribe, who gathered data on local smoking and conducted qualitative interviews with smokers and nonsmokers on intervention approaches and beliefs about smoking and tobacco. This work resulted in a three-year-funded clinical trial called the START project (Stop Tobacco Abuse, Renew Tradition). The purpose of the trial was to test a culturally tailored individual intervention against a standard intervention. The study partners—the researchers, the Menominee Community Advisory Board of elders and younger community members—decided that the best way to tackle the problem was to create a four-session curriculum, delivered by a peer counselor and tailored to Menominee Indian beliefs about tobacco. They designed the intervention to help smokers stop through helping them to see the discrepancy between the sacred nature of tobacco and exploitative commercial purposes and between tobacco as spiritual medicine and tobacco as marketed pleasure. This approach emphasized connectivity to the spiritual world through nature and built on culturally utilized ways of reducing stress and craving. To operationalize the spiritual link, the curriculum drew on the importance of connection to the natural world by inviting participants to choose a stone from a natural site to which they felt connected. Participants were provided the materials to make a traditional tobacco pouch, a symbol of long life, and to ease tension, they listened to American Indian relaxation music (Smith et al. 2014).

This example illustrates some of the important considerations raised earlier. It used a core cultural construct, the idea of tobacco as sacred, and drew on spiritual meanings and spiritual reinforcement as the basis for the intervention content. It also introduced a "critical" component—by asking participants to consider tobacco as a commercial-

profit-oriented commodity—in contrast to tobacco as sacred. Ethnographic research and other forms of data collection carried out by community members contributed to the intervention. The total study population was 101, randomized into two groups, the standard versus the culturally tailored group. Though, in this case, there were no significant differences in outcome between the two groups, the results did show that those with less-positive outcomes had many immediate family members who smoked. While some individual-level interventions work very well as self-help efforts, in this case, the literature suggests that it is much more difficult for people who want to quit smoking to do so when others are smoking around them and tobacco is easily available. This finding suggested to the research team that the study model, based on changing knowledge and attitudes toward smoking and enhancing individual coping behaviors, was not sufficient to make a difference in a setting where tobacco use is ubiquitous. Thus, another level of intervention might be required, by reducing availability (a policy-related intervention) or helping family members stop collectively (a group intervention).

EXAMPLE 6.2

ENCOURAGING THE USE OF INSECTICIDE-TREATED BED NETS TO PREVENT MALARIA

Malaria is a parasitic infection found in many parts of Southeast and South Asia, Africa, and parts of the Caribbean. It is transmitted by mosquitos, and it can be debilitating and cause death in children and in adults during their most productive years. Mosquitos that carry the malaria parasite and transmit it through biting breed in slow-moving or still water in rural and in urban areas. It has been shown for many years that the use of insecticide-treated bed nets is an effective way of preventing malaria. Peak time for mosquitos is early morning and at sundown, but they also bite throughout the night. The bed nets are distributed at low or no cost to households in high infestation areas and are draped over beds. Education programs on the cause of malaria, the efficacy of bed nets, and their proper use are widespread. Bed nets usually are under the control of the household head. While the production, treatment with insecticides, and distribution of bed nets are structural interventions, individuals are responsible for use at the household level.

Many studies have been done to prepare for bed net distribution and to understand who uses them. Most of the studies leave out the behaviors of household members who *don't* use their bed nets, which would help to explain why the education programs are not working very well in some cases. They have found, however, that people know that bed nets are valuable and useful, and often use them. But other factors intervene (Dunn et al. 2011). For example, families living in small dwellings have no privacy for sex. In seeking privacy, they leave the house at night, leaving their children in bed under the bed nets while they expose themselves to mosquitos. Children travel through mosquito-infested areas when they exit the house to go to latrines or distant outdoor waste accumulation locations. Where there are land shortages and farmers have to travel long distances to farm or care for animals, they may remain in their fields overnight, and are thus exposed to mosquitos. In one recent situation, as noted earlier in this book, poor fishermen who could not afford to purchase fishing nets when fish (and cash) were scarce used their bed nets as fishing nets (Gettleman 2015). In these instances, though individual- or even household-level education can be effective some of the time, it may not be sufficient to counter other pressing economic, physical, and social circumstances.

So-called brief interventions designed to change individual behavior can have an effect if carried out in a culturally and contextually appropriate way. Working with married men in Mumbai having relationship difficulties that expressed themselves in sexual dysfunction is a case in point.

EXAMPLE 6.3

STEPS IN THE DEVELOPMENT OF A CULTURALLY TAILORED INDIVIDUAL-LEVEL BRIEF INTERVENTION TO IMPROVE MARITAL COMMUNICATION AMONG MARRIED MEN IN MUMBAI

The cultural basis for this intervention was *gupt rog*, as mentioned earlier in this chapter. The broad partnership that supported this project included a number of individuals with long-standing relationships: Stephen Schensul (University of Connecticut); Bonnie Nastasi, then at ICR; Ravi Verma and Niranjan Saggurti, both at International Institute for Population Sciences (IIPS), Mumbai; Arvind Pandey, National Institute for Medical Statistics, formerly of IIPS; Shubhada Maitra, Tata Institute; and a group of non–allopathic providers in the community who are first-line providers for male health issues.

A Mumbai-based study team guided by this group created a formative mixed methods research design for understanding *gupt rog*. It included key informant interviews with allopathic and non–allopathic physicians, community leaders, and NGO directors. The formative research suggested that *gupt rog* was an idiom of distress, not an infection, and that the stories men told about their lives suggested that *gupt rog* was linked to socially and maritally inappropriate behavior (drinking with friends, seeing women—including commercial sex workers—outside the marriage, and abusing wives). Reasons men attributed to these behaviors were linked to difficulties in their life situation that made it difficult to meet expectations about masculinity related to maintaining family responsibilities, such as having a good job and sufficient income, showing appreciation for their wives or their wives reciprocating, and care of children. These constituted the stimulus for components of an intervention. The study team sought "etic" theories that could underlie a brief intervention approach with these elements. Several cognitive behavioral options were the "Information, Motivation and Behavior" approach (Fisher and Fisher 2000; Osborn et al. 2010); and the Integrated Model of Behavioral Prediction (Fishbein 2008). Both of these approaches hinged on contributors to motivation but did not take into consideration the types of contextual factors suggested by the interviews. One of the investigators had recently been introduced to narrative therapy, a social-constructivist approach to counseling built on clients' own stories and hopes for the future (Freedman and Freedman 1996). This approach offered a strong argument for the use of narrative in a community-based counseling intervention. Narrative was consistent with other approaches to community-based intervention in India, such as street drama, where stories provided the basis for discussions about community problems and solutions (Pelto and Singh 2010). Motivational interviewing, a form of counseling based on client narratives and used often in alcohol-related interventions, offered a good option, but it was not systematic enough (Burke, Arkowitz, and Menchola 2003; Rubak et al. 2005). In place of these, the team came up with the concept of a narrative intervention based on the cultural elements mentioned above. They used Kleinman's concept of explanatory models to create an intervention conceptual model based on the cultural elements (see Figure 6.1) (Kleinman 1980; Weiss 1997).

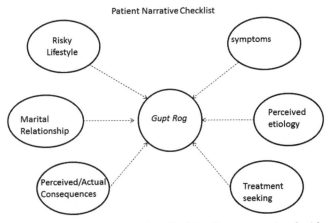

FIGURE 6.1 Patient Narrative Checklist: Factors associated with *gupt rog.*

The intervention followed a protocol for motivational interviewing that begins with the patient's story of *gupt rog* or other concern about masculinity and sexual performance. It then added three critical steps to the typical motivational interviewing process: construction (eliciting the story from the patient's perspective), deconstruction (identifying, based on the model, the main elements that should be addressed in a one-time counseling session), and reconstruction (helping the patient to rewrite the narrative to result in a better ending by changing the elements in his own tailored explanatory model). Of course, motivation and intention to change were central underlying concepts in this approach and were reflected in rewriting the story; but the evaluation did not measure these. Instead, it measured changes in the independent variables (see Figure 6.1) in relation to changes in the dependent variable (*gupt rog*) and changes in desired relational outcomes (better communication and sexual satisfaction with wife, and less sex risk behavior (a reduction in the number of other sexual partners).

The study team learned through key-informant interviews that the best and most sustainable way to implement the intervention was with the alternative non–allopathic providers in the community. Sixty were contacted and invited to a meeting at which the intervention was proposed. Approximately forty agreed to participate. These providers had varying degrees of formal education and knowledge of allopathic medicine; and they had their own ways of treating *gupt rog,* including prescribing medication which was readily obtainable at local pharmacies over the counter. They also wanted to improve their practice, as they were operating on thin profit margins and seeking ways of making their services more attractive and valuable in the community. They were trained and retrained in interactive sessions in which they learned the model, the process of construction, deconstruction, and reconstruction, and the use of queries to make sure that they understood the patient's story. They also added their own insights and experience into the training and implementation process. The study team worked with local NGOs (additional partners) to recruit men to enroll in the study and seek treatment. They then worked with the patient's ideas and resources to reconstruct the narrative, leaving the patient with a new plan of action to improve his relationship with his wife. It was difficult to record the actual sessions, but exit interviews and repeat surveys showed that men found the sessions helpful and that, in the group of more than 450 patients, there were dramatic overall improvements over time in communication with spouses and in reduced drinking.

The study team tried hard to institutionalize the study by basing it with the AYUSH providers and seeking the support of NGOS and a local university to continue training. High mobility among AYUSH providers and inadequate counseling resources at the Tata Institute made sustainability impossible, despite efforts to think about it with collaborators at the beginning of the study. Sustainability of the

intervention to ensure continuing effects is the most challenging aspect of an intervention study, even when it involves collaboration between insiders and "outsiders."

In sum, identifying the components of an intervention targeted toward individual behavior change benefits from an ecological perspective, sufficient ethnographic research in advance and ongoing as process evaluation, a deeply culturally embedded approach, good partners, a mix of local and discipline-based theory, a good evaluation design, and a plan for sustainability.

When researchers and their partners use an ecological framework, it is easy to see why individual-level interventions are important and necessary; but it is difficult to see how they can be sufficient, let alone sustainable, if they are unaccompanied by other approaches. We now turn to group interventions, which do address some of these considerations.

Group Interventions

A group can be defined as an assemblage of people that has one or more things in common. Defining groups is as challenging as defining communities because there are so many ways of doing so. Most groups define themselves in terms of their interests, including recreation, survival exchanges, intellectual pursuits, religious ventures, entrepreneurial activity, and various forms of social activism. They can, however, be given names by others. Usually, these groups are voluntary, though they may be supported by paid staff of organizational sponsors. Friends and families can be considered a group, though family members may be dispersed. A bounded small network or clique including one or more friendship networks also may be considered a group for specific purposes. Groups may be stable or relatively permanent (such as family groups, school clubs, buying clubs, international aid agencies such as CARE and Médecins Sans Frontières, and environmental protection associations), temporary (cleanup groups, environmental crisis intervention groups, parent advocacy

groups, women's neighborhood groups), or transient/
intermittent (groups such Occupy Wall Street, an Internet-based movement that emerges at strategic moments
to protest unequal income and other inequitable resource
allocations). These are all "natural" groups, or preexisting
"communities of identity" that have come together for a
specific activist purpose. They are discovered through ethnographic investigation and are resources for purposes of
a group intervention.

At the same time, there are other "socially constructed"
groups that are convened specifically for intervention purposes. In a fully participatory effort, they may in fact be
the partnerships that will do the research, carry out the
intervention, and evaluate it. Living alliances such as those
we described in chapters 2 and 3 are good examples of
these groups. Other groups are convened through existing organizations, or even by the intervention team itself,
for purposes of understanding what the effects of specific
approaches might be to building group capacity for action
and changing the behavior of individuals within it. These
changes can focus on self-help or social action or both.
Often self-help groups evolve into social-action groups as
their members realize that they can help others beyond
themselves (Encyclopedia.com 2003). Self-help at the individual level would address how group membership affects/
helps the individual. Self-help at the group level questions
how the group intervention improves *mutual* support. Self-
help groups can evolve into social-action groups when a
social-change agenda arises as part of the group's mission.
Social-action groups engage in mutual support and reflection to move collectively toward social activism and social
change. Most PAR groups address knowledge development,
self-help, and social action simultaneously. We describe
these approaches in detail in chapter 9.

Reasons for group interventions include the following:

a. *Norms change.* Individual people are afraid to make
   important and needed changes in their life and norm
   change is required to reduce stigma (e.g., disclosure of
   HIV, changing communication patterns with spouse in
   a gender-inequitable environment).

b. The need for *mutual support*. Lack of community, neighborhood, or friendship supports are an important component of a study mode. Group interventions constitute
efforts to remedy this challenge by creating an environment that enhances mutual support and enables individuals to obtain more resources for themselves and
their families.

c. *Advocacy*. A group intervention, by building mutual support, can create the infrastructure for advocacy efforts
to promote knowledge of an unknown or stigmatized
health problem, to promote improved institutional
responses to health or educational service delivery, or to
advocate for policy change. This type of group intervention is a community-organizing strategy, though often
the process will have an enduring effect on individuals.

d. *Changing behavior of individuals through the group*.
Many culturally or socially undesirable behaviors are
carried out in a group or in a group setting, for example,
using drugs such as alcohol, marijuana, or tobacco, or
overconsumption of fast foods. Thus, it becomes important to modify the context, so that it becomes risk averse
rather than risk proactive, when conducting an intervention with groups of people involved in the behavior or
with the same need.

Figure 6.2 illustrates how and why a group intervention
might be chosen. In this case, the problem is that poor communication exists between parents and elementary school
teachers regarding expectations about children's performance. It arose in a group intervention to address parents'
concerns about adequate preparation for kindergarten. The
first model leading to preparation for kindergarten that the
parents created is shown in Figure 6.2.

If the parents had stopped there, they would have
enhanced these "good parenting" skills, assuming that
their child's performance at school would reflect it. However, they were concerned about teachers' attitudes toward
their apparently nonperforming children. They decided
to speak with teachers about teachers' expectations about
good behavior. Based on their interviews, they found
that teachers expected that children would know how to

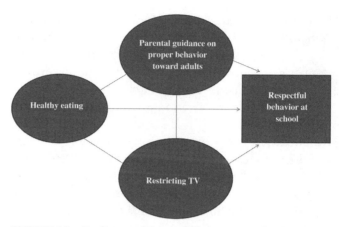

FIGURE 6.2 Predictors of respectful behavior at school.

count, read, and play educational games prior to coming to school, and that parents should know how to "prepare" their children properly for kindergarten/first grade. The parents expanded their model to show different outcome expectations for teachers in contrast to their own, and discussed with the facilitator what to do about the differences in expectations and the poor communication that marked their relationship with the school. They worked as a group to access educational resources for their children, capitalizing on their diverse instructional skills, and went collectively to the school to discuss the differences in orientation they discovered between themselves and the teachers as well as how to negotiate these differences for the benefit of the children.

Henderson describes an ethnographically based approach to develop a culturally "competent" way of forming and working with support groups (Henderson et al. 1993). Assumptions that guide the model include that people will come to group activities if:

- they are introduced in a culturally appropriate way;
- they are recruited by culturally/ethnically and linguistically congruent recruiters using face-to-face approaches;
- the activities are based on collection data from an ethnographic (community embedded) survey that guides the group activities;

Cross Reference:
See Book 3, chapter 9

- the intervention trains peer leaders, who recruit and implement a culturally framed intervention.

At the same time, the reason for the group sessions should be congruent with identified community needs. Henderson does not mention the importance of involving community people in the development of the intervention itself, but we have made it clear that having the endorsement, involvement, and leadership of people at all levels in the intervention is critical, especially when it involves the construction of new groups.

EXAMPLE 6.4

BUILDING A SUPPORT GROUP INTERVENTION FOR WOMEN WITH LYMPHATIC FILIARIASIS IN HAITI

Filiariasis (FL), a parasitic disease transmitted by mosquitos, is a significant health problem that affects mainly women in Haiti. It affects the legs and feet, is very painful, can be disfiguring, and can impair mobility, limit social life, prevent economic activities such as marketing, and may cause women to become completely bedridden. Transmission can be prevented with medication, but it is incurable, and people with enlarged limbs (lymphedema and elephantiasis) suffer from stigma and ridicule. However, a regimen of skin hygiene and physical therapy can significantly reduce secondary infection, symptoms, and suffering. The World Health Organization (WHO) and the World Bank provided support to a research team headed by Jeanine Coreil to develop support groups for women with filiariasis. In in-depth interviews, the women said that they were anxious to share their experiences with other women and, when given choices, preferred women's support groups. Consistent with the reasons for group intervention above, women wanted to share their coping experiences, reduce social isolation because of stigma, observe improvements in others to reinforce confidence in their own treatment, and exchange advice to improve their own and others' well-being (Coreil and Maynard 2009, 198).

Coreil and colleagues expected that group formation would follow the three phases outlined by the American Cancer Society (Herman and Willson 2014):

1. identifying commonalities and finding ways of alleviating problems;
2. providing mutual support, redefining the problem, and finding new coping strategies;
3. consolidating and continuing or ending.

Sixteen support groups consisting of over eighty women were formed with the support of organizations that helped with recruitment, and they began to meet.

Peer leaders presented the problem and showed videos about home care, and participants then were invited to tell personal stories; these activities were then followed by refreshments. The sessions quickly transformed into meetings that included prayer, music, leg massages, practical skills training, and entrepreneurial goal setting. The group intervention was successful at the individual level, improving women's hygiene practice and knowledge, decreasing the frequency of acute attacks, and resulting in their having fewer difficulties living with the disease (Coreil and Maynard 2009, 258). At the same time, discussions, women's growing awareness of the health problems of other women and their structural origins gave rise to formation of a women's health advocacy organization, Femmes en accion pour le development et la sante (Women in Action for Development and Health). Though sustaining the groups was resource intensive, Coreil and colleagues describe the persistence of efforts to initiate entrepreneurial activity, showing how elements of an externally initiated, but culturally embedded, intervention can persist and transform into new ventures over time.

This example, unlike others that begin with a cultural concept, was actually initiated by anthropologists and others who conducted formative research with women sufferers of FL. They identified group intervention (support groups) as a need and included local peer educators in the conduct of the interventions. The actual group process used external models, including that of Henderson, an expert on the formation of culturally centered groups, to develop their approach to group support. The approach was successful in attracting women, even though the experience of support group interventions was new in Haiti. However, once the groups had started, the women "indigenized" the group's process and content, taking the groups over and introducing new elements derived from Haitian culture. They shaped the group sessions toward their needs, which were, in fact, not just to discuss their illness, but to help them to feel physically better, build on their entrepreneurial tendencies to promote microeconomic enterprise, and with newly evolved critical consciousness, develop an organization to promote the health of women like themselves.

Site-Based Interventions

Individual and group interventions take place in "a place," but generally that "place" or site is not thought of as a part of the intervention, even though places like classrooms, dentists' offices, parks, and other locations where individual and group interventions might take place are likely to be prepared as suitable environments for intervention activities. By contrast, site-based interventions take place in locations that are chosen *specifically* because their characteristics are believed to be critical to the intervention or the reasons for its need.

School-based health clinics can be safe havens for teenagers who are searching for counseling and other support or who may simply need a place in their schools where they can "hang out" and feel comfortable with other teens like themselves (CASBHS-UCONN-ICR 2013). School health clinics provide individual-level mental health counseling services to teens. In such cases, the clinic is the location where counseling is offered, but individual counseling models do not utilize the clinic environment in any special way. Similarly, group counseling sessions can take place in these settings, scheduled for particular times and around specific topics that often are identified in advance. In this instance as well, the clinic is "just a place" where group interventions can occur. On the other hand, if counselors know that networks of peers "hang out" in the clinic waiting room and could benefit from group counseling, and if they tried to mobilize informal counseling sessions around these place-based self-convening networks, we could begin to think of this as a place-based intervention because the intervention took advantage of the naturally occurring groups that defined and used the space as their own. Classrooms function in the same way. There are literally hundreds of interventions designed to have an impact on individual students, delivered in a classroom environment. However, when the classroom is viewed as a place where culture is co-constructed by youth through processes facilitated by teachers, changing group norms turns a classroom into a site-based intervention.

EXAMPLE 6.5

SCHOOLS AS PLACES WHERE INTERVENTIONS MAY TAKE PLACE VERSUS SCHOOLS AS SITES THAT OFFER UNIQUE OPPORTUNITIES FOR SOCIAL AND CULTURAL TRANSFORMATIONS

A five-year study conducted by the Institute for Community Research and Yale University School of Medicine and the New Haven public schools was designed to compare a standard "social development" curriculum (a curriculum that was intended to help middle school students change their behavior from defensive and confrontational to negotiating and problem solving) with a new curriculum designed to build group-prevention-oriented norms by viewing classrooms as small groups where the culture of interaction and learning could be changed. In this project, the classroom as a group was the primary unit of intervention, with the effects measured at both the individual level and the group level. Change was assessed through emerging congruence among students in shared perceived norms about substance use, sexual risks, and relationships. In the "standard practice" curriculum, the goal was to change the behavior of individual students. The teacher taught scripted lessons didactically, and students did individualized exercises and activities. The classroom was just a convenient space for reaching a large number of students. In the second approach, the classroom was treated as a community, the members of which (the students) had the power to change themselves and their interactions with each other, and to promote prevention culture, or the valuing of pro-healthy behaviors. The result of the standard intervention was changes in individual beliefs and behaviors. The result of the new approach was a change in the culture of the classroom, which was reflected in a convergence of perceived norms, beliefs, and behaviors—all focused on preventing early sexual initiation and underage drinking. Place (the classroom as a space for changing youth culture) was an essential component of the intervention. And because the intervention was facilitated by trained teachers and took place in all middle school classrooms, it had the potential to reshape the culture of the school.

Several more examples illustrate the importance of sites in overall consideration of intervention strategy.

EXAMPLE 6.6

RESEARCH AND INTERVENTION WITH DRUG USERS IN HIGH-RISK SITES

Between 2001 and 2005, the Institute for Community Research carried out a study of "high-risk" drug using sites under the leadership of medical anthropologist Margaret Weeks. The idea for this study came from the observation, both in Hartford and elsewhere around the country, that users of illegal drugs who inject or inhale heroin, cocaine, or a mix of both often did so in specific, usually private, and hidden locations. Initial investigations with some drug users revealed use patterns and preferences for certain locations, as well as the fact that some "sites" were more exposed and dangerous and more likely to convey risk of HIV exposure than others. One study that followed worked with active drug users to learn about the places they used drugs routinely. The research team conducted observations in sites, often with drug users who guided them and instructed them on how to behave and keep safe in the sites. The sites were found to be quite different, depending on their location, social organization, strength of gatekeepers in the site (apartment owners or renters who controlled behavior in their homes versus "unmanaged" sites in abandoned buildings), and the stability of the sites over time. One marker of stability was whether users were networked and knew each other well or just came to use the site, without any obligation to other users. These factors contributed either to HIV-prevention opportunities or potential for infection. The interaction with drug users as guides to the sites, and their willingness to act as ambassadors who conveyed prevention messages and strategies to other users in the sites that they frequented or managed, led to another study. This study combined prevention actions conveyed through active drug users who took their messages to the sites where they most often used drugs, and to the people with whom they most often exchanged drugs and other resources. Diffusion theory best fit this intervention in which peers conveyed prevention opportunities to other drug users; these peers were already, or became, central to and highly influential in their networks as a means of reducing risk in so-called high-risk sites (Rogers 2003). Peers identified how the intervention should work in specific types of sites, and diffusion theory and DSIT, as noted in the previous chapter, explained it.

In the next example, we consider how residential buildings as sites can be seen as places where important interventions can take place that change the lives of residents as well as their social and health behaviors. Though efforts have been made through government programs to reduce or eliminate public housing complexes, they continue to exist and in many cases to flourish throughout the United States. Some complexes are home to families with children whose incomes meet the requirements; others to older adults; and still others to a mix of families, older adults, and people with disabilities. There are many advantages as well as challenges to working in these sites. First, they are "bounded communities," residents often have lived there for many years; they have a sense of community; they know each other; and they interact in discoverable patterned ways. There also are discoverable "rules" and norms that govern life in residences; these are structured by the management and residents' councils or tenants' associations. Older adults in particular, especially if they do not have access to transportation, may feel isolated and are ready to act as collaborators in approaches that they believe can improve their lives. And they bring cultural and social resources that can enrich intervention activities and assist with outcome evaluations. Finally, it is easier to conduct evaluations in such sites than if a program were introduced in a larger community setting with a dispersed population. This is because many residents can be relatively stable participants for panel studies where evaluation measures are taken at the start of an intervention and then one or more times during and after it has been completed. Two projects situated in public housing settings illustrate the value of site-based intervention for residents.

EXAMPLE 6.7

PUBLIC HOUSING AS INTERVENTION SITES FOR WORKING WITH WOMEN AT RISK FOR DIABETES

A group of Yale researchers working on maternal health, obesity, and diabetes had the unique opportunity to work with a group of public housing units that were scheduled for structural changes to improve opportunities for outside activities (walking, swimming, tennis), all important in reducing potential for diabetes, and for improving diabetes control and avoidance of longer-term cardiovascular and other consequences. The researchers planned to work with residents to design individual and group interventions for all building residents, to see whether the interventions had an effect on use of new facilities, and, conversely, whether the new facilities acted as a motivator for improving diabetes control.

The Institute for Community Research has a fifteen-year history of working in partnership with publicly funded senior housing in the central Connecticut area in partnership with area agencies on aging that serve and are advocates for older adults and other organizations with interest in older adult health.

 **EXAMPLE 6.8**

PUBLIC HOUSING AS INTERVENTION SITES FOR WORKING WITH
OLDER ADULTS ON HEALTH-RELATED ISSUES

In a funded three-year study, ICR partnered with a local psychiatric facility serving older adults, an area agency on aging, a coalition of six mental health clinics serving older adults, and six buildings that were home to older adults. The group focused on depression and access to mental health care among the residents of the six buildings. The topic of depression arose when residents who monitored resident health and safety in several of the buildings expressed concern about the fact that some residents never emerged from their apartments and that several suicides had occurred. Among the many study findings, we discovered that depression was stigmatized, that residents used a variety of terms to express feelings related to depression (*low, drop down, loss, sadness*), and that some residents who did not think they were depressed actually scored as clinically depressed, as measured on two standardized instruments. These residents did not think they were depressed because they had many ways of coping with their feelings. Network analysis typically showed two core elements connected residents, who were both English speakers and Spanish speakers, and that there were a limited number of bridges between these groups. Further, the networks showed the existence of many isolated people who were disconnected from either group. Depression rates also were higher in some buildings than in others, especially where there were no full-time resident coordinators or volunteer committees. At the same time, through in-depth interviews with clinicians and frontline service providers, the team found that clinics were unable to improve their six-month wait times for older adults, and clinic personnel complained of being unable to communicate effectively, especially with Spanish-speaking older clients. The data suggested two directions for intervention. First, the research collaborative worked to reduce the stigma associated with depression and improve communication by bringing a local team of mental health consultants into buildings to deliver culturally appropriate mental health counseling services to people on site. Second, together with residents, they developed social activities that bridged cultural and linguistic groups and drew on cultural heritage and photography to help them create and share their stories and lessons for life with each other to reduce social isolation.

Worksites, prisons, and other bounded residential and work settings also can be important locations for different types of interventions. Sorenson and colleagues at the Harvard School of Public Health have worked with the Healis-Sekhsaria Foundation for Public Health to introduce tobacco-prevention programs in information technology (IT) centers in Mumbai. Schensul, Nastasi, and colleagues with the Mauritius Family Planning Association (MFPA) conducted formative qualitative and quantitative research with unmarried female factory workers in Mauritius to explore their possible exposures to intimate relationships and unprotected sex. The formative research found that women knew little about sex; men and women had different ideas about the meanings of intimate behaviors, which led to misunderstandings about "next steps" in moving toward penetrative sex; and certain sexual behaviors which involved genital touching but not complete penetration were considered "safe" because they did not violate virginity. Based on this information, the MFPA introduced a pilot intervention in several industries that involved separate sessions for men and women in addressing these issues. The industrial setting offered the best site for intervention because the primary opportunities where young men and women could meet and develop intimate relationships were located in the factories and on the way to work. The factory setting could thus become a space where better informed young people could establish sexual safety norms that could protect themselves and others.

In an excellent meta-analysis of worksite interventions focused on tobacco use prevention and cessation, Knowlden and colleagues (2013) note that of the nine programs that met the criteria for inclusion in the analysis, only four of them conducted any formative contextual research focused on the worksite environment. This article repeatedly noted the importance of recognizing that worksites, like other sites, may differ in structural, social, and cultural characteristics. Only one of the approaches, that of Pimple and colleagues (Pimple et al. 2012), used worksite characteristics as moderators of intervention outcome.

In sum, there are good logistical, cultural, and social reasons for partnering with classes or specific types of sites to conduct interventions. These include:

- more effective recruitment;
- capacity to sustain participation in the intervention;

- ready involvement of local teachers, workers, and residents as partners in the study;
- maintenance of high evaluation participation rates;
- good possibilities for introducing environmental change.

At the same time, issues that might adversely affect site-based interventions include the following:

- changes in administration or onsite staffing that are disruptive or not supported by workers or residents;
- potential administrative decisions beyond the control of the researchers and partners that could affect both process and outcome (for example, requiring major curriculum changes and retraining in a school setting, introducing abstinence-only policies for HIV risk prevention, overnight factory closings);
- cohesive internal networks through which negative information about the intervention or study team (e.g., mistakes, misunderstandings, an unhappy participant) could spread rapidly;
- mobility issues (students, residents, and workers shifting sites from one year to the next);
- workplace stoppages or actions such as strikes that can impede the intervention;
- onsite construction or construction delays that impede intervention activities.

Good ethnography and ongoing monitoring can help to avoid, or foresee and address, such problems to minimize their impact on ongoing program activities.

Community Interventions

Community-level interventions are approaches to change that usually involve multiple stakeholders and have the potential for affecting the lives of all people who reside or work or learn in the designated community. These interventions may be designed to:

- change policies (introduce biking paths, community gardens, or charter schools funded with public dollars);
- deliver information through media and social media and face-to-face performance about safety, prevention, health, education, development using various forms of media-based social persuasion;
- diffuse change messages and materials to individuals through peer leaders or communicators through social networks.

Community interventions with broad reach can be generated through "technicians"—researchers and social marketers, but interventions are most effective when they are conducted with the participation of the people who are affected by the problem, who know what will work in their own settings, and who want to change things. In this section, we focus on communications and information-diffusing approaches, leaving policy change for the last part of the chapter.

Communications Approaches

Communication approaches at the community level are large-scale communications events that provide messages to large numbers of people in a target population. They are universal interventions designed to "persuade a defined public to engage in behaviors that will improve health or refrain from behaviors that are unhealthful" (Freudenberg, Bradley, and Serrano 2009) through various forms of media including television, social media, newspapers, films and documentaries, billboards, posters, fliers, brochures, street drama, and murals. The messages are designed to provide new information that counters stereotypes or changes norms. They may be tailored to attract the attention of subgroups or communities of identity within the overall population, or they may be targeted specifically to those groups, even though they reach the entire population. Such communications campaigns serve as enablers, preparing the environment for more intensive interventions that are interactive with groups or individuals on the same topic. As Wakefield and colleagues note (2010), media campaigns are, for the most part, passive efforts that simply make information available, although some campaigns may be accompanied by small-group discussions. Ethnography contributes in significant ways to these campaigns at every level. When conducted with members of the study community, ethnography can produce information that can be converted to messages of local relevance; ethnographic methods also can be used to measure both the process of delivery of campaign messages and campaign outcomes.

Converting data to messages is based on a process in which researchers and community partners (residents, youth, agency representatives, representatives of religious institutions) reflect on their own knowledge base and beliefs about the issue, examine the data, and learn about the issue from others—including scientific experts in the field. A culturally embedded process of converting ethnographic data into campaign messages related to a specific issue or topic can consist of the following steps:

1. Identifying the focus
2. Creating a conceptual model
3. Prioritizing one or more of the predictor variables as a focus
4. Deciding on a guiding theory
5. Identifying and collecting data relevant to the model and potential campaign content
6. Using data related to the model to develop messages for use in the campaign
7. Deciding on means and venues for conveying the messages
8. Developing materials that convey the messages

EXAMPLE 6.9

DEVELOPING A CAMPAIGN PLAN AROUND UNDERAGE ALCOHOL USE

Members of a prevention commission in a northeastern town prioritized underage alcohol use as a major issue in their community. Their initial model argued that two factors—peer norms, and inaccurate perception of harm associated with alcohol consumption in teen years—contributed to high levels of the past thirty days' drinking and to binge drinking (more than four to five drinks at a time). They already were supporting the involvement of youth in a long-term effort to reduce

underage drinking by modifying peer norms and changing the perceptions of harm. One issue that emerged early on in data that teens collected through in-depth interviews, and through a high school survey repeated every two years, was that alcohol was accessible through home parties, with or without parental involvement. With these data, the commission decided that easy access to alcohol at home also was a problem that contributed to underage drinking. Teens conducted a brief intercept survey on a town-wide fair day, asking adults whether they kept alcohol protected or locked in a safe place in their homes. Most parents responded that they did have alcohol, but did not lock it up. In a larger parent survey mounted by the commission through the Internet, 450 parents responded, and again most said that they kept alcohol in the house, but not in a protected place or locked cabinet. The commission then decided to create a message campaign focusing on the home as "drug dealer." After lengthy discussion, as well as consideration of ritual uses of alcohol at religious events held at home, they decided that fear-based messaging was less likely to be effective than "gain-framed messaging." In other words, instead of frightening parents into a defensive fearful posture about hiding or avoiding use of all alcohol in the house, messages encouraging parents to keep their alcohol out of sight and talk to their children about alcohol and its use, as well as establishing strict rules for parties without alcohol, would be a better strategy. Their messages became:

- Is your house safe from underage drinking (below 21 years of age)?
- Make sure your children do not attend home parties where alcohol is available.
- Make and monitor rules governing alcohol among teens during parties at your own home.
- Be sure you are home when your teen invites friends over for a party.

This process involved modeling, gathering data, reviewing literature on the home as a place where illegal substances might be available, examining other similar campaigns, deciding on a guiding or framing theory using their own conceptualization of the theory, and creating messages that could be delivered directly to parents via multiple media venues, including school/parent list serves, town newsprint media, electronic news, booths and fliers at public events, and in face-to-face settings.

Campaigns alone are not the best strategy for bringing about changes in behavior. Even when they mobilize large numbers of people to advocate a policy change (for example, tobacco-control advocacy), participants in a campaign may not themselves change their behavior. However, there is widespread agreement that campaigns change social and cultural norms. Springston (2005) notes that public health campaigns are strategically organized, focused on specific outcomes and large numbers of individuals, and are time bounded. Implementation steps include defining the problem, developing objectives, identifying target audiences, developing message strategies and tactics, selecting appropriate communication channels, implementing the campaign, and evaluating both the process and campaign outcomes. Campaigns may be national or international, but often the most effective campaigns are local (Ettma, Brown, and Luepker 1983; Freudenberg, Bradley, and Serrano 2009; Springston 2005).

Freudenberg, a public health researcher, and his colleagues reviewed twelve national campaigns that attempted to modify the health-related practices of U.S. corporations in the alcohol, automobile, food and beverage, firearms, pharmaceutical, and tobacco industries (Freudenberg, Bradley, and Serrano 2009). The review showed that these national campaigns were moderately effective and that local campaigns were more effective than national ones. Analysis of campaigns mounted against tobacco use in India also showed positive effects across states and regions (Murukutla et al. 2012). Wakefield et al., along with others, concluded that campaigns are generally effective in bringing about change at the population level, but they could be more effective if accompanied by additional services, programs, and policies that support behavior change—in other words, when the campaign is conceptualized as a "multilevel" multidimensional intervention (Snyder 2007; Wakefield, Loken, and Hornik 2010).

Tobacco control provides some interesting examples of nationwide efforts to reduce tobacco use among consumers. Under the WHO World tobacco framework, more than 145 countries have signed an agreement to participate in tobacco-control efforts. These efforts are regulated at the national level. Most require local regulatory action as well as local surveillance to be effective, but some efforts are national in scope. Fear-based messaging with gruesome graphic images on tobacco packages and packets has been shown to be one way of reducing purchase and consumption on a population level. As of 2009, these images had been applied in twenty-eight countries around the world, among which are Taiwan, Mauritius, China, New Zealand, Canada, Chile, Peru, the U.K. Australia, the United States and India. As Fong and colleagues note, "For decades, the tobacco industry has taken advantage of the package as a venue for creating positive associations for their product. The use of graphic pictures is an important means of replacing those positive associations with negative associations, which is far more appropriate given the devastating impact of tobacco products on global health (Fong, Hammond, and Hitchman 2009, 642). India introduced graphic images on cigarette packets in 2009, following examples derived from elsewhere; it used images created by national artists.

EXAMPLE 6.10

A NATIONAL ANTI–SMOKELESS TOBACCO (SLT) CAMPAIGN WITH COGNITIVE AND BEHAVIORAL EFFECTS ON MEN AND WOMEN SLT USERS

While the graphic-images campaign against cigarettes was ongoing, it did not address all forms of tobacco use and was not specifically geared to reach vulnerable rural as well as urban male SLT users and, most especially, women. To do so, physicians and tobacco-control advocates from Tata Memorial Hospital, Mumbai, one of the largest cancer hospitals in the world, used a very different campaign approach. They felt that the best way to communicate with smokeless tobacco users was through stories, photos, and testimony from people who had developed oral cancers because of their smokeless tobacco use. The physician/activists used a theory-driven approach based on the idea that graphic appeals, including those delivered through the testimony of victims of tobacco use, are motivators for health-oriented behavior change (Turk et al. 2012). The campaign also drew on other cognitive behavioral theory to focus on knowledge, beliefs, and attitudes about SLT and drew on social persuasion theory, which directed them to consider the reach of each of the patients and their stories, as well as the influence of the narrator, a cancer surgeon with a high degree of credibility to the target populations. A small crew entered the hospital and, with permission, filmed surgeon-patient interactions and informal interviews with patients about their situation for the purpose of developing public service announcements (PSAs). These films were edited, single photos were selected, and three PSAs developed. The project gave careful consideration to the media used for the campaign, as well as to selecting times and numbers of showings over a six-week period. More than three thousand showings occurred on public television, and rural coverage across the country was achieved through collaboration with private cable and satellite TV stations and the national TV channel, mostly during prime time. A nationally representative survey administered to current smokeless tobacco users who had access to media coverage in households across India in local languages showed that people recalled the campaign announcement, learned new

information about SLT, and changed their thinking about their health and SLT use. In logistic regressions, those who were more campaign aware were more likely to say they had better knowledge of health consequences, had more intention to quit and, had actually tried to quit SLT use. Study results thus show considerable impact of campaign exposure using video PSAs based on real-life situations with patients suffering from oral cancers as a result of their SLT use (Turk et al. 2012).

Multilevel Interventions

Multilevel or systems interventions offer a more holistic and embedded approach to intervention. They are based on the idea that communities or other system are complex, dynamic, and interactive. They take the position that transforming social worlds does not happen by bringing about change in one person or one group at a time, and assume that only comprehensive or holistic change brought about through strategically targeted multiple change efforts can bring about more lasting change. All implementers of multilevel interventions assume that if change occurs at the individual level, it will quickly revert if there are no social and structural supports available at other levels to support or reinforce individual level changes. Further, organizations, governmental bodies, and informal and formal working groups must become involved to ensure necessary policy, structural, and norms changes. These entities may develop different approaches, but the end result moves the community closer toward its vision of change and toward desired overall outcomes. Further, researchers and partners recognize that a critical issue (for example smokeless tobacco use or lack of a high-quality food supply or the school-to-prison pipeline) is complex, consisting of many moving parts. It cannot be addressed with a single intervention. Complex interventions require multiple interactive actions that are driven by theory and research and measured systematically. Finally, multilevel interventions in which all the actions intersect can produce unanticipated results and emergent new directions. Thus, some of the research designs utilized in other forms of intervention do not apply or only partially apply in a multilevel intervention. The metaphors for multilevel intervention that we have mentioned so far all use slightly different language and promote slightly different efforts. They include complicated linear models with organizational and population-dependent variables/outcomes, ecological models, and dynamic systems models. However, they all lead to simultaneously delivered actions and resultant interactions.

Complex linear models use "levels" terminology. They require identifying factors that have to change at the organization (institutional/policy) level, the connection of the organizational issue or problem to population (individuals, households, family networks, kin groups, and voluntary groups), and contributors to the problem at the population level. Complex linear models focus less on the interactions among predictors or contributors across levels and more on what has to change at each level to improve the intersectionality of the two dependent domains. A typical example would be an approach that introduces a new system-wide curriculum that has promise for reducing students' bullying behavior at the institutional level through group exercises to be implemented in classrooms. This might be combined with a household- or community-level intervention that encourages parents to recognize bullying behavior and to stop it wherever they see it.

Ecological models can apply to environmental research that explores and addresses humans' interaction with different features of the natural environment. In such cases, it would not be customary to refer to "levels." Ecological models applied to culturally originating human cognitive and social behaviors, however, are more and more often using the concept of "social" levels—individual, family, peer, organizational (school, church, service program), community (political, recreational resources), media (radio, television, music, etc.), and policy (referring to policies made by larger political entities). These levels are not necessarily hierarchical. As chapter 5 notes, each of the levels in an ecological model should and does interact with the others. As Nastasi and Hitchcock suggest (Nastasi and Hitchcock 2009), however, it is quite difficult to monitor all of the threads of interaction among actions across levels.

Thus, most multilevel interventions frame the interventions according to theories that are appropriate for whatever level they are going to target (peer, media, and policy) and array them independently to have maximum impact on the outcome. The following study of influenza vaccine uptake is a good example of such an intervention.

 **EXAMPLE 6.11**

IMPROVING INFLUENZA VACCINE UPTAKE AMONG OLDER ADULTS—A MULTILEVEL APPROACH

In this multilevel collaborative study, the "vaccine system" included state educators, vaccine suppliers, vaccine deliverers, potential undervaccinated recipients, resident advocates, managers of senior housing, and vaccine researchers. These sectors all met in an alliance to coordinate efforts to improve flu vaccine uptake among older low-income adults in specific senior housing units. The committee agreed on specific theoretically driven goals for each level in the intervention. State educators wanted to expand their capacity to reach underserved older adults through tailored messaging. Vaccine deliverers (Visiting Nurse and Health Care) wanted to streamline the efficiency of their vaccine delivery to older adults by supporting efforts to increase receptivity at vaccine clinics in buildings. Resident advocates wanted to change vaccine norms and increase acceptability of vaccine through peer education. Building management wanted to reduce infectious illnesses in the building and introduce free programming to improve resident satisfaction. Social scientists wanted to use empowerment theory to expand the capacity of resident committees to improve sustainability of the campaign effect. Interventions occurred at each level and were coordinated and documented at committee meetings. Outcomes were measured qualitatively through the achievement of level-specific goals and targets, and quantitatively through counting the numbers of people who attended flu clinics and were vaccinated. The primary outcome was vaccination uptake, but each of the partners had anticipated goals and outcomes that were different from and contributed to both the success of the intervention and to the achievement of other broader flu vaccination uptake agendas (Schensul et al. 2009).

 **EXAMPLE 6.12**

HIV PREVENTION AMONG WOMEN AND THEIR HUSBANDS IN RESOURCE-LIMITED COMMUNITIES

A study of HIV prevention among women and their husbands in resource-limited communities of Mumbai illustrates the same type of approach. The intervention used an ecological framework to identify key components in women's lives that were causing conflict with husbands, thus driving husbands to seek sex with other women. At the community level, the community environment did not favor

gender-equitable norms. At the individual level, the main factors in creating conflict were the women's power-imbalanced relationships with their husbands, economic and other household stressors, stress over the care of children, children's needs for education and especially for girl children, saving for a dowry, and conflict with in-laws and their control over the household. The study wanted to explore whether an individual-level intervention with women alone, or a couples intervention with both husband and wife would have a better effect on improving relationships. The study also changed gender norms by working with mosques and imams to convey gender-equitable messages to the men (the religious level) and with NGOs to promote gender equity among women (the community level). The study thus included multiple levels, with different outcomes measured separately at the community level (a norms change survey) and among the women (a cognitive behavior change survey).

The next example shows how one level may be the primary focus for intervention, but organizations, parents, and media may constitute other ways of reinforcing the primary study outcome in other levels.

EXAMPLE 6.13

TEACHERS AS ROLE MODELS FOR PREVENTING TOBACCO USE IN NORTHERN INDIA

In this five-year study, a collaboration between the Healis-Sekhsaria Foundation for Public Health, Harvard School of Public Health and the Dana Farber Cancer Institute, Boston, used a social contextual model (SCM) approach to create a tobacco prevention/cessation intervention (Nagler et al. 2013). In group discussions, teachers mentioned the importance of acting as responsible role models and contributing to the community. The study team then made the decision that schools were the best locations in which to mount the interventions, and teachers should be the focus of the intervention. They felt that if, as role models, teachers ceased their use of tobacco in any form and functioned as anti-tobacco activists in their schools, the combination of role modeling and social influence to avoid tobacco would have an indirect effect on the students. The intervention focused on seventy-two schools in the northern state of Bihar. Schools were matched and randomized into two groups, one of which was involved in the intervention, and the other acted as a comparison (control). Teachers in the treatment school made a decision to quit the use of tobacco altogether, to model abstinence, and to communicate anti-tobacco messages to students, discouraging them from starting or

continuing to use tobacco. Parents and the media also were involved in supporting the effort, and conveying anti-tobacco messages to students. Results showed favorable reductions in tobacco use among all parties.

POLICY/STRUCTURAL-LEVEL INTERVENTIONS

Much social science research has ended with recommendations for policy change at national, state, and at times, at local levels. Fewer articles describe how policy changes come about and how social scientists working with other stakeholders can influence such changes. Changes in policy occur administratively and through legislation and legislative bodies. Administratively initiated changes in policies *can* be influenced by researchers, especially those working in policy think tanks. Changes can be argued for by evaluating pilot efforts and disseminating the results—for example, changing regulations providing food supports to families with limited incomes, or the utility of income supplementation in stabilizing families—or they can be promoted through legal briefs, literature reviews, meta-analyses, and so on. However, these efforts leave out the voices of the people who are affected. Here we want to focus on approaches to policy change that engage local or national voices.

As some recent national (and global) campaigns have shown, it is possible to mobilize advocates for policy changes from the ground up. Cases in point include global/local movements such as Occupy Wall Street, which mobilized protests against exploitative capitalism and increasing income disparities. The campaign culminated in media attention on the increasing concentration of wealth. Another was ACT UP's advocacy in the mid-1980s in response to the deaths of thousands of gay men, which advocated that more money be designated for HIV research. **Changing policy** from the ground up at any level calls for community organizing through critical analysis, information collection, reflection analysis, and action and the use of social media (Cann 2011). By this we mean:

Definition: Changing policy requires the use of community organizing goals, strategies, and techniques to influence and to change the opinions and legislative action of legislators or other policy makers

- the identification and mobilization of a broad network of stakeholders, especially people affected by the issue;
- appropriate funding that makes possible hiring staffing for mobilization and data collection and analysis;
- ongoing centralized and decentralized activities to engage advocates in information collection, analysis, discussion, and action; dissemination of information via computers, the Internet, social media, mobile phone conferencing, and other mechanisms for sharing information;
- leadership, coordinated action, and preparedness to address opposition voices;
- maintaining and sustaining interest in the issue through ongoing smaller-scale actions;
- integration into policy-making bodies to bring the results of research and advocacy to bear on the right legislation, the right policy makers at the right time.

EXAMPLE 6.14

WHERE'S ROOM 135? CUTTING SHORT THE SCHOOL DAY FOR AT-RISK BLACK STUDENTS

In a seminal book chapter published in 1999, educational researcher G. Alfred Hess described how to conduct policy-related research that influences policy and policy makers. A passionate advocate for educational equity in a segregated Chicago, he discussed how to identify research topics with the potential to influence policy (talk to the people, talk to the policy makers, know where there are inequities in the distribution of time, human resources, intellectual capital, and money). He emphasized the importance of knowing policy makers, participating in "policy clusters," or groups of people with a common interest, in proposing new legislation to address problems. He argued that ethnography helped people understand the processes that explained positive or negative results and reflected the "truth" through the experiences of the people. He described a comparison of Black and white schools that showed that Black schools were releasing students prior to the end of the school day, meaning that the students were being "cheated" out of an hour of instruction daily. A Black newspaper reporter video recorded and interviewed Black students outside one of the schools. One of the students explained for the camera that although they were assigned to study hall—"Room 135"—they knew they were supposed to go home early because the study hall did not exist. The combination of film and study results produced a dialogue that ultimately resulted in the removal of one of the

offending principals and faster movement toward school reform. The chapter went on to discuss how to prepare for and reach the media, work in alliances, practice and offer testimony in local communities, and engage in other activities to link policy research and researchers with the multiple stakeholders important in changing policies and practices in schools (Hess 1999).

Fifteen years ago, Hess's work was on the cutting edge in terms of how to do policy-related research that actually had an effect on policy makers. But his research did not take the additional step of engaging end users in achieving change—the parents of underachieving Black students in underresourced Black schools in a racially segregated and politically charged Chicago environment.

In the next examples, we illustrate how, in different ways, researchers who want to influence policy have worked with communities and policy makers to bring them together in the policy-making process.

EXAMPLE 6.15

AMNESTY FOR CHICKEN KEEPERS—SOCIAL SCIENCE, PUBLIC POLICY, AND RESIDENT ENGAGEMENT

Pima County, Arizona, includes twenty-six census tracts that qualify as food deserts, twenty of which are in Tucson. The city of Tucson is responsive to the needs of local communities and supportive of urban agriculture, and neighborhood residents have a high level of interest in food production through gardens and managing small-animal production, such as raising chickens. Local public-policy processes require including the voices of residents, and policy makers are anxious for their involvement, but the language and formal and informal rules for policy making are difficult to understand. Further, infrastructure for facilitating resident involvement in policy-making bodies did not exist. Given the warm, sunny climate in Tucson and the ability to engage in year-round food production, the Centers for Disease Control (CDC) funded a Tucson-based coalition of agencies and universities to put into place a local food production system that included community and school gardens; home gardens were funded as well as the construction of chicken coops to support chicken keeping and neighborhood egg production. To facilitate resident involvement in the policy process, a policy team was created to educate both team members and target populations about the policy process and assist them in negotiating the policy environment. This team used the following principles:

- a holistic perspective on the community, including all stakeholders;
- facilitation of cross cultural understanding among all stakeholders;
- researching and recognizing community assets;
- promoting community empowerment.

The policy team reviewed multiple policies related to local food production and saw that they had been generated without urban agriculturalists in mind or a perspective on urban agriculture, including animal husbandry. The team then acted as broker, interpreting the policies, and discussing with residents, including Hispanic households, where there were gaps requiring their input. Using ethnographic approaches, the policy team also collected information on best practices in animal keeping with key informants including urban food producers, feed store personnel, a local egg cooperative, and a local food cooperative. The team encouraged and supported community residents in participating in community processes related to the general sustainability plan for the city. It also helped to develop the Pima County Food Alliance, a broad-based grassroots alliance to promote community-based strategies to increase access to healthful food. Finally a Facebook page was created to provide updates on policy developments related to animal husbandry, which was also used to solve problems related to protests against chicken keeping (Eisenberg 2014).

This example illustrates how a social science team utilized networking, policy analysis, and community-based ethnographic skills to broker the various interests of policy makers and residents, especially those locked out of the policy-making process. By focusing on the animal-husbandry interests of those residents, the team was able to engage resident interest in policy and to create new grassroots and informal networks to sustain involvement in both policy and practice. Unlike the first example, this one brings resident voices into the policy-making arena though it does not involve residents in the research designed to improve their knowledge base for advocacy purposes.

Bringing residents into the policy process through research is a challenging enterprise. Two good examples are described in chapter 2 of this book. The first involved researchers, residents, and neighborhood activists in rapid research to evaluate ESL (English as a second language) programs in the Chicago schools, which resulted in a change in superintendents and a shift to bilingual education. The second involved a neighborhood resident research team that conducted a health needs assessment in their housing project and used the results to frame the argument for a much-needed health clinic to serve the residents. The following example illustrates how a group of women resident advocates were able to change the structure of city government to expand and activate a permanent commission on the status of women.

EXAMPLE 6.16

CHANGING CITY GOVERNMENT TO RESPOND TO GENDER INEQUITIES

The Permanent Commission on the Status of Women, State of Connecticut, was very active some time ago, but it catered to the needs of middle-class white women in suburban areas, and not to those of urban women of color. The city of Hartford had a one-person office allocated to addressing women's issues and no capacity to address women's needs. Hartford's women were very diverse, representing Latinos from the Caribbean, South America, and West Indians as well as other Caribbeans, ethnic Europeans, Polish immigrants, and many other groups. The city's women spoke more than fourteen different languages, according to the 1990 census, but little else was known about them. A diverse alliance of women's advocacy organizations and the city and state permanent commissions came together to frame a project that would engage women from the city of all class, racial, ethnic, and linguistic backgrounds in the first-ever development and implementation of an in-depth study of urban women. The goals were to forge networks among women to promote a cohesive advocacy platform for women in the city, to collect important new information about the city's adult (over eighteen) female residents, to share the information with the city commission, to advocate for its expansion, and to use the model as an exemplar for engaging urban women elsewhere in the state.

Over a four-year period, more than one hundred women worked together to create a broad-based analysis of women in the city and then engaged in more focused analyses. Together, they and the members of the supporting alliance underwent reflexive training on women's status, power and capacitation, community organizing, and advocacy. They also developed surveys and interview guides for administration to other women. In the first year of the Urban Women's Development Project, thirty women went through the program. They collected data from women in all of the city neighborhoods on their education, children's education, health, and development needs and presented it to the city council and in many other settings. The result was an expansion of the City Permanent Commission on the Status of Women, which remains very active in developing infrastructure to improve the life of women in the city. In other years, women chose as their topics violence against women, dropping out of school and improving early childhood education. They used survey data in conjunction with interviews and testimony to influence funders and decision makers to support shelters for women experiencing abuse and to support adult education and day care for early dropouts with young children. Over the life of the program, many of the women went on to become neighborhood advocates, obtain higher education degrees, and enter politics and the world of policy (Schensul, Berg, and Williamson 2008).

Reaching Policy Makers Effectively

Communications in writing to the media and to policy makers generally must not be more than one page in length. Press releases and policy briefs should be designed to capture the attention of either media venues or policy makers, or both, and thus must be brief, to the point, and linked to what either or both are interested in. This means homework in terms of what bills are being prepared, which legislators or other policy makers might be interested, and what is newsworthy. Izumi and colleagues (2010) provide assistance for community groups and coalitions to prepare materials and briefs for policy makers. They illustrate with a "one-pager" for use by community and university partnerships in communicating with policy makers. It consists of both a process and an outline for a handout to policy makers. They describe how a coalition of researchers from the University of Michigan worked in partnership with community residents and organizations to improve heart health in Detroit. The steering committee of this entity was charged with examining policies that might have an impact on their goals of reducing air pollutants and improving access to healthful food. Each of their "one-pagers" addressed one of these issues. A subcommittee of the steering committee wrote the one-page brief together, making sure of equitable participation from community representatives (Izumi et al. 2010). The outline for the policy brief is the following:

- Policy statement (either direction or recommenda- tion on a specific bill) with specific action/recom- mendation
- Partnership overview
- Background
- Research findings
- Policy recommendations
- Contact information

Press releases follow roughly the same format. They must be written in ordinary, yet convincing, language. They should frame the problem in a larger context, address disparities, describe the background of the issue briefly, announce some key results or a key event, and include one or more quotes from believable people, such as a community leader, a youth activist, and possibly a researcher, highlighting why the issue is important for the public to know about. More than a policy brief, which is technical, the press release can be a "work of art," formal yet familiar, convincing without being dogmatic, oriented toward the known interests of specific reporters, and with quotes that are pithy and to the point.

Influencing policy makers to act based on the results of research is a challenging task under any circumstances, as we have seen, requiring that researchers and their partners act as brokers between the worlds of research and policy, institutions and communities, with sufficient funding and time to make a real difference. Engaging community residents in the process to speak from an informed platform based on their own experiences, their own and others' research, and their advocacy capacity is even more challenging. It is this latter process that we favor here, for several reasons. First, the voices of people directly affected by a policy-related issue should be heard directly, rather than through the representations of the researchers. Second, the people are likely to be more effective than the researchers alone in appealing to decision makers. Policy makers must respond to the public; using the strategies suggested here represents ways of getting the message across to them from sectors of the public that might not always be heard.

Third, it is always helpful to remember that changing policy requires a broad base of support. Organized residents can utilize the media and community organizing and social movement methods to convey their messages beyond briefs to a broad audience; that audience can also appeal to improved decision making through the electoral process.

Here we have tried to present several models for making this leap across multiple boundaries. The *researcher advocacy model* involves doing research, working with stakeholders, and advocating with multiple sectors to try to change policy. It is researcher driven because the researcher acts as an advocate. The *second model* involves the creation of a brokering structure in which social scientists work with policy makers, translate policy into lay language, and work with and mobilize community members to participate in the policy-making process. Here, the researcher is a cultural broker/mobilizer. The *third model* involves researchers working with community residents to facilitate their own decisions regarding policy change, providing the tools for them to do their own research, and helping them to engage with policy makers directly. This model is citizen-led Participatory Action Research (PAR) for policy change. All of these approaches use a mix of ethnographic research, targeted communication to stakeholders (policy makers, advocacy organizations, and community groups), and community organizing techniques. They all require understanding the worlds of policy, community based ethnography, and community organizing.

SUSTAINABILITY

When we think of sustainability, we often believe that what we are doing can be, and should be, continued just as it is—same people, same activities, same goals and objectives. This form of sustainability is in part a function of the "science" that suggests that the conduct of interventions requires controlling the context to see if the intervention "really works." As so many have realized by now, this is not a realistic way to assess social, structural, and behavioral interventions as they operate in the real world. Nor is it the way culture change occurs—with varying change rates over time and with often unpredictable directions. It is also a reflection of the strategizing of funders who believe that if they invest for three, five, or ten years, the institutional arrangements, processes and outcomes can be ongoing.

We know from field experience and involvement with partners in social settings that things change. Political leaders are replaced, policies are repealed, organizations come and go, public institutions are funded and defunded. When we consider the transformational capacity of systems, we have to recognize that the best operationalized interventions conducted by deeply committed people are not likely to continue in the same way over time. So what, then, does "sustainability" mean when the context of a change effort itself is in constant transition?

As Scheirer notes, sustainability can refer to

a. continuation of activities after the program is over;
b. sustained effects or results after the program is over;
c. the integration of intervention activities into ongoing institutional or cultural arrangements;
d. capacity to respond to changing conditions in order to maintain positive results or achieve new ones (Scheirer 2005).

Most researchers who consider sustainability of effects show that these attenuate over time without continuing inputs. One of the most important lessons to learn from cultural practices is that *they* tend to be sustained over time. We can learn much from cultural rituals that are sustained (rites of passage, housewarmings, wedding practices, birth ceremonies and naming practices, transitions of influence within family structures from one generation to another, and so on). The relative success of simple interventions such as prevention of dengue through use of bed nets and reduction of standing water are based on their cost effectiveness, limited need for continuous monitoring, endorsement by public officials, and incorporation into local cultural practices (Romani et al. 2007). But complex interventions that call for cognitive, social, political, and economic changes in dynamic systems are more difficult to sustain because changes over time in multiple interacting subcomponents or elements of the system make them less stable. In such cases, repetition/replication is less important and self-renewal and community and organizational capacity building become more important. With these capacities, communities and organizations can utilize acquired skills to respond to new circumstances, with the same or different and better results. Asking when the intervention needs to be changed to respond to new conditions, and what a completely new approach might be, are critical components of sustainability in this context, and are the most difficult to achieve. These capacities require committed and visionary leadership, active community participation, sufficient resources, constant training and self-evaluation, and multiple-level inputs and openness to self-reflection, monitoring, and acceptance of feedback (Schensul 2009).

The capacities of an adaptive self-sustaining system utilizing multilevel dynamic systems approaches defined in this way are to:

- identify and model required changes and put them into practice;
- monitor the environment and conduct research to assess if the approach needs to be changed, or there are new problems to address;
- put new policies, regulations, structures, and practices in place in conjunction with people affected by them;
- mobilize to change unwieldy or non-functional elements by participating in movements;
- support constituencies in a process of action research to assess the setting, environmental changes, and opportunities and obstacles;
- detect whether evidence-based interventions imposed on communities make sense, or should be adapted or rejected in favor of approaches that are more culturally or otherwise appropriate.

With respect to social science interventions, Van Willigen, a development anthropologist, asks not "how can we assess existing capacity to accept, conduct and maintain a specific intervention" but instead, "what is important in assessing the capacity of an intervention resource to contribute to (indigenous) community development?" We close this chapter with the components he suggests as crucial to ensuring that interventions fit the needs of local communities:

- the political position and standpoint of the institutional resource (the source of the intervention)— this determines the degree to which the institution is subject to external control;
- the goal orientation of the resource—a broad rather than narrow set of goals allows for greater community involvement; the degree to which the resource focuses on individual versus community (multilevel) welfare; individual-level intervention approaches alone weaken community bonds;
- duration of the resource—the longer the time period allocated for the intervention, the more likely it will be able to contribute to community development;
- the connection of the resource to community organizations—the greater the connection, the more likely the contribution to community development, provided the source is not allied closely with powerful forces that have the potential to undermine community interests or goals.

As Van Willigen cautions, community reliance on external development or intervention resources may be either empowering or disempowering, and the possibilities of disempowerment and/or dependency engendered through reliance on external resources should always be considered (Van Willigen 2005).

SUMMARY

In this chapter we have tried to make use of the lessons learned in the previous three to describe how actions/interventions can be formulated at multiple levels. We have proceeded on the assumption that interventions that take place at one social level can influence changes in other levels and that social, community, or structural interventions may not bring about lasting change because individuals have not permanently transformed their own values, beliefs, and behaviors. In the end, we favor multilevel approaches to social change, especially those that involve dealing with barriers to access and resources and oppressive institutions. We also believe that social researchers and their partners must use ethnography to understand the context, whether the actions they are researching are likely to have an effect, and who their allies and objectors are. These data can be put to use at all levels to enhance potential for success and for sustainability. Those who are dedicated to social change and social transformation want to know whether what they are doing is having an ongoing and long-term effect. Thus, the next chapter addresses the evaluation of interventions at multiple levels, offering a variety of different design options for documenting and calculating both process and outcomes at multiple points in time.

7

DESIGNING EVALUATIONS OF ACTIONS/INTERVENTIONS

INTRODUCTION

In previous chapters, we have reviewed the principles and values of ethnography in action primarily from the viewpoint of ethnographers who create partnerships and collaborations in order to promulgate specific kinds of *change* efforts. These efforts, as we said in chapter 1, are guided by a combination of personal values, social justice concerns, and the goals and needs of communities and institutions that are affected by a situation calling for transformation. We now turn to a discussion of how to assess or evaluate those change efforts.

Evaluation is the act of identifying, questioning, interrogating, assessing, and documenting or measuring a phenomenon that calls for researched action or an action/intervention needing to be researched/evaluated. These considerations occur in the context of:

- what the phenomenon *should* be (the theory, design, or a standard against an expected or hoped-for outcome)
- what it *could* be (imagined options for action)
- what others desire or require (the funder, the public)
- what others want it to be (the participants, recipients, and "beneficiaries" or nonbeneficiaries)

DECIDING ON AN EVALUATION STANDPOINT

Conducting evaluation, like forming partnerships, or identifying intervention topics and approaches, is a political act. When deciding whether to evaluate a program, values come into play in the relationships that are established between the evaluator and those evaluated, processes through which the data are collected, and the way the results are delivered and to whom. Evaluators need to consider whether they like or dislike, approve or disapprove of the institution, program, or activities to be evaluated, and then determine whether their "biases" in that regard will affect the way they conduct the evaluation and represent the result—or even if they can agree to conduct the evaluation at all. Evaluators further must determine what the objectives of the funders are. If evaluators, workers, and participants believe that a program is sound and valuable, but funders do not share that position, evaluators will want to think hard about whether to accept the evaluation assignment.

Anyone contemplating undertaking an evaluation should understand its context even prior to starting. "Pre-ethnography" or what we have called "preliminary fieldwork" in the situation to be evaluated is critical for deciding whether or not a research evaluator is willing to address the issue. Doing an evaluation may involve joining a process already begun, which may be predetermined and immutable, and with which an evaluator does not wish to be associated. Even if that is not the case, the situation is likely to be fraught with differences among stakeholders who have multiple perspectives on what is happening, what success means, and what the outcome of the evaluation should be.

No matter what the approach, the essence of an evaluation is its ability to describe clearly what is going on in the situation, and to attribute causality, if possible, to the designated or emergent outcomes (Dorr-Bremme 1985). This always is a problem. Outside of the laboratory, researchers can only approximate causality. Arguing for the existence of causality and "causal connections" means evaluators would have to have the ability to attribute a set of antecedent conditions to a subsequent outcome. Generally, only controlled experiments can provide some certainty of causality. In non-experimental social science research, however, demonstrating causal connections usually requires first tracking events qualitatively or with mixed methods back and forward over time, describing continuous patterns of association, and then ruling out other explanations. The best that can be achieved is plausible evidence that demonstrates the existence of a connection between events and their presumed consequences. Attributing causality also can be achieved through repeated surveys that assess change in the environment and/or changes in the individual over time. A number of statistical approaches can be used to attribute causality in this way, including structural equation modeling (Judd and Kenny 1981) or mediation modeling (http://davidakenny.net/cm/mediate.htm), and by examining direct and indirect effects of events or cognitions (beliefs, norms, intentions) that occur between the established baseline and later measures.

In intervention work, however, the actions that constitute the intervention are intended to bring about a desired or predicted result. They could, for example:

- demonstrate that the components of an artist's development are improved artist skills and capacities to negotiate their careers;
- show that changing the physical and social structure of a building results in greater numbers of people who socialize with each other;
- show that creating positive public roles for urban youth of color changes public perception of their contribution to society and reverses negative normative behavior (abuse, harassment, expectations of low achievement or violent behavior, and the belief that all urban youth use drugs);
- show that a new curriculum to improve group problem solving in science has a positive effect on individual science performance tests;
- show that a specific approach to education for some children diagnosed with ADHD improves their school performance;
- demonstrate that creating new roles for local residents that let them be cultural guides for tourists

improves their commitment to preserving important aspects of their cultural and physical environment.

At the same time, interventions may contribute to or produce unpredicted or emergent results (Christie, Montrose, and Klein 2005). **Emergent results** are those that evolve from the action, rather than those that are predicted or predictable. They can be welcome surprises, indications that modifications in an intervention are required, or undesirable disasters. In any case, demonstrating all of the causal contributions of an intervention to an outcome involves first measuring the expected outcomes, then looking for other outcomes, whether expected or not, and showing how and why the intervention should and does lead to them. This step often is called "process evaluation" (Bunce et al. 2014; Rasmus 2014). Evaluators then must rule out other plausible explanations for why the desired results did or did not occur and identify contributors to the unexpected outcomes that did occur.

Definition: Emergent results are those that evolve from the action, rather than those that are predicted or predictable

Ethnographic evaluations, like research in general, may be qualitative or may utilize mixed methods. Qualitative evaluations usually are very helpful in understanding processes, participant experiences, and satisfaction (Butler 2005). Their "unobtrusive" measures, including observations, are important in providing information that the sole use of test reports cannot produce (Lee 2000). In general, however, we advocate the use of mixed methods over observation alone. This is because triangulation of different types of data provide a better picture of what is going on and why things are happening than the use of a single approach, such as surveys or tests. It is also because most of the situations that ethnographers initiate or are called upon to evaluate are complicated or complex (Patton 2010). They cannot be understood without using a mix of methods—surveys, observations, interviews, photography, mapping, and so on (Patton 2010). From now on in this chapter, unless we specify otherwise, we will focus on mixed methods ethnographic evaluation of interventions, or those that ethnographers are involved in designing, developing, and implementing.

Bias in Evaluation

The question of bias always arises when those involved in an intervention also are involved in its evaluation; it is particularly tricky because the results of evaluation often mean so much to the designers and implementers who want to see their projects work, to the people who are affected, to the funders who want to see success, and finally, to the worlds of science and practice that want to have sufficient confidence in the results to make use of them. Much can ride on the production of positive, negative, or partial outcome results of a program. At the same time, standing back and taking a critical perspective on one's work is honest, ethical, practical, intrinsically valuable—and necessary.

We have discussed bias in ethnographic research in Books 1, 2, and 6 of the *Ethnographer's Toolkit*. Below, we argue that bias can be addressed in many ways:

- Bias should be embraced and understood by researchers.
- Bias should be formalized into a formative model with hypotheses or hunches to be tested.
- Bias can be limited if methods of data collection are clearly specified. Ongoing discussion with, participation by, and input from people from the study sites can be a check on bias.
- Bias can be explored through ongoing "mini-hypothesis testing" in the field.
- Bias can be identified by using verification techniques such as member checking and social validation.
- Bias also can be controlled by constant self-reflection and awareness of positionality on the part of the ethnographer.

Cross Reference:
See Book 1, chapters 1, 2, and 10; Book 2, chapters 1 and 2; Book 6, chapters 1, 4, 5, 6, 7, and 8

Cross Reference:
See Book 6, chapter 9

Skewing the direction of an evaluation toward positive results by conducting the intervention under the best circumstances, or under conditions where it is most likely to show positive results, is neither good practice nor good science. In evaluation of a partnership, those most immediately affected by the results of an evaluation are the partners/collaborators and the people experiencing the problem. Whether partners/collaborators and/or people experiencing the problem are directly involved in the evaluation or not, they have a significant stake in how their work comes out. Just as an action-oriented implementation team desires to put forward the best possible intervention, it also is deeply invested in the best possible ways of assessing outcomes. No matter whether the evaluation is designed for intervention improvement or for outcomes assessment, its utility still depends on high-quality work, which in turn is the product of solid intervention design and methodology.

APPROACHES TO EVALUATION

There are several different approaches to evaluation, depending on the relationship between the evaluator(s) and the site/setting and people involved in it. At one end of the relationship continuum are those evaluations that are fully participatory and involve all stakeholders, including people who are affected by and trying to address the problem on which the effort is centered. At the other end are those that are driven by outside interests—researchers, funders, and policy makers that want an "objective" external viewpoint. Throughout the *Toolkit* and in this book, we have emphasized the critical importance of collaborative, partnership, and participatory approaches to social change regardless of the level at which they occur. Generally, those involved in the "action" or intervention will want to know about its effects through some form of evaluation (Patton 2010). Among the most common forms of evaluation that involve some form of participation are:

- Participatory evaluations (all partners including those affected participate)
- Stakeholder evaluations (main stakeholders participate but not those affected)
- External evaluations (stakeholders and those affected are gatekeepers for and responders to outside evaluators)

At times, evaluations call for a *participatory model* in which those involved in the intervention also are involved in the evaluation through data collection, analysis, interpretation, and use. When they are designed both to enhance the ability of those affected to improve the process and to improve their own capabilities to act, they are referred to as *empowerment evaluations*. **Empowerment evaluations** are designed to remedy inequities in the power relationship between implementers and participants. Empowerment evaluations give participants a full voice in the implementation/self-direction and the overall change process. One such approach occurs when evaluators teach evaluation methods to people so that they can conduct their own evaluations. In this way they are able to obtain their own critical information about what is and is not working and use it to their advantage (Fetterman 1994; Fetterman 2005). Participatory evaluations are typical in participatory/partnership intervention approaches. Participatory and empowerment evaluations "democratize" by involving participants as lay researchers in evaluation of their own actions (Wandersman et al. 2000). Kim Sabo uses such an approach when working with teens, based on her belief that if teens evaluate programs that are intended for them, they will have a more significant say and more buy-in regarding what the program is and how it is conducted (Sabo 2004). These models also include community-building approaches to evaluation (Hyland and Brimhall 2005).

Other evaluations include *stakeholders* as evaluators. In collaborative intervention research or community development efforts, where stakeholders represent different sectors of a community or other setting, the stakeholders may be involved in designing, supervising, and sometimes implementing the evaluation, and in taking the results into consideration. Fetterman classifies this approach as well under the rubric of *empowerment evaluation* because it empowers implementers to think clearly about their goals, objectives, and actions and raise questions about what they are accomplishing (Fetterman 1994; Fetterman 2005). Another model that involves stakeholders is a collective approach to evaluation in which representatives from different sectors or administrative levels in worksites or other settings come together in a vertical or horizontal alliance to conduct an evaluative self-assessment of process and outcome. This

Definition: Empowerment evaluations give a full voice in the evaluation process and its results to participants who are the recipients of an intervention to ameliorate their experiences of injustice and disparity

approach is successful when the institution is committed to democratic values and to the use of information or data to improve self-management as a means of producing better outcomes (Rapkin and Trickett 2005).

On many occasions, ethnographic evaluators are asked to do *external evaluations* of interventions—programs, services, educational curricula—especially for funders and sometimes for the scientific establishment. Usually ethnographic evaluators accept such assignments when they have a strong affinity for the work and believe in its political agenda, even if they are not an internal player in the project (Gitlin 1994). One such example is Patricia Hudelson's evaluation of ICR's Urban Women's Development Project. Hudelson, whose background was in women's empowerment project development, was engaged as a sympathetic external documenter to meet with women participants from each of the four years of this adult participatory action research program for and with urban women of diverse backgrounds and experiences. Her job was to capture their narratives about the experience of the program and its effects on each of the women, on the group, and on the larger issues they were tackling (Schensul, Berg, and Williamson 2008). Each of these three approaches requires researchers to adopt a different stance or position with respect to evaluation. Anyone who has concerns about the impact of their own or others' actions has probably been involved in all three approaches to evaluation.

TOOLS OF EVALUATION

Ethnography-driven evaluations make use of all of the tools of mixed methods ethnography, the most frequently used of which are described in Books 2, 3, and 4 of the *Ethnographer's Toolkit*. Methods are chosen depending on the questions asked and the nature of the evaluation design (see next section). Common methods used include:

- In-depth individual interviews
- Group interviews

- Narrative observations, ranging from qualitative descriptive to quantified, individual, and setting specific
- Structured observational protocols based on prior observation
- Elicitation approaches (sorts, visual, and oral elicitations of responses)
- Audiovisual forms of documentation
- Collection of project-related artifacts and forms
- Archival retrieval and use of secondary data
- Ethnographic surveys

In Table 7.1, we summarize some of the main uses of these methods of data collection. Then, in examples throughout the chapter, we describe how many of these approaches are used in evaluation.

The approaches to modeling interventions that we describe in chapter 4 of this book are very useful tools in mixed methods ethnographic evaluation of interventions. When researcher/partner teams begin an intervention with a conceptual model, the work of modeling for evaluation is already done. In longer-term, and in larger ongoing development efforts, new program ideas and strategies can emerge at any time, at which point new modeling must be undertaken to guide both future action and its associated evaluative activity.

TYPES OF EVALUATION DESIGNS FOR ASSESSING OUTCOMES

In Book 1, we reviewed different types of evaluation designs. Here we discuss them and apply them to specific examples, including the following:

Cross Reference:
See Book 1, chapter 4

- Case study evaluation designs (one single case as in a classroom, school, community, or business). Case study designs are common in the disciplines of anthropology, political science, and sociology, where researcher interests are in the details of a single case. Case study evaluations may take place over a longer or shorter period of time and may include ongoing measurements or observations of interim and final outcomes. Longer case studies with many

TABLE 7.1 Applications of ethnographic methods in evaluation

Ethnographic Methods	Evaluating Processes	Evaluating Outcomes
Cultural Level		
Key informant interviews (program-level experience)	• Monitor program implementation • Identify need for further training and program modifications • Identify deviations or changes from program plans • Document barriers and facilitators to implementation • Document contextual factors influencing implementation • Monitor program acceptability to facilitators, users, and community	• Document perceived outcomes, expected and unexpected • Assess program acceptability at endpoint • Document efforts to sustain the intervention • Describe relationships between intervention and other community activities
Group interviews	• Monitor implementation • Identify training and modification needs • Identify internal and external changes • Monitor acceptability	• Document perceived outcomes • Assess overall acceptability • Identify external changes affecting the program over time • Examine institutionalization and sustainability
Observations	• Document program implementation and changes. • Document deviations from intention and provide feedback • Identify need for revision, training, and other changes • Use to develop alternative approaches to improve implementation	• Document program integrity/fidelity • Document changes qualitatively and quantitatively • Observe unexpected effects • Identify new directions
Elicitation methods (sorts and visual-oral elicitation of responses)	• Identify and confirm congruence of understanding of key program concepts and within group differences • Use for intervention discussion	• Examine cultural changes in key constructs (program outcomes) • Identify within group differences

(continued)

TABLE 7.1 *Continued*

Ethnographic Methods	Evaluating Processes	Evaluating Outcomes
Audiovisual methods	• Document implementation for coding and analysis • Document intervention settings • Audio-visual recording of interviews for history and analysis of program process	• Document action outcomes for analysis and representation • Prepare dissemination materials for presentation and discussion/data collection
Program/project related artifacts and forms	• Document and record program activities • Record of participants' perceptions of meaningful activities • Preserve materials for display and dissemination	• Evaluate intervention sessions (Use as fidelity checks) • Document changes in target skills • Preserve and display materials
Secondary data/archival materials	• Provide contextual and comparative material for intervention	• Provide larger context for results and results comparison
Individual Level		
In-depth interviews (individual-level experience)	• Monitor program implementation • Identify individual experiences that indicate deviations or changes from program plans • Document barriers and facilitators to implementation • Document how any contextual factors might influence implementation • Monitor program acceptability to users	• Document and provide examples of actual outcomes • Examine cross-program acceptability at endpoint • Document how external changes affect individual or group responses to intervention at endpoint • Document sustainability efforts and links among participants as a result of program or activity
Individual observations	• Observe engagement of sample participants in activities • Observe skills development over time • Observe contextual factors influencing program involvement of individual participants	• Compare observations on individuals over time for program fidelity and individual progress • Document influence of context on individual participation and performance

(continued)

TABLE 7.1 *Continued*

Ethnographic Methods	Evaluating Processes	Evaluating Outcomes
Logs/journals/narratives	• Establish baseline qualitative measures • Support participant reflexivity	• Longitudinal data on participant progress • Identify participant capacity to generalize skills learned • Examine program acceptability
Ethnographic surveys	• Track changes at individual level over time	• Evaluate pre-post or time-series effects/outcomes and mediating factors at individual level • Evaluate sustainability post intervention

subprojects within the larger ongoing development effort can involve all three types of evaluation designs—case studies, pre-post comparisons, and alternative designs.

■ Pre-post comparisons of two or more cases with two or multiple time points. These are designs that involve comparing two or more "cases" that are comparable in nature. The cases are assigned through randomization (that is, assigning individuals, classrooms, youth groups, towns, or businesses on a random basis to intervention and comparison groups). Such designs are often called "randomized controlled trials" (RCTs). Even though they may never involve actual clinics, they might at times be called "clinical trials." Usually, randomized controlled trials involve a much larger number of "cases" to accommodate the requirements of the statistical analyses needed to produce results.

■ Controlled case comparisons. These are yet another way of assigning cases for comparison. Such studies match those cases involved in the intervention against similar cases that are not based on key similarities (age, income, size, type of school, etc.). Comparative designs can be arrayed on a continuum from simple to very complex, and they may also be "pre-post designs," evaluating how cases differ

Cross Reference:
See Book 1 for a number of such examples

between time points. These are often called "case control designs," "quasi-experimental designs," or "alternatives to the RCT" (West et al. 2008).

■ Alternative designs. Alternative designs involve comparisons of slightly different interventions, or components of interventions, against one another.

We summarize these designs in Table 7.2.

In this chapter, we will discuss and give examples of variations in all four designs.

Case Study Evaluations

Case studies are holistic examinations of specific programs or interventions. The case study evaluation design is highly appropriate for community-based interventions that take place in a single community or for specific classroom or program evaluations. This approach is required in a community development effort in a single community when changes over time must be documented. A case study is particularly useful for evaluating programs or interventions:

■ when programs are unique;
■ when an established program is implemented in a new setting;
■ when a unique or unanticipated outcome warrants further investigation;
■ when a program occurs in an unpredictable environment (Balbach 1999, 4);
■ when a program or project or development effort occurs over a long period of time, as in the cases described in chapter 2 of this book.

Case studies do not involve an external comparison group. In fact, no external comparison group *can* exist simply because the community or school is unique, because it is a small initial step toward a larger effort, or because it is a large-scale long-term intervention effort in a single community. Case studies sometimes use pre-post assessments to assess what the status of the situation was at the beginning and again at the end. Such assessments require that

TABLE 7.2 Case study designs with internal comparisons or repeat measures

Type of Design X, Y, Z = intervention 0 = evaluation	Subtype	Description	Methods	Example
X0X0X0X0X0X0	Single ongoing case study	Continuous ethnography	System description Following subsample	Describing curriculum innovation and effects on a small group of students
XXXXXX0	Post-evaluation only	Ethnography plus systematic assessment at endpoint	Mixed methods, quantitative post-assessment	Evaluating the effects of bed net use after introduction with descriptions of use, and a post-introduction survey of use patterns
0 X 0	Single case with observations pre and post	Assessments pre and post the intervention, based on theoretical framework; with or without intervening documentation	Mixed methods; quantitative post-assessment; qualitative process description	Taking a baseline and post-intervention assessment (survey or standardized observations) of a vaccination uptake intervention in a community
0 0 0 X 0	Single case, multiple observations pre, one post	Multiple pre-assessments to show trend followed by one or more post-assessments to demonstrate change in trend	Mixed methods, quantitative post-assessment; qualitative process description	Taking multiple assessments (e.g., grades, birthweight) before the intervention, and one after to see if the intervention bends the trend

X0X0X0X0 Time-series/trend design	Monitoring changes over three or more points in time while the intervention is going on	Mixed methods; quantitative time series measures with qualitative process description throughout	Measuring trends in substance use among high school youth in a community involved in a prevention intervention
Diffusion network ial Diffusion design	Monitoring changes in behavior of interconnected entities (persons or agencies) as a result of an intervention introduced through "seeds"	Mixed methods; quantitative measures of behaviors of linked persons; interviews with a subsample to describe how linkage happens	Measuring the diffusion of HIV risk prevention information through injector networks and relationship to changes in behavior of all network members at different distances from "seeds"
Diffusion network post Diffusion pre-post design Diffusion network pre 	Monitoring changes in behavior of interconnected entities (persons or agencies) as a result of an intervention introduced through "seeds"	Mixed methods; quantitative measures of behaviors of linked persons; interviews with a subsample to describe how linkage happens; adding pre-, post-, or repeated cross sectional surveys at mult ple time points to illustrate changes in general population	Measuring diffusion of AIDS prevention messages beyond networks of "seeds" to general population

meticulous baseline data be collected prior to the start of the project or, at least, as soon after as possible. In some cases, documentary and historical data can supplement the baseline description when ethnographers have not been present at the beginning. Some case studies use the same assessment methods at multiple ongoing time points, to see if things are changing in the hoped for or anticipated direction. If enough time points have been established, the design is called a "time series design." Many case studies use *internal* comparisons, usually by asking whether an intervention achieves and/or has a differential effect on one group versus another. A sound qualitative or mixed methods investigation is essential in a case study approach to determine what happens between time points, especially if unexpected situations occur that might interfere with or speed along the anticipated results. Such an approach, which creates detailed descriptions of the conduct of the intervention as it was planned, as it evolved, and as any conditions in and outside of the community affected it to produce unexpected outcomes at any point along the way, is usually referred to as a *process evaluation*. Process evaluations are essential in explaining *how* and *why* the ultimate outcomes were achieved, whether successful or not.

Any good evaluation must be concerned with linking the intervention's theory and "logic model"—the theory or theories guiding the study, goals, objectives, and actions planned—with a description of how things actually evolved in the context in which the program is set. ***Understanding process is especially necessary in case studies because, since there is no comparison equivalent, we cannot know what likely would have happened without the intervention.*** The logic of causality is wholly dependent on whether the evaluation can trace, from beginning to end, the chain of events that resulted in the outcome, and whether it can document the many possible events that interfered with, diverted, or otherwise changed it. Comparative designs try to control for many of these factors, but case study designs also are compelled to describe them and assess the degree to which they interfere with outcomes.

The role of theory in guiding the intervention methodology cannot be underestimated. Using theory to

 Key point

inform the methods used should produce evidence that produces meaningful results. Good advance planning also can help to avoid designing inappropriate approaches to intervention. But even when the planning is sound, unforeseen circumstances can require small deviations or modifications or, at times, very significant changes to the methods used, even in small-scale studies.

EXAMPLE 7.1

EVALUATING SUCCESS RATHER THAN FAILURE

The nonprofit organization, Movement to End Sexual Abuse (MESA), started as a rape crisis hotline in Boulder, Colorado. Like many such organizations that provide services to people in crisis, it expended a great many resources in training and supporting its volunteers, only to find that they often burned out from the stressful work in less than a year. MESA asked Ann Bruce, one of its volunteers who was looking for a topic for her dissertation research, to evaluate its training program, the conditions under which volunteers worked, and MESA's support mechanisms and then determine what could be done to retain volunteers longer, thereby conserving the organization's limited resources. This was especially important since MESA was being asked to expand the range and type of services it offered. Bruce's initial proposal for evaluation, which her doctoral committee approved, included data showing that more than half of the volunteers failed to complete a full year of service. However, just as she was about to begin, MESA's director called her to say that new data showed not only that volunteers weren't leaving but that other organizations were contacting MESA to find out what they were doing to hold on to their volunteers so effectively. The director wanted her to change the focus of her dissertation to address *that* question, instead of the original one. Ann was fairly sure that the nature of the clients had not changed, but was not sure what else had produced the change in retention rates. The change in focus did not really mandate a change in the evaluation methods to be used, but Ann first had to confirm that the evidence was accurate—that volunteers were, in fact, not leaving. Having done that, she went on to examine the training, support systems, activities, and most important, the emerging culture at MESA for answers to the question and subsequent plans to reinforce both what had led to success and a scalable description that other organizations could use to replicate MESA's success. In both cases, the questions involved what inspired volunteers to stay/leave, and in both cases, the answers related to rituals and practices of support and collegueship that MESA had instituted, or not (Bruce 2005).

In large-scale long-term community development efforts, the understanding of how one set of programs, activities, and political actions leads to others; the networking effects of interactions among organizations as people move from place to place; and the emergence of new forms of leadership can be difficult to understand, especially in the initial stages, and should be documented. The following examples describe sound case study evaluation designs that meet some of the criteria for addressing "causality."

EXAMPLE 7.2

COMMUNITY-BASED SEXUAL RISK PREVENTION PROGRAM FOR SRI LANKAN YOUTH: INFLUENCING SEXUAL-RISK DECISION MAKING

Sri Lanka is a country with a low prevalence of HIV infection, but internal conditions create potentially high risks for HIV transmission were the virus ever to be introduced. These conditions include opportunities for young men and women to get together alone, and even to room together on university campuses, as well as opportunities to engage in intimate behavior in the community. Further, the continuing civil war in the north drew teens into the national army, moving them away from the protective environment of their homes and communities. These settings provided new opportunities for young men and women to interact, but Sri Lankan culture did not provide them with cultural norms and rules to assist them in negotiating intimate relationships and few young people had much understanding about or agreement on what constituted intimacy, sex, and sexual risk.

In an effort to understand and prevent HIV risk exposure in these groups of young people, a group of universities (the University of Peradeniya, Kandy, the University of Connecticut Department of Community Medicine, the School Psychology Program of the University at Albany) and the Institute for Community Research, Hartford, conducted a formative research project using ethnographic mixed methods. The research was funded through the United States Agency for International Development (USAID) to the International Institute for Research on Women (ICRW) and then awarded to the other institutional partners with the grantee organization being the University of Connecticut. The research methods in the Sri Lanka study included observations in places where youth gathered and had opportunity for intimacy, key informant interviews, and in-depth interviews with students and working teens in the city, plus an ethnographic survey with both male and female groups. It produced useful information about intervention sites, modes of delivery, and processes of interaction. The formative model is shown in Figure 7.1.

Based on study findings, the research team created an intervention program for urban youth regarding their lack of knowledge about sex and sexual decision mak-

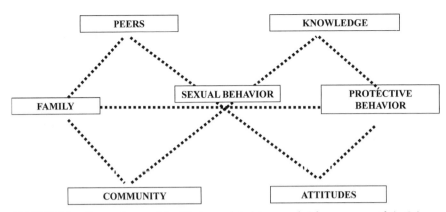

FIGURE 7.1 Formative model of factors related to sexual risk among youth in Sri Lanka.

ing. The intervention helped to fill the gap in opportunities for the youth to interact on these topics and, as well, discuss gender differences in behavioral norms. The intervention was based on the following principles:

1. It had to be focused on sexual knowledge, attitudes, risk perception, decision making, and behavior.
2. It had to be informed by cultural content, the local language, and culturally known modes of interaction.
3. It had to be peer facilitated.
4. It had to use a social construction model of intervention (i.e., use of group process to foster cognitive and behavior change).
5. It had to involve collaboration between interventionists and peer educators to ensure fidelity of implementation.

The intervention was conducted in Tamil and Sinhala, the languages spoken in Sri Lanka, and was implemented by Sri Lankan and U.S. researchers, with the support of local public health instructors and peer educators, who also assisted in recruiting the participants.

The goals of the intervention were:

- to improve communication and social negotiation in heterosexual relationships as antecedents to sexual-risk prevention behaviors;
- to enable avoidance of sexual risk through recognition of the link between sexual behaviors and risky sexual practices;
- to facilitate informed sexual-risk decision making and negotiation with partners by increasing knowledge of reproductive health, STDs, and HIV/AIDS;

- to evaluate the use of vignettes or "dilemmas" as a tool for improving conceptual understanding of sexual risk and the social negotiation skills necessary to avoid risk by choosing safe sexual practices.

A total of 89 participants (41 females, 54 males) attended at least one intervention session. Consistent or regular attendees were defined as those who attended at least 50 percent, or 6, of the sessions, yielding a study population of 66 (39 females, 27 males).

The intervention was located in a community meeting room and it was endorsed by important community leaders having influence on norms related to sexuality and male-female relationships. They included priests, public health personnel, and NGO staff. It involved 12 sessions of 90 minutes each, delivered over 4 weeks. An average of 10 people attended each intervention group. Retention was nearly 100 percent for the women, and 50 percent for the men. Pre-post surveys that constituted the outcome evaluation instrument were administered in the first and last sessions. All but one of the 10 content sessions was conducted in single-gender groups by same-sex peer educators; this allowed young men and women to address knowledge, gender norms, and relationship issues separately and to become familiar and comfortable with the language of intimacy. The eleventh session was conducted by male and female peer facilitators. The four program content modules addressed sexual negotiation, heterosexual relationships, reproductive health and sexuality, AIDS and other STDS, and prevention of AIDS and other sexual risks. The curriculum included individual and group discussions and group problem-solving sessions. Materials used in the intervention served as data to demonstrate movement toward group normative and practice consensus over time.

The evaluation consisted of two parts. First was an in-depth documentation of program implementation focusing on program acceptability, fidelity of implementation, and content delivered and discussed. Data collected were logs, lesson materials, recordings of dialogues, and assessments of satisfaction and knowledge gained from each session.

Acceptability results showed overall satisfaction with the program and interest in expanding some areas, including how to negotiate decisions around sexual intimacy. Session documentation showed satisfactory completion by participants of all program activities, and adherence to facilitator behaviors and group process. Although the program was implemented with integrity across groups, some peer educators were more skillful than others in disseminating information, answering questions, and facilitating group process (e.g., during discussions, negotiation of perspectives, etc.). This was because they were more concerned about conveying health content than peer facilitation.

The second part of the evaluation involved quantitative pre-post measures of sexual knowledge, attitudes, perception of risk, and decision-making skills administered through a self-response survey. Six scales were designed for the study, based on the formative work and intervention content including:

- AIDS Knowledge (8 items, alpha coefficient = .74);
- Condom Knowledge (8 items, alpha coefficient = .69);
- Sex Knowledge (Sex Terms; 7 items, alpha coefficient = .82);
- Sexual Attitudes (7 items, alpha coefficient = .86);
- Perceptions of Future Sex Risk (6 items, alpha coefficient = .86);
- Sexual-Risk Decision Making. The decision-making scale consisted of a scenario (dilemma) based on the formative research and open-ended questions designed to examine perceptions of risk, protections against risk, propose actions that could be taken, and confidence in performing the proposed actions.

The assessment was translated into both Sinhala and Tamil.

Paired-sample *t*-tests were used to compare pretest and posttest means on the three knowledge scales, the attitudes, the perception of future risk measures, and the confidence in decision-making scales. Because of concerns about power due to the small sample size, particularly at the gender-specific level, Wilcoxin signed-ranks tests also were used to test pre-post differences. These analyses yielded similar results. Women's knowledge increased significantly from baseline to posttest, and men's confidence in sexual decision making decreased significantly. Though no other differences were statistically significant, the responses to open-ended questions showed that participants had a more realistic understanding of protective options available to them, and while men declined in certainty about sexual decision making, women's qualitative responses suggested greater capacity and assuredness in ability to negotiate sexual decision making with male partners (Nastasi et al. 1998).

This case example highlights some of the most important aspects of a case study approach. It utilizes a pre-post assessment; it is situated in the community with support of people active in that same community who can provide information on whether other educational programs might have influenced the outcomes (in this case, they did not). The measures are based on culturally appropriate items identified in formative research, and the same formative research provided the basis for culturally relevant content material delivered in a culturally appropriate way. The process evaluation included both satisfaction and fidelity measures, both of which were qualitative and quantitative. Further qualitative materials from the sessions provided support to the quantitative outcomes and, at the same time, illustrated trends in the desired direction, even though the results were not statistically significant. It is important to realize that the ethnographic methods used in this evaluation were in no way contradictory to the use of quantitative methods and statistical tests; their use, in fact, made a strong mixed methods approach possible and provided the crucial information needed.

The next example describes a case study with a pre-post quantitative and clinical assessment, as well as measures that derived from prior ethnographic work with the study population.

EXAMPLE: 7.3

A CASE STUDY OF AN INTERVENTION TO IMPROVE ORAL HEALTH HYGIENE BEHAVIORS IN OLDER ADULTS IN SENIOR HOUSING

In 2010–2011, ICR mounted an intervention focused on improving oral health hygiene behaviors among a diverse group of older adults living in senior housing. The project was conducted in partnership with the management and the residents of senior housing in a community in the central part of Connecticut and the Oral Health Research Strategic Alliance (OHRSA), a coalition of community and state-based advocates for older adult oral health and oral health research. The intervention was focused on feasibility (Could ICR do it?), acceptability (Did the residents like it and want to participate in it?), and efficacy (Could it have the desired effects?). As a bilevel intervention, it involved one-on-one interaction of prevention educators from the community and residents, to help the latter improve their oral health, and a building-level campaign to change oral health norms to favor discussing oral health, brushing, flossing, and seeing the dentist if necessary. The study was conducted in a typical low-income senior building of about 224 apartment units in a town in central Connecticut.

The rigorous research design included a set of clear instructions for interventions at both individual and building levels, evaluation strategies to assess intervention fidelity or faithfulness to the original design, and a pre-post assessment to determine whether the face-to-face intervention and the campaign together had an effect on the oral health of those who volunteered for the intervention. Participants were recruited into the program and either decided to participate in the entire intervention or only the survey. A total of eighty-four residents participated overall in both the pre- and the post-survey, and twenty-nine participated in the intervention. Those in the intervention group also underwent a pre- and post-intervention clinical assessment. The survey-only group constituted a comparison for those who participated in the intervention, but given limitations in resources, they did not get a pre-post clinical assessment. Participants received fifteen dollars for the time they spent completing the survey.

Research staff documented participant needs for improvement of their oral health based on cutoff points for scores on the main intervention domains assessed in the baseline survey. Participants discussed their concerns with the interventionists, and interventionists pointed out their needs as reflected on the survey. Interventionists then recorded the messages they delivered to the participants, showed them the results of the clinical assessment, and instructed them on proper tooth brushing and flossing. Subsequently, they worked with the participants to create an oral health improvement plan. Participants received a copy and a copy was retained for their file. The process evaluation utilized forms to document how the intervention was tailored to individual needs and recorded improvement of skills in tooth brushing and flossing on a mastery assessment consisting of two four-point Likert scores for brushing and flossing teeth. The outcome evaluation assessed cognition and reported behavior, gingival index (GI), and plaque scores (PS) at the beginning and end of the intervention. The results showed very significant improvements in GI and PS in the intervention group from baseline to post-assessment.

This study did not have a randomized control group with "no treatment." It did have a group of voluntary participants who took the pre-post survey but who did not participate in the intervention or the pre-post clinical assessment. Because a clinical assessment with the survey group was beyond the resources of the pilot study, no clinical outcome comparison was possible. However the no-treatment group could be compared to the treatment group on cognitive behavioral predictors. This comparison showed that the intervention group did better on several of these predictors—most specifically on reducing oral health hygiene worries and fears—both scales that were generated based on formative research with the study population. In a final feedback session, all participants and other residents were invited to hear about the results. Subsequently each intervention participant received personal feedback on changes in their PS and GI scores, which almost universally had improved. In in-depth interviews conducted after the study was over, participants expressed a high level of satisfaction with the intervention. Members of the campaign committee then participated in oral health advocacy events statewide and produced the script for an oral health film.

This case study described the fiscal realities that many evaluations end up experiencing in the field. It also shows mixed methods research in action: how the study survey was used to shape the tailored intervention, and how the intervention produced data to evaluate acceptability and approach fidelity with tailoring. It illustrates how an internal comparison can be identified and utilized to help to show outcomes, and how results can be delivered to the intervention group as a whole and to individuals when the study is complete.

These examples show how an effective pre-post design generally is accompanied by extensive ethnographic and other forms of documentation between comparative time points in order to understand the process of moving from one point to another. Ethnographic documentation shows how the sequence of events and activities in the intervention setting show likely causality—that is, which intervention activities lead to the endpoint and how other factors in the setting might contribute to, or detract from or interfere with, desired outcomes.

In some cases, evaluative measures are taken throughout the life of the program. In the single-community study mentioned earlier that engaged women in an intervention to reduce marital conflict and associated sexual risk taking of the husband, a norms survey was administered at three different time points to different samples to assess whether gender norms were becoming more equitable in the general population. The gender norms scale, based on twenty-nine culturally generated items indicating perception of gender equality, was administered to imams associated with local mosques who were involved in delivering gender-equitable messages to men, to NGO staff working with women, and to community males and females at large. The gender-norms survey showed that men and imams had made the greatest progress toward gender equitable beliefs and perceptions; that NGO staffs tended toward support of gender equity and support remained high, and that women improved in their feelings about gender equity, but not very much, suggesting that the community intervention impacted males more than females. Females, by contrast, were affected more dramatically by a face-to-face counseling intervention.

Similarly, the West Hartford, Connecticut, Substance Abuse Prevention Commission (SAPC) generated a survey in 2005 to assess substance use by high school students. The survey drew on national instruments for measuring substance-use patterns, perceptions of risk, and peer norms, as well as some local unique features. Since that time, the survey has been administered to more than 2,500 high school students every two years, and it will continue to be administered. It serves as a time series assessment of changes in these key variables over time. Since 2010, a group of action researchers from ICR has been working with youth and the SAPC to introduce materials, products, and processes that divert teens from underage drinking and binge drinking. These surveys serve as a means of evaluating this long-range intervention strategy, showing stable trends in marijuana use, a downward trend in thirty-day alcohol use, an increase in age of initiation, and an increase in diverted prescription drug use.

Diffusion studies can use similar models to evaluate the "reach" of an intervention delivered by people to others like themselves in their personal networks, who in turn, deliver the intervention to still others. One way of evaluating these diffusion interventions is to track the individuals in networks to see how those at the farthest reaches from the start point (or seed) are thinking or acting. This requires developing a system in which those participating can be tracked. Tracking peer deliverers and receivers of an intervention in this way can only reach as far as an end point (usually no more than six or seven "nodes," or persons at a distance out from the seed). A pre-post survey in the general population of people "like those" to be reached can assess to what extent the intervention has gone beyond the known boundaries of the intervention network. One example is the so-called RAP study conducted by Dr. Weeks and colleagues (Weeks et al. 2009) in conjunction with a group of peer health advocates (PHAs). The study identified drug users who were willing to act as educators in their networks. These users together developed an educational approach to prevent drug users from contracting HIV sexually, as well as through unclean needles, syringes, and other materials used to inject drugs in risky community settings. These users reached members of their networks, who then were asked to reach others in their own networks. Of course, networks varied considerably in size; some ended with the advocate alone while other users had extensive networks. Cross-sectional surveys before and at the end of the intervention period showed that many people actually had come in contact with peer advocates who were not part of the original network intervention, and reported changing their behavior as a result. The pre-post assessment showed that the reach of the intervention was far beyond those trained and beyond the people they approached.

Comparative Designs

Comparative designs always involve at least one intervention group and one control, or comparison, group, but they may be much larger. As Table 7.3 shows, some comparative designs involve matched comparisons where the units are "matched" by a set of criteria considered to be important to hold constant across the groups rather than looking for differences across the groups. Such criteria might be size, age, and education level in an after-school program. For example, in a comparison of teens with ADHD, matching might involve setting up two groups, both of whose members are ages sixteen to eighteen. Crossover designs are useful when it would be unethical or culturally inappropriate to ask one group to hold back and receive no benefits while other groups participate in an attractive effort. A **crossover design** is one in which one group or groups is the intervention and the second is the control. The second is the comparison for the first in short-term outcomes. The second then becomes the intervention group and can be compared to the first post-intervention to see how they differ, against itself or both. Thus, both groups eventually receive the intervention and any benefits it offers. These crossover designs are often used in school or publically funded apartment building studies because they eventually include everyone, something required in the public sector.

Definition: A crossover design is one in which one group or groups is the intervention and the second is the control. The second is the comparison for the first in short-term outcomes. The second then becomes the intervention group and can be compared to the first post-intervention to see how they differ, against itself or both

TABLE 7.3 Comparative designs (two cases or more)

Type of Design X = intervention 0 = evaluation	Subtype	Description	Methods	Example
0 X 0 0 0	Pre-post comparative design, units matched	One group is matched against a second by background characteristics; one receives intervention the other does not	Mixed methods, to measure process/ outcomes, especially to describe differences between matched groups	In an evaluation of effects of Youth Action Research two groups recruited in 3 cohorts and matched by age and ethnicity were compared.
	Case control design	One group is matched against a second based on whether they do or do not share the characteristic	Those with condition and without are identified and compared to explain the difference	Those who failed 9th grade are compared with those who passed, to identify what factors might account for the difference.
0 X 0 0 0 X 0 0 0 0 X 0	Crossover design	One group received intervention and other acts as control. Control receives intervention next. Both interventions are compared against the control (no intervention)	Mixed methods to evaluate process and outcomes. Context must be assessed to reassure that there are no significant differences between the first intervention and second	In an evaluation of an youth campaign intervention in three cities, the second received the intervention after the first post-assessment, and the third received the intervention after the second post-assessment.
0 X 0 0 Y 0 0 0	Pre-post design comparing 2 different interventions against a control	Two matched groups get different interventions against the third, a control	Mixed methods. Documentation accounts for migration of intervention	In an evaluation of culturally appropriate HIV intervention African American and Latino culturally framed interventions in different sites were compared against a third, the "standard."

(*continued*)

TABLE 7.3 *Continued*

Type of Design X = intervention 0 = evaluation	Subtype	Description	Methods	Example
R 0 X 0 R 0 0 R 0 X 0 0 R 0 Y 0 0 R 0 0 0	Pre-post comparative design with randomization (R = randomization)	Two or more groups randomized to treatment/ action and no-action comparison	Mixed methods, for fidelity/ deviation of implementation; survey outcome measures	In an evaluation of married couples' capacity to negotiate, women were randomized into counseling women; counseling couples and standard treatment and outcomes evaluated against the standard "control" couples.

Some designs often referred to as the "gold standard" of evaluation research involve random assignment of units (people, villages, schools) to one condition (intervention situation) versus another or a "control" group (no intervention or business as usual). The randomization process is believed to ensure equal distribution of factors that might bias or influence the outcomes in an unpredictable or undesirable way. Many researchers now recognize that the so-called randomized controlled trial design (RCT) is not suitable under many community or institutional conditions—for example, when people do not wish to be individualized and assigned to one group versus another, when randomization is not culturally understood or acceptable, or when randomization deprives the control group of services that they need or that are legally mandated. In the United States, evaluation of public school reading programs for students whose language is not English cannot ethically include a group that receives no reading instruction at all because such instruction is required by law for all students. The earlier mentioned comparative designs, which pay careful attention to context and process, are now thought to produce equally valid and

reliable evidence in an evaluation, while conforming to ethical standards required by IRBs.

Using Table 7.2, as a reference, several examples can illustrate how these evaluation designs work.

EXAMPLE 7.4

A PRE-POST MATCHED TREATMENT AND CONTROL GROUP DESIGN TO EVALUATE THE EFFICACY OF AN INTERVENTION TO IMPROVE FLU VACCINATION ACCEPTANCE

Influenza is a global problem and a major cause of preventable morbidity and mortality in the United States. It accounts for roughly fifty thousand deaths annually in the United States alone. Ninety percent of these deaths occur among the elderly and most are cardiovascular related (Thompson et al. 2003). Influenza vaccination contributes to reductions in all-cause mortality (Fiscella et al. 2007). Vaccination confers many health benefits, including reductions in acute respiratory illnesses and associated physician visits (Voordouw et al. 2003), fewer exacerbations of congestive heart failure, and fewer heart attacks, strokes, and permanent health problems. While vaccination rates are increasing overall because of more widespread availability and accessibility of the flu vaccine, they are not increasing among older adults, especially older adults of color (Thompson et al. 2004). African Americans and Hispanics consistently report lower rates of influenza vaccination than non-Hispanic whites. For example, in 2004, only 46 percent of elderly African Americans and 55 percent of Hispanics reported receiving the vaccine, compared to 67 percent of non-Hispanic whites. In 2012, the rates had hardly changed (CDC 2013); The current and past rates are well below the approximately 70 percent required to create "herd" or overall immunity for older adults residing in vulnerable communities, or the 90 percent called for by the U.S. surgeon general in 2010.

In the mid-2000s, a strategic alliance of organizations including the state of Connecticut, the Visiting Nurse Health Care program, the UCONN Center on Aging, the Institute for Community Research, and the Hartford Housing Authority mounted an effort to improve vaccine uptake among reluctant residents in senior housing buildings. ICR, with its history of work in residences for older adults, approached two diverse buildings that were part of the Hartford Housing Authority. They were similar in size and roughly similar in population, and ICR had conducted research and programming in them in the past. Building managers, service coordinators, and the tenants' associations were asked to participate in partnership arrangements. The buildings were matched in population size and composition and randomly assigned to treatment and comparison categories. Approximately eighty people were interviewed with cross-sectional surveys in both buildings. The surveys included questions about the perceived risk associated with vaccination, past vaccinations, social influence and vaccination support, beliefs about benefits of vaccination, and history of health problems. An intervention in the treatment building was implemented by residents, who developed and facilitated bilingual pro-vaccination campaigns and vaccination delivery on site. A repeat cross-sectional survey was administered about two months after the program concluded. This survey asked whether the respondents had been vaccinated that year, if they received their vaccination at flu fairs, and whether they had attended the fairs. Rates of vaccination improved significantly in the treatment building in comparison to the control building, and especially with respect to Latinos (Schensul et al. 2009).

This design illustrates a typical quasi-experimental pre-post evaluation design with matched buildings, plus an assessment in each building prior to and after the intervention was implemented. In this case, the buildings were randomized to avoid possible accidental selection for the intervention of a building with the lowest pre-implementation level of vaccination. In such a building, the intervention might appear to be more effective, even with a slight increase, than in a building where levels of vaccination already were 60 percent or above. Also, to expedite the IRB review process, the study obtained data from individuals anonymously and used verbal consents for participation in the survey. This made it possible to avoid IRB delays and to initiate the study quickly, but it meant that researchers could not obtain repeat data from the same individuals they had interviewed at baseline. Thus, the evaluation showed overall improvement in vaccination rates, but because the team could not match respondents, they could not show which individuals were the ones who showed improvement. They were, however, able to match respondents by apartment number and to carry out a comparison of changes by individual (a more accurate way of evaluating change) as well as overall. Results showed that the results for both groups were identical; there was no statistical difference between the two samples. But without written permission from respondents, they could only report on changes in the overall sample, not by individuals. This was a limitation of the study.

EXAMPLE 7.5

A PRE-POST MATCHED TREATMENT AND CONTROL GROUP DESIGN WITH DIFFERENT COHORTS AND FOUR TIME POINTS

This four-year federally funded project carried out by PAR researchers with youth in Hartford evaluated whether participatory action research with teens on substance abuse–related topics could make a difference in their substance use patterns, their feelings of school attachment, and their collective efficacy (perceived ability to work together to carry out important tasks to successful completion). The program was carried out after school several days a week over a school year, at the Institute for Community Research and included three cycles of approximately thirty youths each. Youths in the intervention group were recruited from local after-school programs and through youth networks. The youth could not be randomized into the PAR program or another program because they self-selected into programs based on their preferences—an administrative enrollment process over which the study leaders had no control. So ICR contracted with a partner organization in the Boston area to recruit youth from Springfield as a matched control group. This worked well in the first year. In the second year, recruitment shifted to Hartford youth and a matched control group was recruited after the program group was engaged. Youth were matched by age, grade level, and racial/ethnic self-identity.

The youth were given a survey with questions derived from a national risk assessment and scales developed through prior work with other youth. This survey was required by the funding agency. The survey was administered four times to each cycle or cohort—both the program and the control group youth—before, at midpoint, after the program was over, and six months later. Youth in each cycle thus received four assessments. The data from the treatment and control groups were pooled across cycles. The analysis first compared the treatment and control groups at baseline to identify any significant differences that could affect outcomes. Each cohort was compared with the others to make sure that there was comparability at baseline of all treatment groups and all control groups. After completing that task, the two groups overall were compared on the most important outcomes.

This intervention had several components. First, the youth decided on and modeled a project conceptually. Then they collected and analyzed the data and presented it to the public. Finally, they used the data to take actions to change policy. In this case, the youth in all three groups worked to change policies related to the funding of summer and year-round work opportunities for teens. The results were positive for knowledge and school attachment; the treatment group overall scored higher than the control group. For substance use, youth in the treatment group increased their use at time 3 (T3) and reported reductions in use at the fourth, or final, time point. We interpreted the increase at T3 as a function of participant trust that led to more accurate reporting, and the decrease at T4 as a function of real reductions in marijuana and alcohol use. Finally, collective feelings of efficacy increased at T4 for the treatment group, a response to their capacity to improve funding for summer and year-round youth employment (Berg, Coman, and Schensul 2009).

This design illustrated another quasi-experimental matching process, one in which treatment and comparison individuals were matched and multiple postmeasures were taken to show trends or changes in the primary outcome variables over time. Challenges included recruiting and retaining the participants, especially those in the control group. Even with incentives, it took considerable effort to engage them in repeat surveys. To cope with disinterest and to make sure that the youth understood the questions, the project held "survey parties." At the parties, surveys were read to a group of participants in English or Spanish while they filled in the responses. Other staff supervised to make sure that no one was copying the others' answers. At the end, they had pizza and cake and played music. Sometimes parents came. Participants received a modest incentive for each survey they completed (ten dollars). The design also called for an elaborate process of documenting and scoring facilitation techniques and youth responses to ensure acceptability, social validity, and comparability of evaluation process.

This approach, like the one in Example 7.4, uses a quasi-experimental design, but it matches individuals rather than buildings or schools. Like the first, it involved a program and a comparison group, but unlike the first, the program was offered in three separate cycles. Working with cycles of youth was necessary because of staff and space limitations, the time required to mentor each youth, and the labor-intensive PAR approach. For both reasons, close attention was paid to comparability of membership in each of the groups. Comparability on key dimensions is required to make sure that no antecedent bias, such as big age or grade differences, might affect either the intervention process or outcomes. Unlike the previous example, this project took observations or measures at four time points and matched the youth. Thus, the evaluation could examine how the program was affecting each individual young person as well as how it was affecting the youth as a group. It could also determine how the program affected the youth at each point in time, during, and after it was over. The ability to measure changes over time is an important aspect of

any evaluation because we know that some changes do not occur immediately, especially in counseling and substance abuse prevention work.

The next few designs illustrate the many different ways that comparisons can be set up in community settings. Example 7.6 compares two different interventions against a nonintervention group.

 **EXAMPLE 7.6**

A PRE POST MATCHED DESIGN COMPARING TWO DIFFERENT INTERVENTIONS AGAINST A CONTROL

Public housing sites in a large southern city are being refurbished by a development company that is introducing environmental changes conducive to outside activities and exercise. All buildings will receive these modifications (tennis courts, grassy parks, walking trails, and swimming pools). The residents of these buildings are African American and Latino, and many suffer from type 2 diabetes. Researchers are comparing the outcomes of an individually tailored diabetes lifestyle improvement intervention against a group intervention with some of the same content. Multiple buildings will be randomized into individual- and group-intervention buildings. In addition to evaluating whether one approach is better than another in helping women to manage their diabetes through diet and exercise, the design will assess whether women in the interventions are using the new outside facilities more than women in the control buildings, which experience no interventions.

 **EXAMPLE 7.7**

A CROSSOVER DESIGN COMPARING THE RESULTS OF AN INTERVENTION ACROSS THREE CITIES SEQUENTIALLY: XPERIENCE

Xperience was a three-year communications intervention based on the principles of "edutainment" and youth-driven prevention messaging. The intervention involved the formation of youth prevention groups that were interested in improving their artistic skills and delivering prevention messages around marijuana and alcohol through performance. Youth were recruited and assisted by experienced artists to develop spoken-word, rap, dance, and other musical performance skills and to write or design their own works of art. Other youth developed graphics and marketing to reach a broad audience of youth and adults. Performances were recorded in a professional sound studio and CDs were given to audiences along with program T-shirts and other callouts and giveaways at CD release shows. The comparative study design called for intervention in three cities sequentially, with one city serving as the comparison for the others and all cities eventually getting the intervention. The evaluation was based on assessing changes in substance use norms and perceived harm and was to be administered in the form of a survey in all cities at the same time. All cities thus were to respond to surveys at baseline, at post–first city, post–second city, and post–third city.

This design was creative but very costly to implement. Thus the intervention was perfected in three cycles in one city instead of three, and youth, their networks and an independent group of afterschool youth were evaluated after each CD release show. The shows were wildly successful and attended by hundreds of youths and parents. Many had to be turned away at the door. Xperience showed both the energy and enthusiasm created by involving youth in the development of prevention messages through art. But it also showed the challenges and human and financial costs of doing broad-based surveys to gauge exposure and changes in substance use norms and perceptions. The best designed evaluations cannot be conducted without sufficient resources, so evaluators and intervention designers must be careful not to make promises they cannot keep.

There have been many questions raised about the feasibility and ethics of randomizing individuals into program and comparison groups in a community setting because randomization with a control or comparison group ends up depriving the control group of whatever benefits the intervention might bring. The next example shows how individuals can be randomized to different intervention groups in a community environment.

EXAMPLE 7.8

RANDOMIZING INDIVIDUALS IN A CONTROLLED TRIAL IN A COMMUNITY SETTING

Women in a low-income, predominantly Muslim community in Mumbai were offered a culturally based counseling intervention to address their *tenshun,* or emotional consequences of life stresses and marital conflict. The intervention offered two alternatives: a multisession individual counseling intervention and an intervention for couples in which the men and women attended four sessions separately and then joined together for the last two sessions. Women who came in with white discharge, a symptom of life stress or *tenshun* that had no biological basis in infection, were recruited into the program. If they were willing to join, they all received a physical exam and were asked if they were willing to be randomized into one or the other of the interventions. Almost all women who were able and willing to join agreed. Women were then randomized into either the treatment groups or a treatment as usual (visit with doctor and prescription) group. These groups were compared to see which of the two interventions was more effective in reducing marital conflict and improving communication and marital intimacy. All participants were assessed at three time points, before and after the intervention, and approximately six months later. Both the individual and the group intervention were effective, and the evaluation found that attendance at even a small number of sessions made a difference in outcome. No problems arose as a result of the randomization process because all service personnel agreed to its importance and were involved in making sure it happened and all women received some form of treatment.

In our final example, we illustrate a group, randomized, quasi-experimental trial design in which schools are randomized. This design could apply to villages as well, such as those in which Sorensen and colleagues conducted their study in India, with teachers serving as role models for quitting smokeless tobacco use.

   **EXAMPLE 7.9**

A GROUP RANDOMIZED TRIAL DESIGN IN MULTIPLE SCHOOLS

In this case, twelve middle schools in a central Connecticut city were matched and randomized. Through a prevention intervention program, we rewrote a social development curriculum to shift from individual self-management to the creation of group norms for social problem solving, managing interpersonal conflict, substance use, and AIDS risk. The program was implemented in half of the schools by training and coaching teachers. Curriculum components were evaluated qualitatively by documenting classroom processes and coaching, and by collecting information from workbooks and discussion sessions with students. Outcomes were evaluated with the use of an instrument already in use by the school district to measure trends in these variables; it was administered to all eighth-grade, tenth-grade, and twelfth-grade classes. This instrument allowed analysts to compare across classrooms, schools, and grades and to even to match many of the students so as to compare their changes in measures of concern over a two-year period, from eighth to tenth grade.

Alternative Designs

Definition:
A "segmented
linear," or
factorial, design
tries to disaggregate
and separate the
components of a
larger intervention
and measure their
separate effects on
a desired outcome.
An "interactive
systemic" design
views a community
or system such as a
school as bounded and
consisting of multiple
interconnected
subsystems in
constant interaction,
sometimes in favor
of and sometimes in
opposition to desired
change, with resultant
emergent and
often unpredictable
outcomes

The term used here—*alternative designs*, shown in Table 7.4—refers to one of two optional directions in evaluation: evaluating the individual contributions of components of a more comprehensive intervention at one point in time, or showing the effects of a systemic intervention by modeling or projecting alternative outcomes *over time*. Each of these approaches can be said to represent a different view of the world: the first can be described as "segmented linear" and is often referred to as a *factorial design*. Factorial designs are associated with complex interventions. The second can be referred to as an *interactive systemic* design. A "**segmented linear**," or factorial, design tries to disaggregate and separate the components of a larger intervention and measure their separate effects on a desired outcome. This is the approach that Ann Bruce's study of MESA, in Example 7.1, could have taken (Bruce 2005). An "**interactive systemic**" design views a community or system such as a school as bounded and consisting of multiple interconnected subsystems in constant interaction, sometimes in favor of and sometimes in opposition to desired change, with resultant emergent and often unpredictable outcomes. In a segmented linear, or factorial, intervention, the "package" of elements has had a positive effect on desired outcomes, and the researcher wants to know whether some or all of the elements in combination have the best effect on an outcome (table 7.4, first example). In another version (table 7.4, second example), the researcher wants to determine which elements in a complex intervention are likely to have more impact separately or packaged. Thus, the intervention is unpacked—that is, the key elements believed to be important in leading to outcomes are identified. Identification is facilitated by the development of a prior formative and predictive model informed by theory. These elements then are evaluated against each other and/or against a control situation to see which has the best outcome.

Cross Reference:
See Book 2, chapters 4 and 5

TABLE 7.4 Alternative comparative designs

Type of Design X, Y, Z = action 0 = evaluation	Subtype	Description	Methods	Example
0 X 0 Y 0 0 Y 0 X 0	Comparing components and sequencing	Intervention components sequenced differently and outcomes measured at first and second time points	Mixed methods with quantitative outcome measures	An intervention to improve oral health in older adults has two components: face to face and campaign. Design considers differential effects of each, and whether long-term effects of differences in sequencing matter
0 X 0 Y 0 Z 0 0 Z 0 X 0 Y 0 0 Y 0 Z 0 X 0 0 0 0 XYZ 0 0 0 0 0	Comparing components and sequencing	Three intervention components sequenced differently; the fourth packaged, assessed against a control	Mixed methods with quantitative outcome measures	An intervention to assess relative contribution of three different interventions to improve HIV adherence, sequenced differently, against a "packaged" comparison and control
System dynamics (SD) designs	Examining how factors intersect in feedback loops and with time lags to model long-range outcomes	Building an SD model with trend data and hypothesizing or showing how interventions can change long-range outcome predictions	Mixed methods and secondary data showing trend lines or reference modes	Modeling alternative interventions to assess their outcomes; introducing multiple interventions to change long-term outcomes

In segmented linear or factorial designs, it is important to specify in advance what the constituent components of a multifaceted intervention are and how they are theoretically driven. What makes the first two designs in Table 7.4 alternative designs is that in addition to comparing the core elements at post-assessment, they are sequenced differently. The reason for this is to see whether the cumulative effect varies if the elements are sequenced in different ways. Sequenced designs allow for comparing each component against the other, and for examining the ways in which the different elements interact to influence the outcomes differently over time. In addition, the second design in Table 7.4 also compares three different forms of sequencing to a "basket" or packaged approach in which all components are introduced at the same time. This design allows for a comparison of the effects of each of the three main components of the intervention separately and in different sequences, against all of them together, as well as a treatment-as-usual control group. While most of the case study designs and many of the comparative designs can be conducted in a natural environment, stacked designs require a lot of staging and good management of many moving parts, especially if the components operate at different "levels" in a system.

In the following we describe an example of Table 7.4, Design 1 and Design 2.

EXAMPLE 7.10

GOOD ORAL HEALTH, A BI-LEVEL INTERVENTION USING A "STACKED" FACTORIAL DESIGN (DESIGN 1)

In its pilot phase, Good Oral Health, an NIH-funded participatory intervention trial with older adults in senior housing, combined a local campaign (two resident-driven oral health fairs emphasizing oral health and hygiene knowledge, reduction of oral health fears and worries, and skills practice) with a one-on-one intervention based on motivational interviewing, tailored to individual knowledge gaps, concerns, and skills development. The intervention had very positive outcomes, showing significant across-the-board improvements in plaque removal and in the status of the gums around the teeth as well as in promising declines in oral health worries and fears—the key predictor of skills improvement. Because the intervention was packaged (campaign plus face to-face-intervention, administered simultaneously) and the sample size was small (only twenty-seven people in the intervention overall), we could not separate out the effects of the campaign from those of the face-to-face intervention.

In the larger study, we wanted to address which intervention—the campaign or the face-to-face intervention—was most effective. So we created a design that allowed us to compare the campaign (fairs) against the face-to-face intervention. At the same time, though we had strong reason to believe that each of the components was significant in producing positive outcomes, we did not know whether the order of introduction of the components would make a difference. Would the tailored intervention, if conducted first, bring more people to the campaign, which would then reinforce the results of the face-to-face session? Or would the campaign, if conducted first, build the basis for greater receptivity to the face-to-face intervention by reducing fears and worries? Which of the two would create an environment of support for sustainability of personal behaviors?

The evaluation included the following:

1. Initial assessments (a clinical assessment of oral health status; an assessment of tooth brushing and flossing skills, and a knowledge, fears, and oral dental behavior survey) administered before any activity, after the first component (to compare components against each other), after the second component (to evaluate the short-term effects of different sequencing of components), and six months later (to evaluate sustainability).
2. Fidelity checks by collecting copies of materials used during the tailored intervention and a "passport." This card lists all campaign activities and exhibits. Each participant receives one, and attendance at each exhibit or event is stamped in the passport. In this way, exposure to different campaign activities could be calculated for each attendee.
3. Audio recording of the face-to-face intervention (for fidelity and self-correction and for future research on the process of the intervention).

The following example shows how a similar design used a similar type of comparison to examine the differential effects of three interventions conducted separately and sequenced differently against all three of the interventions conducted at the same time and a control group that received only standard treatment until the very end.

EXAMPLE 7.11

IMPROVING MEDICATION ADHERENCE AMONG MEN LIVING WITH HIV IN INDIA USING A "STACKED" FACTORIAL DESIGN WITH A "BASKET" COMPARISON (DESIGN 2)

Many years of prior research on HIV and alcohol consumption in low-income communities of Mumbai produced several useful approaches to intervention in local health care and community settings. These interventions were offered at the individual, group, and community level. Individual and group interventions used a motivational interviewing counseling approach based on co-construction of knowledge and interactive exercises; the community-level interventions consisted of delivering messages intended to promote gender-equitable norms by specifying the value of open communication, mutual support between married men and women, and men's concerns about women's health and well-being. The interventions targeted alcohol consumption as an undesirable means of coping with stress or *tenshun*. Alcohol research results showing links between drinking and risky sexual behavior were disseminated, spreading harm-reduction messages through street dramas in study communities. These general approaches were integrated into a study to reduce alcohol consumption among men taking HIV medication.

The Indian government requires that men obtain HIV medication from government clinics. The clinics include counselors whose role is to review adherence and provide brief counseling. The counseling model does not include concerns about alcohol as a contributor to nonadherence. The clinics also include case coordinators who are available to conduct group interventions; clinics also are linked to government service centers that offer outreach capacity to try to bring people who are not adherent to the clinic to pick up their medication monthly.

The alcohol and antiretroviral (ART) adherence study design calls for collaboration with clinics and patient advocacy organizations to participate in the development and implementation of an (1) individual- and a (2) group-counseling intervention and, as well, to work with NGOs to deliver a (3) community-level intervention. Based on formative interviews and surveys with similar men, the individual and group interventions must address alcohol and medication adherence, but can do so by asking about other known concerns, for example, self-stigma because of HIV status, shame and fear of disclosure, depression because of infection, managing interpersonal relationships so as not to disclose HIV status, and maintaining medication adherence. The group intervention also focuses on healthy lifestyles, disclosure practices, and internal stigma; the community intervention focuses on reducing stigma associated with HIV. The design calls for working with five centers. The centers are randomized into five conditions: individual first, community first, group first, one-time packaged intervention, and treatment as usual. Four of the centers receive all three interventions in different ways; the fifth will receive the package after the study is completed.

The study is a panel study, which follows a group of 188 men from each center throughout the life of the project. A **panel study** follows the same group of people and assesses them at different points in time. For the outcome evaluation, men are assessed before any intervention and, after the first, after the second, and after the third intervention. A process evaluation will assess the individual and group interventions for fidelity and substantive content, using a handheld tablet for the individual intervention and curriculum recording sheets for the group intervention. The community intervention, delivered through outreach workers to local NGO, business, and community cultural settings, will be assessed in a grid that records type of message delivery by type of site by number of encounters. Context will be monitored by research staff and a national list serve (AIDS-INDIA) that document main issues and trends in HIV-related activities, policies, and advocacy efforts around the country. The diagram for this intervention is shown in Figure 7.2.

Definition: A panel study follows the same group of people and assesses them at different points in time

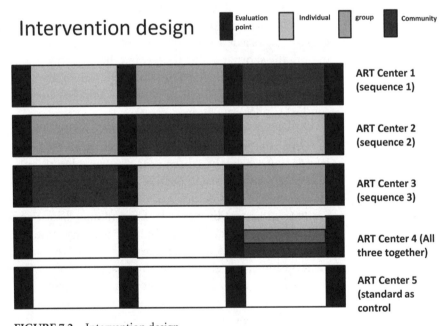

FIGURE 7.2   Intervention design.

System Dynamics Designs

The second general approach to alternative evaluation design is a system dynamics design. System dynamics (SD) approaches are useful in understanding complex problems in which multiple variables interact in an ongoing (dynamic) way over time. We have described SD approaches in chapters 4 and 5. SD approaches are inherently evaluative. They tend to be introduced when a problem is complex and intransigent, when a "system" is the focus of the examination, and when there is widespread agreement that prior or initial efforts to address the so-called cause or causes of the problem have not been effective in solving it. As Metcalf and colleagues have noted, **system dynamics is concerned with the identification and modeling of feedback relationships and delays that characterize a particular problem.** By linking the structure of complex systems to their behavior over time, system dynamics modeling helps policy makers assess the impact of different interventions in both the short and long term (Metcalf, Northridge, and Lamster 2011, 1821). Modeling also helps community partners in a community-based participatory modeling exercise conduct similar evaluations.

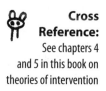

Cross Reference:
See chapters 4 and 5 in this book on theories of intervention

Key point

Key point

Modeling involves the identification of feedback loops that link components of a system around a specific problem. SD approaches have been used to address health, substance use, and business, industrial, and military problems. One case in point is dental health. In older adults, dental health (tooth retention and lack of periodontal disease and tooth decay) is affected by the ability or inability to obtain proper dental care (dental care access, insurance/reimbursement options); it is also affected by a variety of other factors, including other chronic illnesses such as diabetes and cardiovascular disease, multiple medications, physical disability, cognitive impairment, and social isolation. Further, knowledge of, access to, and ability to prepare high-quality foods, as well as transportation to community activities also can affect oral health. These factors can be considered separately, but once recognized, it is clear that they all interact in ways that may reinforce or undermine oral health status over time. Metcalf and colleagues note that different components or subsystems intersect during the aging process: (a) chronic illness, (b) quality of nutrition, (c) oral health promotion, and (d) social support.

They argue that chronic illness interacts inversely or negatively with oral health, that is, with increasing chronic illness, oral health declines and its decline further contributes to the exacerbation of chronic health conditions. A reinforcing feedback loop shows that healthy food choices improve nutrition, which improves cognition, which in turn contributes to healthy food choices. Negative loops can interact with positive loops so as to undermine positive results: as oral health deteriorates, it may have a negative effect on cognition, which in turn could deteriorate over time, interrupting the positive feedback loop that links cognition to healthy eating and good food choices. Real-world data provide the basis for understanding subsystems and how they interact over time. Baseline models can be used to estimate the range of variation in the variables, and the strength of relationships among the variables is estimated with functions. Together, these calculations estimate changes in the outcome variables (oral health, tobacco use, etc.) over time. The original models with estimations serve as baseline assessments against which interventions such as new additions to the system or components that modify existing variables, for example, increasing food accessibility and availability through local community gardens, plus work in those gardens, which also improves chronic health conditions, can be evaluated. These models, which are fundamentally ethnographic, allow researchers and their partners to see communities or any bounded "systems" holistically and to evaluate or predict in advance, and then in real time, how changes affect population health, demographics, and general welfare.

SUMMARY

In this chapter, we have defined *evaluation* as the examination of intervention directions, processes, and actions against a designated or desired outcome. We have noted that some evaluations are not theory driven—that is, that they are intended to "find" the theory or model and relate it either to anticipated or unanticipated outcomes. Many evaluations are required to find promising or significant differences across time points. Anticipated outcomes do occur, and they can be determined to be significant as measured by mean differences between groups experiencing different interventions or conditions. The theories that drive these evaluations are considered to be sufficient to explain why the outcomes occur. However, *how* and *why* the outcomes occur, above and beyond the intervention theory, are important to consider. And the links between the beginning and the end state are not very well understood and they may not match the theories of implementation

Throughout, we have tried to show that the typical evaluation designs require documentation of what actually happens between "baseline" or pre-intervention circumstances and subsequent consequences. ***Understanding the "process" of an intervention, especially a complex one, requires systematic ethnography—planned attendance at important events, interviews, collection of small "satisfaction" or other types of surveys, photographic documentation—and many other means of recording both the process and the context of the activities as well as the responses of individual "units" (persons, classrooms, alliances, clinics, etc.) involved in the venture.*** It also is more and more expected that interventions will collect both *acceptability* and *fidelity* data. Acceptability data record whether those involved are interested and engaged—if and how much they care about the intervention. Fidelity data record whether the intervention was implemented as planned and whether the implementation was consistent across administrations. This may not be relevant to one-time interventions. However, in community development efforts, or programs such as Xperience or the town hall meetings held to dialogue about substance abuse prevention in West Hartford, there often is a "script," protocol, plan, or blueprint for intervention that should and can be followed. The degree to which consistency approaching perfection in implementation is required is highly variable, depending on the situation and the funder. Usually, the more medicalized the intervention, the more the intervention must be applied consistently across units such as people or clinics.

 Key point

Almost any evaluation can fit into the categories that we have defined. All of the evaluation designs that we have described here call for mixed methods research. As we have described elsewhere in the *Ethnographer's Toolkit* series, we define *mixed methods* as a combination of qualitative, quantified qualitative, and quantitative research. We also argue that ethnography itself always has been a mixed methods design. Mixed methods are useful in preparing for any approach to intervention at the individual, group, community, or broader level. ***Mixed methods are critical in the formative work that improves the measures used, and qualitative research as well as quantification are important in documenting intervention processes and in triangulating intervention outcomes.*** In addition to text based and visual forms of data collection, mixed methods health evaluations often complement survey research with clinical data and biomarkers evaluations. Clinical assessments can include functional ability (ability to walk, move, lift), mental health status (depression, anxiety, *tenshun*/tension), substance abuse (alcohol and drug use), and biomarkers. **Biomarkers** are, like unobtrusive social science measures, indicators of health problems noted through blood, urine, hair samples, and other body tissues and processes.

Key point

Definition: Biomarkers are, like unobtrusive social science measures, indicators of health problems noted through blood, urine, hair samples, and other body tissues and processes

No researcher interested in intervention/action for social, educational, and health change can avoid evaluation. But we can choose what we evaluate, with whom, and in what ways, and best of all, we can partner with others to develop and participate in approaches to change that are most meaningful, to improve what we do and to tell us whether what we are doing is having an effect. In chapter 8, we turn to various ways of sharing the results of our work with different audiences. Evaluation participants and partners are two such audiences, but there are many others—community residents, politicians and policy makers, service organizations, and social media. As a consequence, we consider modes and forms of dissemination, potential audiences, and desired impact.

8

SHARING RESEARCH RESULTS WITH MULTIPLE PUBLICS

INTRODUCTION

In prior chapters of Book 7 of the *Toolkit* and in other books, we have discussed the many steps required in the development and conduct of research in and with communities and other partners. Our conversations have covered the formation of research alliances, approaches to theory development including development of intervention theory, intervention approaches, and ways of analyzing data. In this chapter, we concentrate on methods and approaches for sharing research results with others, and not just with the scientific community through books, conference presentations, and papers in peer-reviewed journals alone. We also are concerned with sharing research results with specifically targeted publics, evaluation recipients, repeat-research audiences, and the public in general.

It is important to distinguish between three main types of research results:

- Results that emerge from "basic research" that answer questions identifying the need for interventions (or more research). These research results should be shared with members of the communities or other institutions that participated in the research, with the public at large, and with actors, activists, newspaper reporters, and policy makers who can utilize the results to improve their policy making.

- Results that emerge from different types of evaluations with multiple stakeholders, each of whom may need different kinds of information.
- Results that emerge from "applied" research that answers questions about how to create transformative changes with individuals, groups, organizations, communities, and policies, especially those changes that remediate injustices and contribute to improving social, economic, health, and legal conditions.

While it may seem that we have implied above that each type of result is designed for a specific audience, in actual fact, all of these results should be shared with members of the communities who participated in the intervention activities and with other publics. This is so that the intervention or other results might be adapted in other settings, or shared with other potential implementers via consultancies, manuals, social media and websites, and technical assistance.

The first section of this chapter focuses on ways of sharing the results of "basic" or formative research. **Formative research** is ethnographic (mixed methods) research that helps to map out dynamics and descriptors of a community or problem, generate information for an initial model, and provide the basis for constructing an intervention in different formats and with different audiences. The second section of the chapter reviews the challenges involved in sharing the results of evaluations with multiple stakeholders—funders, administrators, people who are the beneficiaries or participants in various types of innovations or social and environmental change programs, local residents, school children, policy makers, the media, and many other potential audiences. Here we will review main approaches, and common challenges.

The third section focuses on dissemination and implementation science. These terms, which we define below, refer to sharing information about researched

Definition: Formative research is ethnographic (mixed methods) research that helps to map out the dynamics and descriptors of a community or problem, generate information for an initial model, and provide the basis for constructing an intervention

Definition: Dissemination is the purposive distribution of information and intervention materials to specific audiences. The intent is to spread information about evidence-based interventions

Definition: *Research* on dissemination examines how information on any intervention is created, packaged, transmitted, and interpreted among a variety of stakeholder groups and audiences

Definition: Implementation is the use of strategies to adopt, adapt, and integrate evidence-based interventions so as to transform or change practice patterns within specific settings

Definition: Implementation *science* explores the process through which interventions carried out in one location can be adapted to another, and to what extent such interventions can be integrated into the ongoing life of the new setting

and evaluated interventions with others so that it can be applied together with people/partners in a new setting and reevaluated. In this way, the process through which these research-based intervention approaches are integrated into and implemented in other settings can be studied. **Dissemination** is the purposive distribution of information and intervention materials to specific audiences. The intent is to spread information about evidence-based interventions. *Research* on dissemination examines how information on any intervention is created, packaged, transmitted, and interpreted among a variety of stakeholder groups and audiences.

Implementation is the use of strategies to adopt, adapt, and integrate evidence-based interventions so as to transform or change practice patterns within specific settings. The "evidence" in "evidence based interventions" may consist of any and all credible sources of information that can convince reviewers that the plans enacted have been effective or useful. **Implementation** *science* explores the process through which interventions carried out in one location can be adapted to another, and to what extent such interventions can be integrated into the ongoing life of the new setting.

TAKING RESEARCH RESULTS TO THE PUBLIC: PURPOSES, AUDIENCES, MESSENGERS, AND FORMATS

Ethical considerations in contemporary research call for sharing results with participants (AAA February 2009; Fernandez, Kodish, and Weijer 2003; Fluehr-Lobban 2013). An ethical *requirement* of collaborative research is that research be shared with patients, students, community residents, students, and other partners (Banks et al. 2013; Fernandez 2003; Flicker and Worthington 2011). Community or stakeholder dissemination differs from sharing data through publications because its purpose is not simply to communicate to scholarly audiences. Rather, it is both to inform and to inspire viewers to think, inquire, critique, and even to mobilize them to effect changes in programs, policies, service delivery, or the environment. As Roger Sanjek notes, social science researchers "should" communicate beyond their disciplinary colleagues and to "the public sphere" (Sanjek 2004, 452). The dissemination process should be informative, dialogic, and politically and socially motivated and motivating, and it often can be transformational.

Any effective efforts to share the results of research require consideration of the purposes of the dissemination effort, the audiences who will be the recipients of the information, the types of participants who will engage in discussion about results and their possible uses, which participants will convey the results, and what formats should be used to convey them. Purposes of dissemination include:

- improving knowledge;
- informing communities for whom the research is relevant about the results and engaging them in dialogue;
- convincing the public that research can be useful;
- persuading audiences to take action because of the urgency of the results;
- convincing politicians and policy makers that policies and regulations need to be changed;
- shedding light on historical or current but unknown or unrecognized disparities or injustices, often as a wake-up call to action;
- persuading the news media that the research story is worth promoting through newspaper and television reports and programs.

The first three bullets can be classified under the rubric of "engaged social science"—they rest on conveying important research results and information to a general audience without the requirement that action follow. Roger Sanjek (2004) tells us that there are many ways that research can be shared with public audiences including:

- writing books that can be read by non–social scientists in contemporary language;
- getting the attention of various publics and leaders by sending research results to newspaper editors, television and radio talk shows, book review editors of nonacademic publications, organizational leaders,

government officials and their staffs, and popular magazines;

- appearing on radio and television talk shows;
- testifying at government hearings, commissions, and community-sponsored events;
- acting as a source to reporters;
- serving as an expert witness.

To Sanjek's list, we add

- sending out press releases;
- creating blogs and posting on social media such as YouTube, Twitter, and Facebook;
- engaging with main social and scholarly network sites such as LinkedIn and ResearchGate;
- creating and circulating research briefs or summaries, project newsletters, and policy recommendations.

A brief publication by CARE, a community-based research center at Yale University, provides useful tools and checklists for considering dissemination goals, audience, medium (ways of reaching the audience), and execution. The guide includes tips that are useful when writing materials for dissemination, suggesting that text materials be responsive to the audience, concise, interesting or compelling, logical, directed (that is, with key points highlighted), useful, attractive, and with clear recommendations for action (CARE 2012, 2–3). For dissemination to multiple audiences, an adapted version of the CARE checklist is shown in Table 8.1.

Taking Research Back to the Community Where It Was Done

Beyond outreach to the general public, probably the first and most likely audience for community researchers is the community or institutional setting in which the research has been conducted. The approach that we have taken in this book as well as in others in the *Toolkit* calls for creating partnerships with organizations and with community leaders and change agents. Often these partner-

Cross Reference:
See chapter 3 of this book

TABLE 8.1   Steps to consider in dissemination of research results to the community

Know about the dissemination program	This requires working with partners to identify lists of invitees, and means through which they can be invited including networking, fliers, posters, media
See that it is relevant to their interests	Promotional materials and messages must appeal to community concerns
Make sure key players are encouraged to attend	Invitations should be extended repeatedly and through multiple channels, especially face to face or by phone/cell phone; in some cases transportation may be required; timing maximally convenient
Assure that audiences receive the information in formats that are understandable, enjoyable, believable, and appropriate for the cultural setting	Results can be delivered through animated PPT slides Films made by local people on the results Performances based on interviews and survey results Graphic interpretations of quotations and statistics Formats must be manageable in the setting (e.g., availability of electricity; air-conditioning, fans or outside presentations in extremely hot weather; audibility) (limitations on background noise); formats can include local theaters and street displays
Create opportunities so audiences can engage in questioning, discussion, and dialogue about the findings	Presentations can include questions for audience Create openings for audience questioning Large and small group discussion opportunities Feedback times
Make sure audiences derive benefit from the experience	Through social interaction; incentives (food, music)

Source: Adapted from CARE 2012.

ships take the form of alliances, research advisory boards, or full participatory arrangements. The principles of good partnership require involving partners in all aspects of research, including analysis and assembly of results. Thus, partners are the first and ongoing recipients of research results, presented in formats that are readily understood by study "insiders." However, though the partners may act as planned on the results, they do not always share them with the larger community. The public health and social science literature is filled with excellent examples of alliances and collaborations that have made policy recommendations or otherwise acted upon the research results to promote policy, improve health service delivery, and stimulate other structural changes without actually disseminating the results to the community at large. Researchers Chen and colleagues (2010) conducted a survey of authors who had published articles on community-based health research and dissemination in peer-reviewed journals and found that, though many of the respondents were positive about dissemination, including to local communities, they encountered many obstacles. These included lack of recognition by universities of such dissemination as a valuable research-related activity, the cost and time required to prepare materials for dissemination, language/literacy constraints of the study team in relation to the language requirements of the community, insufficient funding for proper dissemination efforts, and changes in personnel or receptivity by local community partners.

Disseminating research results to the study community, regardless of what the research is about, is an ethical imperative as well as a practical matter. It is especially important because research partnerships and alliances are formed to address specific issues that affect people directly; it is those people who may be in the best position to act on the results or to forge relationships with others who can work with them to do so. As we noted earlier in this book, communities and other organizations are complex. Most important, reading reports does *not* usually constitute a major activity in the daily life of community residents, community organizations, and other institutions that partner in research. The relative ages of participants; the composition of the community audience; differences of language, educational level, and culture; and other factors will shape how the information should be presented, who presents it, who should receive it, and how.

There are many ways in which research results can be shared with study populations in an interactive way. These include creating:

- easy to understand presentations in PowerPoint or a similar computer presentation program or on newsprint;
- performances and street plays;
- dialogues/conversations;
- banners, posters, and panels;
- gallery exhibits and installations;
- films and photovoice.

Reaching the study population requires a different kind of effort from standard academic formats to make sure that the participants and others know about the dissemination events, recognize their importance, are encouraged to attend, and are offered information in a form that is relevant and appropriate and that ensures their understanding and engages them in conversation about the results.

Sharing information with participants and others in the study community can produce many good ideas, additional data, and suggestions for intervention. The following example illustrates how dissemination in a complex study community engaged three main audiences: the women who were the subjects of study, service providers and community educators working with them, and commercial establishments selling unhealthful products.

   **EXAMPLE 8.1**

DISSEMINATING RESEARCH RESULTS TO THE STUDY COMMUNITY: SMOKELESS TOBACCO USE AMONG WOMEN

Results of this mixed methods study conducted in Mumbai between 2010 and 2013 showed that approximately 23 percent of women of reproductive age used smokeless tobacco (SLT) daily, and one-third of chewers, including those who rubbed powdered tobacco on their gums, were users of multiple types of tobacco on the same day. More than half of the women in the study started their tobacco use late (mean age twenty) and after marriage, and of those, one-third started during pregnancy. Women reported consuming smokeless tobacco at the same rate during pregnancy as otherwise, were not impeded in their use by negative norms, saw few risks in use, and were able to purchase their tobacco themselves or through their underage children in shops very close to their homes. Women had no notion that the use of smokeless tobacco products might affect fetal health or create problems at birth such as low birth weight and premature birth. Shop owners reported that they felt no responsibility to limit the sale of tobacco; they felt that use was the responsibility of the user.

The study team led by Jean Schensul and Saritha Nair decided to disseminate these results to three groups in the community that were active in the study: community health workers and women leaders (key informants), tobacco sellers, and the women SLT users themselves. Two different strategies were prepared for these groups. The first involved using the study results to create a semi-scripted drama highlighting how a woman first learned to use tobacco (through her mother-in-law's advice to solve her gum problem during pregnancy), how she became addicted, and what happened to her during pregnancy (having a very low-birth-weight baby). The study team performed this play in multiple sites in the study community, with invited key informants and with community women who were informed about, and recruited to, the performance sites by the research team and key informant helpers through study networks. More than two hundred women attended the performance. After the presentation, several presented underweight babies to the study team as examples of what happens when women chew SLT. Subsequently, women discussed the need for help in quitting the use of SLT.

Approaching tobacco sellers required a different strategy because some of them earned their entire income from the sale of tobacco. Thus, the team decided to appeal to their sense of responsibility by showing study results in a professional-office setting with a PowerPoint presentation. The team discussed the legal implications of selling tobacco to minors, which could result in damage to mothers and children. After watching the presentation, these men moved from initial indifference to agreement that refusing to sell tobacco to children would not impair their business; they could, they said, replace the gap in revenue with the sale of other products. The results of the dissemination are being transformed into a *multilevel intervention* approach for use in communities where women are frequent users of SLT.

This dissemination effort was created on a very limited budget. The play was created and enacted by talented members of the study team who were intimately familiar with both the data and study community. The stage props

were minimal. The study team members knew, and stayed in touch with, key informants, shopkeepers, and women through repeated visits in a small geographic area. Thus, it was easy for them to recruit study participants and their friends to the events. The community sites were donated and spread throughout the study community so no costs were incurred for transportation. The only cost to the study was for refreshments.

Two related art-based dissemination efforts on youth culture and substance abuse, one involving animated panel displays and gallery exhibits and the second involving a film based on the study in question, took place in Hartford, Connecticut, and in other locations around the United States and Canada. The following example describes both of these as linked efforts.

EXAMPLE 8.2

DISSEMINATING NARRATIVES OF YOUTH CULTURE AND SUBSTANCE USE TO THE STUDY POPULATION

Between 1999 and 2010, the Institute for Community Research carried out three studies on emerging adult lifestyle and substance use. These studies took place during a period when drug selling was decentralizing from larger gangs to smaller crews, substances of choice were changing to include ecstasy (MDMA) and other club drugs and diverted prescription drug use, and PCP use was widespread, but little was known about it. The first study followed the circumstances under which young urban adults age sixteen to twenty-four became involved in drug use and drug selling and eventually were drawn into injection drug use. The second focused on club drug use and the "club" scene with the same population. The third considered the underground use of the drug ecstasy (MDMA) for sexual enhancement and its role in sexual risk. In all studies, many inequitable dimensions of urban life that young minority adults have to face every day came into play. The first study focused on the role of drugs in an underground economy within a formal economy that lacked employment opportunities for young people. The second study addressed the lack of available information about club drugs and their risks in formats that urban youth customarily utilized, as well as the ways in which the city manipulated young people's desires for inclusion while building a vibrant downtown economy. The third study explored the use of MDMA to reduce symptoms of depression in youth who had no access to treatment and wanted to negotiate challenging and potentially risky intimate relationships. The study team, made up of researchers from the city's neighborhoods, artist Colleen Coleman, study director and physician Raul Pino, and anthropologists Jean Schensul and Sarah Diamond decided to work with youth from the study population to tell the story of how use of the main substances, MDMA and PCP, interacted with the lives of young people in the city. These substances were chosen because they are opposite in effect and play very different roles in drug selling and social life. PCP is associated with violence; and MDMA is associated with fast friending, interpersonal intimacy, and sexuality.

The project was built upon a 2005 dissemination project featured in the ICR gallery, which illustrated the situations facing women infected with HIV in Africa. It featured stories and photographs of women infected with and affected by HIV on three-foot-by-ten-foot laminated panels. In 2005–2006, the ICR study team decided that a portable version of this format would allow the research team to "drop" panels on street corners and other public locations where youth in the study population gathered, in order to foster dialogue along the lines of ACT UP, an AIDS activist organization based in New York City (Murphy 2013), and other users of guerrilla art as protest forms. Though we were not allowed to place the panels we created on street corners in public places, we did manage to work with a team of young people and a young animator from Hartford to produce thirteen laminated three-foot-by-nine-foot panels that told the story of youth, lifestyle, drug selling, and drug use in the broader context of economic decline/development in an industrializing urban center. The panels illustrated in Figure 8.1 included national and local history, narratives of six characters, data in the form of simple graphics and drawings, and quotations from actual interviews about drugs, risks, and the situation facing youth in the city.

These panels were featured first in an interactive exhibit in the ICR community gallery (see Example 8.3 for details about the gallery) along with other accouterments of the "club scene" and club drugs, including videos, club fliers, rave toys, animated novels, replicas of MDMA, and a guide to club drugs and their risks. The opening brought in many people from the community, including study participants. The panels were later shown at events in the local convention center where they were accompanied by an informational treasure hunt, a guide to panels, and an assessment. Youth from many other sites across the city, including galleries, youth centers, and city hall, came to see the panels and reflect on their messages of risk exposure, struggle and achievement, and the omnipresent appeal of drugs that have useful functions in clubbing and sexuality, as well as drugs and the underground economy. The exhibit traveled elsewhere in Connecticut and with staff to Los Angeles, Vancouver, and Minneapolis (Schensul et al. 2012; Schensul et al. 2005).

A student and a member of the research staff subsequently decided to use material from in-depth interviews to create a film about the risks of using MDMA. They created a script in partnership with a group of young adults involved in street-violence prevention who knew the cultural setting from which the data had been collected. The team selected de-identified quotes from the study archives, took photographs of the city, integrated the quotes into the script, and recorded it. The film,

FIGURE 8.1 Two Rollin' and Dustin' panels.

entitled *Borders Beyond Bliss* was shown along with PowerPoint presentations to many groups of young people throughout the city, followed by discussion about the findings and implications for intervention.

Unlike the dissemination in Example 8.1, the panel exhibit was quite expensive and was funded with the dissemination budget included in NIH grants, as well as supplemental funds from NIH for minority summer youth research education experiences. The panels are still being

used to inform young people about Hartford youth history and substance use and to help youth to recognize that there are forces beyond those of their peers that have an effect on their decisions about drug use. The film was created with no budget at all. In each case, access to the study population was enabled by taking the panels, the film and the PowerPoint presentation to places where young adults gathered or were likely to visit. In both cases, researchers and youth from the study population facilitated discussions around the materials that were intended to highlight the context of substance use, social influences on youth, and myths about the economy of drug selling and the broader political arena of illegal drug use and markets in the United States.

Taking Research and Results to the Broader Public

A third example highlights the ways in which information about the latest prevention research on HIV can be shared with a wide variety of community publics over time.

EXAMPLE 8.3

ENGAGING PUBLICS, INCLUDING RESEARCH PARTICIPANTS AND OTHER STAKEHOLDERS, IN DISSEMINATION OF HIV STUDY RESULTS

In the early 1990s, the Institute for Community Research opened its gallery, a community art space. The purpose of the ICR gallery was to create a safe and open space for dialogue between researchers and community stakeholders on important issues affecting the local community. It also was intended to help integrate the dialogue with performances and displays of material culture. ICR researchers and board members believed that a variety of art forms not only appealed to different learning styles but also stimulated emotional responses to the topics addressed, and encouraged intimacy across cultural and other boundaries through personal stories, beautiful objects of art made by local artists, and music and dance. The gallery offered an excellent opportunity to highlight ICR's prevention research on HIV, a then-seemingly intransigent problem that was increasing ethnic/racial disparities in the area and affecting active drug users, women exposed to transactional sex, and men having sex with men.

The first opportunity arose in response to World AIDS Day, which roughly coincided with the Mexican Day of the Dead. In honor of both, ICR decided to host an exhibit with multiple components: artwork by local artists who were HIV-

infected; artwork by professional artists whose work made a statement about the devastating impact of HIV on these communities; a living altar, which offered anyone the opportunity to show objects, poems, stories, and memorabilia about their loved ones taken by AIDS; and a local quilt made by family members of infected people. A well-known curator, Sal Scalora, worked with HIV-infected artists to curate the work; the altar drew hundreds of people from Hartford communities who left mementos and attended the exhibit/installation. Accompanying programs offered a mix of attractions. Two workshops presented data from area studies designed to appeal to a wide variety of audiences; at two special events, volunteers presented testimony about their loved ones, describing their lives and helping the public to recognize that regardless of the source of infection, those infected were talented, intelligent, loving human beings with families who cared.

"Giving Women Power over AIDS" (2005) linked a traveling exhibit in the ICR gallery, based on photographs of a woman living with HIV in Zimbabwe, to the importance of women's ability to protect themselves from HIV. The exhibit, entitled "In Her Mother's Shoes," was created by its two photographers to convey the challenges that women face, regardless of their country, in coping with their illness, working, and dealing with stigma and discrimination, while at the same time sustaining their families (GCM 2002). The exhibit was shown in conjunction with a panel highlighting the importance of female-controlled prevention technologies, an important area of emphasis in ICR's work, including microbicides, female condoms, and more recently, PrEP or pre-infection prophylaxis. All of these technologies are controversial, regardless of efficacy, because of their capacity to enable vulnerable women to make decisions about their own protection independent of their male partners. The exhibit and a panel discussion focused on gender inequity, the root cause of women's vulnerability, and women's limited ability to ensure their own safety from infection. Panelists included researcher and anthropologist Margaret Weeks, two HIV-prevention counselors from different clinical services, and Bindiya Patel, then North American Sites Coordinator for the Global Campaign for Microbicides. It was moderated by Laurie Sylla from the Connecticut AIDS Education and Training Center. The event attracted a highly diverse public consisting of both women and men stakeholders in the fight to help women to maintain their sexual independence and their sexual safety and health.

Another event in 2008 involved a group of peer health advocates (PHAs) working to promote syringe safety and sexual protection against HIV infection among drug users in the community as part of a study funded by the National Institute on Drug Abuse (NIDA). Risk Avoidance Partnership (RAP) PHAs decided that they wanted to expand their leadership capacity. With the support of community installation artist and ICR gallery curator Colleen Coleman, they created works of art that made their own statements to the public about themselves and their lives. A press release described the event as follows:

> The exhibit includes collage, masks, posters, paintings and fabric art. An AIDS Awareness quilt created by the PHAS and ICR staff will be on display. Portraits of the artists with personal quotes that describe their participation in Project RAP and present hopeful messages about the power of change, memories of family, and the importance of faith also are included in the exhibit. Curator Colleen Coleman: "We all could see the interest and excitement growing within the group as the PHAs began to open up about their life experiences while developing ideas for their artwork. One PHA told me this project allowed him to sit with his mother for the first time in many years, because she was helping him to sew his quilt square." One artist featured in the exhibit had been HIV positive for 21 years. She said "I am a survivor, not a victim . . . for me, this exhibit is my way of telling my families and the community that I'm doing something positive."

These vignettes illustrate just how important the availability of public exhibit spaces that are embedded in community settings can be. With such spaces, it is possible to bring together researchers, study participants, other stakeholders, and social justice motivated artists and curators to develop mixed media events that integrate research methods and results with social gatherings. These events allow people to cross cultural, racial/ethnic/age/lifestyle and other boundaries in ways not possible in other more traditional or formal ways. There are many such spaces that can be found through creative searches—in unused downtown space; in the exhibit spaces and entryways of large new urban libraries, book stores, and other cultural centers; in youth-serving organizations; in old warehouses, beauty salons, bowling alleys, coffee shops, and restaurants; and on school and college campuses. All it takes is social capital and a little bit of venture capital to secure such spaces and to find artists who can connect with social issues to create works of art with high emotional and intellectual appeal.

A final example illustrates an interesting process that used the results-dissemination event with community stakeholders as an opportunity to help participants consider possible actions to be taken to address the problems raised and examined by the study.

EXAMPLE 8.4

COMMUNITY-BASED DISSEMINATION OF RESEARCH RESULTS IN LUSAKA, ZAMBIA

Dr. Lwendo Moonzwe carried out her dissertation work in the largest migrant community in Lusaka, Zambia. In looking for factors that contributed to women's empowerment and their ability to avoid sexual risk in this very resource-limited community, she sought partners among the international and local service agencies and political leaders working in the community. These included CARE, zone leaders, the Ward Development Committee, and local informal leaders. Born in Zambia though raised in the United States, Moonzwe returned frequently to Lusaka, where she had many friends and relatives. Her study took place over a year and involved interviewing men and women key informants, participant observation in the community, and an ethnographic survey based on the interviews. Her results show that positive male-partner relationships and joint decision making by women and partners reduced violence, men's sexual risk behaviors, and women's risk of HIV. However, food insecurity, abuse, and greater support-seeking actions from friends and family were associated with greater sexual risk, which limited women's abilities to use their networks for support.

To disseminate study results, Dr. Moonzwe returned to Lusaka and set up two dissemination events and a follow-up event. The first dissemination event presented feedback to representatives from the study community; the second was directed to NGOs, community-based organizations (CBOs), and government ministries; and the third was directed to community representatives who discussed community problems and identified resources to help to solve them. For the first, an interactive PowerPoint presentation with time for dialogue was combined with composite case studies read to the gathering by residents. The event ended with a discussion about the findings, in which four groups discussed what strategies could be put into place to equalize gender norms, support women's empowerment, improve male-female relationships and prevent HIV. Some of the community residents met the next day with the NGOs and government organizations. A summary of the previous day's activities was presented along with the PowerPoint presentation, and the conversation that followed focused on women's empowerment and how men should be brought into efforts to empower women. The community representatives also described how government institutions whose obligations were to provide services and infrastructure, including education and economic development, failed to do so, shortcomings which had not been recognized earlier. All parties agreed that more community involvement in women's empowerment issues would be an improvement over current practice. The agenda for the last meeting was to engage representatives of both groups, including all the stakeholders, in drafting a proposal to present to the authorities.

Cross Reference: See Book 2, chapter 9, and chapter 4 of this book   The meeting introduced to stakeholders the systems analysis approach described in chapter 9 of Book 2 and again in chapters 4 and 6 of this book. This type of analysis begins with identification of issues that need to be addressed in the community, plus a topic to address. Participants in this case chose the increasing rate of HIV infection among youth as a topic. The exercise called for the participants to identify issues leading to HIV infection among youth at the "organizational" level (gaps in government institutions, poor education, inadequate service delivery from international NGOs) and at the community level (women's groups need support, CBOs lack resources, local political action groups do not include women). Next, the group was asked to identify resources at the organizational and community level available to address these gaps. These included women's groups, cultural traditions such as rites of passage for women, churches, the local ward officials, and trained professionals. Finally, the group was asked to consider how these resources could make a difference in reducing the factors identified as contributing to HIV among youth. This produced an action plan that the joint group was able to present to the multiple sectors represented among stakeholders. This model of dissemination, ending with an analytic strategy in which all stakeholders are able to participate regardless of educational level or other factors, can be used in any setting where the goal is to share information and, at the same time, support local capacity for resource assessment and problem solving.

TAKING RESEARCH AND RESULTS TO POLICY MAKERS AND INCITING ACTION

In their 2010 exploration or scoping review of publications on approaches to dissemination, Wilson and colleagues found that most dissemination efforts directed to public audiences were based on communications theories (Wilson et al. 2010). Cognitive behavioral theories based on beliefs, values, knowledge, motivation, and intention underpin most efforts to persuade audiences to engage, and to transform themselves and their behaviors. The most highly referenced family of communicative theories are cognitive behavioral theories. These theories seek to modify or transform thinking and behavior through appeals to norms (customary practices), beliefs, perceptions of self efficacy (ability to actually make the change), and motivation to change. They also include stages of readiness to change (Prochaska, Prochaska, and Levesque 2001). Other theories involve risk and benefit assessment (Hawkins, Catalano, and Arthur 2002).

Cross Reference: See chapter 5 of this book

Diffusion theories are the second most frequently cited. Diffusion theories are based on the idea that information and persuasive influence flows through social networks (Rogers 2003). Some diffusionists believe that opinion leaders convey persuasive messages best, as they are role models already identified as those to whom others look for advice and guidance. Others think that the opinion-leader concept is both too narrow and too unstable and that everyone in a change community has the potential to convey information and persuade others, especially if they are clustered in small subnetworks (Pfeffer and Carley 2013).

Both creative problem solving and persuasive communication are required to take dissemination to the next step: influencing policy makers and motivating people to action. Persuasive communication, the most frequently cited, and one of the oldest theoretical frameworks, includes using emotive and empathetic qualities to attract, engage, and ultimately encourage audiences to change or act. These qualities often can be conveyed by using the artistic media we have described earlier; they engage audiences and are usually culturally based, holistic, and appealing to heart, mind, and values. It is partly for this reason that well-known media personalities and performers are chosen to model behaviors desired by public health authorities, such as vaccinating one's children or using condoms. They also are used by corporations to promote undesirable behaviors such as drinking a particular

brand of alcohol or consumption of sugary highly caffein-
ated energy drinks by teenagers. While these approaches
are often considered appropriate for the dissemination
of qualitative research results, they can be used with all
forms of research results, depending on the audience.

Persuasive communication, as first described by
McGuire (1961; 1969), and since noted by virtually all persuasive communications theorists, rests on five attributes
or strategic considerations: the source of communication,
the message to be communicated, the channels of communication, the characteristics of the audience (receiver), and
the setting (destination). Each of the considerations mentioned above requires thinking about who the audience
should be and how that audience can best be reached. For
example, sharing information for general knowledge might
simply involve presentations at local colleges, in NGOs,
local libraries, in university centers devoted to the topic,
or public fora organized by others. However, persuading
policy makers to take on an issue emerging from a research
project calls for other strategies, including press releases
and press conferences, face-to-face engagement with policy
makers, using persuasive arguments, lobbying, presenting
testimony, publicizing findings on social media, and other
community organizing strategies.

**Cross
Reference:**
See Example
6.14 of this book, on
changing educational
policy in Chicago

Sometimes change cannot be incited simply by persuading policy makers alone to act. Some policy makers
rely on authoritative sources and wait for the endorsement
of science and scientists before they can be persuaded to
act. Influencing the scientific community and scientists
through publications and presentations in respected
journals or widely read books is often required in addition to other direct actions to convince policy makers of
the legitimacy of an argument. However, such approaches
are not at all effective with so-called science deniers; such
people reject the findings of science and foment "cultural
wars" that are based on beliefs, opinions, ideological commitments, deep-seated values, and religious fervor rather
than science findings and facts. These wars are increasingly fought on global Internet sites, through social media,
and in blog discussions.

DISSEMINATION RESEARCH: ADAPTING AND RETESTING OR COMPARING AND SCALING UP INTERVENTIONS

In the previous pages of this book, we have described many different successful projects, research programs, and approaches, most of which have been carried out as a result of short- or longer-term "immersion" experiences in local settings and in collaboration with partners in those settings. Regardless of duration or scope, it is always desirable to share what happened in these experiences so that their successful processes and outcomes can be reproduced in other similar or even different settings. However, because our focus is on "communities," and not clinical or laboratory settings, we must caution readers that duplication is not always possible; we cannot control for the multitude of events and forces that could or do impact on our efforts, even in the best of situations. Further, once we attempt to try out our accomplishments with partners in other settings, no matter how similar, we invariably must go through a process of exploration and discovery, using ethnographic methods, in which differences between the original and subsequent sites and problems will emerge. These will necessitate adaptation of approaches and methods to record what has happened, what should be done, and how outcomes can be assessed.

Extending and Adapting Approaches Used in One Setting to Another Setting

To initiate this discussion, we begin with the idea that approaches that evolve in communities and community development in one place can lead to similar efforts in other settings. Here, we are referring to the kinds of situations that we described in chapter 2 of this book—long-term experiences in community development. Taking as an example the action research projects in Chicago described in Example 2.1, we now examine efforts to adapt these projects to fit conditions in Miami, Florida, and Hartford, Connecticut.

All adaptation/replication efforts require the identification of "key components of the intervention." Identifying these key components is required in order to confirm just how similar or dissimilar a site is to the original, and to assert convincingly that a repetition has been attempted. The Chicago Mexican American community development experiment migrated first to Miami and later to Hartford. Below we list key components of this long-term intervention that needed to be present for replication or adaptation elsewhere.

- Identification of key community actors and activists in ethnic/racial communities
- Identification of core community organizations concerned with community development on multiple fronts
- Interest within the community in using research as a means of identifying issues and new directions to resolve them
- Interest in collaboration across disparate sectors
- Availability of outside funding to support innovative programs
- Sufficient politicization within the communities that people would be willing to demand rights in relation to dominant political and economic forces
- A felt need for community development in areas of education, health, mental health, and culture
- Minimum negative opposition to community development

These core elements were applied first in the city of Miami. In this extraordinarily multiethnic and Latin American–oriented city, six or more different ethnic/racial groups are vying for recognition, resources, and cultural presence. The Chicago approach applied to Miami in the 1970s identified some key actors in each of these communities; however, these key actors were arrayed in a hierarchy dominated by Cubans and their African American partners, who in turn were allied with the entrenched white power structure. Nascent community organizations existed, but they were too poorly developed to represent assertively the cultural and other interests of communities such as West Indians, Haitians, Puerto Ricans, Cubans, and other African Americans. While research was viewed as an asset, some key gate-keepers believed that providing mental health services was more important than doing research, given that the program implementing community development was funded through community mental health dollars. So it was difficult to mount the kind of research efforts needed to assess programmatic needs. Other than existing alliances created for political purposes, the Miami community had created no efforts to collaborate across ethnic/racial lines. In addition, during the mid-1970s, federal funding policy shifted from supporting community development to service delivery—an approach designed to treat the symptoms of an ailment rather than cure the underlying problem—followed by a dramatic decline in public sector support for services to people who needed them. Community development was no longer perceived to be a major issue. In this conservative state, political mobilization was limited by a political environment in which "deals" were arranged behind closed doors and little overt public political activism existed. Community development was needed, but unlikely to take place except through channels that supported neither research nor advocacy. The transfer of the "Chicago Model" to Miami was unsuccessful because the requisite core components were missing.

In Hartford, Connecticut, however, the story was somewhat different. Community advocates in both the Puerto Rican and African American communities existed and were visible. Their organizations already were attempting to promote community development, and they had a strong commitment to research. An umbrella organization had already brought Black and Puerto Rican advocates together to fight for community development; it had developed strong plans for acquiring outside funding. Communities had learned how to fight for their rights in the late 1960s and were highly politicized. In several cases, the developmental priorities had already been identified (e.g., in the Puerto Rican community, priorities included economic development, housing, education, and health). The environment was ready for further development, especially in the areas of health and culture. The effort proceeded in a manner comparable to the Chicago approach: identification of key partner advocates and their organizational bases, development of participatory research efforts to highlight needs and issues, creation of new advocacy teams and organizations serving the community, and promotion of community-based participatory research for community development. This comparison reminds us that it is critically important to use ethnographic skills to determine whether the core components of a long-term community development effort are viable and whether using them is practical. There is little in the way of useful literature that compares and contrasts the longer-term community development interventions we outlined in chapter 2; this makes it difficult to suggest either what the core components of such interventions might be or which qualities might make them most effective over time. Perhaps the best summary is that of van Willigen. His seminal chapter on community assets and the community-building process uses a six-point rating mechanism to rate assets from the perspective of building on community capacity in his work with Arizona's Native American Tohono O'Odham community. It included these points:

- The internal (to community) location of the implementing institution identified as a resource. Internal was rated as higher because of the community's ability to maintain control over it.
- The focus of the resource on community rather than individual goals; a focus on community was rated higher.
- The generality of the goal orientation—the more general the goal orientation, the greater the opportunity for the community to plan and include its own priorities, and the higher the rating.
- The longer duration of the funded program effort—financial resources without deadlines would allow greater community participation, and garner a higher rating.
- The capacity to link a resource with the community's organizations. Stronger and more numerous linkages received higher ratings.

- The formation of new roles within the community; the more new roles created, the higher the rating (van Willigen 2005).

Van Willigen suggests that strategies for implementing both long- and shorter-term interventions be considered in light of these criteria. He also notes the importance of community institutions, local knowledge, physical infrastructure, and history, suggesting that these are critical in addressing community development goals.

Other dissemination efforts reflect the shorter-term, more project-oriented programs that are more typical of participatory and collaborative interventions in community, school, and clinic settings. The key point is that ***whenever interventions are successful, they need to be disseminated and shared with others, and then adapted to be usable in different settings and with different populations.*** As we explained earlier in this chapter, *implementation science* is the term given to the area of research that examines the process by which adapting and transferring specific interventions from one location, often an ideal one, to another which may be less ideal or different in many other ways, occurs. The term *implementation science* is often used to refer to so-called **evidence-based interventions**, which means that they have been evaluated empirically using standardized and, almost always, quantitative measures to be effective in line with their expected outcomes. Most of these interventions are generated by psychologists or by interdisciplinary public health teams, though some are developed by anthropologists, sociologists, other social scientists, and educators. There are now compendia, archives, Internet storage sites, and other locations where researchers and policy makers can find interventions that they would like to adapt, adopt, and evaluate in their own settings.

The process of adapting, adopting, and evaluating these existing interventions and programs utilizes a specialized language summarized in Table 8.2 (Pemberton 2012).

Key point

Definition: Evidence-based interventions are those that have been evaluated and determined to be effective, based on their ability to achieve their desired goals

TABLE 8.2   Key terms in dissemination (adaptations and implementation) of successful programs and projects (interventions)

Key terms	Definition
Core elements	Required elements that represent the intent, theory, and internal logic of the intervention and are thought to result in the intervention's main effects. Core elements define an intervention and must be implemented as specified in the original intervention to increase the likelihood that program outcomes in community settings will be similar to those demonstrated in the original research.
Key characteristics	Key characteristics are important, but not essential, attributes of an intervention's recommended activities and delivery methods. They may be modified to be culturally appropriate and fit the risk factors, behavioral determinants, and risk behaviors of the target population and the unique circumstances of the venue, agency, and other stakeholders. Modification of key characteristics usually do not compete with or contradict the core elements, theory, and internal logic of the intervention.
Capacity	An organization's motivation and ability to identify, select, implement, evaluate, and sustain effective interventions. Capacity can also refer to an organization's ability to adapt an intervention prior to or after it is implemented, and to generate new interventions based on assessed community need.
Community	A group of people or organizations defined by function, geography, shared interests, or characteristics, or by a combination of these dimensions in which members share some sense of identity or connection.
Context	The environment in which participants exist or reside that affects the usability and applicability of the treatment intervention. Context may include (a) social organizational factors; (b) economic factors; (c) political factors; and (d) spiritual factors including religious practices/rituals and concepts of the supernatural.
Dissemination	The spreading of innovations from the originators or developers to the intended users and beyond. More generally, this can refer to the targeted distribution of intervention information or materials to a specific public health or clinical practice audience.
Efficacy	The extent to which an intervention works in a highly controlled setting.
Effectiveness	The extent to which an intervention works in a real-life situation.
Implementation	A specified set of activities designed to put into practice an intervention of known dimensions in a specific setting.
Innovation	New programs, processes, policies, and principles that can be useful in social-change efforts.
Translation	The process of converting (translating) scientific knowledge into practitioner-friendly products to be used for implementation.

Source: Adapted from Pemberton 2012.

It also utilizes common sense. Proctor and colleagues help us to consider the elements in implementation (Proctor, Power, and McMillen 2013). They propose the following guidelines to consider.

1. **Name it.** Name the intervention strategy. Proctor et al. suggest using language consistent with existing literature; but naming also should be consistent with local language and meaning.

2. **Define it.** Define the implementation strategy and any discrete components operationally—that is, in ways that they can be actualized in behavior.

3. **Specify it.** Identify the *actor*—the person who enacts the strategy (e.g. teachers, counselors, advocates, residents, peer educators); identify the *action*—specify the specific actions, steps or processes that need to be enacted; identify the action target (who it is to be directed to); identify the *units* important in measuring outcomes. Specify exactly *when* the strategy is used (e.g., time of day, sequence in the overall intervention); specify *how much* it is to be used (e.g., frequency of delivery, amount of delivery, number of times delivered over a designated period of time); *justify* the choice of strategies both locally and through the literature.

Good intervention researchers know how important it is to study the context, the "delivery setting" (clinic, school, community organization, group), and the people involved when adapting an intervention for dissemination. Various researchers who do participatory dissemination work make it clear that all three—context, setting, and participants—need to be considered in detail and engaged as much as possible to ensure that an intervention shown to be effective elsewhere is feasible, acceptable, cost effective, likely to have good outcomes, minimally buffeted by external forces that could undermine it or negatively affect desired outcomes, and owned and embraced by those to whom it matters most.

Top-down approaches to dissemination of interventions generally are driven by social scientists who may work with people in local communities to make adjustments to the intervention delivery process, content, setting, language, and other aspects of the program. Often in such cases, communities or schools or clinics are not given the option to choose from a variety of interventions. Instead, they are offered one approach that the social scientist is interested in. If the community is interested, the intervention is implemented and evaluated. However, whether that intervention actually was the best possible choice seldom is sufficiently evaluated ahead of time, especially if financial incentives of funding are attached to adoption of the intervention! This top-down and non-collaborative process really is not consistent with the egalitarian partnership approach that we have emphasized in this book and elsewhere in the *Toolkit*.

A more effective approach, although one that is rarely tried, is to involve communities, public health departments, parents, and other stakeholders in the selection of several possible intervention options, and to provide them with or help them to build criteria that help them to choose what works best for them. Layde describes an approach called the "community health improvement process" (CHIP) that involves stakeholder participation in defining the context and problem, choosing evidence-based options and alternatives, and evaluating them. The "EdCHIP" approach identifies critical health issues and stakeholders, evaluates community assets and health, participants' educational levels, and other available secondary data, and then identifies relevant interventions from an inventory based on these priorities and desired outcomes. The data utilized by the stakeholder group is collected from secondary sources, and the assets are determined depending on the knowledge and resources possessed by the stakeholder group (Layde et al. 2012). While this approach reaches a broader swath of the community, it still does not guarantee that the voices of those experiencing educational or health inequities or other forms of disparity will be heard.

A fully participatory approach which does ensure the full engagement of marginalized communities is one in which community members generate an explanatory model for a health or other disparity of their choice, conduct their own research, and (based on their own data as well as other secondary sources and the literature) determine what kind

of interventions they think would be beneficial, and how to identify or to create them. For this purpose, they can use any of the tools and techniques outlined in this book for generating local theory, linking it to "etic" or disciplinary theory, identifying intervention components, and even identifying interventions.

The following example shows how this approach can work for local residents.

 **EXAMPLE 8.5**

LATINO PARENTS OF PRESCHOOL CHILDREN DO RESEARCH AS THE BASIS FOR CHOOSING THEIR PREFERRED INTERVENTION MODELS

In the late 1990s, the Center for Substance Abuse Prevention offered a unique two-year opportunity to communities to study with the creators/developers of six social science–based cognitive behavioral interventions for strengthening families. The goal was preventing substance abuse in the future. In a national convening, representatives from communities awarded grants by the Center for Substance Abuse Prevention were to come together to choose one of the six interventions. The Institute for Community Research in Hartford, Connecticut , together with a local Latino mental health and substance abuse facility, received an award. Most of the parents of young children involved in the center did not speak English and had not heard of prevention before. Under the leadership of Marlene Berg, a participatory researcher at ICR, and the center director, parents concerned about their children's future substance use came together to determine what they wanted. The six parents who attended the convening could not decide on a single program. Instead of choosing one of the preexisting interventions, the parents created their own conceptual model of what constituted a healthy family and a healthy home. Choosing elements from three of the six programs, they integrated them into a new intervention, "Encontrando el Poder Dentro de Ti" (Finding the Power Within You), that worked for them. They tested the model through in-depth interviews and a survey of other parents of young children. After triangulating the data, they defined what they considered to be a healthy family and a healthy home and drew up a statement that could be used at the convening as they looked for appropriate programs.

The approach of the Hartford parents was quite contrary to the principles of "dissemination science," especially its emphasis on fidelity (consistency of implementation with the original model), but it fit well with the notion of enabling communities and groups to develop their own approaches to intervention rather than being dictated to by the scientific establishment.

"Scaling Up": Expanding the Scope of a Program or Movement to the State or National Level or Globally

So far, we have been discussing different ways of expanding the settings in which interventions can be redefined, adapted, repeated, and assessed. We've also mentioned that by using the tools of research, communities and educators can become empowered to choose from a wide variety of interventions. With proper preparation and facilitative expertise, they even can choose elements from multiple interventions to craft their own. The final stage in dissemination is "scaling up," a term that refers to broad implementation of an intervention across multiple settings and units. For example, the intervention known as GEMS (Gender Equity Movement in Schools), a successful program that promotes gender equity in educational settings, is being implemented in many schools in the Indian state of Maharashtra, with minor process and outcome assessments. The All Stars program, a successful tested and evaluated substance-abuse-prevention program for middle school students (age eleven to fourteen) is designed to prevent and delay the onset of high-risk behaviors such as drug use, violence, and premature sexual activity. The program focuses on (1) developing positive ideals that do not fit with high-risk behavior; (2) creating a belief in conventional norms; (3) building strong personal commitments to avoid high-risk behaviors; (4) bonding with school, pro-social institutions, and family; and (5) increasing positive parental attentiveness, such as positive communication and parental monitoring.

The All-Stars curriculum includes highly interactive group activities, games and art projects, small group discussions, one-on-one sessions, a parent component, optional online activities and worksheets, and a celebration ceremony. Its thirteen forty-five-minute class sessions can be delivered by teachers, prevention specialists, or social workers. Multiple packages of student materials are available to support implementation, either by regular teachers or prevention specialists. The materials are meant to be administered without external facilitation.

Programs that are "scaled up" usually have a set of unique features. They are packaged so that they can be self-administered without much, if any, facilitation; they make sense to a broad spectrum of implementers in the settings for which they are intended; they are cost effective, especially in resource limited settings; they can be implemented by many different actors because they don't depend on a narrow range of professionals; they can readily be culturally adapted to specific groups in specific settings; and they are often translated into multiple languages. Scaling up programs takes a considerable amount of financial support for the first few years, for packaging, testing, training, and evaluation. Thus, those who wish to scale up their programs will find that good results are not good enough—they must be able to find donors, or government or business sponsors, who will help them to package their work. For example, the developer of a successful participatory intervention to reduce obesity among African American women, created with an alliance of Black churches in Connecticut, was able to find support for scaling up the program through Empire Blue Cross/Blue Shield, the company that provides insurance for New York's state employees.

SUMMARY

In this chapter, we've discussed the variety of ways that researchers and their partners can and should share the results of their research and their successful interventions with others. In the first part of the chapter we argued that researchers have the responsibility to share the results of their work with the broader community in which it was carried out, and most especially with the community of participants. We've suggested that this is an ethical requirement for researchers, regardless of the degree to which they are partnering with local settings. This is because partnerships cannot and do not include everyone in a community, school, or clinic. Thus, it is not enough to share the results with partners and legislators. We have suggested a variety of ways in which research results can be shared, from various forms of media and face-to-face communication to more formalized planning to develop interventions and advocacy approaches based on the results.

In the second part of the chapter we discussed the growing field of "dissemination/implementation science." This field began to emerge more than four decades ago, as information about successful approaches to education, and later to health and other service areas, were piling up in articles, on bookshelves, and in funders' archives but were not being shared with the public. Public funding was not producing public benefit. The net result of dissemination/implementation science is a rapidly expanding set of approaches to adapting interventions for use in multiple settings and a new language of dissemination to and with "end users"—the people for whom the interventions are intended so as to ameliorate their social, environmental, health, educational, and mental health suffering. These approaches also include ways of creating community infrastructure for choosing interventions, for supporting communities and other users to use research methods as well as secondary data sources and opinion, and to assess their own settings and population to determine what approaches suit them best.

In the next chapter, we discuss Participatory Action Research with adults and youth—a fully participatory approach that "teaches" action-oriented citizen groups concerned with social justice issues to use research as a means of assessing their environment in order to change it. In the PAR model, participant activists are the drivers of the research and intervention process, using all of the tools and methods we have described throughout the *Toolkit* to do active research on their environments, determine their assets and resources, decide what they need, and make intelligent and informed decisions with respect to social-change strategies.

9

PARTICIPATORY ACTION RESEARCH IN COMMUNITY SETTINGS

INTRODUCTION

So far, throughout Book 7, we have discussed a variety of strategies for building partnerships; developing theoretical and methodological approaches in collaborative research; and creating, implementing, and evaluating interventions at multiple levels in complex community and institutional settings. In this chapter, we shift to approaches that capacitate community partners—adults and youth—to take leadership in the conduct of research on issues that affect them in order to transform them and their communities. We call this approach Participatory Action Research or PAR. PAR extends the collaborative approaches that we have described so far by demonstrating how formally trained researchers can work with lay or community researchers and enable them to take leadership roles in research integrated with action steps to address or ameliorate social, health, cultural, economic, and political injustices. This methodology utilizes all of the components of research as described throughout the book, but is structured in such a way that community residents, teachers, cultural workers, or others can readily understand and fully participate in all aspects of the research/action cycle.

DEFINITIONS

Participatory Action Research is an approach to research that integrates research with action and social transformation and unites formally trained researchers in and outside of academic settings with the people affected by an issue that they wish to change or transform. PAR is an emancipatory process that places actors affected by an issue at the heart of the research endeavor, thus equalizing the balance of power between themselves and academically trained researchers. In PAR, those affected by the problem embrace or admit the existence of that problem and declare that their goal is to ameliorate it by changing the conditions that cause it. Researchers assist by joining forces and integrating research methods and tools with their own and participants' lived experience. In the process, research becomes the means by which community research groups critically analyze, reflect, and act upon the problem they want to solve. Their cultural and social capital brings forward the insights and resources needed to mobilize a directed transformation process (Cornwall and Jewkes 1995, 833). Reason and Bradbury suggest that action research "is not so much a methodology as an orientation to inquiry that seeks to create participatory communities . . . in which qualities of engagement, curiosity and question posing are brought to bear on significant practical issues" (Reason and Bradbury 2006). Using systematic research approaches, PAR researchers and university-trained researchers co-construct strategies and identify problems together, using "official scholarly knowledge" (Schensul 2015). In this way, PAR validates and promotes the voice of local communities and marginalized groups, as well as their "authority to determine truth" as they see it (Rodríguez and Brown 2009, 23). The following statement illustrates ways in which PAR gives voice to community issues. It was written by the research director of the Highlander Research and Education Center (http://highlandercenter.org/), a well-recognized community-based research organization (CBRO) with a forty-five-year history of activist work including PAR directed toward social and economic justice in Appalachia and other areas of the South.

EXAMPLE 9.1

ACTION RESEARCH IN APPALACHIA

"A community called Bumpass Cove became the defining experience in learning about another kind of research, a research dedicated to honoring people's own knowledge and empowering them with the ability to access and interpret information they need to act on their problems—a kind of 'research literacy.' Bumpass Cove is a small Tennessee mountain community. Its mines had long closed, and many people had moved away before a company bought some land for dumping 'household garbage.' Most people were happy, because it provided some jobs, and they believed officials who assured them that nothing dangerous would be dumped there. Only when spring floods washed some barrels out of the landfill and down the creek, and churchgoers became ill with the fumes, did the community come to recognize the problem, and turned out en masse to close down the landfill.

"But even when the landfill was closed the problem was not solved, for at the head of the hollow were still buried an unknown mix of chemicals with the potential to harm humans and the environment. Research was a crucial tool in the residents' struggle to clean up the landfill. Four people from the community group formed a research team. Two went to Nashville to search the files of the state health department for any records relating to the Bumpass Cove landfill. All four then brought to Highlander the two-foot-high stack of photocopies they had made. We sat around a table in the library, sorting through the documents. We made an index card for every instance of chemical dumping we could document. Then we used a chemical directory, a medical dictionary, and a regular dictionary to identify the chemicals and their potential health effects. None of us had formal scientific training, and most of the research team had not graduated from high school—two later enrolled in their local ABE program, and one has just obtained her GED.

"It was my first experience of the literacy of reading both the 'word' and the 'world.' As we read, the group used their local knowledge to make meaning: they knew people who had experienced many of the symptoms we were now documenting, they remembered some of the unusual loads going into the landfill, they knew barrels had fallen off a truck at a bend in the road, where nothing would now grow. Their own knowledge gave the official knowledge meaning.

"Around the same time, in a mountain community in Kentucky, Yellow Creek Concerned Citizens (YCCC) was fighting another chemical pollution problem and provided support and encouragement for the Bumpass Cove group. YCCC went a step further and conducted their own health survey of residents along contaminated Yellow Creek. With guidance from health professionals at Vanderbilt University, YCCC members developed a questionnaire and went door to door to collect information. What they found may not have been strictly 'scientific' in the model of epidemiological studies, but it was a valuable tool in their legal battle against the company responsible for

the pollution during their political battle to get local and state government to act, and in their organizing of community residents" (Merrifield 1997).

 Cross Reference: See Book 2, chapter 3 on research modeling

 Cross Reference: Review these methods in Books 3 and 4

 Cross Reference: Review analysis techniques in Book 5

All forms of participatory action research involve group participation in conceptualization, research design, information collection, plans for remediation, and resultant action (Foster-Fishman et al. 2010; Hovmand 2014; Kemmis, McTaggart, and Nixon 2014; Torre, Cahill, and Fox 2015). We can conceptualize the PAR process as a spiral linking research and action in an ongoing way throughout the duration of a project or program of change. It moves from group inquiry and identification of a common issue through conceptual modeling, early identification of desired outcomes, data collection methods, and to group data analysis. At each step of the way, research activities are linked to reflection and planned actions, including building relationships with allies and other actors; presenting persuasive, data-based messages to people of influence; mobilizing community responses; and communicating with the media. In the process, actions produce responses, which are then documented, leading to more questioning, systematic inquiry, data collection, reflection/analysis, and action planning, moving toward the desired goal or outcome. Figure 9.1 re-illustrates this process, first presented in chapter 1 of this book, showing how observation and data collection (observe) require analysis and thoughtful consideration (reflect), leading to planning (plan) for action (act). These processes are arrayed along a spiral, indicating that they are interactive and ongoing. The horizontal axis concerns building evidence; the vertical access concerns building allies. Together they lead to strategic action for systems change (diagram created by Heather Mosher and Jean Schensul for ICR PAR program).

PAR has been used in many settings and with many different groups (Greenwood and Levin 1998; LeCompte and Schensul 2010; Schensul et al. 2004a), but it is most often applied with those who have been politically, economically, and culturally marginalized and who come to see research as informing actions leading to their advancement through

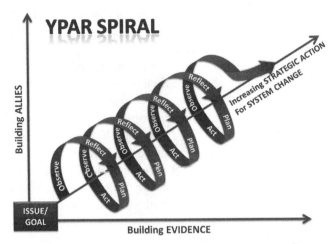

FIGURE 9.1 The Youth-Led Participatory Action Research (YPAR) spiral. Mosher and Schensul.

intervention, advocacy, and policy change (Cornwall and Jewkes 1995). Most people who actively choose PAR as a research approach are politically motivated to transform repressive or inequitable policies, institutional practices, and resource allocations that produce social and emotional suffering. Thus, PAR has a specific change-oriented, social justice agenda (Brydon-Miller 1997; Cahill 2007; Cammarota and Romero 2009; Fals Borda and Rahman 1991; Nygreen 2009–2010; Torre, Cahill, and Fox 2015).

The PAR process uses a critical ecological approach, collectively exploring and seeking to transform oppressive or discriminatory components in multiple subsectors of a system and at multiple levels, often with a strong community-organizing and mobilization component added (Schensul 1978; Schensul and Schensul 1978; Sohng 1996). In their ICR curriculum, Schensul et al. use the term *eco-critical approach* (Schensul, J. et al., 2004). Prilleltensky, a community psychologist, uses a parallel term—"psychopolitical validity"—by which he means "the extent to which research and action take into account power dynamics in psychological and political domains affecting oppression, liberation, and wellness at the personal, group, and community levels" (Morsillo and Prilleltensky 2007). Lather applies a similar concept, "catalytic validity," meaning research that has the capacity to generate activism against oppression or marginalization by those who experience it. The research is defined as having validity if it stimulates people to take action on their own behalf (Lather 1986). PAR integrates the passion of researchers to reverse the inequities of power, dominance, and control that typify any form of research in which populations are viewed as subjects, with the goals of those affected by structural inequities to move to the center using a combination of knowledge and political organizational capacity (Hall 2005). PAR democratizes science—to place the theories, methods, and techniques of science in the hands of those who have been excluded, to raise issues, speak to power, and advocate for change (Schensul 2002).

A truly transformational PAR project adds to participatory research methods other strategies for bringing about social change. These include community-organizing approaches and participation in social movements (Lipschutz 2004; McCormick 2007), political and social communications campaigns with persuasive messaging (Freudenberg, Bradley, and Serrano 2009; Wakefield, Loken, and Hornik 2010), community-engaged activities (Snyder 2007), and media-rights efforts (Dharod et al. 2004; Martínez-Hernáez 2010; Rael 2009). PAR efforts that have produced transformative change include educational institutions and practices, disability research and advocacy (e.g., autism, etc.), programs for reproductive health, tobacco-use prevention, mental health, community development, environmental advocacy, prisoners' rights, HIV prevention and treatment, educational reform, older adult health (Blair and Minkler 2009), and many other topics (Balcazar 2006; Buettgen et al. 2012; McCalman 2009).

PAR topics often favored by youth are sexuality, pregnancy, and sexual risk (Winskell and Enger 2009), stress and suicidal considerations (Downs et al. 2009), violence, guns, and bullying (McIntyre 2000), and illegal activities such as hustling or substance use. Youth also typically express interest in changing unjust school policies ranging from academic tracking and poor quality lunchroom food to inappropriate suspension in school; conflicting policies regarding work, school, and daycare for young mothers;

racism, and racial, linguistic, and other forms of discrimination (Krueger 2010; Morgan et al. 2004; Ozer, Ritterman, and Wanis 2010; Rubin and Jones 2007; Stovall and Delgado 2009; Wilson et al. 2007), income inequity, unwelcoming environments, gaps in adequate food supply (Breckwich Vasquez et al. 2007), and inadequate service delivery (Cooper 2005; Maglajlic and Tiffany 2013). The following brief example illustrates this type of approach.

EXAMPLE 9.2

A PARTICIPATORY ACTION RESEARCH PROJECT WITH HIGH SCHOOL YOUTH TO STUDY YOUTH PERSPECTIVES ON RACIAL AND CLASS-BASED INJUSTICES

During the three-year period from 2001 to 2004, CUNY Graduate Center researchers Michelle Fine and colleagues were invited to join an educational research team to explore test score gaps across ethnic/racial groups. They agreed to do so provided they could work with students from urban and suburban high schools in New York and New Jersey to study youth perspectives on racial and class-based injustices in schools and the nation. They identified a core of youths from six suburban high schools and three urban schools to study what the youths named as "the opportunity gap." Students participated in two-day research camps to deconstruct the concept of research; and learn about social justice theory, research methods, race and class issues, struggles in public education, and the civil rights movement. They also discussed educational justice for LGTBQ (lesbian, gay, bi, trans, and queer or questioning) youth, second-language learners, and students with disabilities.

The youth designed a survey together with the adults; it was translated into Spanish, French-Creole, and Braille and distributed to ninth and twelfth graders across thirteen urban and suburban districts. In subsequent research camps, youths analyzed qualitative and quantitative data from a total of 9,174 surveys, 24 focus groups, and 32 in-depth interviews with youth. Students and faculty together read extensively from archival and historical materials on related topics (e.g., the existence of the prison-industrial complex; federal policies that exclude poor and working-class students from educational opportunities). Students and faculty "created an empirical map of the Racial, Ethnic and Class In/Justices in secondary public schools focusing on structures, policies and practices, including inequitable distribution of urban/suburban resources, the dismantling of desegregation, tracking systems based on race, students' differential experience of respect, implications of teaching/testing and discriminatory disciplinary action." Together they took the results to urban and suburban schools and to educational policy makers. In order to maximize their potential for achieving public awareness and garnering action to remedy the structural injustices the faculty decided to transform their working knowledge and findings into performance. To accomplish this goal they recruited youth from many different youth groups and schools in New York and New Jersey. From project archives and interviews with older civil rights advocates, thirteen youths created a multimedia performance which they called "Echoes of Brown," to celebrate the fiftieth anniversary of *Brown versus the Board of Education*, which was later published along with the project archives as a DVD (Fine et al. 2004).

In their write-up of this project, which extended over more than four years and crossed multiple schools and states, the authors reflect on involving youth in research on injustices (Fine et al. 2007). In doing so, they make several critical points. First is that in the study of injustices, it is important to include a diverse group of youths (or adults), in order to understand that injustices are impersonal and affect everyone; second is that the research must help researchers learn about successes in strategic activism for change in order to ensure that they engage in critical hopefulness (Christens, Collura, and Tahir 2013). That is, they must be able to see possibilities and promise in their own and others' actions.

Participatory Action Research is now a truly interdisciplinary, intersectoral approach; it cuts across the social, environmental, and health sciences, cultural development, and educational change efforts, and it broadly encompasses a wide range of constituents and stakeholders in the community. Any and all of these questions can be addressed using a set of theories and methods tailored to the setting and to developmental, contextual, and cultural characteristics of participants.

BRIEF HISTORY OF PARTICIPATORY ACTION RESEARCH (PAR)

The origins of PAR often are attributed to Kurt Lewin, a German-Jewish psychologist who fled Europe during World War II to work in the United States in the 1930s and 1940s. Lewin's commitment to social justice focused on efforts to equalize relationships among groups with differential power. One of his early publications criticized the value of conversations among such unequal groups, in particular between middle- and upper-class white organizations and low-income African Americans in New York City. Instead of conversations between groups possessing asymmetrical power, and in sympathy with an incipient civil rights movement, he advocated giving priority to activities that fostered stronger intragroup identity and self-esteem through engagement in the struggle for group civil rights. He argued that fighting for recognition and rights was central to gaining equality in decision making, and that it should be reinforced through research and reflection. Lewin was a visionary social scientist who connected research to activism and Western colonial policies to inequitable policies and practices within the United States—a nation founded upon racially discriminatory practice and policies. Lewin's emphasis on reclaiming histories and identities through struggle underpins all community-action research efforts to the present (Lewin 1946).

In the 1950s, Sol Tax, a well-known anthropologist at the University of Chicago, evolved an approach which he called "action anthropology" based on his students' work with the Mesquakie Indians. The students viewed oppressive Mesquakie/white relationships to be a major problem. After engaging in inappropriate, naïve, and unsuccessful efforts to improve those relationships, the students learned from the Mesquakie Indian tribe itself how to help them to move their own economic development plan forward (Gearing, Netting, and Peattie 1960). Some of his students, including Fred Gearing and Lisa Peattie, went on to promote activist research in educational anthropology and urban planning (Peattie 1968).

PAR approaches evolved rapidly in the 1960s and 1980s, a time marked by civil rights movements in the United States and Canada and anticolonial, independence, and indigenous movements in Latin America, the United States and Canada, Africa, Australia, New Zealand, and South Asia (Fals-Borda 1987; Freire 1973; Tandon 1981). PAR became widely recognized as a means of strengthening the capacity of those with limited opportunity to record, conserve, document, control, or represent their historical experiences and cultural capital, and to argue for their own interpretations of causality and the futures to which they aspired (Schensul, Berg, and Williamson 2008). PAR is rooted in the struggles of marginalized working-class people, minority racial/ethnic groups, people with disabilities, sexual minority groups, girls and women, and indigenous populations around the world to improve their condition through structured inquiry and strategically planned action (Barnhardt and Kawagley 2005; Grayshield and Mihecoby 2010; Lea 2008; Maguire 2006; Simonds and Christopher 2013; Tuck 2009).

This form of PAR has an international history, supported by sociologists (Brydon-Miller 1997; Hall 2005), feminist theorists (Brydon-Miller, Greenwood, and Maguire 2003; Harding 2006; Maguire 2006), popular educators (Brydon-Miller et al. 2008; Duncan-Andrade 2004; Freire 1973), and many anthropologists and activists in countries around the world.

PAR operates at three levels (Burgess 2006):

- first person (individual learning, personal reflection, and development)
- second person (development of group consciousness, mutual support, and co-construction of new knowledge)
- third person (engagement in research and organizing for action on behalf of others)

Changes targeted by PAR may be focused on reframing or revising policies, introducing new institutions and improving service delivery, reversing the structures of power, influence and economics impeding freedom of decision making, political advancement, and social action, or supporting indigenous communities in their quest for land, water, and other natural resource rights. At the same time, as Berg and colleagues note, joining forces to analyze inequitable situations and advocate for transformative changes can bring about significant changes not only in structural and social conditions but in those who themselves are research/activists in the action/research process (Berg, Coman, and Schensul 2009).

While community-based participatory research (CBPR) and PAR share some similarities, they differ in some critical ways. CBPR involves "community partners" in all aspects of the research. In most cases, however, the goal of CBPR is to forge a compatible working relationship between activist partners and university-based researchers. This involves knowledge sharing, but the goal is to marry the research strengths of the university with the activist and organizing strengths of the community partners. It tends not to involve training community members to become researchers themselves; consequentially, community members do not become fully prepared to drive the research agenda. PAR, on the other hand, recognizes that knowledge derived from science-based inquiry *is* power and is specifically oriented to shifting research and research-based knowledge and practice directly into the hands of communities of adults and youth who, through the process, gain critical consciousness and come to recognize that they have the right and the capacity to use research to transform their world. In the words of Fine and Torre, "Cultivated on the spikes of social injustice, participatory action research projects are designed to amplify demands and critique from the 'margins' and the 'bottom.' ... Legitimating democratic inquiry, PAR signifies a fundamental right to ask, investigate, dissent and demand what could be" (Fine and Torre 2006).

The approach that we outline in the next part of the chapter reflects the experiences of organizations around the country and elsewhere in the world that have been promoting PAR as an opportunity to do research on the world in order to change it. It also draws from the nearly thirty years of experience of the Institute for Community Research, a Hartford, CT, based, community-based research organization that has conducted short- and long-term PAR programs for youth and adults since 1988. ICR's approach is both consistent with and different from other transformational PAR centers, such as those at Cornell and the CUNY Graduate Center. ICR is a community-based, community-situated organization. As such, it can hire and train community residents and activists to conduct research. And it can translate research and community organizing technology into usable tools so that community participants—residents, activists, leaders, youth, children—can use research as a means of achieving personal, community, and social transformation based on their lived knowledge and new knowledge acquired through their own inquiry. ICR is not bound by academic cycles or university hiring policies, and it can support research innovations without anyone having to worry about promotion, tenure, or faculty criticism. ICR research personnel have conducted PAR with adults and youth (Schensul, Berg, and Williamson 2008; Williamson and Brown 2014) and trained youth workers, teachers, and college and university educators. ICR also has worked with community organizations in Connecticut, across the United States, and in Europe using its youth curriculum. Most recently ICR's PAR curriculum for youth has been adopted and adapted for use by the Oregon Health Authority (Mosher and Schensul 2014), where ICR staff has been involved in training OHA youth workers to use it with teams of young people both face-to-face and through online distance training.

PARTICIPATORY ACTION RESEARCH THEORY AND METHODS

As we have stated above, PAR involves far more than the mere group conduct of research. PAR is designed to build strong individual identities, self-efficacy, and critical consciousness. PAR facilitation processes also are designed to collectivize the research experience, to co-construct knowledge for action through interactive data collection and analysis, and to forge a strong *group* identity, mutual support, and willingness to work together for a common goal. The theories and methods used as well as the facilitation techniques required to enable youth and adults to do PAR are fundamentally similar.

Theories

Cross Reference: See Book 1, chapter 3 and chapters 4 and 5 in this book

A number of theories underpin PAR work, and we summarize them here. Additional descriptions of most of the research-related theories can be found in Book 1, chapter 3 and this book, chapters 4 and 5. Pedagogical theories that are central to PAR as an educational approach include the following:

- critical theories
- theories of identity and positionality
- ecological theories
- theories of power and empowerment
- cultural theories
- pedagogical/instructional theories

Because we have described some of these theoretical orientations in earlier chapters and books, we focus here only on two with immediate relevance: critical and pedagogical or teaching/learning theories.

Critical Theories

Critical theories focus on structural barriers to achieving greater equity, and point PAR projects to a critical analysis of the structures of power, dominance, and oppression. These theories argue that conducting an initial analysis of power and oppressive structures provides the basis for taking action to change such structures. First used with impoverished and illiterate farmers in Brazil, Paulo Freire's often-cited approach was to create the visual and cognitive tools, including reading, writing, and research, that enabled groups to analyze structural and experiential contradictions in their lived experience. The knowledge thus constructed led them to incite radical change in the landholding practices in Brazil that gave most land to the Catholic Church and wealthy ranchers and left the majority of farmers with insufficient land on which to make a living (Freire 1973; Ledwith 2007). Agency, or the idea that individuals can think and act for change even in difficult circumstances, is undergirded by "hope" (Canaan 2005), a concept that connects structural analysis to action and empowerment. "Hopeful" resistance to structural limitations and barriers occurs through examining, reflecting, and acting to change institutions that obstruct creation of more equitable distribution of resources (economic, educational, social, informational, etc.) across communities or groups (Ledwith 2007) and then never giving up on efforts to change them. This is especially important with respect to doing research with young people, who should be supported and encour-

Cross Reference: See Book 1, chapter 2 and chapter 5 of this book

aged in their efforts to change their worlds, but who can be impatient with the pace at which change occurs.

Instructional and Learning Theories

PAR first and foremost is an educational experience for facilitators and participants regardless of participants' ages or circumstances. Key to the process is full engagement of participants. Theories of instruction and learning guide facilitators to draw on participant capacities and involve them in socially situated learning/action activities. Useful pedagogical theories include those addressing the social construction of knowledge, social and sociocultural learning, theories of multiple intelligences, experiential education in community settings, and cooperative learning.

Constructivist theories position social learning theory within the social construction of knowledge. A constructivist perspective argues that individual understanding and cultural creation and transmission are mediated by the knowledge bases and concepts people already hold and are generated during the process of interpersonal exchanges (Berger 1990; Rogoff 2003; Vygotsky 1978; Wertsch 1985). Thus, they occur through mediated learning. Its proponents hold that engaging in communication, collaborative problem solving, negotiation of divergent perspectives, and the joint construction of new ideas and norms will result in higher forms of reasoning (using information and problem solving while making decisions about action), new interpersonal skills (idea negotiation, persuasive communication, and consensus building), and new cultural constructions. These skills are critical in improving educational performance and in supporting activist-oriented social-change efforts.

PAR also draws heavily on the concept of multiple intelligences, a notion that stemmed from Sternberg's Triarchic Theory of Human Intelligence (Sternberg 1985). Sternberg believed, and tried to demonstrate, that intelligence could be organized and measured under three rubrics: analytic (academic problem solving), creative (ability to respond to novel situations), and practical (the ability to grasp, understand, and deal with everyday tasks). Howard

Gardner followed with the idea that multiple intelligences, or sensory modalities, are preferred ways of learning and relating to the world. These "intelligences" include musical/rhythmic, visual/spatial, verbal/linguistic, mathematical, bodily/kinesthetic, interpersonal, intrapersonal, and naturalistic (Gardner 1993), as well as emotional intelligence. Gardner's work illustrates that people prefer to learn in one or two of these modalities, but he emphasizes that everyone is capable of learning through each of them. The concept of multiple intelligences is pedagogically relevant, in that it suggests that full involvement of all learners requires facilitators to offer learning experiences in more than one modality (Waree 2013). Social learning/development theory takes the position that learning occurs in communities of learners—in social settings and in interaction with others, both formally and informally (Kozulin 1990; Lave and Wenger 1991; Wenger 1998). These include such settings as:

- workshops, kitchens, greenhouses, and gardens used as classrooms;
- ordinary classrooms;
- stand-up role playing in real world settings, including most military training (much of which, though, takes a behaviorist approach);
- field trips, including archaeological digs and participant-observer studies in cultures different from those of the learners;,
- on-the-job training, including apprenticeship and cooperative education;
- sports practice, music practice, and art, which involve situated learning *by definition,* as the exact actions in the real setting are precisely those with which novices practice—and with the same equipment or instruments.

PAR approaches are uniquely well suited to projects initiated in such settings.

Cooperative learning is a specific application of social learning theory that involves providing guided activities for collaborative learning and problem solving through individual, small-group, and large-group exercises. Moving away from the traditional and authoritarian idea of teachers or leaders as "sage on the stage" and toward notions of the "guide on the side," cooperative learning positions the teacher or leader not as the ultimate authority but as a guide who provides assistance to learners who work in groups to solve problems or engage in learning activities. However, it involves much more than simple learning in groups. Key components are positive interdependence, individual accountability, equal participation, and simultaneous interaction in groups. Individuals in these groups usually differ with regard to their ability in the specific learning activities, so that more competent learners can assist those who are still novices. Additionally, while each group member offers specific areas of competence, all members of the group learn and practice all the skills involved in solving the specific problem posed. Experiences at each level are coordinated to reinforce decision making, analytic and self-reflection skills, interpersonal communication, and persuasive argumentation. The overall goal is for each member of the group to master all of the skills needed to solve the problem.

PAR INSTRUCTIONAL TECHNIQUES AND FACILITATION SKILLS

PAR facilitation skills and instructional techniques are derived from the theories we have just outlined. They build on the ideas of helping learners move from novice to expert status in skills that are acquired through observing how expert teachers or guides model desired behavior, practicing those skills themselves, then learning to assist others in communities of learning and practicing doing so. Of crucial importance in the co-construction of knowledge and action is that power sharing should occur between facilitators and PAR researchers. Reluctance to relinquish power to learners is a challenge to facilitators' ability to implement emancipatory PAR (Galletta and Jones 2010; McHugh and Kowalski 2011; Sánchez 2009). Facilitators use specific skills and techniques to engage participants in guided learning, to encourage dialogue, to foster problem solving and argumentation skills, to build consensus, and to reinforce power sharing in the collaborative learning and action venture. Facilitation skills include:

- guided learning through questioning, providing new or contrasting information to create disagreements/discussion, suggesting options for research and action, and offering feedback to enhance participant-led inquiry;
- scaffolding—building on and extending ideas and experiences presented by group members, and linking knowledge to be acquired to prior knowledge and experience possessed by the learners;
- modeling—demonstrating how an exercise or learning process is done;
- explication—explaining or summarizing and synthesizing points made by the group;
- reflection—group and individual deconstruction and analysis of experiences to further learning and individual and group development (cf. Nastasi and DeZolt 1994).

In response, PAR participants are expected to ask questions, gain and organize information, exchange ideas, engage in **argumentation** to promote their own carefully thought-out opinions, and participate in exercises that help them to arrive at consensus. They also reflect on their values, biases, learning process, accomplishments, emotions, relationships with others, and the degree to which they are moving toward accomplishing their personal and group goals.

Definition: Argumentation is a process of discussion, disagreement, and debate based on logical reasoning to arrive at a mutually acceptable conclusion

EXAMPLE 9.3

FACILITATING A PAR SESSION

In a prevention study designed to improve communication between Latina and African American mothers/"other mothers" and their daughters, one of the issues that created conflict between girls and their female caregivers was boyfriends and dating/parties. Behind the mothers' immediate concern was a fear that their daughters would find themselves in a compromised position, pregnant, and having to "put their lives on hold." One component of the curriculum involved protection against sexuality-related risks and HIV. Facilitator Evelyn Baez worked with a group of heterosexual adolescent girls to encourage them to think about how to protect themselves from HIV and how to communicate their protection goals to their boy-friends (fictitious or otherwise). The process ensued as follows:

Evelyn: *Have any of you had a boyfriend that you felt close to or that you thought about getting close to?*

Group responds one way or the other. They discuss.

Evelyn: *Can you think of what you would consider to be "getting too close to you"? For example, if your boyfriend wanted to be alone with you when your mother was out.* (guided learning)

Group discusses examples of "getting too close." Each person lists an idea; one idea follows and builds on another. (scaffolding)

Evelyn: *Let's discuss these examples. Let's take them one by one. We can think about examples of when each of these might be getting too close or not. Everyone's opinion counts. Our goal is to discuss and understand what we mean by these situations and come to a decision about when they might be risky or uncomfortable and why.* (explication)

Group discusses: Being alone when no one is home
Being alone after a party in a car
Wanting to talk about sex
Putting pressure on to have unwanted sex
(other examples are brainstormed)

Once the listing exercise and discussion are completed, and no new ideas come forward, the conversation proceeds as follows:

Evelyn: *So let's summarize the discussion. What do you see here?* (guided learning)

Group: They mention that all situations can be risky, that there are different kinds of risk and that sex is not the only risk. One says, "I might not be able to say no even if I know I could get pregnant or I could get AIDS, because he wants me to."

Evelyn: *So it's important to assess the situation, and to keep in mind all the possible things that could happen when you are in one of them.* (explication) *What can you do when you feel you can't say no?*

Group: We could avoid the situation; we could be prepared with a condom; we could stay with our friends.

Evelyn: *For example, I could say that I need to stay by my girls at the party so I can't leave now* (modeling). *What are some other solutions that would work and you would be OK with?*

Group: Lists and discusses solutions.

Evelyn: *Let's take a moment. Write down on this card one or two things that you have learned from this discussion (probes for listening, offering ideas, responding to ideas, letting people finish their thoughts, helpful solutions).* (reflection)

PAR METHODS

PAR methodology builds on the theories described above to ensure group participation. It also creates participatory ways of using all of the methods and tools of ethnography and inputs of multiple disciplines to assist members of a PAR group to learn about and find ways of addressing social justice issues through social and political forms of action. But PAR groups are not simply classrooms; they are self- or socially constructed research/action groups. Thus, good research for action must be embedded in methods of group development and identity construction. Core elements of PAR methodology, as detailed in Table 9.1, include:

- Individual identity exploration
- Group/team building
- Understanding the value of research
- Introduction to research methods
- Identifying/building a research/action model
- Data collection and action approaches linked to models
- Group data and action analysis
- Representation of results
- Group action decisions

TABLE 9.1   Participatory Action Research core methods

PAR Methodology: Core Elements of Participatory Research	Participatory Activities
Individual identity	• Photographs or photovoice • Personal timeline • Auto ethnography (telling or acting one's story) • Letter to friend or relative about self and situation • Identity thermometer or chart • Identity collages or models • Identity installations (life-size dolls or other personal images) • Multiple intelligences or capacities assessment • Personal poem • Journaling
Group identity	• Group icebreakers • Creating a collective symbol and explaining it • Creating a group product • Doing group activities
Defining research and researchers	• Simulation showing its utility • Defining research • Drawing or acting out images of researchers and debunking myths • Showing work of other PAR groups
Introduction to research methods	• Brainstorming and scaffolding methods options • Research stations
Identifying a research problem through consensus	• Individual inquiry using photographs, artifacts, poems, or other personal/experiences or observations • Using a small group Delphi process • Using whole group brainstorm, discussion, and prioritization process • Group free listing, pile sorting, and consensus analysis
Building causal research action models	• Ecological modeling • Simple linear modeling with hypotheses, goals, and action options • Complex linear modeling with hypotheses, goals, and action options • System dynamics modeling with hypothesized links among components, and desired outcomes and positive and negative feedback loops
Data collection approaches: Throughout, these data collection approaches are all geared toward identifying information, allies, resources, potential actions, feasibility of actions, and obstacles to action.	• Observations and unobtrusive measures (individual, group, visual recording; audio recording, counting) • Interviews (individual, group) • Elicitation methods (pile sorts, collages, responses to images, objects, or actions) • Mapping (locating events, demographics, interactions, people, or reactions/emotions/consequences on a body or geographic surface) social, hand drawn, GIS or geographically accurate mapping • Surveys (internet or paper/pencil) • Secondary sources (archives, Internet, national and state data sets, town and city maps, articles, and summaries) • Videos and films

(continued)

TABLE 9.1 *Continued*

PAR Methodology: Core Elements of Participatory Research	Participatory Activities
Participatory analysis/ reflection	• Informal reviews of research experiences • Transcriptions and coding • Analysis of quantitative data • Linking results to research model and hypotheses • Identifying actors and resources for action
Representation and action	• Face-to-face presentations of results and continued data collection through responses to different audiences • Public media campaigns • Community mobilization • Appeals to policy makers

Individual Identity Exploration

Individual identity exploration uses an interdisciplinary constructivist perspective including multiple intelligences and culturally specific social, emotional, and cognitive competencies. Some examples of methods to promote exploration of identity are:

■ Using photographs to highlight ideas, contextual elements, or material items important to an individual and sharing them with others (a form of photovoice). This was illustrated through an ICR program called "Recipes for Life" in which older adults were given cameras and took photographs of people, places, and things important to them, which they then shared in an exhibit along with quotes about their lives.

Cross Reference: See Book 4, chapter 9, for details of this method

■ Using a personal timeline to do autoethnography and sharing it (Boylorn and Orbe 2013; Chang, Ngunjiri, and Hernandez 2012). In a project to build community leadership through PAR, Puerto Rican parents created their own lifelines showing when they migrated to the United States. Then they compared their collective lifelines to an historical timeline showing waves of migration to the United States, the conditions under which it occurred, and the economic, social, and psychological consequences for those who came and those who remained.

■ Writing a letter or telling a story to a relative in another location in the country or world about one's situation. The immigrant parents above presented their stories and lifeline in a letter to their children telling them about their personal histories.

- Using an identity "thermometer" to identify location on the LGTBQ "coming out" continuum. Each week, young adults in an LGTBQ of Color PAR group rated themselves on a thermometer that stretched along the wall, ranging from heterosexual to lesbian/gay. During a period in which identities as lesbian, gay, or transgender were emergent, they could see how their perceptions of their gender identities shifted and changed in a nonlinear manner over time.

- Building "identity" collages and describing them to others. This activity is enhanced by a collection of found objects that can be used to create small two- or three-dimensional images that represent the multiple personas of the makers. For example, young people have made three-dimensional collages of found objects and paper in empty pizza boxes. Adult community health advocates and active drug users utilized found objects to make auto-representative, two- or three-dimensional works of art, which they exhibited with personal statements about their lives and themselves.

- Building life-size models of imagined selves and exhibiting them in a gallery format. In a program to reinforce self-efficacy, teen girls used thick cardboard to create bigger than life-size "dolls" as representations of themselves. They dressed the dolls according to their vision and hopes for themselves in the future.

- Taking a multiple-intelligence or other capacities assessment that evaluates learning styles (Gardner 1993). This approach is based on instruments designed to measure eight different forms of intelligence or proclivity for learning and relating to the world. Participants rate themselves on subscales for each type of intelligence and compare themselves to the mean; they also rate themselves using a Delphi strategy, by placing up to three stickers next to a maximum of three different intelligences, from eight to eleven in all, arrayed in a chart on the wall.

- Keeping a personal journal on things learned and experienced and plans for future.
- Writing a poem based on "I am . . . statements." Statements are:

  - I am (two special characteristics)
  - I wonder (something you are curious about)
  - I hear (an imaginary sound)
  - I see (an imaginary sight)
  - I want (an actual desire)
  - I am (the first line of the poem restated)
  - I pretend (something you pretend to do)
  - I feel (a feeling about something imaginary)
  - I touch (an imaginary touch)
  - I worry (something that really bothers you)
  - I cry (something that makes you very sad)
  - I am (the first line of the poem repeated)
  - I understand (something you know is true)
  - I say (something you believe in)
  - I dream (something you actually dream about)
  - I try (something you make an effort to do)
  - I hope (something you actually hope for)
  - I am (the first line of the poem repeated)

Here is an example of an I-AM poem.

I Am

I am sharp and focused
I wonder what the camera really sees
I hear the buzzing bee
I see flowers in early morning light
I want to stop time in a box
I am sharp and focused
I pretend to be a statue
I feel the shakes inside
I touch the shutter button
I worry about the blurry result
I cry that the moment has forever passed
I am sharp and focused

I understand moments in time
I say let's freeze them forever
I dream of watercolor effects coming to life
I try to see all the soft muted edges
I hope it happens someday
I am sharp and focused

(http://ettcweb.lr.k12.nj.us/forms/iampoem.htm)

Group Team Building

A strong sense of group commitment is critical to a sound PAR team. A sense of group identity should be instilled from the first moments of a PAR effort, through references to the importance of working together, developing mutual understanding, and addressing and negotiating differences. Group team building is based on recognizing and building on individual strengths for collective good. Group team building for learning and action is a critical component in PAR, and more so since participants are unlikely to have acquired much prior experience or practice with cooperative or collaborative group learning, problem solving, and/or action in their formal schooling or work settings. Some activities promoting team identity are:

- introducing group icebreakers that demonstrate how a goal requires the participation of all team members (unraveling a net or solving a puzzle);
- creating a group name, concept, or brand;
- creating a collective symbol;
- generating a group product (e.g., a social map of a city, collective migration routes on a map, the "ideal school").

Group activities should not be implemented only at the beginning of a project; they should carry on throughout the life of the PAR effort to continually reinforce the sense of group identity.

Understanding the Value of Research

Many people enter into a PAR project without fully understanding what research is or why it is valuable. They also may bring with them myths, misunderstandings, and negative stereotypes about what research is and who can do it. They may feel that they are not capable of doing research, or they may want to go right into "action" because they do not necessarily understand the value of prior field investigations and exploration. It is important to disabuse group members of these myths, misunderstandings, insecurities, and natural inclinations by explaining that, especially now, successful efforts to bring about change require knowledge of community issues and inhabitants as well as personal experiences and activist mobilization. Such knowledge consists of learning about policies, institutions, people, and the opinions and experiences of others. Armed with this knowledge, people gain a better understanding of how to take action, with whom, and in what settings. Both youth and adults are listened to and "heard" if their arguments are bolstered with systematically collected information as well as case studies and testimony. Some ways of introducing PAR participants to the meaning of research and why they should and can conduct research of their own are:

- Simulations illustrating why more systematically collected information is necessary to come to a decision or create a project. Examples include holding a "mock court" that offers a jury of peers insufficient information to come to a decision, or posing a complex problem such as deciding where to locate a garbage dump or a mall and why or how to improve school lunches or reduce teen dating violence.
- Sentence completion exercises. Facilitators can ask group members to respond in a call out (or in writing) to the statement: "research is". . . followed by guided discussion.
- Presentation of a drawing of a stereotyped image of a researcher (e.g., male, white coat, in a laboratory) and explaining the thinking behind the drawing to

the group, followed by a discussion of why everyone has the power, ability, potential, and right to do
research on issues that affect them.
■ Examples of others' PAR research.

The first goal of such exercises is to demonstrate to the group
that everyone, including the disenfranchised, nonliterate,
racially and ethnically marginalized, and all others without
perceived power have the right and the responsibility to conduct research on issues that have a profound impact on their
lives, and do something about them. The second goal is to
illustrate why people need to collect more information before
they can act effectively. The third goal of the exercises is to
show that research is an everyday activity that everyone is
capable of doing to reach an important goal.

Identifying a Research Problem

Like any research project, PAR begins with the identification of a problem or issue to explore. In chapter 5 of this
book (the participatory modeling chapter), and in Books
1 and 2, we have discussed the many possible sources of
potential research problems or targets. However, in PAR,
the participants themselves, not the researchers, identify
the issue, which emerges from their own lived experiences
and observations of disparities or things they would like
to change in their own communities or other settings. It
is important for facilitators to find ways of enabling group
members to observe and reflect on these issues. Facilitators
can use collaborative or individual + group strategies that
highlight important problems. Individual + group activities require more time than group exercises alone, especially if they call for individuals to explore their physical
as well as psycho-social environment, take notes—field
notes—on them, and share the results with the group.
However, collective strategies also have some limitations.
When they are based on brainstorming and discussion,
they run the risk of constraining issue identification to
what participants already know. When they are based on
group exploration of the external environment, they are
constrained by time, resources for transportation, permis-

sions (in the case of underage youth), and the challenges of organizing group visits to specific locations where participants can observe, compare, and analyze what they see. Some techniques to help participants identify the issues of priority to them are:

- asking participants to take photographs of situations with high-impact value that can be printed, displayed, and discussed (gang graffiti, an important neighborhood mural, deteriorating buildings, children playing near illegal drug refuse or a garbage dump, schools with and without playground equipment, open second and third floor windows without screens, sculptures or murals with historical significance, e-cigarette ads in neighborhood shop windows, etc.);
- showing preselected images representing an array of positions or indicators of a problem (images of alcohol or expensive cars projected in magazines, on billboards, and other print material);
- arranging group visits to sites differentiated by class or culture that create opportunities for participants to observe and interrogate differences and inequalities (e.g., communities where clustering of liquor stores occurs in some but not all neighborhoods; differences in food quality, variation, type, and price in suburban versus urban supermarkets; differences between school facilities in inner city neighborhoods and more affluent suburbs, etc.);
- organizing walks through neighborhoods to observe and discuss what they see (beautiful buildings or buildings in disrepair, high quality food sources or corner stores, school yards and parks with different types of equipment, etc.);
- making visits to key informants to find out about differences in perspectives on proposed changes in policies such as legalization of recreational marijuana;
- group listings and prioritization of issues or problems, elaborated discussion, and subsequent negotiation to consensus.

Creativity is called for in inventing activities that are appropriate to the developmental stage of PAR participants, group characteristics, time of year, and resources at hand. Activities arranged for elementary- and middle school–age youth are likely to be different from those prepared for ninth or eleventh graders. Further, facilitators must work hard to encourage consensus within the group without alienating any group members. It's best to emerge from the issue-identification process with only one key issue if possible, since working on a single important issue builds group identity, consensus and power, and avoids unnecessary strain on staff and other resources as well as potential division and competition among groups.

Introduction to Research Methods

Most members of a PAR group have had formal experience gathering some form of information in school or in life (for example, gathering documents during immigration processes, getting a driver's license, finding out about the quality of neighborhood schools, or assembling an application for school entry or a job). They have had to engage in systematic inquiry to accomplish these goals. Thus, research as inquiry should not be unfamiliar to most people in a PAR group—especially if these activities are called to their attention and identified as information gathering. However, *systematic group inquiry* that uses research methodology and different approaches to data collection to provide the rationale and information needed for social change will be a new experience for many. To assist group members to understand research methodology, a tried-and-true strategy is to demonstrate that all action/researchers need a "methods" roadmap, by rotating them through "research stations." Research stations run by the facilitators or experienced community or youth PAR co-facilitators expose small groups of participants to brief ten-to-twenty-minute research exercises, in a three-to-six-hour experiential-learning role play. While facilitators can be creative about designing this instructional experience depending on the situation, staff resources, and their own comfort level, research stations usually include the following components:

- Problem identification—at this station, group members are asked to brainstorm an important issue that needs to be addressed in their community or a change they wish to make. Group members quickly discuss and prioritize.

- Systems modeling (ecological, linear, or system dynamics models)—at this station, group members are asked to put the issue or change goal from the prior station in a box (dependent variable), or on a trend line, and identify several causes of the problem or contributors to the change goal (independent variables). They are asked to discuss and then explain the links between independent and dependent variables—thus creating hypotheses. They learn the language of modeling, practice assembling models, and leave the station with a workable one.

  Cross Reference: 𝍫
  See chapter 5 in this book for a discussion of such models

- Research methods stations—several stations offer small groups exposure to different approaches to data collection and analysis. Usually these are face-to-face brief informal interviews that the facilitators model; surveys, in which participants develop a brief survey based on their dependent domain and one or two independent domains; exposure to visual materials such as maps, overlays with instruction; and photographs and videos. Participants learn how to use different types of these materials with an experienced facilitator, discuss the pros and cons of data collection using the materials, and practice learning to do free lists and sorting activities. In the process, they learn how to collect data related to their model at the individual, cultural, and structural levels, and how to use the data collection process to analyze the potential of their data to instigate change and to identify both available resources to support the change, and allies and obstacles to its implementation.

  Cross Reference: 𝍫
  See Book 4, chapter 3, for a discussion of free lists, pile sorts, and similar strategies

- Representation—at this station, participants learn about the different change strategies available to them as well as multiple ways of using their results to persuade or promote change at multiple levels.

Identifying a Research/Action Model

In chapter 4 of this book, we described a variety of ways of developing indigenous or local research models. Facilitators can be creative in devising interactive exercises to help groups create these models. Some strategies that have been found to be useful are:

- *Eco-modeling games,* in which a large size (4-foot-by-6-foot or larger) bull's-eye representing an eco-map is hung or placed on the floor or wall with levels predefined (individual group, organizational, media, community, policy, etc.). Participants take turns drawing cards with instructions or statements. One set of cards identifies possible issues. From this set each group member chooses one card. Each member of the group then throws a large set of dice. The issue card of the person with the highest score is placed in the center of the eco-map. The second set of cards identifies many possible strategies for resolving issues. The third set identifies many possible causes of issues. Each participant chooses one card with a strategy for solving the problem or a contributor to the problem, decides if the card is appropriate for the issue, and places the card in its proper level and explains why. The process goes on until there is at least one strategy, and cards are completed. Some cards will be relevant to the issue, others will be discarded. The facilitator summarizes by pointing out connections between causes, strategies, and the issue and the need for more information to determine how causes and strategies might really affect the issue.
- *Performing a linear model.* The facilitator asks the group to identify an important issue and invites a volunteer from the group to become the "dependent variable" and describe it to the group. The facilitator then invites the group to identify "causes," or independent variables. The individuals who identify each cause/independent variable are positioned on the floor, as in a performance space, in relation to one

another as actors, acting out the role of their variable domain and describing what it is and why it is connected to other domains—including the initial problem domain. The facilitator then debriefs the group and they discuss the process and what they have learned.

■ *Brainstorming a linear or complex model.* The facilitator asks members of the group to identify an issue quickly. Then each member is asked to think about possible causes and write them on sticky notes, which are placed one by one on the wall to the left of the issue (dependent variable) with explanations (hypotheses). Next, the group is asked to think about possible "causes of the causes," thus extending the model. The facilitator can then transform this into a multilevel model or a system dynamics model.

Data Collection and Action Approaches

In most PAR group projects, there is too little time to try out all possible data-collection methods. Thus, groups must decide which ones to use and why, and connect their choices to their model. Choices will depend on facilitator comfort with implementation of the method and analysis of the data collected, time available, weather conditions (for outside data collection), access to respondents or observation sites, technical skills of the group, and resources (e.g., film editing, drawing, obtaining maps and secondary data). For youth groups, face-to-face interactive methods such as face-to-face interviews and pile sorts are a priority because they offer opportunities for young people to improve their social and inquiry skills and to meet key people who could be instrumental in their action strategy. Surveys and videoed interviews are important in convincing audiences, including policy makers, of the depth and scope of an issue and its recommended solutions. In general, we recommend choosing at least one type of open- or semi–open-ended interview, a paper/pencil or electronic survey, and a visual method (video, film, photography). Participants can then work together in staging data collection or can divide into working groups and triangulate

Cross Reference: See Books 3 and 4 for a discussion of various approaches to data collection

their results at the end. As part of their in-depth orientation to the method, it is important to explain to participants how the data will be analyzed. Facilitators also should be sure that the group understands how the data they want to collect relates to their model and be ready to help them to prepare the tools necessary to collect the data. Morgan and colleagues, and Schensul, and colleagues include good overall explanations of this process (Morgan et al. 2004; Schensul, Berg, and Nair 2012).

Participatory Analysis

Conducting participatory analysis of data collected by group members poses a challenge to most PAR facilitators. Simple and straightforward approaches are best. In group analysis, group members should meet to discuss what they have collected and why. Working with the facilitator's guidance, the group then reviews steps in the analysis of each type of data, thus making sure that all participants have a clear understanding of what data have been collected, why they were collected, and how to analyze it. They then enter their data into software that facilitates analysis of text, elicitation data, and quantitative data. Free software for these functions is available on the Internet, and word processors or text management programs can be used as well. Interview data, which must be in text form, must be coded for analysis. This does not have to be done with a computer, especially if the amount of data is small. However, computers can facilitate the process. Hand coding on paper involves entering letters or numbers denoting specific items or using color coding for key concepts, highlighting relevant text where the concept appears. Color coding makes it possible to count the number of times a concept is mentioned, explore the nuances of a block of text, and extract quotes to make key points. Sometimes cutting apart a hard copy of differently colored coded text blocks and grouping them is an easy way of actually visualizing how often a concept is mentioned—as well as what is in it. Survey data can be counted for simple frequencies or cross-tabulated. Excel is useful for creating and displaying frequencies. Photographs can be documented, classified, and arranged to tell a story. These activities should all be carried out by participants with guided facilitation. In-depth interviews with individual respondents can be reviewed for examples of specific cases, life histories, or other illustrative materials. Most of the chapters that cover different mixed methods ethnographic approaches to data collection in Book 4 of the *Toolkit* also include information about how to analyze these data. This information can be adapted for use by different lay researchers across the developmental spectrum. Book 5 provides a variety of approaches to the analysis of mixed methods data which also can be readily adapted and apply very well to working in a participatory manner with community youth and adults. Foster-Fishman and colleagues also provide a good description of how to organize and conduct thematic analysis with youth (Foster-Fishman et al. 2010).

Cross Reference:
See Book 4, all chapters, and Book 5, all chapters

Once the data are analyzed, methods groups should present their results to the entire group for discussion. There are many ways of "disseminating" these data, including public presentations, workshops, performances, and visual presentations. Chapter 8 in this book provides some general ideas about sharing information with public audiences, and advocating for specific desired results, that can be adapted for use with lay groups. In preparation for sharing, the discussions should focus on ways of representing the results, summarizing them, and presenting whatever has been learned about actual or potential actions to address the issue.

CONTINUING THE ACTION RESEARCH CIRCLE

Some approaches to PAR training limit themselves to the use of knowledge that is co-constructed by the group without engaging in additional data collection. Some PAR groups have a short life and, for reasons of funding or other resource constraints, do not continue beyond the initial data collection/action period. Their effect is limited to what they can do with media and policy makers or peers during the time they have available. Others operate on the basis of annual cycles in which new members are recruited, bringing with them new issues and concerns.

The mission and commitment to change continues, but the groups vary. Others have the resources and membership to continue, but are faced with the loss of initial members—those who have actually identified the issue under consideration, suggested the directions for change, implemented an action strategy, and collected and represented the data to the public. While the group and/or its facilitators may want to continue, they must recruit and orient many new members who may want to change the framing of the original problem, or may want to collect their own data and devise their own action strategies.

One way to address this dilemma is to conceptualize PAR groups as part of a larger movement. This can be challenging, because movements are issue, not method, based. An important tenet of PAR is that community groups identify their own issues. Larger movements, such as immigration or school reform, pre-frame the issues, thus circumscribing or limiting who might be interested in joining. Further, most movements already have defined how they want to go about addressing their issues. While they often are heavily committed to community organizing, they may be little or not at all interested in the added benefits of inquiry, even if it served to adapt the movement better to the local setting. Finally, many movements like the food justice movement are slow to include the voices of those marginalized by race/ethnicity, identity, or income.

Another response is to build local PAR groups into a *local* movement. This can be done if facilitators have a stable base and can work with PAR groups to help them see that their issues can be incorporated into higher-order concerns. For example, a substance abuse prevention program based on youth PAR in the town of West Hartford, Connecticut, parlayed the work of young people into a youth-invented and youth-driven high school substance abuse prevention campaign which they called "Lead by Example." This campaign became integrated into the public schools as a set of youth-led clubs, and the concept of "lead by example" diffused to a larger effort to change and improve the school environment at both the high school and middle school levels.

It is not difficult to conceptualize the potential connections between PAR and social movements that are undergirded by community organizing to promote social justice–oriented change. However, PAR fundamentally also is an educational strategy, helping participants to deepen their critical consciousness, collective identity, and feelings of efficacy. PAR reframes power relationships by enhancing participants' power through increasing their knowledge, building allies, and promoting change. Practically, however, linking macro-movements at the national and international levels with local PAR activist and social justice–driven efforts is likely to remain a challenge.

DEVELOPING AND SUSTAINING PAR FACILITATORS

Developing a cadre of effective PAR facilitators is the first and most important step in the organization of an effective PAR program (Amsden and Van-Wynsberghe 2005), whether working with youth or adults (or both). Effective involvement in PAR requires dedication to social justice issues and an activist stance; deep understanding of and experience with ethnographic research methods; knowledge of pedagogical theories and developmental approaches appropriate for youth and adult experiential learning; understanding of local community cultures—including their residential variability, history and politics; and the desire not only to *do* research but also to *teach* research in a non–academic setting for a sustained period of time. PAR participants bring knowledge, lived experience, and cultural richness to their groups. At the same time, they may have limited literacy or cognitive or information-processing skills; or they may bear the emotional scars of forced immigration, historical trauma, exposure to civil, social, or interpersonal violence, stigma, discrimination, exclusion, or continued negative feedback and criticism of their language and culture. On an ongoing basis, PAR facilitators must assess the skills and abilities of participants and determine how to integrate their lived experiences, personal struggles, skills, and educational gaps into the work. Recruits to PAR facilitation may have several, but often do not have all, of these characteristics. Thus, finding, training, and retaining PAR facilitators remains a significant challenge.

Adult facilitators of youth PAR require both formal and site-specific training. Their training should include all the skills that they need to work with youth and adult groups:

- the ability to engage in reflection on positionality and power
- pedagogical techniques that make possible knowledge co-construction in group settings
- methodological training
- empathetic knowledge-based ability to relate to group members

Thus, it is critical to select, train, support, and pay facilitators to ensure that they have the skills and continuing motivation to do their work.

One way of supporting community-based PAR facilitators is to link them to sympathetic college and university faculty in the local setting. Some examples of such linkages include the association between Marlene Berg, an ICR-based ethnographer dedicated to youth PAR, and Evelyn Phillips, an anthropologist based at a state university with a commitment to school-based youth PAR. Establishing such linkages is a good idea and attempts should be made to overcome the difficulties encountered in attempting to build them. The main difficulty is finding interested faculty with the time and the skills to participate consistently over time, and students for whom they can provide supervision and mentorship. Younger faculty tend to be interested in PAR outside the academy, but work with PAR often is not valued by promotion and tenure committees, making it difficult for these faculty to find the time and support to engage in it. Nevertheless, as more universities move toward valuing community-engaged work, and are more able to bend promotion and tenure rules, it may become easier to forge PAR partnerships between community facilitators and university faculty across disciplines. One practical way of furthering the dialogue is to integrate PAR courses and practica into social science, critical methods, and foundational education curricula in institutions of higher education. We discuss how this has been done in the next chapters.

ETHICAL ISSUES IN PAR

While the usual ethical issues important in community-based ethnographic research come into play in PAR, both youth PAR and adult PAR introduce some new ethical considerations. Youth PAR is intended to enhance young people's ability to make informed judgments about social and environmental injustices that affect them and their communities. The approaches youth select may be critical of school or other institutional policies and actions, or youth may want to do something about the failure of the social service system to serve them adequately (Cammarota and Romero 2011; Cammarota and Romero 2009; Morsillo and Prilleltensky 2007). For these reasons, ethical considerations require assurance that the research young people undertake does not place them in positions of undue risk as individuals, within their families or in their schools and communities. This means that it must both result in some intended benefit, and allow the youth to engage in activities that engender a feeling of empowerment without getting them into serious trouble (Ritterbusch 2012). Schools might disallow research and action on topics that youth suggest, such as youth suicide or depression, violence or drug selling in school settings. When authorities disallow either youth-selected topics or the methods the youths choose for collecting data, or do not permit them to present their data, the experience is very discouraging and can contradict the positive effects the projects intend to foster.

During the process of collecting data, youths may be asked to present their work or speak about their concerns to important stakeholders. These stakeholders may be the same people who are critical of youth, especially those who drop out of school, underperform, or who are otherwise perceived as incapable, inadequate, or socially undesirable. Preparing them well in advance can avoid reinforcing such stereotypes or making mistakes that could have a negative effect on their work. Beth Krensky's arts-in-action project with disaffected Latino/a middle schoolers described in

Example 11.12 in this book shows how a researcher avoided such pitfalls. Finally, youth-PAR groups often include young people who are facing difficult life situations, such as extreme poverty, poor housing, or abusive parents, that affect their concentration and their ability to relate to other group members. It is important to find ways of helping such youth cope with these issues in positive ways. Krensky's PAR project also illustrates how such preparation can literally transform attitudes, not only of once-criticized youth but also of the city officials and other authorities who held them in disesteem.

Both youth and adults can collect information from their peers and others in their own community, but they should be aware of the requirements for using human beings as research subjects. Special attention should be paid to training PAR members to avoid any violations of confidentiality, which could be detrimental both to the group and to the community at large (Chabot et al. 2012). Helping PAR members become knowledgeable about ethical and human-subjects issues can be facilitated by requiring both youth and adult researchers to obtain a formal certificate from a legitimate National Institutes of Health or university institutional review board to indicate that they have undergone human-subjects training. This training usually is provided by online courses that are sponsored by IRBs and easily accessed by participants. We have found this to be advantageous in introducing them to the importance of recognizing the risks and benefits of research and to understanding just what risks might inhere in the data-collection techniques they want to use. It also is helpful in conveying why their current work is a response to unethical and exploitative research practices in the past.

SUMMARY

In this chapter, we have focused on Participatory Action Research as a method for transferring power over research methodology and results to communities and groups affected by specific social justice–related problems that they wish to reverse. We've focused less on the issues and more on the process of how to discover and represent disparities and possible solutions. We have said that the PAR approach differs from other collaborative approaches in that community groups are not only partners in the co-construction of knowledge and its uses but also take leadership in both, with the support of experienced facilitators. We have referred to the theories behind this approach and showed how it applies to both youth and adults. We have outlined specific methods and tools for a fully participatory PAR process, by paralleling chapters in other books of the *Toolkit*, but gearing this chapter especially to lay research/ activists and facilitators.

Sustainability is important in PAR work, since it concerns creating knowledge for social change, which takes place over time. The chapter discusses some of the challenges in addressing sustainability, including the time- and program-bound nature of some PAR efforts, and the difficulties of linking local PAR efforts that are community driven with larger social movements. Though PAR is subject to general ethical considerations in community-based research, in this chapter we have reviewed some ethical considerations that are specific to PAR, both with youth and adults. Finally, since proper facilitation is key to good PAR programming, we discuss the characteristics of PAR facilitators and how to train and support them. One such way is to link community-based PAR efforts and facilitators to local university faculty and students. In the next chapter, we describe approaches and programs in post–secondary educational institutions that help to build capacity for PAR in community settings.

10 ━━◆━━◆━━◆━━◆━━

INSTITUTIONAL INFRASTRUCTURE FOR TEACHING PARTICIPATORY ACTION RESEARCH IN HIGHER EDUCATION SETTINGS

INTRODUCTION

In this chapter, we address the departmental and university structures and processes we think are needed to support higher education faculty who want to offer students experiences in meaningful collaborative and participatory ethnography in action. We discuss this issue because we believe traditional university training and structures are seldom hospitable to real and ongoing collaborations with communities. In fact, universities and their programs often have hostile, exploitative, or competitive relationships with the (often limited resource) communities that surround them. Further, the cultures of communities and those of the academy differ widely and can be incompatible, especially with regard to the conditions required for collaboration and participation among various sectors of the community, community members, and academic researchers such as:

- constraints imposed by structures of hierarchy and privilege;
- rigidities of time, schedules of courses and assignments;
- requirements for grading and other constraints.

All of these factors can make it almost impossible for even the most well-intentioned and committed faculty members to introduce collaborative and Participatory Action Research into their program offerings.

Notwithstanding the challenges, university/campus involvement in community engaged research (CER or CE) for social change has a long history, bolstered by a number of national organizations and foundations as well as arguments by engaged scholars for diverse approaches to CER. Following are some good examples of efforts that support these approaches:

- Community-Campus Partnerships for Health (CCPH), established in 1997, is a national non-profit membership organization that promotes health equity and social justice through partnerships between communities and academic institutions. CCPH organizes, educates, advocates, and conducts research on issues affecting community-campus research partnerships. It also offers seminars, webinars, an annual conference, and technical assistance to campuses, especially health-related schools and universities that want to form research collaborations with community partners. CCPH has worked to change and broaden guidelines for promotion and tenure for researchers building community research infrastructure; it initiated CES4Health (http://www.ces4health.info/), a program that peer reviews materials produced through community-university partnerships that are not publishable in journals so that faculty can use them as article equivalents when seeking promotion and tenure. It also posts these materials on its website to highlight the work of community partners. Each year CCPH holds a conference, often with counterparts in Canada, Latin America, and Europe, highlighting good community-university research partnerships and their results. CCPH envisioned the Community Network for Research Equity and Impact (CNREI, a network of community-based research organizations (CBROs) with very diverse constituencies that advocates regionally and nationally for better research relationships with university partners and more social justice research (https://ccph.memberclicks .net/about-us).

- Campus Community Compact is a national coalition of nearly 110 colleges and universities, the mission of which is to "advance the public purpose of colleges and universities by deepening their ability to improve community life and to educate students for civic and social responsibility." Dedicated to campus-based civic engagement, Campus Compact enables campuses to develop students' citizenship skills and forge effective community partnerships by offering resources and support to faculty and staff to pursue community-based teaching and scholarship in the service of positive change. Community Compact is a strong supporter of service learning (www.commu nitycompact.org), but is less focused than CCPH on social justice, disparities, and rights issues.
- The Carnegie Foundation for Advancement of Teaching initiated its community engagement classification in 2010. The classification is voluntary and requires an application (http://www.carnegie foundation.org/). As of 2015, 361 campuses across the country have been awarded the community engagement classification. Community engagement is defined as "collaboration between institutions of higher education and their larger communities (local, regional/state, national, global) for the mutually beneficial exchange of knowledge and resources in a context of partnership and reciprocity. The purpose is to enrich scholarship, research, and creative activity; enhance curriculum, teaching and learning; prepare educated, engaged citizens; strengthen democratic values and civic responsibility; address

critical societal issues; and contribute to the public good (http://carnegieclassifications.iu.edu/).

- The Consortium for Practicing and Applied Anthropology (COPAA) is a consortium of universities and departments dedicated to collectively advance the training of students, faculty, and practitioners in applied anthropology. COPAA offers a variety of resources for university programs, including a visiting fellows program that brings well-known applied researchers to departments to talk with students and faculty, tenure and promotion recommendations, best practices materials in applied research, and guidelines for training practicing anthropologists. For students, it offers network opportunities, distance learning opportunities, and distance mentoring (http://www.copaa.info/index.htm).

CCPH's emphasis is on research partnerships to address health inequities. Both CC and the Carnegie Foundation have a teaching goal that is not specifically concerned with educational or other forms of systemic inequity; however in its general comments to campuses that did not receive the Community Engagement (CE) designation in 2015, the Foundation notes that some campuses have involved minority students in community efforts to address disparities or social injustices. It argues that these efforts must not be marginalized or remain isolated from the mainstream of campus community engaged work; instead, they must be integrated into community outreach efforts overall.

Derek Barker offers a useful overview of the political context of community engaged research and a framework that makes it easy to situate our argument for action research in community engaged scholarship (Barker 2004). Among the reasons he gives for promoting more engaged university scholarship are the decline in public commitment to public education, the isolating effects of siloed disciplines, the failure to prepare students for real-world life after college or graduate school, and student desire for more interactive forms of teaching and learning engagement. Action-oriented research and related activities falls into the second row in Barker's table, Table 10.1.

TABLE 10.1 Approaches to engaged scholarship

Practice	Theory	Problems	Methods
Public scholarship	Deliberative	Complex public problems requiring deliberation	Face to face open forums
Participatory research	Participatory democracy/social justice	Inclusion of specific (excluded) groups	Face to face with specific publics
Community partnerships	Social democracy	Social change/ structural transformation	Working with intermediaries
Public information networks	Democracy broadly understood	Problems of networking and communication	Data bases of public resources (network building)
Civic literacy scholarship	Democracy broadly understood	Enhancing public discourse	Communication with general public

Service and experiential learning can take many different forms, most of which offer opportunities for student placements that do not always require much faculty involvement or supervision. Once research enters the picture, especially when issues of disparities are concerned, faculty must be involved, and universities should be able to offer faculty who are concerned with improving community life and addressing inequalities some assurance that they will be supported and protected while establishing training opportunities for their students. In this chapter, we highlight ways that colleges and universities can provide such support to faculty and students.

Below we cover faculty needs, challenges, and models of successful teaching/training structures, and the difficulties of establishing appropriate experiences to students, both at the university and the department/program level and through programmatic centers and field schools. Finally, we discuss briefly some of the ways in which action-oriented applied research and training efforts can be funded or otherwise supported. We are very optimistic that, given the current emphasis on using engaged research to address injustices and social disparities, universities as well as funders will expand their attention and their resource allocations to include action research goals and ethnography in action.

OPPORTUNITIES AND CHALLENGES IN BUILDING INFRASTRUCTURE FOR TEACHING PARTICIPATORY ACTION RESEARCH IN HIGHER EDUCATION SETTINGS

University training must offer a range of guided and supervised learning experiences designed both to initiate would-be collaborative and participatory researchers into the research process and to help them hone their intellectual and practical skills in real-life applied settings. To organize such experiences, departments and faculty should consider the following:

- Whenever possible, hiring new faculty across disciplines who have had experience in research methods and community-based applied research
- Creating time and financial incentives for faculty who want to build research infrastructure and partnerships in community settings
- Developing courses, course sequences, and workshops for students so that they gain maximum exposure to research methods, field experiences, and responsible research with research partners
- Building opportunities for students to create group projects on their own
- Creating a campus environment favorable to engaged research with local partners, including community-campus exchanges around important social, health, and other disparities
- Establishing parity in the faculty reward structure between traditional academic research and publication and engaged research with local community partners
- Making sure that adequate infrastructure exists for seeking grants and other financial resources to support community partnership projects
- Supporting the establishment of field schools, training programs, and other experiential educational opportunities for students and appropriately rewarding faculty for running them

The key principles guiding instruction in community-based action-oriented research require:

- creating environments in which students can pursue relevant knowledge and skills;
- developing relationships of collaboration and solidarity with the study community;
- learning about, assisting in obtaining information for, and engaging in, social justice actions that communities or organizations want to pursue;
- "engaging in collaborative action that wins victories and builds self-sufficiency" (Stoecker 1999, 845).

In this context, research becomes a method, along with others, to achieve social-change goals. It also helps students learn how to do research of social significance in the context of larger community, health, or educational change efforts.

The terms most often applied to experiential teaching/learning designed to encourage research and social change are *action research, participatory action research, community-based participatory research (CBPR)*, and *service learning*. Action research/articipatory action research (AR/PAR) is the term favored by social scientists, primarily sociologists, anthropologists, and geographers, for activities that connect participatory place-based research with meaningful social-change-oriented action. The term *community-based participatory research* is favored by public health researchers as well as some others; it generally refers to collaborations between university researchers and communities of "identity" that integrate research with interventions and policy changes to remedy health disparities and injustices. Service learning has the longest and best articulated tradition of integrating classroom learning and community practice. As we will note in the next chapter, service-learning approaches guide students to individual or group service that can take many forms. It generally involves college undergraduates and K–12 students in a community-based learning exchange in which they can make a social contribution (provide a service) and reflect both on their experience and their roles and responsibilities as members of a civic society (Bonsall, Harris, and Markzakym 2002; Ward and Wolf-Wendel 2000).

Strand and colleagues have noted several different challenges that instructors face when teaching CBPR/service learning courses at the undergraduate level. The first is finding a disciplinary link between courses, including research methods courses and community issues or needs. The second is finding the time and space for community-based research in curricula that are restricted by the requirements of degree and certification requirements, specific coursework demands, and scheduling. Ensuring student readiness, structuring the experience for students, managing team projects, troubleshooting, and evaluation are all responsibilities that instructors must come to terms with during a single semester or summer program (Strand et al. 2003).

Experienced postsecondary faculty who want to train students for effective involvement in community action and change efforts must first prepare themselves for instruction. As faculty, they themselves should have or seek experience and reflexivity by engaging in action research–based social change pursuits together with communities. They should have research and facilitation skills, recognize their identity and positionality relative to both students and the community in which they are working, and be prepared to learn about appropriate change goals and processes from people in the setting. They should be change, rather than charitably, oriented (Lewis 2004; Marullo and Edwards 2000) and at the same time should be flexible about their philosophy of change. Faculty without any experience can learn from others and also can learn from entering the field with their students, so long as they keep in mind Stoecker's basic criteria, listed above.

It's best—especially at the levels of MA and PhD coursework—if faculty members themselves develop the field sites and collaborations within which their students will work toward social change. This means finding time to develop the relationships that are essential for building long-term programs of action research. Many universities are committed to community-engaged research and have been endorsed by national organizations such as the Carnegie Institute for their efforts to build interdisciplinary links and connect their students to local settings. Engaged scholarship and much service learning, however, covers a wide variety of short-term activities, from serving in homeless shelters or senior centers to environmental cleanups and capturing oral histories. Often liaisons are appointed for the purpose of identifying these settings and matching students for limited assignments. Liaisons may connect students to field settings, but this does not accomplish the goal of long-term collaboration with communities for addressing ongoing development, change, and social justice issues. Creating these relationships really requires the time of dedicated action-research-oriented faculty who are committed to local change efforts.

Building the infrastructure for social change efforts takes time, and often involves participating in non-research activities such as attending community meetings, joining sports teams, going to political rallies, and meeting community leaders and activists. Though they are time-consuming, these activities build the network of relationships crucial to effective collaborative projects; they also demonstrate to critical communities that faculty members are serious about their commitments. Faculty from private colleges and larger private and elite state universities may need to overcome stereotypes about "helicopter researchers" who hover over a research site without really engaging with it. They also may face overresearched communities that have not reaped benefits from decades of surveys conducted on—not with—their residents. Further, universities have uneven and sometimes conflictual relationships with local communities. Many universities have expanded their real estate holdings through the purchase of nearby land and housing, a process which increases the cost of living, including rents and property ownership costs, and often results in dislocation of residents who are forcibly moved, whose housing has been demolished to make way for construction of university facilities, or who can no longer afford to live in their neighborhoods.

Faculty members who would like to offer mentored experiences in a globalized world must establish international field settings either by connecting with foreign campuses and establishing exchanges, or by creating their own joint international projects within which students can be

placed. These activities also are time-consuming. They require some financial and other resources, and ideally, the backing of departments and the institutions themselves. Faculty can face difficult challenges when they represent an institution that has a history of noninvolvement or lack of commitment to remedying social or other injustices and that responds negatively when asked to support a local joint venture. Newer faculty who also are the most likely to reach out to build community relationships must achieve tenure by doing their "own" research and publishing single-authored papers. Institutions that make it easier for these new faculty members to receive credit for and build a strong base for student training are those that are inclusive in their promotion and tenure reviews, recognizing the importance of partnerships and disparities research and action. In sum, it is challenging but certainly not impossible in many cases for university faculty to find the time, resources, and support to build the required community infrastructure for sound community-research placements.

CASE EXAMPLES: ESTABLISHING INFRASTRUCTURE FOR PAR/CBPR IN COMMUNITY SETTINGS

Fortunately, there are a number of models that offer positive examples of departmental and university-wide commitments to action-oriented "service learning." These departments and universities are concerned about learning, but their emphasis is on action—combining research and action to accomplish a social or environmental or health goal—or at least on the provision of research results that stem from community or stakeholder needs that can be used immediately.

EXAMPLE 10.1

COMMUNITY-BASED RESEARCH IN SERVICE LEARNING

From 2003 to 2005, Duke University sponsored a program of mentored internships in a community organization, followed by a semester of community-based research intended to deliver a product to the community partner hosts. The program was part of a larger effort run through the Program in Education and the Department of Psychology and hosted by the Duke Neighborhood Partnership. It was funded by the Kellogg Foundation to provide programs and services to Durham, North Carolina, children. From three to five students each year spent the summer in one of three youth programs or camps. They chose research projects during the fall semester that responded to organizational interests as well as their own and that of their mentors in education and psychology. The community organizations partnered with the fall CBR course and their members attended some classes to strengthen collaboration. The students did literature reviews, collected data, and provided recommendations and materials. More important than the recommendations were the products or materials created by the students. These included a collaboratively developed summer literacy program, which students from the first and second cohorts implemented the following year, a social development curriculum and peer mentoring model, which also was implemented and evaluated, and a cultural competency program implemented with program staff and evaluated over the course of the three-year program. Thus, by combining a mentored summer experience with a semester of classroom-based research training, students were able to immerse themselves in a community organizational service setting, identify a joint project, do research with the partner organization to support it, and create a product useful for and desired in the setting. The ability to continue the program over several years made it possible to build on the products of the first year and, through later cohorts, implement the pilot interventions and evaluate them in collaboration with the organizations. Though this program was not focused on social justice per se, it did give undergraduate students experience with the full community-based partnership research and action continuum (Stocking and Cutforth 2006).

While the effort we have just described stemmed from programs in education and psychology, and the products reflected these disciplines, PAR/CBPR is global and such programs can be found in many disciplines and most countries around the world. The example below highlights a similar program in environmental and geographical sciences, conducted at Bournemouth University, United Kingdom.

EXAMPLE 10.2

THE BOURNE STREAM PARTNERSHIP

The Bourne Stream Partnership (BSP), a broad-based long-term partnership among political bodies, environmental advocates, and Bournemouth University, was launched in 2002. The aim of the BSP is to "enhance the environmental quality and amenity value of Bourne Stream through sustainable development." The partnership has offered many opportunities for research on water quality, ecological assessments, and other topics for undergraduates and master's degree students. The BSP takes an integrated holistic approach to water quality issues and a linked educational strategy involving affiliation with local educational institutes (Shah and Treby). The stream is within walking distance of the Bournemouth campus. Several "live projects" illustrate the links between teaching and research, including a six-week placement for ten undergraduate and MA students. The students explored a variety of different topics such as an assessment of water quality and highway runoff (with the Environmental Agency); habitat quality in constructed wetlands as part of a sustainable urban drainable system (with the local Council); and the recreational potential of Poole Park, including a user survey (with the BSP).

The "use water wisely project." Twenty-three undergraduate applied geography students in a fieldwork placement were supervised by two MA-level students to construct and administer a survey to determine what went wrong in a water company campaign to increase awareness of the need for water conservation in the Bourne Stream community. The data received international visibility and were used in a student report to the BSP and Water UK, the organization representing the water industry.

The Bournemouth University water audit. Twenty-two PhD students responded to the university's request to audit water on campus to see if it was being wasted and whether attitudes toward water would need to change. The students participated in a "taught unit" that enabled doctoral-level students to use their geographical skills to understand environmental problems and recommend solutions. Students worked in groups of five to six to become oriented to the project, develop a study, collect data, and analyze it; they then made a presentation.

A mixed methods evaluation of these experiences using observations of students in their "live projects," informal feedback, semi-structured interviews with host organizations, and a student questionnaire showed that students were motivated by live projects, appreciated involvement of outside organizations as experts, were anxious to provide meaningful findings to organizations, felt more prepared for work, and appreciated the widespread applicability of geography. As their comments demonstrated, "We hadn't realized that you can apply geography to everything" (Shah and Treby 2006, 41).

Anthropologists Simonelli, Earle, and Story describe quite a different situation with respect to reframing service learning to suit the mission and philosophy of Zapatistas in Chiapas. Students participated in a two-week summer program for which they had to prepare by developing a research proposal required for travel support.

EXAMPLE 10.3

LEARNING TO LISTEN AND GIVE VOICE AS SERVICE WITH THE ZAPATISTAS IN CHIAPAS

The purpose of the "El Horizonte" program, a collaboration of Wake Forest University and the University of Texas, El Paso, was to "provide a community-authored service-learning experience in the Zapatista jungle communities of Cerro Verde and Tulan" (Simonelli, Earle, and Story 2004, 44). The two-week program was organized by two more experienced students who had gone through a well-established Maya summer study program in Guatemala. Faculty members Simonelli and Earle had both worked in the frontier regions of Chiapas and had a long-standing interest in the ways that community development and NGO interventions could be helpful without hurting community individuals or groups (Simonelli and Earle 2001). They were interested in the Zapatista development model and the relationships among processes of peace, conflict, and development.

The area they chose was one characterized by autonomous municipalities consisting of Zapatista support bases and resistance communities. The Zapatistas were very concerned whether informed community development could encourage peaceful interactions among parties in conflict. Simonelli and Earle were interested in research on this topic and saw it as an opportunity to introduce students to "internally authored development." With an initial service learning model (learn and help), Simonelli, Earle, and the eleven students who participated raised money to help rebuild a school. Further, the students came with specific research projects to be executed that had undergone a difficult IRB review process. The students were proposing ethnography, an approach that challenged standard forms of research practice. What they learned during their stay in these two communities was that, for Zapatistas, service was not constituted by a single action such as building a school, but rather by "witnessing." This involved observing and learning about the Zapatista style of governance and collective development, building a long-standing relationship with members of the community, and then telling the story to others—a form of engaged anthropology and service. They also learned that they could not obtain individual signed informed consent documents from members of the Zapatista community because the

Cross Reference: See Book 2 for a discussion of safety in the field and Book 6 for a further discussion of ethical and consent issues of research in non-Western or indigenous societies

community considered them unsafe. Instead, consent had to be negotiated with and granted by the community, not by individuals.

The study site was socially very complex, and the principles of service and learning called for obeying the will of the community (*acompañar obediciendo*). Much of the two weeks was spent observing, listening, learning, and conversing with local people about how the Zapatistas acquired sufficient autonomy to make independent political decisions and the right of community members to negotiate their lives as they wished. Further, the students learned that assistance might be direct or through a sister-city relationship, which the Zapatistas preferred. The students and faculty observed as Zapatistas trained the local communities in self-governance in the context of the larger resistance movement, and in how to identify old governance practices to be discarded. The authors report that the visit was "helping the municipality to probe at a model of where and how outside help should fit into their programs" while making sure that the so-called help actually reached the communities without being diverted to NGO administration. With respect to rebuilding the school, the students were guided to recognize that more important than a school was long-term educational development, so that the school funds became an investment in enhancing human infrastructure for the area, rather than simply a building (Simonelli, Earle, and Story 2004).

In their reflection on these experiences, Simonelli and Earle note that over and above evaluating how to provide service to an autonomous rebel organization, they had to consider other factors: how to prepare students with background readings to enable them to understand the context and reasons for the Zapatista rebellion as well as how to live in the jungle; how to provide a rich immersion experience without overwhelming students; how to balance and schedule encounters and private time with group experiences and opportunity for individual conversations; how to manage safety concerns and logistics with students and at the same time, allay the concerns of the students' parents. The primary take-away message, however, for the El Horizonte group, was that their service was far less important than their learning. Labor, cash, and supplies were far less important than presence, sociability, engagement, understanding, witnessing, and giving voice, and in this way assisting in the "cultivation of international solidarity." For the Zapatistas, this is a strategy for political survival.

At the same time, consistent with other action-research strategies, the students were able to identify and assist in responding to community interests. They worked with one of the communities to develop a business plan for marketing their honey, obtained a small grant to cover shipping, and distributed and sold the goods following Zapatista guidelines for capitalism with socialist goals, consistent with self-development rather than "development done by others." These students learned the lesson that Sol Tax's students learned in the 1950s, and that van Willigen described in 2005: If you wait, listen, learn, participate, then change opportunities consistent with communities seeking autonomy will emerge. In these examples, we have discussed programs and projects run by individual faculty members or joint program efforts. However, what does it look like when an entire school, especially one characterized by privilege, develops an overall approach to community organizing and community development? And what happens when that commitment changes over time?

EXAMPLE 10.4

APPLIED ANTHROPOLOGY AT THE UNIVERSITY OF MEMPHIS

The Department of Anthropology at the University of Memphis (then Memphis State University) was founded by anthropologist and civil rights activist Dimitri Shimkin. Shimkin's view was a radical one, which identified three major components of social justice anthropology and action anthropology:

1. Documenting the "traditional and emerging cultures" of the Mid-South region, urban and rural, Black and white
2. Inducing academic institutions to take leadership in working with communities to develop problem-solving centers with other government and private institutions
3. Conveying new approaches to cultural context and practical problem solving to be "conveyed to young people and to the general public" (Register and Hyland 1978, 32; Shimkin et al. 1978).

Strikes and civil rights activities in the late 1960s and early 1970s had involved various sectors of the university; as a consequence, the university was open to new forms of engagement with local Black communities. In 1972, the Department of

Anthropology was formally established and opened its doors in the 1970s as an applied department with a clear mission to continue development work in Memphis and the Mississippi Delta. The university endorsed a model of anthropology that focused on doing anthropological fieldwork in its own backyard. The new anthropology department hired Thomas Collins, an activist ethnographer who "came to the University of Memphis in 1972 ready to do anthropology 'out of his door'" (Collins 1977; Collins 1980). His fieldwork focused on labor movements, desegregation, and identity issues and emphasized the voices of the workers. He later turned to other issues related to desegregation and its uneven effects on education and employment equality. His critical work led to the development of the MA program in applied anthropology, with a special emphasis on research on important regional issues, placements of students in local organizations, and the beginnings of a model that offered an alternative to traditional antipoverty approaches that actually perpetrated and perpetuated economic and political traditional hierarchies, rather than alleviating poverty. The MA program justified its existence appropriately, based on its social relevance and potential for offering career-oriented employment opportunity to alumni.

Coursework in the anthropology program included an urban concentration. In coordinating it, the director, Stan Hyland, generated internships for students, drawing on urban studies and anthropology and addressing problems of adequate housing, lack of coordinated service delivery, and marginalization of neighborhood leadership. The department quickly found that, as students completed practica that addressed critical problems within the Mid-South, meaningful and long-term relationships could be established and maintained with community-based organizations. These, in turn, led to jobs for students. By 2012, more than 150 alumni, half of them employed in the local area and working directly with the anthropology department, were recognized at the department's thirty-fifth anniversary celebration. In addition to formalizing a broader strategy for urban development, Stanley Hyland, the long-term faculty member in the Department of Anthropology, became head of the School of Urban Affairs and Public Policy, thereby expanding the scope of development work through that school and its connections. In recent years, the University has formed a school of public health, drawing from applied anthropologists and other social scientists to continue its engaged research tradition. The university has established itself as an institution on the cutting edge of fostering urban development and engaged social science and public health, offering technical assistance and consultation to other universities interested in community-engaged research and community-driven development.

The next example illustrates the challenges of maintaining strong community development–oriented local university-community links over time. This is especially crucial in the face of shifting external politics and an increasing emphasis on global university partnerships, expanding U.S. campuses to other countries, and building opportunities for U.S. students to experience semesters abroad.

EXAMPLE 10.5

A COLLEGE COMMITMENT TO URBAN DEVELOPMENT

In the mid-2000s, Trinity College, a private undergraduate school located in Hartford, Connecticut, sought and obtained federal Housing and Urban Development (HUD), Kellogg Foundation, and other funding to improve and expand its relationships with the city of Hartford. Trinity College was located in the heart of the south end Puerto Rican community in Hartford. At the time of this initiative, the college had a strong commitment to equitable urban development through close collaborations with local community development organizations and the city of Hartford. The external funding was used to hire a very experienced community liaison who connected faculty with promising opportunities for joint service-learning ventures in Hartford, staff from the community to train students in understanding the city and in community organizing, and a digital café, open to both students and community residents and headed by a former student, a bilingual Puerto Rican city resident and educational activist. Faculty members were encouraged to respond to community needs for service and information and they placed many students in community-based organizations and other city settings to work and learn. Student experiences were integrated into classroom work by dedicated social science faculty members. Faculty members sought out opportunities for their students to become involved in significant urban development efforts.

Prior to this development, Sandra Sydlo Ward, a Trinity student who liked African dance, sought to learn African dance with the Artists Collective, a local African American–oriented arts and teaching organization. She did so against the advice of her faculty advisors, who felt that she was entering into "unsafe territory." However, through this connection, she discovered the Institute for Community Research (ICR) and asked for an internship there. The internship evolved into a job as the director of youth Participatory Action Research programs. For students under Trinity's new urban initiative, such linkages became much easier to locate. For example, in the early stages of this development, a Trinity student was placed at the Institute for Community Research because of her interest in adolescents. There she negotiated to have her senior psychology thesis focus on an evaluation of problem-solving-skills development among youth in ICR's PAR program. She used vignettes in her analysis. This experience, mentored by ICR PAR researchers Schensul and Berg, had an enduring effect. Some years later, after completing a clinical psychology PhD degree, she returned to Trinity as a faculty member in a tenure track position and reestablished contact with ICR, both to place her students in a community research setting and to explore joint opportunities. Two of her students coded qualitative interviews on smokeless tobacco use and presented the results to their class. Two others worked with a study of MDMA use in urban young adults, checking transcriptions against audio recordings of interviews in this strictly qualitative study. One of the students created a film entitled "Borders without Bliss," a study about ecstasy (MDMA) use in the Hartford/Greater Hartford area, which she based on interviews she conducted for her senior thesis. The film became one way of disseminating the results of the MDMA study to city residents and college students. An organization dedicated to fighting against gang and street violence, whose young staff was hired from the study population, did voiceovers of interview extracts for the film. During that time, several Hartford PAR students were hired at ICR by researchers Schensul and Sarah Diamond with National Institute of Drug Abuse (NIDA) supplemental funding to develop a foundation for an intervention study with low-level urban alcohol/marijuana users. The students helped to brand it as "Xperience: For Those Who Choose Not to Use" and developed a logo for the program. These students decided to continue their applied research and entered Trinity College as undergraduates. Trinity's historical commitment to the city and faculty involvement with ICR converged to result in positive developments for Trinity students, ICR research, and urban youth with the desire to become students at this city-situated private undergraduate school.

The story does not end there, however. In later years, Trinity shifted its priority from "urban" and "local" initiatives to global education, and began to establish campuses and learning opportunities in urban areas throughout Europe. At the same time, the university pursued its interest in acquiring land and housing in proximate neighborhoods and constructed a permanent fence between its campus and the rest of the city, presumably to ensure the so-called safety of its students. Like many institutions of higher education, Trinity lost its prior sensitivity to local conditions in ways similar to other universities in Connecticut and in common with cities elsewhere. Now Trinity faculty are encouraged to send their students to off-campus semester-long experiences in cities abroad, and students are hard pressed to find placements for local learning in a university now situating itself in a global world. This shift from local to global differs little from other undergraduate and graduate examples that privilege international experiences and those who can afford them over learning about disadvantage and marginalization at home. Perhaps most important, the shift to global also obviates field experiences for low-income and nontraditional students who can only afford to carry out field placements if they exist in the local area.

The primary message here is that university-based community-engaged (CE) work is a "moving target" responding to constituent interests, needs, funding sources, university marketing strategies, and local pressures. Universities may be open to local CE at one time, and less so at another, leaving faculty with ongoing CE commitments with the need and the responsibility to continue their advocacy for this approach while maintaining their links with local (and international) communities.

OTHER UNIVERSITY STRUCTURES THAT FOSTER PAR/CBPR WORK

Universities have a variety of ways of creating opportunities for students to become engaged in socially responsive activist research. Some, such as the University of Washington, Seattle, the University of Michigan, and the University of Connecticut, work with organizational stakeholders from many different sectors to build independent community alliances or consortia. These consortia act as critical gatekeepers, initiating and participating in joint research efforts, and helping to place students in settings where they can both gain community insights and utilize community research skills.

Centers

Universities, such as Tufts and Loyola and the Universities of Arizona, Kentucky, South Florida, and Wisconsin, have created centers whose mission is to create research partnerships between the centers, faculty, and local communities. One of the best known of these centers is the Bureau of Applied Research in Anthropology (BARA) at the University of Arizona.

 **EXAMPLE 10.6**

BUREAU OF APPLIED RESEARCH IN ANTHROPOLOGY (BARA)

The Bureau of Applied Research in Anthropology (BARA) is a unique academic research unit within the School of Anthropology at the University of Arizona. BARA's mission is to place anthropology at the service of contemporary society, prepare the next generation of professional anthropologists, advance knowledge of the human condition, and address the pressing issues of local communities. BARA faculty and affiliates carry out research, teaching, and outreach activities within Arizona, throughout the country, and internationally.

BARA's cultural resources program focuses on the national need to assure the preservation of Native American cultures and languages. A long history of misguided policy making and disregard for native cultures in this country created marginalized and dependent peoples with severe economic disadvantages and little control over their own destiny. Federal legislation, such as the American Indian Religious Freedom Act of 1978 and the Native American Graves Protection and Repatriation Act (NAGPRA) of 1990, has attempted to redress the situation and establish new policy paths that emphasize tribal empowerment and cultural respect. BARA has contributed to these new directions by developing standard procedures that assure the full participation of Native American tribes in the process of identifying and controlling their comprehensive cultural resource inventories. In this program, BARA researchers facilitate the interaction of tribes with government and private agencies.

BARA researchers, undergraduates, graduate students, and postdoctoral fellows have assisted communities to reconstruct their cultural histories, made geographical information systems (GIS) technologies available to tribes wanting to identify and maintain their cultural landscapes, and have worked to address language shift through the development of dictionaries and the promotion of language literacy on reservations. The program has generated genuine, mutually respectful, and productive partnerships between the university and Native American tribes. BARA has conducted critical applied research in over twenty sites in the United States, involving undergraduate and graduate students, faculty of the university, and postdoctoral fellows (http://bara.arizona.edu/about).

Field Schools

Field schools are another very important mechanism for training students and faculty, as well as community members in community-based action-oriented research.

Field schools are short-term, four-to-six week intensive immersion training programs designed to introduce students from a single university or from many different places to a specific geo-cultural location where research is ongoing and to involve them in it. Field schools are not semesters abroad; they are more focused efforts to provide specific skills training to students under guided faculty supervision. Establishing a field school is an elaborate process in which faculty set up a learning program to teach language, culture, politics, methods, and relationships methods in a site where they have preexisting associations. Students then become part of a team that becomes integrated into the community, learning and, ideally, serving. Most field schools do not specifically include a service component; the balance of service and learning is heavily weighted toward the learning end; further, they are generally not based on the principles of participatory research for action.

Field schools that include PAR require special conditions. Local people need to participate in the education program. In PAR field schools, the community members co-teach with the faculty. Thus, they are directly involved in shaping the topic that is to be studied and acted upon; they also are invested in the resulting action. In such field schools, students ideally should reside in the study community and be part of it. And the students should work as a group. These conditions call for significant faculty responsibility and time commitments.

EXAMPLE 10.7

THE MONTEVERDE FIELD SCHOOL

Drs. Nancy Romero Daza and David Himmelgreen, project directors; Sarina Ergas, Department of Civil and Environmental Engineering; and colleagues from the University of South Florida's Department of Civil and Environmental Engineering jointly direct the "REU Site, Globalization and Community Health Field School: Combining Social Science and Engineering." The NSF-funded field school is now six years old and is embedded in a history of research and collaboration with the Monteverde Institute of Costa Rica, which is hosting the field school, including the current three-year research project funded by NSF on the impact of tourism on food security in the area.

The nine-week summer program provides students with rigorous training on both qualitative and quantitative methods from anthropology and civil and environmental engineering to conduct community health research in areas of the world undergoing rapid change as a result of globalization. Students from diverse disciplinary backgrounds live in Monteverde, participate in community life, learn about institutional structures in health, and link with personnel from the Ministry of Health, the School of Public Health at the University of Costa Rica, and community organizers. Thus, they begin to see interdisciplinary health issues from a systems perspective. Engineering, social science, and health sciences students work together on projects that are community priorities and present their results in both academic and community settings.

EXAMPLE 10.8

THE TALLAHASSEE FIELD SCHOOL IN A HISTORICALLY BLACK COMMUNITY

Another action-oriented community-based research field school is based in Tallahassee, Florida. Also NSF funded, this University of Florida field school is conducted in collaboration with Florida A&M University, a historically Black college, and the activist residents of Frenchtown, a historic African American community near the heart of Tallahassee's downtown. In its first year, the program focused on food insecurity. In the second, residents and faculty decided together to focus on racism. In its third year, the topic selected was "Race, Space, and Place." The school serves a mixed group of committed students from all over the country; from those who apply, approximately twelve are selected. The students live in Frenchtown for six weeks. Residents and faculty of Florida A&M University join with the students in making the curriculum happen, by starting with relationships. Clarence Gravlee, a faculty member at the University of Florida and both an expert on race and the principal investigator of the NSF training grant, is much appreciated in the community and helps to facilitate relationships among the students, other faculty, and community residents. Sarah Szurek, formerly a postdoctoral student at the University of Florida and a prior field school assistant, directs the field school. The relationships are solidified by the learning of community and city history through the lens of the residents and Florida A&M faculty and by means of ongoing socialization in the community. Guest faculty are invited to share weeks with the group, bringing and sharing their different approaches to participatory ethnography and social justice research. In 2014, visitors included anthropologists Krista Harper, Jean and Stephen Schensul, and Tony Whitehead.

Several elements make this field school unique. Some of the community activists also are local historians, artists, and public health scholars. They are committed to preserving Frenchtown as a space and place that symbolizes the com-

plexities of African American identity, history, and cultural persistence in a city that overtly seems receptive, but at the same time is deeply racist. The research that students conduct with these community activists reveals important theoretical and practical insights about community conservation in the face of cultural, political, and other forms of encroachment. It results in products that community members can use to argue for Frenchtown's place in the history of the city and African American presence in central Florida. A description of the 2014 field school experiences with articles co-authored by students and community residents has been published in a 2015 issue of *Practicing Anthropology*, one of the journals of the Society for Applied Anthropology. The issue is entitled "Integrating Methods Training and Community-Based Participatory Research: Lessons from the Ethnographic Field School in Tallahassee, Florida" and is edited by Sarah M. Szurek and Clarence C. Gravlee.

RESOURCING COMMUNITY-BASED PARTICIPATORY ACTION RESEARCH EFFORTS

Financial resources are required to support both faculty and institutional efforts to train students effectively. Often these resources can be identified within the university itself. Many universities provide ongoing core, or sustaining, funds for centers on their campuses whose mission is to promote service learning or engaged scholarship. Carnegie funding, and more recently Carnegie endorsement as a community-engaged campus, can assist in advocating for endowment or legislative funding for such centers.

A second source of funding comes from national public funders of intervention, applied, and collaborative research. These include the National Science Foundation, which funded the Florida field school, and the National Institutes of Health, which funds centers on various topics including cancer prevention, HIV prevention, and disparities research and intervention. The U.S. National Institutes for Health consist of more than twenty-five different disease- or topic-oriented institutes that develop grant-funding programs every three years.

NIH also funds special initiatives and centers, longer-term (three-to-five-year) individual or group/cluster studies, groups of studies, and longer- and shorter-term training programs of various sorts. Over the last decade or so, a very substantial amount of funding has gone to universities to build translational research centers (CTSAs or Centers for Clinical and Translational Research). These centers are mandated to include community-engagement components or cores. Over thirty-six such centers have received from four to sixty million dollars to move research from laboratories and controlled settings into clinics, hospitals, and communities. A few such centers not have well-developed community-engagement arms. Universities such as Duke, Minnesota, Michigan, UCSF, and Wisconsin have developed their community relationships to go far beyond recruitment into studies and clinical trials. In these locations, faculty and community partners are building strong partnerships and equitable arrangements for doing good translational research together to address health disparities and the structural injustices that produce them.

The Centers for Disease Control (CDC), another large federal institution, has funded four major urban research centers based on principles of collaboration, giving places like the University of Washington and the University of Michigan opportunities to establish urban collaborative research alliances focusing on reducing health disparities in communities, districts, or neighborhoods. The CDC continues to fund prevention research centers (PRCs) at universities with schools of public health, and community research collaborations—another mandate of the CDC program as well. The National Park Service has also been very creative in its approach to supporting local cultural resources in partnerships between researchers and cultural stewards; for two decades, the National Park Service has made grants available for work in collaboration with local cultural experts and community historians to reconstruct the stories and historic sites that represent important moments in the history of African American, Native American, and other marginalized groups in the United States.

Because the NIH, NSF, and CDC are publically funded institutions, they must respond to public influence through appeals to Congress as well as individual discussions with directors, branch chiefs, and project officers. Organizations like CCPH, Campus Compact, and CNREI, and Concerned Scientists do educate and lobby Congress to promote community responsive research topics and relationships. Public influence, along with programs such as the Carnegie CE designation promoting and recognizing the importance of research engagement have had considerable effect on NIH funding streams. Publications also affect funding decisions. A report commissioned by the director of NIH, Francis Collins, which was released August 18, 2011 (http://nih .gov/news/health/aug2011/od-18.htm) showed clearly that Black applicants were less likely to receive NIH grants than white applicants (NIH 2011), initiating NIH programs to address this disparity. A feature article on the report was published in *Nature* magazine the same day (Corbyn August 18, 2011). Foundations such as the Robert Wood Johnson, Kellogg Foundation, and Gates Foundation have provided substantial support for training community-based researchers to develop research collaborations over the past decade. Other possibilities exist for supporting international exchanges through USAID and other government exchanges, as well as the Rockefeller and Ford Foundations. Each institution has its own assets and considerations, and can and must work with researchers, its research foundation, and politicians to find innovative ways of providing sound infrastructure for good community-based research for social change purposes.

SUMMARY

In this chapter, we have argued that behind most research conducted with and in communities are people who are committed to addressing social issues, resolving injustices, and working directly in communities. Such highly motivated people can do sound research with community partners only if their universities and their faculty advisors are able to create opportunities for them to learn. This means that universities and colleges must work hard to provide the institutional infrastructure—the programs, the partnerships, and the regulatory action—that are needed so that faculty can build the partnerships they need to train their students well, while offering substantial benefit to communities that want research to help them to develop new programs, advocacy efforts, and political stances. We have outlined some of the structures that need to be in place; given examples of research-based service-learning programs, including those with far reaching political implications; and described centers, field schools, and other organizational structures that help to support community-based participatory research in local, or in international settings. In the next and final chapter of Book 7 we consider what needs to happen in classroom and training settings to support student learning.

11 ━━◆━◆━◆━

TEACHING COMMUNITY-BASED APPLIED ETHNOGRAPHY IN HIGHER EDUCATION

INTRODUCTION

In the previous chapters, we have provided numerous examples of participatory and collaborative intervention and action research projects with community partners that represent structural commitments by departments, universities, disciplines, and advocacy organizations for community-based action research for social justice/social change. In chapter 10, we described infrastructure that should be in place so that faculty can give students the best possible individual and group experiences at each level in order that students learn that community needs and struggles come first, *before* considerations of student learning. We have argued, at the same time, that collaborative research is a negotiated dance designed to ensure a win-win situation for communities and students alike. In chapter 9, we've described how to engage in mutual teaching and learning through PAR instruction and facilitation with adults and youth in various community and other nonacademic settings.

While young people and community members can learn to carry out many or most of the tasks involved in a research/action project, in all of the examples we have presented skilled ethnographers/action researchers, usually based in universities or research organizations, are needed to initiate, guide, and implement such projects. However, such people do not grow on trees.

In this chapter, we ask, "How do new ethnographers learn in their academic programs to apply mixed methods research with multiple stakeholders to make a difference in communities and other settings?" To answer this question, we move to university classrooms and university faculty because most of the people who have led action research and multi-stakeholder intervention projects have been trained in university programs by faculty who are supportive of and often involved in such research themselves. Below we explore how the skills needed to engage in participatory and collaborative action research can be taught in university settings that are linked to opportunities for field experiences.

Participatory and activist-oriented ethnographic research in action can be taught at all levels of postsecondary/higher education, and through a variety of different approaches. However, those we endorse are ongoing and involve faculty and students in learning to do and use research along with other strategies to further community agendas and build community and student skills. Here we use case descriptions to illustrate such training at the undergraduate, graduate, and postgraduate levels. Throughout, we remind readers of the crucial nature of the infrastructure we describe in chapter 10 of this book; such infrastructure is a requisite to support faculty and students in their pursuit of experiences in ethnographically based research for social action and social justice.

INITIAL FORAYS INTO COMMUNITY SETTINGS: SERVICE LEARNING

Some college students already have gained a great deal of volunteer or other experience in community organizations or other settings in high school. Others have almost none. An initial exposure opportunity such as service learning in communities different from the students' own socioeconomic, cultural, and ethnic background can help these inexperienced students. Service learning resembles and is a successor to volunteer work, but it requires more sensitivity to what services the community needs, rather than what the volunteer wants to do or needs to learn. It also can be focused on achieving social justice for communities. Volunteers have to study the culture, history, and demographic characteristics of the people they are serving and, more importantly, get an idea of the social structural genesis of the conditions in which the people they are "serving" or learning about live. It inspires students to ask questions such as: What has led to the fact that people are living in substandard housing? What might explain why children cannot read by fourth grade? Why are food banks and soup kitchens needed? Why does it feel so unsafe to go from one side of this neighborhood to the other? What explains the existence of a toxic waste dump on the edge of town, and what are its consequences? Why do children play in the streets where many are injured by cars? What explains the absence of high quality fresh fruits and vegetables in neighborhood stores?

Service learning increasingly is becoming a requirement for high school graduation and for successful completion of many college classes. It is built into many alternative education programs, including overseas experiences and Semester at Sea. It can serve as a way to begin learning how to negotiate access to a community, develop relationships, and acquire sensitivity to the concerns and issues of others—all initial skills needed to become good ethnographers.

Service learning also involves self-reflection, where the persons providing service engage in a systematic exploration of their reactions to the experience, begin to identify and explore their biases and the impact of their preconceived notions and prejudices, and look at their own roles and privileges through the eyes of the community. The goal of such activities is to develop what Paolo Freire called *transformative consciousness*, in which social problems are seen as the consequence of social injustice and inequity, rather than as the fault of individuals (Freire 1970; Freire 1981).

Effective service learning projects occur when the organization receiving services identifies what it needs, and volunteers/students engage in activities that fulfill those needs. Since most first-time service learning participants are not experienced either in ways to engage with communities or to identify community needs, faculty should provide them with an array of already vetted organizations and let them choose the ones with which they would like to be associated. Example 11.1 below describes how students were prepared for a service learning experience in the classroom and in linked field site placements, which they chose from a predetermined list. This service learning project gave teacher-education students a feel for the "field" and let them develop relatively long-term interactions with people from communities and backgrounds very different from their own, and become more familiar with the challenges they would face among their own students when they became teachers. They had to work through differences of race, class, language, immigration status, sexual orientation, and physical and mental abilities between themselves and the children in their sites, and also to learn to be more careful, critical, and analytical observers of the conditions in which people live.

All of these skills are important foundations required for doing fieldwork. However, undergraduate students often know very little about research methods. The best that service learning experiences can do is to open their eyes, reduce some of their preconceived notions, assist them in learning how to find out what communities need, and figure out how to help them meet those needs. The course described below did not teach actual research methods other than sensitizing students to better observations. Other strategies are needed to teach them how to actually do the ethnographic research that leads to action ethnography.

 **EXAMPLE 11.1**

SERVING COMMUNITIES ON THE WAY TO BECOMING TEACHERS: EASING UNDERGRADUATES INTO SERVICE AND SOCIAL JUSTICE

"School and Society," the first required class in an undergraduate teacher-preparation program, focused on the context in which schools operate—the history, politics and finance, philosophies of curriculum, and the demographics of students and the teaching force—everything that affects what goes on in classrooms and that would-be teachers normally ignore. The class required students to perform twenty hours of service during the semester with a community organization serving low-income, at-risk, disabled, minority, or immigrant children, not only to experience working with real children, but also to understand the many forces impinging on students' ability to succeed academically. Students had to choose placements serving people who were different culturally from themselves and with whom they had not worked before, and they had to involve actual interaction with children, rather than simply handing out food at a soup kitchen or similar activity involving one-way interaction. Three hundred students were enrolled each semester in the course—which was taught in ten to twelve sections of thirty or so students each—so the logistics of the field experience had to be structured carefully.

Students chose their placements from a list of options created by the course supervisor. These sites had already been visited by the faculty supervisor and assessed for appropriateness of clients and suitable structure. The professor also negotiated in advance the tasks and activities in which the students would be engaged. One requirement was that the sites and activities be able to facilitate rather extended periods of interaction with children, including times for informal exchanges. This was important in making it possible for students to build relationships, whereas an activity such as cleaning up lunch or organizing classroom materials was not conducive to sharing experiences and did not allow students to learn from others. The activities included such things as tutoring for immigrants and students performing poorly in school, at an immigrant newcomer's center; providing recreational activities for children at several local trailer parks; and working with non-English speakers at the high school ESL center. Other placements included working with an after-school program for teen parents and their babies, working on playgrounds and recreational centers as coaches for after-school programs for developmentally challenged and low-income students, participating in youth-run community gardens and after-school arts programs for at-risk youth, and mentoring adjudicated youth through the juvenile probation system. Students kept structured diaries of their experiences, documenting their reactions from the very first day, and noting how they changed over time. They were guided by their instructors in regular debriefing sessions where they could discuss problems, challenges, and successes, and they were coached on issues to observe and questions to explore. These debriefing sessions were designed to help students understand the genesis problems and inequities they observed, and to prevent them from seeing all negative behaviors as the fault of the children or their parents.

Students' work was graded by the instructor, based on their journals and class discussions that drew on their experiences in the field sites. They also were evaluated separately by the community organization using a rating scale devised by instructors in the course and approved by the organizations; it included everything from punctuality, appropriate dress, and flexibility in coping with challenges to actual competence in the tasks assigned. These ratings figured into the students' course grades. In only a very few cases, students were removed from field placements because of personality or political conflicts, failure to perform adequately, or because they or the site could not adapt to the class requirements. In some cases, field sites were dropped for the same reasons.

Service learning supporters generally agree that service learning has several critical components:

- Connecting with a community to determine "needs" and desired outcomes;
- Involving students in the selection, development, and evaluation of service experiences (and sites);
- Including process and outcome evaluation of the experience (objective assessments);
- Including reflection sessions linking service experiences, critical analysis, and academic subject matter;
- Constructing service learning curricula that increase the learning potential of the experience.

Despite much discussion about whether service learning is elitist or whether it intentionally or unintentionally reinforces existing power structures, many faculty and the schools that support it view learning through strategic placements in community settings to be a useful way for students to begin to understand different perspectives and bridge class, racial/ethnic, and other social and cultural divisions. Etmansky and colleagues, as well as others, describe a form of service learning that extends the classroom into practice settings where students can use their academic learning while engaging in struggles for social change (Berg 2004; Etmanski, Hall, and Dawson 2014; Keene and Colligan 2004; Schensul and Berg 2004). These authors redefine the concept of "service," with its potential for privileging academic scholarship over community needs, by framing it as learning from the setting and from shared inquiry into how to forge alliances to undo injustices. Regardless of disciplinary source and terminology, there are now many examples of student learning in the context of ongoing efforts to improve health and educational policy and practice, recapture archaeological and oral history, learn about the making of civil democracy in a revolutionary setting, and other topics (Nassaney 2004; Wood and Samuel 2012).

As Etmansky and colleagues point out, most universities have requirements that students must, or at least should, engage in experiential learning through various forms of interdisciplinary collaboration with local communities. The demands placed on faculty in fulfilling these requirements is high because creating learning environments that are truly transformative for faculty, students, and communities is fraught with multiple difficulties. Obvious links between classroom learning and community praxis may seem tenuous or nonexistent. Faculty may not really like or want to participate in community placements or social justice programs. Discipline-based classroom learning may be too limiting for the interdisciplinary and intersectoral experiences students desire. Students may not be prepared effectively for the "field" and may be asked to do more than they are ready or able to do. Also student projects that are required by their classes, capstone projects, and senior theses may constrain what students actually can choose, do, and learn. Faculty and community organizations may be uninvolved or too busy to mentor students properly. And students may be placed in settings as individuals rather than as working groups, thereby obviating valuable group learning, research, and reflection processes (Stocking and Cutforth 2006). These obstacles can be overcome by dedicated faculty and university administrations willing to make institutional and personal commitments to the process of linking academic resources to community well-being.

DESIGNING AND ORGANIZING COURSEWORK IN PARTICIPATORY AND APPLIED ETHNOGRAPHY

Like learning to do action research in community and other field settings, learning to do ethnographically driven action research from an academic base is subject to some advantages and some special constraints as well. Action research usually begins with a problem in need of resolution, located within a community or other setting affected by that problem. *Participatory or collaborative action research usually means that researchers and members of the community work together to identify ways to address a specific problem and, sometimes, to collaborate in the actual identification of the problem itself. Teaching participatory and collaborative action research at the university or college level presents a considerably different starting point.* Teaching action research, especially at the undergraduate and graduate levels, often begins with a research methods, or applied research class, rather than a specific problem. The class may or may not extend into the community. Often the class is designed to convey a good sense of the main issues that emerge in the conduct of action research, as well as to provide experiences designed to permit students to dip their toes into the stream of action. Ideally, faculty have links with community, clinic, school, research, or service settings, and can create space and time in their courses for students to really learn about the setting, figure out how to experience and negotiate differences, and come to see the world through the eyes of the people who are their guides. Classes also are designed to convey basic research skills and give students some practice in using them before undergoing a total immersion in a field project. In fact, about the worst thing that would-be teachers of action research can do to students is to throw them unguided and unprepared into a project before they are ready even to tread water. Sadly in some cases, students are placed in learning settings and expected to "learn by doing" without proper preparation and guidance. Unsupervised placements are now viewed as unethical because they take advantage of communities; use scarce community resources to accommodate students or, at minimum, to keep them from getting into trouble; and seldom, if ever, produce work of much good to the communities being studied. Further, novice researchers can put themselves into precarious positions, and their mistakes can poison the well, annoying and even damaging community members so much so that further researchers are excluded from working there again. Finally, immersion experiences intended to help reduce social distance, prejudices, and biases held by both students and their community

Key point

counterparts have the potential for reinforcing these biases unless students are carefully guided and mentored so that they understand what they are observing and experiencing and where and when it is appropriate for them to both observe and act.

Not only can students learn only a small part of what they need to know in just one or two courses, but their quarter- or semester-long classes often really do not permit sufficient time to delve deeply into learning about a community and developing relationships within it. *As a consequence, students who are properly guided often rely on the relationships and trust that their professors have developed in gaining participatory field experience. This places the onus on the faculty who are teaching action research or intervention research methods to be involved themselves in applied efforts.* In this way faculty can create opportunities within which students can become engaged in useful mentored work without having to do it all themselves.

 Key point

Students may end up working in a setting where the partnership relationships have already been established, the problem or issue already has been identified, and research and intervention work already begun. But faculty members may have opportunities to introduce students at the beginning of a research partnership or even before it is formed. And there are times when students create projects of their own, sometimes against the advice of faculty who feel that the students may be diverted from the real work of "finishing."

The first thing that interested faculty must consider is where to introduce the ideas, skills, and brief engagements that can best help students to be successful in the field. Classroom preparation focuses on:

- kills development (participatory research methods);
- substantive knowledge (e.g., soil quality, aging in place, asthma);
- a working knowledge of the community in which students will be working (through brief involvements or site visits to local organizations or landmarks, unobtrusive observations, interviews with gatekeepers, mapping activities, language exposure, etc.);

- and, reflection on the root causes and experiences of inequality through readings, discussion, site visits, films, and classroom speakers and practice.

Fields such as sociology, communications, anthropology, and cultural geography often require their undergraduate majors to take courses in research methodology, including introductions to statistics and qualitative methods. Qualitative methods research courses involving participant observation, interviewing, photography, and other skills development can create spaces for students to gain access to and build relationships within communities; listen to community residents; and participate in identifying issues, collecting data, and searching for feasible actions.

Often schools combine classroom work with field-based practice. In the very early stages, field-based practice might be nothing more than a two-hour placement each week in a local organization under the supervision of organizational staff, to review data, help prepare meetings, sit in on project meetings, or transcribe interviews. These brief placements can result in longer internships later on.

EXAMPLE 11.2

COMBINING CLASSROOM WORK WITH FIELD-BASED PRACTICE

In the state of Connecticut, Trinity College, a four-year undergraduate private school, asks community organizations involved in community-based research to host students for very short-term placements. In one such example, two Trinity undergraduates reviewed the transcriptions of digitally recorded interviews with young adults in Hartford who had used the drug ecstasy, to make sure they were accurate. The students reviewed interviews each week for two hours. By the end of the semester, they had completed a review of more than forty interviews. The following year, one student returned for the summer to help recruit and interview, and she completed her senior honors thesis the following year. Other students were involved in similar initial projects in organizations throughout the greater Hartford area.

Cross Reference:
See Example 10.5 of this book

Skills, prior experience, and specific interests of students differ and develop as students move through the undergraduate, MA, and PhD coursework and placements. Some students come into higher education wanting to know how to "change the world." Such students can be led carefully into projects that involve learning the initial stages of ethnographic research: how to observe systematically, interview people and construct structured questionnaires, and assemble useful current documents and historical materials. Undergraduate courses can offer brief mentored field experiences along with classroom introductions. However, it is easiest to build field-based learning upon service learning programs and into senior or honors theses for which students are expected to devote more time.

At more advanced levels, students focus on topical interests and research methods, and more intensive field placements and internships, which may be team based. Often, despite the current need in the STEM (science, technology, engineering, mathematics) fields to develop team-based science, students at the PhD level are socialized into individual research projects driven by faculty interests rather than being group initiated and group based. However, doing Participatory Action Research for social change usually requires teamwork. Faculty will find that it is not difficult to introduce team-based projects or activities within the PhD program, even when individual students are expected to write their own dissertations. At all levels, faculty teaching students to do participatory ethnography or PAR for social change should consider:

- useful skills students must learn;
- student orientation to the field setting;
- ways of integrating field experiences into classroom learning, theory, and dialogue; and
- balancing student learning and community benefit.

Student Skills

 Key point

Before students at any level enter the field, it is valuable to assess their skills and learning needs. *A skills assessment can explore social skills, topical interests,*

methodological capacities, teaching and writing skills, computer skills, and other skills that could be useful in a field placement. Classroom instruction can be directed to some of these areas, such as research methods and writing. Subject-specific methodology also can be helpful; for example, classroom instruction can provide introductions to pedagogical theory and practice in education, or methodological approaches or theoretical lenses in medical anthropology. Some colleges offer cultural-competency training for students and faculty to introduce them to different cultural experiences and settings. Topical or substantive knowledge also is useful, so students could be encouraged to take courses on "the city," or the history and politics of ethnicity in the area where the university is located and/or the work is to be accomplished. Student interests also are important. One undergraduate student at a local university who had an interest in epidemiology volunteered to work in an oral health study at ICR and is learning how surveys collected in the field are transformed into data for analysis. Students may or may not have experience in crosscultural/multiethnic, and cross-class situations, and they may hold inherent biases regarding the superiority of their own experience to that of others. As Budd Hall, an experienced Canadian community-based researcher and activist puts it:

"The key learning objectives in my teaching about CBR are the following: (1) knowing who we are, (2) learning to listen, (3) understanding the centrality of values and commitment, (4) recognizing that there are multiple ways to create and represent knowledge, and (5) understanding the role and meaning of action" (Hall 2014).

Skills-building courses are always included at the master's level in applied fields such as education, applied anthropology, sociology, and public health. These almost always include theory, logical thinking, and writing, and often require both qualitative and quantitative research methods. Several examples of such courses in education and anthropology are described below.

EXAMPLE 11.3

MOVING TO THE MASTER'S LEVEL: A SURVEY COURSE TO GIVE MA STUDENTS THE BASIC TOOLS OF RESEARCH PRACTICE

Margaret LeCompte regularly taught a course called "Introduction to Disciplined Inquiry" to MA students in the School of Education. The course included a survey of research designs from ethnography and historiography to systematic surveys and experiments; it familiarized students with the research methods used for each, and it required students to learn about and practice basic skills such as taking field notes, designing a survey, and learning about archives and the use of second-ary data. It also covered the epistemologies informing each design type. Students were required to design and write up a proposal for a study that interested them, though they weren't required to execute it within the semester. These proposals included the research question, the theoretical frameworks informing the study, the specific variables of interest, and a data collection matrix (LeCompte and Schensul 2010; Schensul, Schensul, and LeCompte 2012) that specified the kinds of data collection methods to be used. LeCompte structured the proposals around the components required for an IRB proposal to make sure that the students really thought through what their project needed to entail. Students also had to obtain certification to do research from the university's IRB. This gave them real-world experience with research ethics and approval to proceed as researchers, in case they wanted to seek IRB approval for their project and actually conduct their study. A number of such students did exactly that as a culminating activity for their MA degree, after the class was over.

Most applied MA degrees in anthropology, such as those offered at the University of Maryland, and the University of Memphis, offer a variety of skills-building classes. Anthropologist Dan Jordan, currently working with a diverse group of urban and suburban high school students to develop PAR-based advocacy campaigns, took research and evaluation courses at the University of Maryland's Department of Anthropology. During his program, he used his newfound skills in a community evaluation placement where he studied the process and results of a GED program in Baltimore. Below we describe another class that helped practicing professionals improve through learning to use research.

EXAMPLE 11.4

MOVING TO THE MASTER'S LEVEL: GUIDING TEACHERS TO DO RESEARCH ON THEIR OWN PRACTICE

Sherri Ludwig taught an MA-level class in research methods with a slight twist. Called "Teacher as Researcher," it was located in a school of education and targeted practicing teachers who were working on MA degrees in their substantive subject area, and it was required for their degrees. In the course, students were asked to design and complete a mini-ethnography in the schools or classrooms where they worked. Ludwig made this stipulation not only because she knew that the single semester allowed for the course would not permit wide-ranging fieldwork, but also because she firmly believed that teaching teachers to identify problems or issues they faced in their own schools, and to study and evaluate their own practice, would contribute powerfully to their insights as teachers and activists in their communities. One of Ludwig's students, for example, learned that her school included a number of immigrant children from Somalia. Her study for Ludwig's class was a mini-ethnography of their culture. Another was interested in where her Spanish-dominant students from Central America were finding opportunities to practice English. Yet another, the principal of his high school, wanted to explore how to get a school garden growing in his community, located in an arid semi-desert where few grocery stores sold fresh local produce. Ultimately, he was able to persuade the superintendent of his district to develop school gardens at all the secondary schools. Produce from the gardens was used in the school cafeterias and sold to people in the local community, thus improving their diet and health; children also learned how to prepare and eat "strange" but healthful foods they had never considered edible. In addition, the school gardens tried to focus on plants that indigenous people in the area had grown and consumed historically. His most recent activism involved running for, and winning, election to the position of the city's mayor.

Student Orientation to the Field Setting

There are many ways to orient students to a field setting. Other researchers who have worked in the setting can be invited to speak to students about their work. Site visits can introduce students to important community people or other stakeholders with whom they might need to work or conduct interviews and who could help them to feel comfortable and safe in the setting. Immersion exposure in structured discussions with organizational staff or community leaders or activists can give students an intimate feel for the field situation, which can go a long way to motivating them to get there on their own! Site visits also help students to examine their biases and explore myths about the community and its people; they also generate questions in students' minds about what they want to learn and look at, as well as what is needed in the setting. However they are implemented, orientations *always* should include information about the history and current situation in the field setting as well as the project in which the student will be involved. Our applied classes have often involved walks through neighborhoods where research and advocacy are ongoing, or "drive-throughs" if the area is too large. Using these methods, students learn to understand the geography of the setting and to get an initial sense of how geography—the interaction of built environment with places where people can shop, gather, eat, interact, play, grow food, and so on—might play a role in such things as access to high quality food, the nature of interracial relations, or the existence of public violence. Faculty or more senior students who have experience in the study community are best suited to orient students working whenever possible with local residents.

Balancing Student Learning and Community Benefit

Many teachers of the "service learning" approach to social justice– and community change–oriented field placements have expressed concern about the balance between student learning and community benefit. Overall, the primary goal of the university and its departments is to make sure that students learn—not necessarily to provide benefit to communities. While much literature exists on how much students *can* learn through doing "ethnography"—that is, participating in the lives of communities—through semesters abroad and other immersion experiences, less has been written about how much these experiences offer to the local setting. Faculty members often ask local organizations to "take" students and provide them with a learning experience. This practice can be quite annoying to those organizations that receive few resources in return and that also may find themselves confronted with students who have little useful knowledge, and are not always consistent in their schedule, or diligent in the work they are asked to do.

However, as we tried to show in chapters 2 and 10 of this book, many universities have established long-standing sets of relationships with community partners and alliances, as well as many different kinds of ongoing exchanges—for example, campuses that host community events, joint art exhibits of community artists in university galleries, joint research projects, and joint advocacy and policy-change efforts. Such institutions have much more flexibility in what they can ask their community colleagues to do. An organization that has had the benefit of a productive student volunteer's work for fifteen hours a week one year is very likely to be willing to accept several students for two hours a week the next year. Thus, establishing long-term relationships can open many opportunities for student placements and learning under the critical mentorship of engaged faculty.

Integrating Field Experiences into Classroom Learning

Integrating field experiences into classroom learning can be challenging but, with some creativity, can happen in many different ways. As demonstrated in Example 11.1, service learning classes should build into the curriculum regular opportunities for students to discuss and reflect on their field experiences. Students can be instructed to keep journals or field notes and can be asked to prepare reports based on their experiences for discussion in class. Discussions can follow a sequenced guide, helping to orient students in what to look for, offer, and experience in the field, and how to reflect on their experiences. If students are doing a participatory study, classroom sessions can be oriented around data collection and data analysis and the results reported back to the partners.

It is more difficult to integrate student experiences into topical or theoretical courses than in substantive classes like "School and Society." The former generally are not field oriented, though the goal of a field experience could be to integrate classroom knowledge into field experiences and observations. Psychologist Laura Holt offers this opportunity to her community psychology students, who do brief weekly placements in action research settings, and try to apply what they see and learn to the psychosocial theories they are reading about in their course. Teacher educator Shelby Wolf customarily assigned her students in elementary reading and writing methods classes to follow a primary school student for a semester, observing where, how often, and for what purposes children engaged in reading and writing. These activities helped prospective teachers develop strategies for better integrating reading and writing into their students' daily activities. Often these courses are critical antecedents to a more extended field placement, including participation in a field school.

Most science is conducted in teams; thus, the more students experience team work in their undergraduate and graduate education, the better prepared they will be for future work in actual research and action teams. A good way for students at all levels to practice ethnography is to work with a professor on his or her research projects. Many students get considerable valuable team field experience in this manner.

EXAMPLE 11.5

GETTING FIELD EXPERIENCE: TEAM RESEARCH FOR A NAVAJO SCHOOL DISTRICT'S UNANSWERED QUESTIONS

Margaret LeCompte was involved in a multiyear collaboration with a small school district in the Navajo Nation. Her task was to assist the district in school reform efforts, most of which were designed to more fully integrate Navajo cultural ways of teaching and learning, as well as information about the Navajo language and culture, into the curriculum at all grade levels. Over the years, LeCompte, who had very little funding to support her work with the district, brought teams of her doctoral students with her to help design and implement studies that answered questions the district administrators generated. She used her small-grant funding to pay for motel rooms and a van for transportation to the community, and the students worked for free—with LeCompte's promise that they would have both a good time and a powerful learning experience in crosscultural immersion and in doing real research. Among the questions administrators asked were: Why do certain teachers at the high school resist implementation of overall "block" scheduling that gave them a full two periods for each class? Why were so many high school seniors failing classes they needed to graduate, when their grades indicated that they should be passing? Why were so few of the middle school teachers actually implementing "site-based management" (a pet project of the superintendent designed to give schools more autonomy in how they operated)?

LeCompte's students conducted observations at the high school and interviews with teachers about block scheduling. These interviews revealed that while social studies and science teachers loved the changed schedule and used it for experiential projects, those most antagonistic to it were in subject areas where teachers customarily taught by using drill sheets, memorization, and practice. Block scheduling was designed to change that, making teachers more innovative in how they taught. But foreign language and math teachers couldn't figure out what to do to fill up all the time in the blocks. "We can't just do worksheets for two hours!" said one math teacher. "The kids get bored just learning vocabulary!" exclaimed a French teacher. Staff development helped the teachers learn how to use their longer periods more productively.

Interviews and focus groups with high school students revealed that many were failing because of excessive unexcused absences—ten such absences meant a grade of "F." These interviews also revealed that many students were absent when the school buses could not pick them up because of bad weather or washed-out roads. While the bus drivers were supposed to report which students had not been picked up so that their absence could be recorded as excused, it turned out that most drivers had simply failed to do so. Checking the bus schedules against weather reports corrected the records of students who were wrongly reported absent, and enforcing the reporting rule solved the problem in the future.

The failure of teachers to support site-based management was a bit more complicated. The district's administration described itself as "fully site-based." However, there was a considerable gap between administrator pronouncements and school-level practice. LeCompte's team interviewed all the teachers at the middle school, as well as the principal. Most of the teachers said that either they had never heard of site-based management or had only heard it in their teacher-training classes and never really understood what it meant. None had heard that it was supposed to characterize practice in the Pinnacle district. It seemed that they had received no staff development to learn what it was or how to implement it. When they were told by the interviewers that it meant giving teachers more voice in deciding how to run the school and what to teach, the teachers almost universally rejected the idea, saying that they already had too much work without being asked to "run the school" as well. The final piece to the puzzle involved interviewing the administrators, especially the superintendent and his assistant. They seemed to feel that proclaiming a reform made it a reality. As a consequence, no special training was given to principals or teachers in how site-based management was to work. Staff development might have helped the teachers and principals better understand the concept, but teacher antagonism, unearthed in the interviews, doomed it to failure in the end.

The experience of students in the medical anthropology program at the University of Connecticut offers another good example of activist-oriented team research experiences.

EXAMPLE 11.6

MENTORED GROUP PLACEMENTS AT THE UNIVERSITY OF CONNECTICUT

In the early years of the medical anthropology program at the University of Connecticut, PhD students worked in teams in newly emerging action research field settings in Hartford, Connecticut. One group of students worked at a new community health clinic established by a group of residents and faculty of the School of Medicine, including Stephen Schensul. The students played a key role in the formation of the health clinic, and several did dissertation work designed to answer questions about health problems (asthma) and patterns of health care use (by ethnicity) for the board and staff of the clinic. A second group was assigned to work on studies and developments that supported the action research program of the Hispanic Health Council. These students conducted interviews for the Council's first mental health study, assisted with data analysis on a variety of projects, taught research methods to community members, and worked on grants and projects. Their work resulted in several additional dissertations, including one on communication patterns between staff of a neonatal intensive care unit and Puerto Rican mothers, another on asthma, and a third on public health clinic utilization patterns.

The University of Connecticut Master's Program in Public Health offers students the opportunity to do theses or capstone projects, carried out in group projects. The program describes its approach as service learning with a strong commitment to producing students who are oriented to collaborative applied research and practice. The approach used by the program integrates substantive issues and methodology across the program and is focused on civic engagement, public service, and the reduction of health disparities. Community preceptors or supervisors work with students on action research projects and make policy recommendations. During the second year of the program, a group practicum is offered. The group practicum is interdisciplinary, faculty mentored, collaborative, and cumulative across the semester. Students develop a project, identify a field preceptor, do a "logic model" to guide the study (a form of research/action proposal summary that includes goals and objectives, an action plan, methods, and outcomes), figure out how to work together, and generate a contractual statement for their work. Student teams have

focused on a number of projects, including childhood obesity and acceptability of the Human Papilloma Virus vaccine (Gregorio, DeChello, and Segal 2008).

Most doctoral-level courses in ethnographic methods require students to conduct a mini-ethnography during the course. A typical course or course sequence permits students to choose their own site and topic. This is not so problematic if the course covers two semesters or quarters. The first semester provides enough time to read ethnographies and find out what they look like, learn and practice skills, seek out a site, organize a project, produce a proposal, and obtain IRB approval—needed if students ever hope to present their research to an audience other than their own classmates, which most do. The second semester is used to collect and analyze data and write up the results. However, getting all of the foregoing activities completed within one semester can be quite challenging.

 **EXAMPLE 11.7**

DOING ETHNOGRAPHY IN A SEMESTER: A DOCTORAL-LEVEL COURSE IN ETHNOGRAPHY

LeCompte dealt with this problem by recruiting students for the class in the semester before they enrolled, and making admission to the class contingent upon their having already selected a topic, located a site, and developed a preliminary IRB proposal for their project work. The latter requirement is necessary because of the time required to obtain IRB approvals. The IRB proposal was submitted during the second week of the semester. Students who already had taken a class such as LeCompte's "Disciplined Inquiry" course or who already had contacts with groups they wanted to study did not find this impossible, but students who had not taken such a course or who lacked contacts with a group to study needed considerable coaching from LeCompte during the previous semester to meet the requirement. Another solution is to have the course designed around development of a full proposal for an ethnographic dissertation study, including conducting the preliminary fieldwork necessary to gain access to the site and develop relationships with potential participants. However, while many students may want to learn how to conduct an ethnographic research study, not all want to do so for their dissertation.

Cross Reference: See Books 1 and 6 for detailed descriptions of sensitive topics and vulnerable subjects—the types of investigations that usually are more time-consuming than can be carried out in one semester

Cross Reference: See Book 2 for a description of how to prepare an application for IRB review

A final solution to the time crunch is for the professor to decide upon a general topic and to negotiate a site in advance. This is a case in which the students depend on the professor's contacts and community knowledge. While they can choose different aspects of the site to study, all of the students are required to work in the same place, often as a team. This obviates their being able to pick their own site and topic—often a process too time-consuming to complete in a single school term. In addition, to save time in the IRB process, all of the projects must comply with the requirements for "expedited" review by the IRB, which means that they cannot involve sensitive topics and in most cases, must avoid recruiting vulnerable subjects. One exception is projects using child participants, *if* those participants are engaged in normal instructional activities, including sports, school or community gardens, or extracurricular activities such as art or theater productions or cheerleading; these usually are not considered "sensitive." A major challenge in all of the options described above is that in order to produce an ethnography, students need to have already acquired a considerable number of research skills, including how to do structured observation, produce field notes and conduct interviews and surveys, and also to at least do preliminary analysis of qualitative data. In most cases, students end up *doing* their ethnography at the same time they are beginning to learn *how to do* ethnography.

HONORS THESES, CULMINATING PROJECTS, MASTER'S THESES, AND CAPSTONE PROJECTS

Requirements for honors theses, final summative, or capstone projects are the culmination of many undergraduate and MA/MS-level programs. These projects require that students spend more time in the field, generally as individual students rather than in teams. However, on some occasions, teams of students can work on projects together and also negotiate group work—especially if they clarify their contributions by dividing up the work. For these longer-term projects, students, with faculty mentorship, negotiate placements in field settings. Often they return to the familiar settings where they have been interns and where they feel that their research can be of immediate benefit to the setting as well as to their own careers.

Honors Theses

Honors theses and other special projects provide an opportunity for motivated undergraduate students to get one-on-one mentoring by their thesis faculty chairperson or other committee members. Honors theses are important rites of passage for undergraduate students, allowing them to integrate exercise of their skills with development of relationships with collaborators and the production of useful materials and approaches that serve community needs. They also may address health, social service, educational, and social disparities.

EXAMPLE 11.8

DOING AN HONORS THESIS BASED ON A COMMUNITY INTERNSHIP

Noelle Bessette, a Trinity College student aiming for a public health career, built her honors thesis at the Institute for Community Research with youth who used the drug ecstasy. She began with a short-term placement reviewing the transcriptions of digitally recorded interviews with young adults in Hartford who had used ecstasy, to make sure they were accurate. The young adults came each week for two hours. The following year, she returned for the summer on a paid internship to help recruit and interview downtown young professionals who were using MDMA. This led her to design a senior thesis based on her work. She worked with the study team to create a film about MDMA and the risks associated with its use, based on a script derived from the study's in-depth interviews, which she had read earlier. She has subsequently gone on to a public health career and is employed in Communicable Disease Services, Department of Public Health, New Jersey.

EXAMPLE 11.9

AN HONORS THESIS STUDYING HOW TEACHERS ESTABLISH RELATIONSHIPS WITH OTHER IMPORTANT PEOPLE IN THEIR SETTING

Sociology major Elizabeth Patino was interested in community building and, for her honors thesis, proposed to study how teachers in elementary school classrooms established linkages and partnerships with parents, their teacher aides, community members, and the students in their classrooms. Elizabeth had taken one undergraduate class in qualitative methods and a course in statistics, but had no hands-on experience doing fieldwork. As the only sociologist at the university with an interest in education, Margaret LeCompte was asked to chair Elizabeth's honors thesis work. LeCompte knew of one teacher whose reputation for skill in such community building was well-known throughout the community. She contacted the teacher, Craig Yaeger, and facilitated a meeting between him and Elizabeth. Yaeger's class also was interesting because he worked with a co-teacher in a classroom with sixty children. Elizabeth negotiated an agreement with Yaeger and his co-teacher that involved her being able to observe the classroom several days a week, and to interview the adults who worked as volunteers and aides with Yaeger, as well as have ongoing conversations with Yaeger himself and his co-teacher. In exchange, she would provide him with feedback on what she observed and would help out as needed in classroom tasks, such as helping on the playground, making copies, and reading stories to children. Elizabeth had to submit a proposal for her project to the university's IRB; doing so required that she make her plan for collecting data very explicit regarding who and what she would observe and when and where, who she would interview and about what, and how she planned to analyze the data. More than any other task, completing the IRB proposal made Elizabeth cognizant of all the steps required for doing acceptable research and the level of specificity her plans needed to have before they were approved by the IRB. Elizabeth clearly benefitted more from her collaboration with Yaeger than he did from her actions, but he also was motivated by the opportunity to have an additional enthusiastic aide in the double class of sixty children. As a former student and instructor in the School of Education, he also was motivated to support the learning activities of University of Colorado students.

Capstone Projects and Master's Theses

Capstone projects are an option for MPH (master of public health) students in public health programs. Capstone projects are problem oriented, and usually involve some form of collaborative research. They require a considerable amount of time and can involve writing about and solving a significant problem in an ongoing collaborative research effort, preparing a proposal for work in a field setting elsewhere, and presenting the results in an annual student research program or conference.

 **EXAMPLE 11.10**

A CAPSTONE PROJECT IN UGANDA

Kelsey Drake's capstone project, for which she won an award from the Johns Hopkins University Bloomberg School of Public Health, was a well-crafted proposal to address obstacles to accessing emergency care for residents of a district in rural Uganda who were unaware of emergency room services in a nearby center, unable to reach the ER in a timely manner, or unsure about when definitive emergency care was required. Most of the time, as she noted in her capstone proposal, such emergencies occurred outside of a health care setting, especially in resource-limited or rural areas where health centers or health professionals are sparse. Thus, a truly comprehensive system would incorporate multiple pre-hospital components in addition to definitive care at a hospital or health center. Her thesis examined the question of what pre-hospital components such as emergency roadside or village intervention were needed, and whether education programs to identify emergencies were necessary in order to reduce morbidity and mortality of medical or traumatic emergencies (Drake 2012).

 **EXAMPLE 11.11**

COMPLETING AN MPH THESIS

Dr. Lwendo Moonzwe Davis, a university of Connecticut MPH/PhD student, completed an MPH thesis by building on field research in an ongoing collaborative intervention study to understand women's empowerment and its relationship to health, mental health, and sexual health. She focused on the association between women's empowerment and women's self-reported general health status and health status reported during pregnancy. Her thesis used qualitative interviews with 66 married women and a survey of 260 married women from three communities. The results were the reverse of what would be expected. Non–pregnant women with higher levels of empowerment reported more general health problems, but pregnant women with high empowerment experienced fewer pregnancy-related health problems. Her reading of the field situation and the qualitative data suggested that empowered pregnant women received more social support and were expected to seek health care if they needed it, while empowered non–pregnant women received less attention, worked harder, and were expected to put their children's health before their own. She argued that feelings of empowerment are situationally and contextually defined rather than a measurable absolute (Davis et al. 2014).

DISSERTATIONS

Coursework and actual practice prepare aspiring researchers for the components of doing ethnography with practical significance. However, the actual conduct of a study requires putting all of these pieces together and implementing them over the course of a project. Below are three examples of major ethnographic projects. The first is a PhD dissertation study with practical benefit; the second as an action research project that built on work begun in a dissertation study; and the third is a full-scale participatory action research dissertation with a video feedback component.

EXAMPLE 11.12　　　

BUILDING THE PEACE PARK: A YEAR-LONG SCHOOL-COMMUNITY COLLABORATION
AND DOCTORAL ACTION RESEARCH PROJECT

Artist-activist Beth Krensky and cofounder with Carole MacNeil of Project YES!, an arts outreach program for disadvantaged and at-risk youth, wanted her dissertation research to develop a model for community-based arts education that would help to solve a community problem. Beth already had taken a course in ethnographic methods, a survey of research designs, and several courses in statistics. Also, she already was a community activist with a strong belief in the power of community-based arts projects. She proposed to develop such a project and, concurrently, evaluate its effectiveness as her dissertation topic. She wanted to enlist a local school, parents, students, and community businesses and volunteer organizations as partners in the effort, and she herself engaged in an ethnographic study for the evaluation. The problem soon emerged. She was familiar with the Lafayette, Colorado, community and its schools, having worked there for several years with Project YES! One key problem at Angevine Middle School was the large number of Latino/Latina children who were acting out at school and failing academically. Meeting with them and their parents, Krensky learned that the nearby low-income trailer park community where many of the children lived was isolated from transportation and lacked any play facilities for children. The school was across a very busy highway and too far away for children to walk to its playground; public transportation to the school or other parks was cost prohibitive for the families. Gang activity in the neighborhood meant that parents kept their children inside after school for safety. Parents decided that acquiring a safe play area for children to expend energy was a crucial need, and they named the project the "Peace Park" in hopes that it would quell the violence in the neighborhood and develop both inner and interpersonal peace for the youth living there. The problem was to find a space. Parents and Krensky learned that a trash-filled vacant lot adjacent to the trailer park and the nearby lumberyard and railroad tracks actually belonged to the trailer park's owner. They persuaded him to donate the land for a playground, promising that doing so would lower delinquent behavior and perhaps even stem gang violence.

Krensky then worked with two sixth-grade classes to start the initial design for Peace Park. The idea was that they would work with a playground design company that volunteered to help, identifying the kinds of activities and equipment they felt the community needed. They also would create a plan for the park and create artwork and a landscaping design. They would have to solicit donations of plants, landscape materials, and playground equipment, and to raise funds for needed expenses.

After six weeks of working with the teachers and youth from the middle school, Krensky and her team from Project YES! recruited youth from the trailer park to complete planning for the Peace Park and build the site. Krensky described the first days of working with the youth as totally chaotic; they fought, punched the walls, and refused to participate until Krensky brought in the tools they would have to work with—sharp and possibly dangerous power and carving tools, messy paint and clay, and other materials most often used by adults and forbidden to children. Krensky told the children that they could be trusted to work with these materials, but only if they learned how to use them safely. Gradually, the children became more engaged, and their brainstorming with designers yielded a plan: a castle-like entry way denoting that the place was a "Peace Park" for all, decorated benches, trash cans and other artworks, a basketball hoop, swings and other playground equipment for "little kids," appropriate safe surface coverings and "fall areas," and a plan for assuring that people—parents and volunteers from the neighborhood—would monitor the park once it was completed. As they mastered the tools and began making the art pieces, the children also brainstormed sources of funding or sponsorship, including the local chamber of commerce, the city council, and the mayor of the town. To do this, they had to master communications technology and gain confidence in making oral presentations to adults. The entire community rallied around the Peace Park. Parents monitored it and helped with construction. Children learned landscaping skills and helped with the heavy lifting of spreading pea gravel and mulch and planting shrubs and flowers. Parents and children negotiated with gang leaders to assure that the Peace Park would be safe for little children, as well as provide a place for older teens to shoot hoops. Activities culminated when the children made a formal presentation to the City Council, which declared that day "Peace Park Day" and accepted the park on behalf of the community. Newspaper articles expressed astonishment at the maturity and poise of young teens who had so recently been viewed as a community menace. A tribute to the enduring nature of the relationships built during the project is that more than ten years later, the Peace Park still exists (Krensky 2002).

EXAMPLE 11.13

A DISSERTATION STUDY LEADS TO CREATION OF A VILLAGE: BUILDING EDUCATIONAL OPPORTUNITY FOR IMMIGRANT MAYA CHILDREN THROUGH A COMMUNITY INTEGRATION PARTNERSHIP

Q'anjob'al-speaking Maya from western highland villages in Guatemala began arriving in Colorado's San Luis Valley and its main town, Alamosa, in 1979. Initial immigrants came to escape death and enforced military service during the thirty-six-year civil war that decimated villages in rural Guatemala. More came later, finding seasonal work in the potato fields and year-round employment at the local mushroom farm. The initial Maya immigrants were very visible because they often were so poor that they had no clothing other than their distinctive handwoven garments. The local Catholic Church reached out to them, offering shelter and other assistance, even housing some in the church basement. However, they and their children were alienated from a school system that ignored them and an economic structure that left them with the poorest paying jobs, if they were employed at all. In 1987, Alamosa's Christian Community Services facilitated creation of a grant-funded community entity, the Immigrant Resource Center (IRC), to provide legal assistance to undocumented immigrants seeking amnesty or citizenship, and social aid to victims of domestic violence. However, the IRC did not concern itself with educational matters.

Not until 2006, when Sherri Ludwig arrived in Alamosa to take a position in the school of education at Adams State University, did any focus on education for immigrant children begin. Ludwig took the position in part because the existing Maya community in Alamosa gave her a chance to continue her investigations of Maya people in diaspora. That had begun while she taught in a Denver middle school serving many Guatemalan immigrant children and continued with her dissertation in Guatemala (2006), studying indigenous and formal modes of teaching and learning experienced by the Maya. However, her colleagues at Adams State told Ludwig not to bother working with the school district, as it "never was going to change." Nonetheless, Ludwig's interest was piqued when several elementary school teachers told her they were worried about the "Mexican" students in their classes who spoke neither English nor Spanish. It turned out that they were monolingual speakers of Q'anjoba'l Maya, and the teachers did not know what to do with them. Ludwig then began a multiyear collaboration between groups of parents, emerging Maya organizations, the local Immigrant Resource Center (IRC), the Adams State University Teacher Education Department (ASUTED), teachers in several public schools, and a national group, Pastoral Maya, to develop strategies for better addressing the needs of the Maya children and their community overall.

The needs of various community components differed. The school district wanted to stem the extremely high rates of school dropout among Maya children. Teachers wanted to devise effective teaching strategies to boost the children's performance; eventually, they also wanted to learn more about the Maya community and its origins. To that end, Ludwig organized a trip to Guatemala for teachers in partnership with the Universidad del Valle in the Guatemalan highlands, where teachers could see how children were taught in Guatemala and could learn more about the heritage of their students.

Maya parents knew their children were unhappy and lost at school. They wanted them to succeed in school, but they also worried that their children had begun to lose a sense of "respect" for parents, the environment, and their culture. Parents also wanted to maintain some ties to their original community in Guatemala at the same time that they advocated for a strong Maya identity among themselves and young teens and high school students. However, supporting their children in school could be dangerous because it meant undocumented Maya parents risked exposing their status. All of them faced barriers of language, education, and status in dealing with the schools other ethnic groups in the area.

The Maya community was committed to preserving its language and cultural practices and passing them on to their children; they also hoped for a sense of acceptance and integration into the Alamosa community. Social service agencies wanted strategies to help Maya women who spoke neither English nor Spanish and who suffered isolation and depression as a result. Maya students wanted teachers who would spend sufficient time to help them achieve, an end to racial harassment and marginalization in the schools, a chance to be proud of being Maya, and to feel legitimate in the Alamosa/American community.

In 2007, the Immigrant Resource Center received a four-year Community Integration Grant to fund local efforts to integrate immigrant populations with the mainstream community, and Adams State University's Teacher Education Department (ASUTED) received a five year Title III grant to support more coherent practices for the Maya community. The result was a community-based participatory research study which supported Ludwig's work with the schools serving Maya students and their teachers, and creation of a Southern Colorado Educational Consortium. Ludwig and her co-PI, Dr. Joel Judd (from Adams State), conducted an ethnographic evaluation of the project, which initially involved simply enumerating the Maya children in the schools, difficult, because school data made no distinctions between them and "Mexicans."

The Maya community began to develop visibility through high status but authentic cultural activities that fostered student cultural groups, helped youth reclaim their language and heritage, and created student agency in seeking high school graduation and college. In 2003, for example, Guatemalan immigrants dressed in authentic folkloric clothing joined the Fourth of July parade, performing traditional dances all the way down Main Street, bravely announcing their presence in the community. Subsequently, a "Chapines" (the nickname for people from Guatemala) club was organized for high school students.

Working jointly with the IRC and the elders of the local Guatemalan community brought Ludwig into contact with a national organization, the Maya Project, sponsored by Kennesaw State University in Georgia and Pastoral Maya, a movement sponsored by the Maya Project and the Catholic Bishops in Washington, DC. Pastoral Maya brings together leaders of Maya organizations from around the United States to collaborate in strengthening the more than forty local Maya communities in the U.S. In 2007, by sheer luck, an elder of the Alamosa Maya community who was unable to drive and who had planned to attend the annual Pastoral Maya conference in Atlanta, needed a ride to the airport in Denver. Ludwig jumped at the opportunity to drive him there. She was rewarded for her willingness to be the airport chauffeur with an invitation to attend the Pastoral Maya conference; this began Ludwig's ongoing association as "our American teacher" with Pastoral Maya and its activities.

Over time, local Maya began to move into leadership roles within the local Catholic Church and the Immigrant Resource Center. Then, Maya community members founded La Puente (the Bridge), an organization devoted to the growing number of homeless in the valley, especially newly arrived immigrants, many from Guatemala. Using traditional Maya leadership models, they organized a council that elected a community leader; the objective of the council, the Authentic Eulalian Q'janoba'l Maya (Espiritu Maya), was to assist the Maya in the difficult task of adjusting to life in a new and very different culture (Ludwig 2012). The work of maintaining Maya "respect" also has been taken on by this organization and Pastoral Maya. It initiated Q'janob'al lessons at the Catholic Church, inviting all community members to learn the language, and organized an annual Fiesta of Santa Eulalia, a Maya community event for their patron saint to which mainstream community members are always invited.

The Immigrant Resource Center helped the community obtain a grant to buy authentic Maya clothing (*traje*) from Guatemala so a Maya *folklorico* dance troupe could be created. With additional grant funds, a marimba—the national instrument of Guatemala—was purchased and imported to the San Luis Valley from Guatemala. Marimba groups were formed, and children learned ancient dances and how to play the marimba. Now, marimba groups are often asked to perform during ESL (English as a Second Language) Parents' Nights at local schools and during Hispanic Heritage Month celebrations at the local university and in the community.

Though initially organized to support Maya immigrants, today Pastoral Maya supports teaching and understanding of cosmological meanings of Maya ceremonial customs, adding depth to the understanding of Maya history and cultural roots. The Maya now recognize that they will be staying in the United States and, not only that their children will live and work there, but that they will be able to be proud of their special Maya identity.

Heather Mosher's dissertation was a collaboration that describes the formation, evolution, and development of a community forged by homeless people.

 **EXAMPLE 11.14**

PARTICIPATORY ACTION RESEARCH DISSERTATION IN DIGNITY VILLAGE

The context for the dissertation is the rising numbers of homeless people in the United States and a national movement in which disenfranchised unhoused people are striving to build for themselves democratically governed communities of affordable housing. Dignity Village of Portland, Oregon, is one of the oldest and best organized self-help housing communities in the nation. These housing communities emphasize membership and participation in humane and dignified "self-help micro-housing" communities such as Dignity Village as key steps away from homelessness. Heather worked collaboratively with Dignity Village on a Participatory Action Research project aimed at both understanding and facilitating processes for mobilizing community and sociopolitical engagement. Her dissertation specifically explored the role of PAR as a strategy to facilitate community empowerment. Her team research approach involved twenty-four Dignity Village–based co-researchers/residents (nine of whom attended meetings regularly) gathering together once weekly over fifteen months, with consultation from the broader Dignity Village community throughout. The research followed a participatory-systems approach to creating a number of action tools as multiple points of leverage to create long-term positive change within the community. These tools included: (1) a diagram of the Dignity Village orientation process, protocols, and practices at the start of the research; (2) a list of "problem areas" or "areas for improvement" in the orientation process where changes might help to increase participation in the community; (3) possible options for solutions to improve the process; (4) a step-by-step implementation action plan for one of the solutions, which was considered a top priority; and (5) an orientation video (Mosher 2010, 270).

The development and use of the action tools was documented as part of the study to assess how they affected the process of developing a democratic pathway to stable housing. One point of leverage utilized participatory video methodology to co-create a video action tool as an orientation video for newcomers. The video is intended to build cooperative relationships and facilitate empowerment within the community. The impact of the research process was documented on multiple levels in the community using video, field notes based on observation of meetings and unfolding events, and reviews of records related to the history of Dignity Village. Data collected through the process were analyzed inductively to identify key themes and processes that influenced participation and empowerment in the community. The results showed three paradoxical tensions, participation, power, and embeddedness, that were creating barriers to change in the community, and the PAR process attempted to create movement beyond these barriers. Findings suggested that four main changes occurred in the community during and after the research: (a) an increase in collaborative participation, (b) enhanced engagement and sense of community, (c) an emergence of critical consciousness, and (d) changes in the organizational leadership/power structure (Mosher 2010). One interesting feature of the dissertation, above and beyond its collaborative and action-oriented methodology, was that the results were co-constructed and represented in video format to enhance report accessibility for community partners and other nonacademic audiences. Heather now lives three thousand miles away from Dignity Village and does PAR work at the Institute for Community Research in Hartford with teens and adults in Connecticut on issues of unstable housing and homelessness, but she still stays in touch with her dissertation PAR collaborators in Oregon.

TRAINING FACULTY AND POSTDOCS FOR CBPR

Many postdoctoral students, clinical fellows (primary care physicians interested in research in communities), and new faculty members want to establish their own partnership research in local settings and to train students as members of their team. A number of support mechanisms exist for training these post-PhD personnel. One is the Robert Wood Johnson Clinical Fellowship offered by the RWJ Foundation. In the past, these fellowships were given to clinicians interested in public health research, but RWJ recently has revamped its program and may be highlighting more specifically the central role that communities and clinics play in training clinicians to do good action-oriented public health research that meets their needs. Another means of training support is the National Institutes for Health (NIH) T32 postdoctoral training program. Institutions that obtain T32 funding can pay for a number of postdoctoral positions. Most postdoctoral opportunities involve working in a laboratory or with a faculty member on his or her own research. When located in a university that is community oriented, the T32s can attract trainees who are interested as a group in a community-specified research effort focused on disparities. This rarely happens because, in fact, postdocs are an inexpensive source of skilled labor for senior researchers and they may not be encouraged to do their own work, but it does provide a potential source of support for community-based collaborative action research.

NSF also has funded summer training institutes in research methods for many years, conducted by various universities, but spearheaded by the University of Florida. These one-week institutes offer training for new faculty in mixed methods research "Methods Camps" are now going digital and are being offered via the Internet. Another opportunity to develop training programs is the NIH R25. This training mechanism, often focusing on a topical issue relevant to the funding institute (for example, the National Institute of Allergy and Infectious Diseases, the National Institute on Mental Health, the National Institute on Alcohol Abuse and Alcoholism, the National Institute on Minority Health Disparities), especially addresses training to remedy health disparities and produce more health-disparities research and diverse researchers. Training programs geared to instruction in research methods appropriate to the study of disparities in marginalized or underserved populations—defined by history of poverty, ethnic minority status, disability, or sexual preference—are popular. At least until recently, some R25s included funding for pilot studies. Investigators based in universities or other independent research centers can apply, often with other partners. If they receive a training grant, they recruit new faculty members of diverse backgrounds with promising futures for a one- to six-week training program. Those accepted attend classroom lectures from senior faculty and other community representatives, may make local site visits to expose them to local community issues, and write a proposal to support a pilot study which they then are expected to carry out One such program is described below; there are many others around the country.

EXAMPLE 11.15

COMMUNITY-BASED RESEARCH TRAINING FOR DIVERSE SCHOLARS

From 2010 to 2015, the National Institutes of Health, National Institute on Mental Health (NIMH) funded a joint training program for a consortium of organizations that included the Yale University School of Nursing, the Yale Center for Inter-disciplinary Research on AIDS, the Institute for Community Research, Hartford, and the Center for Health and Prevention (CHIP) at the University of Connecticut. Each year, the PIs, Barbara Guthrie, associate dean, Yale School of Nursing, and Jean Schensul, senior scientist, Institute for Community Research, selected four or five candidates from a pool of approximately twenty very diverse candidates. All were required to be postdocs or new faculty in tenure track positions and able to remain in the program for two years, with potential to apply for NIH grants from their organizational base. The program was not restricted to candidates from universities, and several came from clinic, hospital, or community organizational bases. The recipients were mainly African Americans and Latino/Latinas from a number of social science and public health disciplines.

During the first year of each of four cohorts, the candidates took seminars and visited the participating consortium sites and communities. The interactive curriculum involved them in discussions of community, structural contributors to HIV and related health issues, HIV and co-morbidities, community-based research design, model development, methods and measures, ethical issues in CBR, and how to write research grants. A requirement of the program was to write **Cross** a concept paper with all of the components of a research **Reference:** grant. Each student's concept paper was reviewed by the See Book 2, project officer and others at NIMH. When it was approved, chapter 3 scholars transformed their concept paper into a full-scale proposal for a pilot grant to conduct a small community-based study on HIV and disparities in the area of their institutional base with a local institutional mentor. This grant was submitted to the Yale IRB and to their own institutional IRB for approval from both IRBs. The two PIs and other faculty members acted as program mentors to the participants. Mentors chose their candidates, and cross trained, providing support and feedback to their designated mentee and also to the others as needed. Mentorship involved assistance with conceptualization of the research question, analysis of the setting, model development, methods, analysis approaches, and writing the prospectus and the proposal.

When participants were in the field, they communicated with their mentors on issues that arose. The following summer, they returned to the Yale base for a six-week residency to write up their results and prepare a paper and proposal for funding. Later, this period was reduced to three weeks since much of the assistance that trainees needed could be provided online. Over the five-year period, scholars conducted participatory research projects with communities on many salient topics, including HIV prevention through Black churches, coordinated transitional support for HIV infected men released from prison, access to care for rural African Americans who are HIV positive, and prevention of risk behaviors among men who have sex with men in San Juan, Puerto Rico, among others.

Of course, there were some challenges in making this program happen. Not all the mentor/mentee arrangements worked out well; one candidate passed away at the end of the first summer. Several participants lost their jobs during their data-collection year and could only complete part of their data collection. Other participants changed jobs or took time from their research schedules in the last year of their postdoctoral program to look for academic positions. All the participants were accomplished, but, because of the economic recession, finding good jobs with potential for continuing their research was quite difficult. The curriculum initially was too didactic and too comprehensive; and it included topics with which the participants already were familiar. Over time, the curriculum benefited from feedback from successive cohorts and became more interactive and group driven. Overall, however, the program was immensely successful. At the end of the first five-year period, all participants were in tenure track positions and several had been promoted. Some have published one or more articles in peer-reviewed journals, and one scholar completely changed her career orientation from analysis of quantitative primary and secondary data to field-based research in rural communities in the United States and Africa. She also received several grants to support research in Africa!

Programs such as these, funded either privately by foundations such as Robert Wood Johnson or Kellogg, or by state and federal government agencies, go a long way toward addressing structural inequities that make it very difficult for African American, Native American, Asian Pacific, Latino/Latina, and first-generation researchers to compete for funded research grants. These agencies typically use a bi-level approach, first supporting individual researchers or groups of researchers, then building supportive networks of researchers with common interests and struggles, and finally influencing the institutions that employ them to mentor African American and Latino/Latina faculty properly and move them to achieve tenure.

Teaching students to do community-based action-oriented research is a complex venture, with many different desired outcomes. Though there is a tradition of evaluation in service learning, much of it is concentrated at the K–12 level (Eyler and Gyles 1999). In this chapter, we have focused on postsecondary education and have described the main outcomes that we would like to see from students as they grow through the various stages of developing CBPR/

PAR skills. Among them are improved cross-cultural communications skills and increased critical consciousness, reflexive capacity, participatory mixed methods research skills, and foreign language acquisition. Further, we would like students to be able to enter new cultural worlds, critically perceive and confront power differentials and inequities through research and advocacy, gain perspective on broader political and structural dynamics and their influence on local settings, define useful projects with local partners, and carry them out to completion in order to contribute to or effect change. *These outcomes cannot be fully assessed using standard quantitative methods.* Proper evaluation requires mixed methods research that includes personal records, portfolios, intermittent in-depth interviews, qualitative monitoring over time, observations and reflections on performance, photographs and videos of work carried out, network analysis, and any other means that can help to capture the existential experiences. It also requires the skills acquired by students in CBR courses and programs (Polin and Keene 2010). Finally, proper assessment includes the capacity to continue programs that assist students and faculty to take seriously community-based research to counter inequities and contribute to community development requires advocacy. It should be the responsibility of established researchers who want to see PAR, CBPR, and other forms of action research continue to find ways of advocating for it with their community partners who see its value. More organizations like the Community Network for Research Equity and Impact, that represents coalitions that value community-based research and want to see it happen, are needed. Maintaining the pressure on research funders to continue support for community-based research, to encourage research linkages from "lab" to community *as well as* from "lab" to clinic or school, and to balance the distribution of funding along the continuum from the cellular level to the community level, is essential.

 Key point

SUMMARY

In this final chapter of the *Ethnographer's Toolkit*, we have reviewed the many different ways that community-based, action-oriented, ethnographic research can be taught and shared with students at all levels and of all ages. We have described in-classroom and out-of-classroom experiences, internships, and field schools. We have alluded to the intensive mentorship that is required if students are to learn as apprentices in the field. And we have discussed in detail the obligations and responsibilities of faculty to make the learning experience as rich, as meaningful, and as balanced, in terms of research and service/action, as possible.

We end the *Toolkit* where we began, with the strong belief that collaborative mixed methods ethnography is the best, most valid, and most ethically responsible form of research, especially in communities that are underserved, marginalized, minoritized, racialized, and otherwise subjected to forms of disrespect, disparity, and inequity. In such settings, the first issue to address is trust. Ethnography, with its dedication to continued presence, its commitment to the building of interpersonal relationships, and its balance of intimacy and confidentiality in face-to-face communication, is unique in its ability to build trust. The mixed methods that ethnography makes available are easily made participatory, and most people in most communities around the world can "get them," can get access to them, and can use them well. Triangulation of data along with the intuitive interpretation that comes from immersion in the setting produces highly robust results. And in this book we have shown that participatory ethnography has the capacity to produce culturally and situationally relevant interventions, informed political action, and other approaches to multilevel transformational social change.

Finally, we believe that embodied experience with it is the best and deepest way to know inequality and to find the internal drive, passion, and the external networks needed to do something about it. Reflexive ethnography offers us the opportunity to search within ourselves and our settings and with friends, partners, and fellow activists, and to find the methods and tools to improve social conditions and attempt to reverse injustices in this world.

REFERENCES

AAA. February 2009. *Code of Ethics of the American Anthropological Association*. American Anthropological Association.

Abelson, R. P. 1981. "Psychological Status of the Script Concept." *American Psychologist* 36:715–29.

Abraham, R. 2014. "Agent-Based Modeling of Growth Processes." *Mind, Brain, and Education* 8:115–31.

Abusharaf, R. M., ed. 2006. *Female Circumcision Multicultural Perspectives*. Philadelphia: University of Pennsylvania Press.

Agar, M. 2004. "We Have Met the Other and We're All Nonlinear: Ethnography as a Nonlinear Dynamic System." *Complexity* 10 (2): 16–24.

———. 2005. "Local Discourse and Global Research: The Role of Local Knowledge." *Language in Society* 34:1–22.

Allen, M. L., M. V. Svetaz, A. Hurtado, R. Linares, D. Garcia-Huidobro, and M. Hurtado. 2013. "The Developmental Stages of a Community-University Partnership: The Experience of Padres Informados/Jovenes Preparados." *Progress in Community Health Partnerships: Research, Education, and Action* 7:271–79.

Amsden, J., and R. Van-Wynsberghe. 2005. "Community Mapping as a Research Tool with Youth." *Action Research* 3:357–81.

Anderson, T., and J. Shattuck. 2012. "Design-Based Research: A Decade of Progress in Education Research?" *Educational Researcher* 41:16–25.

Andreasen, A. R. 2006. *Social Marketing in the 21st Century*. Thousand Oaks, CA: Sage.

Balcazar, F. E., C. Keys, D. Kaplan, and Y. Suarez-Balcazar. 2006. "Participatory Action Research and People with Disabilities: Principles and Challenges," http://home.iI?-terlog.com!-kroghlKroghlPgl05.html

Banks, S., et al. 2013. "Everyday Ethics in Community-Based Participatory Research." *Contemporary Social Science: Journal of the Academy of Social Sciences* 8:263–77.

Barker, D. 2004. "The Scholarship of Engagement: A Taxonomy of Five Emerging Practices." *Journal of Higher Education Outreach and Engagement* 9:123–37.

Barlas, Y. 1996. "Formal Aspects of Model Validity and Validation in System Dynamics." *System Dynamics Review* 12:183–210.

Barnhardt, R. 1977. *Field-Based Education for Alaskan Native Teachers. Cross-Cultural Issues in Alaskan Education*. Fairbanks, AK: University of Alaska.

———. 1999. "Preparing Teachers for Rural Alaska." *Sharing Our Pathways* 4:1–3.

———. 2002. "Domestication of the Ivory Tower: Institutional Adaptation to Cultural Distance." *Anthropology & Education Quarterly* 33:238–49.

———. 2005. "Creating a Place for Indigenous Knowledge in Education: The Alaska Native Knowledge Network," in *Local Diversity: Place-Based Education in the Global Age*. Edited by G. Smith and D. Gruenewald. Hillsdale, NJ: Lawrence Erlbaum Associates.

———. 2008. *Culture, Chaos and Complexity: Catalysts for Change in Indigenous Education*. Alaska Rural Systemic Initiative, Fairbanks, AK: University of Alaska.

Barnhardt, R., and A. O. Kawagley, eds. 2010. *Alaska Native Education: Views from Within*. Fairbanks, AK: Alaska Native Knowledge Network.

Barnhardt, R., and O. Kawagley. 2005. "Indigenous Knowledge Systems and Alaska Native Ways of Knowing." *Anthropology and Education Quarterly* 36:8–23.

Barnhardt, R., O. Kawagley, and F. Hill. 2000. "Educational Renewal in Rural Alaska." International Conference on Rural Communities and Identities in the Global Millenium, Nanaimo, BC, CA, pp. 140–45.

Baron, D. 2009. "Community Health Assets Key to Innovative Community-Based Health Research Project," in *The Irwin W. Steans Center*. Chicago: DePaul University.

Barrette, K. 2015. *Approaches to Community Organizing: Theory and Practice*. Hartford, CT: Institute for Community Research.

Bartunek, J., and M. L. Louis. 1996. *Insider/Outsider Team Research*, vol. 40. *Qualitative Research Methods Series*. Thousand Oaks, CA: Sage.

Batterman, S., L. Du, E. Parker, T. Robins, T. Lewis, B. Mukherjee, E. Ramirez, Z. Rowe, and W. Brakefield-Caldwell. 2013. "Use of Free-Standing Filters in an Asthma Intervention Study." *Air Quality, Atmosphere & Health* 6:759–67.

Beck, S., and C. Maida, eds. 2015. *Public Anthropology in a Borderless World*. New York: Berghahn Books.

Beebe, J. 2001. *Rapid Assessment Process*. Lanham, MD: AltaMira.

Beresford, Q. 1996. *Rites of Passage: Aboriginal Youth, Crime and Justice*. South Fremantle, Western Australia: Freemantle Arts Centre Press.

Berg, M. 2004. "Education and Advocacy: Improving Teaching and Learning Through Student Participatory Action Research." *Practicing Anthropology* 26:20–24.

Berg, M., E. Coman, and J. Schensul. 2009. "Youth Action Research for Prevention: A Multi-Level Intervention Designed to Increase Efficacy and Empowerment Among Urban Youth." *American Journal of Community Psychology* 43:345–59.

Berg, M., and J. Schensul. 2004. "Participatory Action Research with Youth." *Practicing Anthropology* 26.

Berger, P. L. 1990. *The Social Construction of Reality: A Treatise in the Sociology of Knowledge*. Edited by T. Luckmann. New York: Anchor Books.

Bernard, H. R., and C. Gravlee, eds. 2014. *Research Methods in Anthropology*, 2nd ed. Lanham, MD: Roman & Littlefield.

Blair, T., and M. Minkler. 2009. "Participatory Action Research with Older Adults: Key Principles in Practice." *The Gerontologist* 49:651–62.

Bonsall, D. L., R. A. Harris, and J. N. Markzakym. 2002. "The Community as a Classroom." *New Directions for Student Services* 100:85–95.

Borgatti, S. P., and D. S. Halgin. 2011. "Consensus Analysis," in *A Companion to Cognitive Anthropology*. Edited by D. B. Kronenfeld, G. Bernardo, V. C. Munck, and M. D. Fischer, pp. 171–90. Hoboken, NJ: Wiley-Blackwell.

Borofsky, B. 2011. *Why a Public Anthropology*. Honolulu, HI: Center for a Public Anthropolgy-Hawaii Pacific University.

Boylorn, R. M., and M. P. Orbe. 2013. *Critical Autoethnography: Intersecting Cultural Identities in Everyday Life*. Walnut Creek, CA: Left Coast Press.

Breckwich Vasquez, V., D. Lanza, S. Hennessey-Lavery, S. Facente, H. A. Halpin, and M. Minkler. 2007. "Addressing Food Security Through Public Policy Action in a Community-Based Participatory Research Partnership." *Health Promotion Practice* 8.

Bretherton, L. 2012. "The Political Populism of Saul Alinsky and Broad Based Organizing." *The Good Society* 21:261–78.

Bronfenbrenner, U. 1989. "Ecological Systems Theory," in *Annals of Child Development*, vol. 6. Edited by R. Vasta, pp. 187–249. Greenwich, CT: JAI Press.

Brown, A. W., and D. B. Allison. 2014. "Using Crowdsourcing to Evaluate Published Scientific Literature: Methods and Example." *PLoS ONE* 9:1–9.

Bruce, A. E. 2005. An Examination of Factors Facilitating Successful Induction and Training of Volunteer Counselors in a Rape Crisis Program. Unpublished doctoral dissertation. Denver: Denver University.

Brydon-Miller, M. 1997. "Participatory Action Research: Psychology and Social Change." *Journal of Social Issues* 53:657–66.

Brydon-Miller, M., I. Davids, N. Jaiti, L. Brinton, J. Schensul, and S. Williams. 2008. "Popular Education and Action Research: Voices from the Field," in *Handbook on Educational Action Research*. Edited by S. Noffke and B. Somekh. Thousand Oaks, CA: Sage.

Brydon-Miller, M., D. Greenwood, and P. Maguire. 2003. "Why Action Research." *Action Research* 1:9–28.

Bucholtz, M. 2002. "Youth and Cultural Practice." *Annual Review of Anthropology* 31:525.

Buettgen, A., J. Richardson, K. Beckham, K. Richardson, M. Ward, and M. Riemer. 2012. "We Did It Together: A Participatory Action Research Study on Poverty and Disability." *Disability & Society* 27:603–16.

Bunce, A. E., R. Gold, J. V. Davis, C. K. McMullen, V. Jaworski, M. Mercer, and C. Nelson. 2014. "Ethnographic Process Evaluation in Primary Care: Explaining the Complexity of Implementation." *BMJ Health Services Research* 14:607–17.

Burgess, J. 2006. "Participatory Action Research: First-Person Perspectives of a Graduate Student." *Action Research* 4:419–37.

Burke, B. L. 2011. "What Can Motivational Interviewing Do for You?" *Cognitive and Behavioral Practice* 18:74–81.

Burke, B. L., H. Arkowitz, and M. Menchola. 2003. "The Efficacy of Motivational Interviewing: A Meta-Analysis of Controlled Clinical Trials." *Journal of Consulting and Clinical Psychology* 71:843–61.

Butler, M. O. 2005. "Translating Evaluation Anthropology." *NAPA Bulletin* 24:17–30.

Cahill, C. 2007. "Doing Research with Young People: Participatory Research and the Rituals of Collective Work." *Children's Geographies* 5:297–312.

Cahnmann-Taylor, M., S. Bleyle, Y. Hwang, and K. Zhang. 2014. "Writing Poetry to Create New TESOL Futures," in *American Anthropological Association*. Washington, DC.

Cammarota, J., and A. Romero. 2009. "A Social Justice Epistemology and Pedagogy for Latina/o Students: Transforming Public Education with Participatory Action Research." *New Directions for Youth Development* 2009:53–65.

———. 2011. "Participatory Action Research for High School Students: Transforming Policy, Practice, and the Personal With Social Justice Education." *Educational Policy* 25:488–506.

Canaan, J. 2005. "Developing a Pedagogy of Critical Hope." *LATISS: Learning and Teaching in the Social Sciences* 2:159–74.

Cann, A. 2011. *Social Media: A Guide for Researchers*. Leicester, UK: University of Leicester.

CARE. 2012. *Strategies for Disseminating Research Findings*. New Haven, CT: Yale Center for Clinical Investigation-Community Alliance for Research and Engagement.

Carrete, L., and P. Arroyo. 2014. "Social Marketing to Improve Healthy Dietary Decisions." *Qualitative Market Research: An International Journal* 17:239–63.

CASBHS-UCONN-ICR. 2013. "Connecticut School Based Health Centers Engage Adolescent African-American and Latino Males in Mental Health Services." *Issue Brief-Connecticut:* www.cthealth.org/wp-content/uploads/2011/04/IssueBrief_web2-Final.pdf.

Catania, J. A., T. J. Coates, S. Kegeles, M. T. Fullilove, J. Peterson, B. Marin, D. Siegel, and S. Hulley. 1992. "Condom Use in Multi-Ethnic Neighborhoods of San Francisco: The Population-Based AMEN (AIDS in Multi-Ethnic Neighborhoods) Study." *American Journal of Public Health* 82:284–87.

CDC. 2013. "Health, United States, 2013: Table 79." Edited by DHHS, pp. 270. Washington, DC: Centers for Disease Control National Center for Health Statistics.

Chabot, C., Jean A. Shoveller, Grace Spencer, and Joy L. Johnson. 2012. "Ethical and Epistemological Insights: A Case Study of Participatory Action Research with Young People." *Journal of Empirical Research on Human Research Ethics: An International Journal* 7:20–33.

Chakraborty, B., L. M. Collins, V. J. Strecher, and S. A. Murphy. 2009. "Developing Multicomponent Interventions Using Fractional Factorial Designs. *Statistics in Medicine* 28:2687–2708.

Chang, H., F. Ngunjiri, and K.-A. C. Hernandez. 2012. *Collaborative Autoethnography*. Walnut Creek, CA: Left Coast Press.

Chapman, D. J., and R. Pérez-Escamilla. 2013. Acculturative Type Is Associated with Breastfeeding Duration among Low-Income Latinas. *Maternal & Child Nutrition* 9:188–98.

Chariyeva, Z., C. E. Golin, J. A. Earp, S. Maman, C. Suchindran, and C. Zimmer. 2013. "The Role of Self-Efficacy and Motivation to Explain the Effect of Motivational Interviewing Time on Changes in Risky Sexual Behavior among People Living with HIV: A Mediation Analysis." *AIDS Behavior* 17:813–23.

Chaskin, R. J. 2001. "Building Community Capacity: A Definitional Framework and Case Studies from a Comprehensive Community Initiative." *Urban Affairs Review* 36:291–323.

Chavez, L. R., F. A. Hubbell, and J. M. McMullin. 1995. "Structure and Meaning in Models of Breast and Cervical-Cancer Risk-Factors: A Comparison of Perceptions among Latinas, Anglo Women, and Physicians." *Medical Anthropology Quarterly* 9:40–74.

Chedekel, L. 1998. "Health Center to Remain Open," in *Hartford Courant, January 9, 1998.*

Chen, P., N. Diaz, G. Lucas, and M. S. Rosenthal. 2010. "Dissemination of Results in Community-Based Participatory Research." *American Journal of Preventive Medicine* 39(3):37–78.

Chilisa, B. 2012. *Indigenous Research Methodologies*. Thousand Oaks, CA: Sage.

Christens, B. D., J. J. Collura, and F. Tahir. 2013. "Critical Hopefulness: A Person-Centered Analysis of the Intersection of Cognitive and Emotional Empowerment." *American Journal of Community Psychology* 52:170–84.

Christie, C. A., B. E. Montrose, and B. M. Klein. 2005. "Emergent Design Evaluation." *Evaluation and Program Planning* 28:271–77.

Clarke, C. 2013. *Be the Change: Saving the World with Citizen Science*. Kindle Edition.

Cobb, P., J. Confrey, A. diSessa, R. Lehrer, and L. Schauble. 2003. "Design Experiments in Educational Research." *Educational Researcher* 32:9–13.

Collins, T. 1977. "Unionization in a Secondary Labor Market." *Human Organization* 36:135–41.

Collins, T., ed. 1980. *Cities in a Larger Context*. Athens: University of Georgia Press.

Combs, C. J. 1999. Theories of Group Intervention. *Transplantation Proceedings* 31:46S–47S.

Cooper, E. 2005. "What Do We Know about Out-Of-School Youths? How Participatory Action Research Can Work for Young Refugees in Camps." *Compare: A Journal of Comparative Education* 35:463–77.

Corbyn, Z. August 18, 2011. "Black Applicants Less Likely to Win NIH Grants." *Nature: International Weekly Journal of Science.*

Coreil, J., and G. Maynard. 2009. "Indigenization of Illness Support Groups for Lympathic Filiariasis in Haiti," in *Anthropology and Public Health: Bridging Differences in Culture and Society.* Edited by R. A. Hahn and M. C. Inhorn. New York: Oxford University Press.

Cornwall, A., and R. Jewkes. 1995. "What Is Participatory Research?" *Social Science & Medicine* 41:1667–76.

Dalle Molle, D. T., B. J. Kuipers, and T. F. Edgar. 1988. "Qualitative Modeling and Simulation of Dynamic Systems." *Computer and Chemical Engineering* 12:853–66.

D'Andrade, R. G. 1992. "Schemas and Motivation," in *Human Motives and Cultural Models.* Edited by R. G. D'Andrade and C. Strauss, pp. 23–44. Cambridge, UK: Cambridge, University Press.

———. 1995. "Moral Models in Anthropology." *Current Anthropology* 36.

Datnow, A., L. Hubbard, and H. Mehan. 2002. *Extending Educational Reform: From One School to Many.* New York: RoutledgeFalmer.

Davis, M. L., S. L. Schensul, J. Schensul, R. K. Verma, B. K. Nastasi, and R. Singh. 2014. "Women's Empowerment and Its Differential Impact on Health in Low-Income Communities in Mumbai, India." *Global Public Health* 9:481–94.

Davis, S. M., and R. Reid. 1999. "Practicing Participatory Research in American Indian Communities." *The American Journal of Clinical Nutrition* 69:755S–59S.

De Leeuw, S., Emilie S. Cameron, and Margo L. Greenwood. 2012. "Participatory and Community-Based Research, Indigenous Geographies, and the Spaces of Friendship: A Critical Engagement. *The Canadian Geographer* 56:180–94.

Demiris, G., D. P. Oliver, D. Capurro, and E. Wittenberg-Lyles. 2014. "Implementation Science." *Gerontologist* 54:163–71.

Dharod, J. M., R. Pérez-Escamilla, A. Bermúdez-Millán, S. Segura-Pérez, and G. Damio. 2004. "Influence of the Fight BAC! Food Safety Campaign on an Urban Latino Population in Connecticut." *Journal of Nutrition Education & Behavior* 36:128–34.

Diamond, S., J. J. Schensul, L. B. Snyder, A. Bermudez, N. D'Alessandro, and D. S. Morgan. 2009. "Building Xperience: A Multilevel Alcohol and Drug Prevention Intervention." *American Journal of Community Psychology* 43:292–312.

Doan, L., T. Robins, S. Batterman, B. Mukherjee, G. Mentz, X. Ren, S. Grant, E. Parker, and T. Lewis. 2012. "Asthma Control In Detroit Children Is Associated with Exposure to Highway Traffic." *American Journal of Respiratory and Critical Care Medicine* 185:A2474.

Dorr-Bremme, D. W. 1985. "Ethnographic Evaluation: A Theory and Method." *Educational Evaluation and Policy Analysis* 7:65–83.

Douglas, M., and A. Wildavsky. 1982. "How Can We Know the Risks We Face? Why Risk Selection Is a Social Process." *Risk Analysis* 2:49–58.

Downs, T. J., L. Ross, S. Patton, S. Rulnick, D. Sinha, D. Mucciarone, M. Calvache, S. Parmenter, R. Subedi, D. Wysokenski, E. Anderson, R. Dezan, K. Lowe, J. Bowen, A. Tejani, K. Piersanti, O. Taylor, and R. Goble. 2009. "Complexities of Holistic Community-Based Participatory Research for a Low Income, Multi-Ethnic Population Exposed to Multiple Built-Environment Stressors in Worcester, Massachusetts." *Environmental Research* 109:1028–40.

Drake, K. 2012. "A Lay Training Program in Basic Emergency Care and Danger Sign Recognition in Rukungiri District. Uganda: Recommendations for Global Emergency Care Collaborative's Pre-Hospital Emergency Resources Project (Program Plan)." Johns Hopkins Bloomberg School of Public Health.

Du, L., S. Batterman, E. Parker, C. Godwin, J.-Y. Chin, A. O'Toole, T. Robins, W. Brakefield-Caldwell, and T. Lewis. 2011. "Particle Concentrations and Effectiveness of Free-Standing Air Filters in Bedrooms of Children with Asthma in Detroit, Michigan." *Building and Environment* 46:2303–13.

Duncan-Andrade, J. 2004. "Your Best Friend or Your Worst Enemy: Youth Popular Culture, Pedagogy, and Curriculum in Urban Classrooms." *The Review of Education, Pedagogy, and Cultural Studies* 26.

Dunn, C. E., Ann Le Mare, and Christina Makungu. 2011. "Malaria Risk Behaviours, Socio-Cultural Practices and Rural Livelihoods in Southern Tanzania: Implications for Bednet Usage." *Social Science & Medicine* 72:408–17.

Dushay, R. A., M. Singer, M. R. Weeks, L. Rohena, and R. Gruber. 2001. "Lowering HIV Risk among Ethnic Minority Drug Users: Comparing Culturally Targeted Intervention." *American Journal of Drug & Alcohol Abuse* 27:501.

Eddy, E. M., and W. L. Partridge. Editors. 1987. *Applied Anthropology in America.* New York: Columbia University Press.

Edgar, T., and M. A. Fitzpatrick. 1993. "Expectations for Sexual Interaction: A Cognitive Test of the Sequencing of Sexual Communication Behaviors." *Health Communication* 5:239–61.

Eisenberg, M. 2014. "Social Science, Public Policy and Amnesty for Chickens." *Practicing Anthropology* 34:6–11.

Ejima, K., K. Aihara, and H. Nishiura. 2013. "Modeling the Obesity Epidemic: Social Contagion and Its Implications for Control." *Theoretical Biology and Medical Modelling* 10:17.

Encyclopedia.com. 2003. "Self-Help Movement," in *Dictionary of American History.* http://www.encyclopedia.com/doc/1G2-3401803797.html.

Engel, L. J. 2002. "Saul Alinsky and the Chicago School." *The Journal of Speculative Philosophy* 16:50–66.

Epstein, J. S. 1998. *Youth Culture: Identity in a Postmodern World.* Edited by J. S. Epstein. London: Blackwell.

Escueta, M., and S. Butterwick. 2012. "The Power of Popular Education and Visual Arts for Trauma Survivors' Critical Consciousness and Collective Action." *International Journal of Lifelong Education* 31:325–40.

Etmanski, C., B. L. Hall, and T. Dawson, eds. 2014. *Learning and Teaching Community Based Research: Linking Pedagogy to Practice.* Toronto: University of Toronto Press Scholarly Publishing Division.

Ettma, J. S., J. W. Brown, and R. V. Luepker. 1983. "Knowledge Gap Effects in a Health Information Campaign." *Public Opinion Quarterly* 47:516–27.

Evelyn, D. 2004. "Telling Stories of Research." *iCONN OneSearch Video* 36:1–18.

Eyler, J., and D. E. J. Gyles. 1999. *Where's the Learning in Service-Learning?* San Francisco: Jossey Bass.

Fals-Borda, O. 1987. "The Application of Participatory Action-Research in Latin America." *International Sociology* 2:329–47.

Fals-Borda, O., and M. A. Rahman. 1991. *Action and Knowledge: Breaking the Monopoly with Participatory Action Research.* New York: Apex.

Farney, D. 1989. "River of Despair, Along the Rich Banks of the Mississippi Live the Poorest of U.S. Poor." *Wall Street Journal,* pp. P. 1., A16.

Farquhar, S. A., E. Parker, A. Schulz, and B. Israel. 2005. "In Their Words: How Detroit Residents Perceive the Effects of Their Physical Environment." *Local Environment* 10:259–74.

Fernandez, C. V., E. Kodish, and C. Weijer. 2003. "Informing Study Participants of Research Results: An Ethical Imperative." *IRB: Ethics and Human Research* 25:12–19.

Fetterman, D., ed. 1984. *Ethnography in Educational Evaluation.* Beverly Hills, CA: Sage.

Fetterman, D. 1994. "Empowerment Evaluation." *Evaluation Practice* 15:1–15.

———. 2005. "Empowerment and Ethnographic Evaluation." *NAPA Bulletin* 24:71–78.

Fine, M., R. A. Roberts, M. E. Torre, J. Bloom, A. Burns, L. M. Chajet, Y. A. Payne, and T. Perkins-Munn. 2004. *Echoes of Brown: Youth Documenting and Performing the Legacy of Brown v. Board of Education.* New York: Teachers College Press.

Fine, M., and M. E. Torre. 2006. "Intimate Details: Participatory Action Research in Prison." *Action Research* 4:253–69.

Fine, M., M. E. Torre, B. G. Stoudt, M. Fox, A. Burns, and Y. A. Payne. 2007. "Youth Research/Participatory Methods for Reform," in *International Handbook of Student Experience in Elementary and Secondary School.* Edited by D. Thiessen and A. Cook-Sather, pp. 805–28. New York: Springer.

Fink, E. L. 1996. "Dynamic Social Impact Theory and the Study of Human Communication." *Journal of Communication* 46(4):4–12. February 1996. DOI: 10.1111/j.1460-2466.1996.tb01500.x.

Fiscella, K., R. Dressler, S. Meldrum, and K. Holt. 2007. "Impact of Influenza Vaccination Disparities on Elderly Mortality in the United States." *Preventive Medicine* 45:83–87.

Fishbein, M. 2008. "A Reasoned Action Approach to Health Promotion." *Medical Decision Making* 28:834–44.

Fishbein, M., and I. Azjen. 2010. *Predicting and Changing Behavior: The Reasoned Action Approach.* New York: Routledge.

Fisher, J. D., and W. A. Fisher. 2000. "Theoretical Approaches to Individual-Level Change in HIV Risk Behavior." *CHIP Documents, Paper 4,* http://digitalcommons.uconn.edu/chip_docs/4.

Flicker, S., and C. A. Worthington. 2011. "Public Health Research Involving Aboriginal Peoples: Research Ethics Board Stakeholders' Reflections on Ethics Principles and Research Processes." *Canadian Journal of Public Health* 103(1):19–22.

Fluehr-Lobban, C. 2013. *Ethics and Anthropology: Ideas and Practice* Lanham, MD: AltaMira.

Fong, G. T., D. Hammond, and S. C. Hitchman. 2009. "The Impact of Pictures on the Effectiveness of Tobacco Warnings." *Bulletin of the World Health Organization* 87:640–43.

Ford, D. N., and J. D. Sterman. 1998. "Expert Knowledge Elicitation to Inform Formal and Mental Models." *System Dynamics Review* 14:309–40.

Forrester, J. 1968. *Principles of Systems* (2nd ed.). Portland, OR: Productivity Press.

———. 2007a. "System Dynamics: A Personal View of the First Fifty Years." *System Dynamics Review* 23:345–58.

———. 2007b. "System Dynamics: The Next Fifty Years." *System Dynamics Review 2* 3:359–70.

Forrester, J. W., and P. M. Senge. 1980. "Tests for Building Confidence in System Dynamics Models," in *TIMS Studies in the Management Sciences,* vol. 14. Edited by A. Legasto, A. Jr., J. W. Forrester, and J. M. Lyneis. New York: North-Holland.

Foster-Fishman, P. G., K. M. Law, L. F. Lichty, and C. Aoun. 2010. "Youth ReACT for Social Change: A Method for Youth Participatory Action Research." *American Journal of Community Psychology* 46:67–83.

Freedman, J., and J. Freedman. 1996. *Narrative Therapy: The Social Construction of Preferred Realities* (1st ed.). New York: Norton.

Freeman, D. 1983. *Margaret Mead and Samoa: The Making and Unmaking of an Anthropological Myth.* Boston: Harvard University Press.

Freire, P. 1970. *Pedagogy of the Oppressed.* New York: Herder and Herder.

———. 1973. *Education for Critical Consciousness* vol. 1. New York, London: Continuum.

————. 1981. *Education for Critical Consciousness*. New York: Continuum.

Freudenberg, N., S. P. Bradley, and M. Serrano. 2009. "Public Health Campaigns to Change Industry Practices That Damage Health: An Analysis of 12 Case Studies." *Health Education & Behavior* 36:230–49.

Frith, H., and C. Kitzinger. 1997. "Talk about Sexual Miscommunication." *Women's Studies International Forum* 20:517–28.

Gaglio, B., J. A. Shoup, and R. E. Glasgow. 2013. "The RE-AIM Framework: A Systematic Review of Use Over Time." *American Journal of Public Health* 103:E38–E46.

Galletta, A., and V. Jones. 2010. "'Why Are You Doing This?' Questions on Purpose, Structure, and Outcomes in Participatory Action Research Engaging Youth and Teacher Candidates." *Educational Studies* 46:337–57.

Galman, S. C. 2007. *Shane, the Lone Ethnographer: A Beginner's Guide to Ethnographic Research*. Walnut Creek, CA: AltaMira.

Gardner, H. 1993. *Frames of Mind: The Theory of Multiple Intelligences*. London: Fontana Books.

Garro, L., and C. Mattingly, eds. 2000. *Narrative and the Cultural Construction of Illness and Healing*. Berkeley: University of California Press.

Gaviria, F. M., G. Stern, and S. L. Schensul. 1982. "Sociocultural Factors and Perinatal Health in a Mexican-American Community." *Journal of the National Medical Association* 74:983–89.

GCM. 2002. "In Her Mother's Shoes: Giving Women Power Over AIDS." Edited by G. C. f. Microbicies. Global Coalition on Women and AIDS. http://www.global-campaign.org/exhibit.htm.

Gearing, F., R. M. Netting, and L. R. Peattie, eds. 1960. *A Documentary History of the Fox Project, 1948–1959: A Program in Action Anthropology*. Chicago: University of Chicago Press.

Gennep, A. V. 1960. *The Rites of Passage*. Edited by M. Vizedom and G. L. Caffee. Chicago: University of Chicago Press.

Gettleman, J. 2015. "Meant to Keep Malaria Out, Mosquito Nets Are Used to Haul Fish In." *New York Times*, January 24, p. 1.

Ghorbani, A., G. Dijkema, and N. Schrauwen. 2015. "Structuring Qualitative Data for Agent-Based Modelling." *JASSS-The Journal of Artificial Societies and Social Simulation* 18.

Gibson, M. A. 1985. "Collaborative Educational Ethnography: Problems and Profits." *Anthropology and Education Quarterly* 16:124–48.

Gigerenzer, G., and W. Gaissmaier. 2011. "Heuristic Decision Making." *Annual Review of Psychology* 62:451–82.

Gilmore, S., J. DeLamater, and D. Wagstaff. 1996. "Sexual Decision Making by Inner City Black Adolescent Males: A Focus Group Study." *Journal of Sex Research* 33:363–71.

Gitlin, A., ed. 1994. *Power and Method: Political Activism and Educational Research*. New York: Routledge.

Glanz, K., and D. B. Bishop. 2010. "The Role of Behavioral Science Theory in Development and Implementation of Public Health Interventions." *Annual Review of Public Health* 31:399–418.

Gnuschke, J. E., S. Hyland, J. Wallace, and S. Smith. 2008. "Still a Long Way to Go for the Lower Mississippi Delta." *Journal of Health & Human Services Administration* 31:72–104.

Goldblatt, E. 2005. "Alinsky's Reveille: A Community-Organizing Model for Neighborhood-Based Literacy Projects." *College English* 67:274–95.

Goleman, D. 2011. "The Brain and Emotional Intelligence New Insights" (1st ed.). Northampton, MA: More Than Sound.

Gonzalez, E. R., C. S. Sarmiento, A. S. Urzua, and S. C. Luevano. 2012. "The Grassroots and New Urbanism: A Case from a Southern California Latino Community." *Journal of Urbanism* 5:219–39.

González, R. J. 2008. "Human Terrain." *Anthropology Today* 24:21–26.

Goodman, R., A. Wandersman, M. Chinman, P. Imm, and E. Morrissey. 1996. "An Ecological Assessment of Community-Based Interventions for Prevention and Health Promotion: Approaches to Measuring Community Coalitions." *American Journal of Community Psychology* 24:33–61.

Grayshield, L., and A. Mihecoby. 2010. "Indigenous Ways of Knowing as a Philosophical Base for the Promotion of Peace and Justice in Counseling Education and Psychology." *Journal for Social Action in Counseling and Psychology* 2:1–15.

Greco, M., and P. Stenner. 2013. *Emotions and Social Theory: A Social Science Reader*. New York: Routledge.

Green, L. W., and R. E. Glasgow. 2006. "Evaluating the Relevance, Generalization, and Applicability of Research: Issues in External Validation and Translation Methodology." *Evaluation & the Health Professions* 29:126–53.

Greenspan, P. S. 2014. *Emotions and Reasons: An Inquiry into Emotional Justification*. New York: Routledge.

Greenwood, D., and M. Levin. 1998. *Introduction to Action Research: Social Research for Social Change*. Thousand Oaks, CA: Sage.

Gregorio, D. L., L. M. DeChello, and J. Segal. 2008. "Service Learning Within the University of Connecticut Master of Public Health Program." *Public Health Reports.* 123 (S2):44–52.

Grier, S., and C. A. Bryant. 2005. "Social Marketing in Public Health." *Annual Review of Public Health & Place* 26:319–39.

Gruber, C. W. 2012. "Humanistic Cognitive Behavioral Theory, a Value-Added Approach to Teaching Theories of Personality." *Procedia—Social and Behavioral Sciences* 46:252–59.

Guarnaccia, P., R. Lewis-Fernández, and M. Marano. 2003. "Toward a Puerto Rican Popular Nosology: Nervios and Ataque de Nervios." *Culture, Medicine and Psychiatry* 27:339–66.

Habib, F., I. Etesam, S. H. Ghoddusifar, and N. Mohajeri. 2012. "Correspondence Analysis: A New Method for Analyzing Qualitative Data in Architecture." *Nexus Network Journal* 14:517–38.

Hall, B. L. 2005. "In from the Cold? Reflections on Participatory Research 1970–2005." *Convergence* 38:5–24.

———. 2014. "Learning to Listen: Foundations of Teaching and facilitating of Participatory and Community-Based Research (Chapter 7; E-book)," in *Learning and Teaching Community-Based Research: Linking Pedagogy to Practice*. Edited by C. Etmanski, B. L. Hall, and T. Dawson, Location 2750. Toronto: University of Toronto Press.

Harding, S. 2006. *Science and Social Inequality: Feminist and Postcolonial Issues*. Chicago: University of Illinois Press.

Harrison, B. 2001. *Collaborative Programs in Indigenous Communities: From Fieldwork to Practice*. Walnut Creek, CA: AltaMira.

Hastings, G., and N. McLean. 2006. "Social Marketing, Smoking Cessation and Inequalities." *Addiction* 101:303–4.

Hawe, P., A. Shiell, and T. Riley. 2009. "Theorising Interventions as Events in Systems." *American Journal of Community Psychology* 43:267–76.

Hawkins, J. D., R. F. Catalano, and M. W. Arthur. 2002. "Promoting Science-Based Prevention in Communities." *Addictive Behaviors* 27:951–76.

Hays, P. A., and G. Y. Iwamasa, eds. 2014. *Culturally Responsive Cognitive-Behavioral Therapy: Assessment, Practice, and Supervision* [electronic resource]. Washington, DC: American Psychological Association.

Henderson, J. N., M. Gutierrez-Mayka, J. Garcia, and S. Boyd. 1993. "A Model for Alzheimer's Disease Support Group Development in African-American and Hispanic Populations." *The Gerontologist* 33:409–14.

Herman, T., and M. Willson. 2014. "Learning CBR through Community Organizing: Reflections on Struggles for Essential Health Services for People Who Use Drugs," in *Learning and Teaching Community-Based Research: Linking Pedagogy to Practice*. Edited by C. Etmanski, B. L. Hall, and T. Dawson. Toronto: University of Toronto Press.

Hess, A., Jr. 1999. "Reporting, Dissemination and Utilization," in *Disseminating and Utilizing Ethnographic Data* (1st ed.). Edited by J. J. Schensul and M. D. LeCompte. Walnut Creek, CA: AltaMira.

Himmelgreen, D. A., and M. Singer. 1998. "HIV, AIDS, and Other Health Risks: Findings from a Multisite Study—An Introduction." *American Journal of Drug & Alcohol Abuse* 24:187–97.

Hirsch, G., J. Homer, B. Milstein, L. Scherrer, C. Ingersonll, L. Landy, J. D. Sterman, and E. Fisher. 2012. "Understanding and Influencing Local Health System Change." 30th International Conference of the System Dynamics Society, St. Gallen, Switzerland, 2012.

Holland, D.C., and N. Quinn. 1987. *Cultural Models in Language and Thought*. New York: Cambridge University Press.

———. 1998. *Identity and Agency in Cultural Worlds*. Cambridge, MA: Harvard University Press.

Holmes, D. 2014. "David Napier: Cultivating the Role of Culture in Health." *Lancet* 384: 1568–68.

Hovmand, P. S. 2014. *Community Based System Dynamics*. New York: Springer Science-Business Media.

Hovmand, P. S., D. F. Andersen, E. Rouwette, G. P. Richardson, K. Rux, and A. Calhoun. 2012. "Group Model-Building 'Scripts' as a Collaborative Planning Tool." *Systems Research and Behavioral Science* 29:179–93.

Hovmand, P. S., L. Brennan, and N. Chalise. 2011. "Whose Model Is It Anyway?" 29th International Conference of the System Dynamics Society, 2011.

Hyland, S. 1979. "Multi Urban Power Structures: The Impact of Neighborhood Associates in Memphis." *Tennessee Anthropologist* [Miscellaneous Paper] 4:18–28.

———. 2008. "Commentary: Reflections on the Culture of the Lower Mississippi Delta: Challenges and Opportunities." *Journal of Health & Human Services Administration* 31:156–67.

Hyland, S., and L. Bennett. 2013. "Responding to Community Needs through Linking Academic and Practicing Anthropology: An Engaged Scholarly Framework." *Annals of Anthropological Practice* 37:34–56.

Hyland, S., and R. E. Brimhall. 2005. "Evaluation Anthropology in Community Development/ Community Building." *NAPA Bulletin* 24:125–37.

Hyland, S., and K. Maurette. 2010. "Developing Poverty Reform Efforts in the Memphis Region: Lessons for an Engaged Anthropology." *Urban Anthropology and Studies of Cultural Systems and World Economic Development* 39:213–64.

Hyland, S., and M. Owens. 2005. "Revitalizing Urban Communities through a New Approach to Computer Mapping," in *Community Building in the 21st Century*. Edited by S. E. Hyland and L. Bennett, pp. 101–33. Santa Fe, NM: SAR.

Hyland, S., and M. Timberlake. 1993. "The Mississippi Delta: Change or Continued Trouble," in *Forgotten Places: Uneven Development in Rural America*. Edited by T. Lyson and W. Falk, pp. 76–101. Lawrence, KS: University Press of Kansas.

Hynie, M., J. E. Lydon, S. Cote, and S. Wiener. 1998. "Relational Sexual Scripts and Women's Condom Use: The Importance of Internalized Norms." *Journal of Sex Research* 35:370–80.

Iris, M. 2004. "Fulfilling Community Needs through Research and Service: The Northwestern University Ethnographic Field School Experience." *NAPA Bulletin* 22:55–71.

Isom, D. A. 2003. "'Me, I got a lot of parts'; Tainted by, Struggling Against, Striving for: Racialized Gender Identity Constructs in African American Children," Doctoral Dissertation, pp. 174. Chicago: Loyola University.

Israel, B., E. Eng, A. J. Schultz, and E. A. Parker, eds. 2012. *Methods for Community-Based Participatory Research for Health* (2nd ed.). San Francisco: Jossey-Bass.

Israel, B., J. Krieger, D. Vlahov, S. Ciske, M. Foley, P. Fortin, J. R. Guzman, R. Lichtenstein, R. McGranaghan, and A. Palermo. 2006. "Challenges and Facilitating Factors in Sustaining Community-Based Participatory Research Partnerships: Lessons Learned from the Detroit, New York City and Seattle Urban Research Centers." *Journal of Urban Health* 83:1022–40.

Israel, B., R. Lichtenstein, P. Lantz, R. McGranaghan, A. Allen, J. R. Guzman, D. Softley, and B. Maciak. 2001. "The Detroit Community-Academic Urban Research Center: Development, Implementation, and Evaluation." *Journal of Public Health Management & Practice* 7:1.

Israel, B., A. J. Schulz, L. Estrada-Martinez, S. N. Zenk, E. Viruell-Fuentes, A. M. Villarruel, and C. Stokes. 2006. "Engaging Urban Residents in Assessing Neighborhood Environments and Their Implications for Health." *Journal of Urban Health* 83:523–39.

Israel, B., J. Schulz, E. A. Parker, and A. B. Becker. 1998. "Review of Community-Based Research: Assessing Partnership Approaches to Improve Public Health." *Annual Review of Public Health* 19:173.

Izumi, B. T., A. J. Schulz, B. A. Israel, A. G. Reyes, J. Martin, R. L. Lichtenstein, C. Wilson, and S. L. Sand. 2010. "The One-Pager: A Practical Policy Advocacy Tool for Translating Community-Based Participatory Research Into Action." *Progress in Community Health Partnerships: Research, Education, and Action* 4:141–47.

Jacobs, E. 1987. "Traditions of Qualitative Research: A Review." *Review of Educational Research* 57:1–50.

Jørgensen, T., et al. 2013. "Population-Level Changes to Promote Cardiovascular Health." *European Journal of Preventive Cardiology* 20:409–21.

Judd, C., and D. Kenny. 1981. *Estimating the Effects of Social Interventions*. Cambridge, MA: Cambridge University Press.

Junker, A. 2012. "Optimism and Caution Regarding New Tools for Analyzing Qualitative Data." *Sociological Methodology* 42:85–87.

Kaufman, C. E., A. Litchfield, E. Schupman, and C. M. Mitchell. 2012. "Circle of Life HIV/AIDS-Prevention Intervention for American Indian and Alaska Native Youth." *American Indian and Alaska Native Mental Health Research (Online)* 19:140–53.

Kazantzis, N., M. A. Reinecke, and A. Freeman. 2010. *Cognitive and Behavioral Theories in Clinical Practice*. Guilford, CT: Guilford Press.

Keene, A. S., and S. Colligan. 2004. "Service-Learning and Anthropology." *Michigan Journal of Community Service Learning* 10:5–15.

Kegeles, S. M., R. B. Hays, and T. J. Coates. 1996. "The Empowerment Project: A Community-Level HIV Prevention Intervention for Young Gay Men." *American Journal of Public Health* 86:1129–36.

Keim-Malpass, J., R. H. Steeves, and C. Kennedy. 2014. "Internet Ethnography: A Review of Methodological Considerations for Studying Online Illness Blogs." *International Journal of Nursing Studies* 51:1686–92.

Kelly, J. A., J. S. St. Lawrence, T. L. Brasfield, L. Y. Stevenson, Y. E. Diaz, and A. C. Hauth. 1990. "AIDS Risk Behavior Patterns among Gay Men in Small Southern Cities." *American Journal of Public Health* 80:416–18.

Kemmis, S., and R. McTaggart. 2005. "Participatory Action Research: Communicative Action and the Public Sphere," in *The SAGE Handbook of Qualitative Research*. Edited by N. K. Denzin and Y. S. Lincoln. London: Sage.

Kemmis, S., R. McTaggart, and R. Nixon. 2014. *The Action Research Planner: Doing Critical Participatory Action Research*. New York: Springer.

Kilgore, S. 2010. "Modern Red School House," in *Encyclopedia of Educational Reform and Dissent*. Edited by T. C. Hunt, J. C. Carper, J. L. I. Thomas, and D. C. Raisch, pp. 567–70. Thousand Oaks, CA: Sage.

Kleinman, A. 1980. *Patients and Healers in the Context of Culture: An Exploration of the Borderland between Anthropology, Medicine, and Psychiatry*. Berkeley: University of California Press.

Knowlden, A. P., M. J. Ickes, and M. Sharma. 2013. "Systematic Analysis of Tobacco Treatment Interventions Implemented in Worksite Settings." *Journal of Substance Use* 19(4):283–94. DOI: 10.3109/14659891.2013.799240.

Knowles, M. 1980. *The Modern Practice of Adult Education. From Pedagogy to Andragogy* (2nd ed.). Englewood Cliffs, NJ: Prentice Hall/Cambridge.

Kostick, K. M., S. L. Schensul, K. Jadhav, R. Singh, A. Bavadekar, and N. Saggurti. 2010. "Treatment Seeking, Vaginal Discharge and Psychosocial Distress Among Women in Urban Mumbai." *Culture, Medicine, and Psychiatry* 34:529–47.

Kostick, K. M., S. L. Schensul, R. Singh, P. Pelto, and N. Saggurti. 2011. "A Methodology for Building Culture and Gender Norms into Intervention: An Example from Mumbai, India." *Social Science & Medicine* 72:1630–38.

Kotler, P. 1989. *Social Marketing: Strategies for Changing Public Behavior*. Edited by E. L. Roberto. New York: Free Press.

Kozulin, A. 1990. *Vygotsky's Psychology: A Biography of Ideas*. Cambridge, MA: Harvard University Press.

Kretzman, J., and J. L. McKnight. 1993. *Building Communities from the Inside Out: A Path Toward Finding and Mobilizing a Community's Assets*. Evanston, IL: Institute for Policy Research.

Krueger, P. 2010. "It's Not Just a Method! The Epistemic and Political Work of Young People's Lifeworlds at the School-Prison Nexus." *Race, Ethnicity & Education* 13:383–408.

LaFrance, J., and R. Nichols. 2009. *Indigenous Evaluation Framework: Telling Our Story in Our Place and Time*. Alexandria, VA: American Indian Higher Education Consortium.

Latane, B. 1996. "Dynamic Social Impact: The Creation of Culture by Communication." *Journal of Communication* 46:13–25.

Lather, P. 1986. "Research as Praxis." *Harvard Educational Review* 56:257–77.

Latuszynska, M., and J. Lemke. 2013. "Validation of System Dynamics Models: A Case Study." *Journal of Entrepreneurship, Management and Innovation* 2:45–59.

Lave, J. 1985. "Introduction: Situationally Specific Practice." *Anthropology & Education Quarterly* 16:171–76.

Lave, J., and E. Wenger. 1991. *Situated Learning: Legitimate Peripheral Participation*. Cambridge, UK: Cambridge University Press.

Lavine, H., and B. Latane. 1996. "A Cognitive Social Theory of Public Opinion: Dynamic Social Impact and Cognitive Structure." *Journal of Communication* 46:48–56.

Layde, P. M., A. L. Christiansen, D. J. Peterson, C. E. Guse, C. A. Maurana, and T. Brandenburg. 2012. "A Model to Translate Evidence-Based Interventions Into Community Practice." *American Journal of Public Health* 102:617–24.

Lea, T. 2008. "Housing for Health in Indigenous Australia: Driving Change When Research and Policy Are Part of the Problem." *Human Organization* 67:77.

LeCompte, M. D., and J. P. Goetz. 1981. "Problems of Reliability and Validity in Ethnographic Research." *Review of Educational Research* 52:31–60.

LeCompte, M. D., P. Judith, and R. Tesch. 1993. *Ethnography and Qualitative Design in Educational Research* (2nd ed.). San Diego, CA: Academic Press.

LeCompte, M. D., and J. Schensul. 2010. *Designing and Conducting Ethnographic Research* (2nd ed.). Lanham, MD: AltaMira.

Ledwith, M. 2007. "On Being Critical: Uniting Theory and Practice through Emancipatory Action Research." *Educational Action Research* 15:597–611.

Lee, R. 2000. *Unobtrusive Measures in Social Research. Understanding Social Research.* Buckingham, PA: Open University Press.

Lehmann, W. 2004. "'For Some Reason, I Get a Little Scared': Structure, Agency, and Risk in School-Work Transitions." *Journal of Youth Studies* 7:379–96.

Leischow, S. J., and B. Milstein. 2006. "Systems Thinking and Modeling for Public Health Practice." *American Journal of Public Health* 96:403.

Lewin, K. 1946. "Action Research and Minority Problems." *Journal of Social Issues* 2:34–46.

Lewis, O. 1951. *Life in a Mexican Village: Tepoztlan Restudied.* Champagne-Urbana: University of Illinois Press.

Lewis, T. L. 2004. "Service Learning for Social Change? Lessons from a Liberal Arts College." *Teaching Sociology* 32:94–108.

Lin Chih, A. 1998. "Bridging Positivist and Interpretivist Approaches to Qualitative Methods." *Policy Studies Journal* 26:162–80.

Lipschutz, R. D. 2004. "Sweating It Out: NGO Campaigns and Trade Union Empowerment." *Development in Practice* 14:197–209.

Liu, S. 2014. "Crisis Crowdsourcing Framework: Designing Strategic Configurations of Crowdsourcing for the Emergency Management Domain." *Computer Supported Cooperative Work: The Journal of Collaborative Computing* 23:389–443.

Lopez, I., R. Ramirez, P. Guarnaccia, G. Canino, and H. Bird. 2011. "Ataques de Nervios and Somatic Complaints Among Island and Mainland Puerto Rican Children." *CNS Neuroscience & Therapeutics* 17:158–66.

Low, S., and S. Engle Merry. 2010. "Engaged Anthropology: Diversity and Dilemmas: An Introduction to Supplement 2." *Current Anthropology* 51:S203–26.

Ludwig, S. 2012. "Supporting Respect: Community Partnership in Alamosa, Colorado." *Practicing Anthropology* 34:1.

Luke, D., and A. Stamatakis. 2012. "Systems Science Methods in Public Health: Dynamics, Networks, and Agents." *Annual Review of Public Health* 33:1–25.

Luna-Reyes, L. F., and D. L. Andersen. 2003. "Collecting and Analyzing Qualitative Data for System Dynamics, Methods and Models." *System Dynamics Review* 19:271–96.

Mackie, P. F.-E. 2009. "Grassroots Community Practice: Applying Alinsky's Rules in the 21st Century." *Reflections: Narratives of Professional Helping* 15:47–59.

MacQueen, K. M., E. McLellan, D. S. Metzger, S. Kegeles, R. P. Strauss, and R. Scotti. 2001. "What Is Community? An Evidence Based Definition for Participatory Public Health." *American Journal of Public Health* 91:1929–38.

Maglajlic, R. A., and Jennifer Tiffany. 2013. "Participatory Action Research with Youth in Bosnia and Herzegovina." *Journal of Community Practice* 14:163–81.

Maguire, P. 2006. "Uneven Ground: Feminisms and Action Research," in *Handbook of Action Research*. Edited by P. Reason and H. Bradbury, pp. 60–71. Thousand Oaks, CA: Sage.

Martínez-Hernáez, A. 2010. "Dialogics, Ethnography and Health Education." *Revista de saude publica* 44:399–405.

Marullo, S., and B. Edwards. 2000. "From Charity to Justice: The Potential of University-Community Collaboration for Social Change." *American Behaviorial Scientist* 4:895–912.

Mayock, P. 2005. "'Scripting' Risk: Young People and the Construction of Drug Journeys." *Drugs: Education, Prevention and Policy* 12:349–68.

McCalman, J., et al. 2009. "'Bringing Back Respect': The Role of Participatory Action Research in Transferring Knowledge from an Aboriginal Men's Group to Youth Programs." *Australian Psychiatry* 17:59–63.

McCormick, S. 2007. "Democratizing Science Movements: A New Framework for Mobilization and Contestation." *Social Studies of Science* 37:609–23.

McFall, R. M., T. A. Treat, and R. J. Viken. 1997. "Contributions of Cognitive Theory to New Behavioral Treatments." *Psychological Science* 8:174–76.

McFate, M., and A. Jackson. 2005. "An Organizational Solution to DOD's Cultural Knowledge Needs." *Military Review,* 85:18–21.

McGraw, S. A., K. W. Smith, J. J. Schensul, and J. E. Carrillo. 1991. "Sociocultural Factors Associated with Smoking Behavior by Puerto Rican Adolescents in Boston." *Social Science & Medicine* 33:1355–64.

McGuire, W. 1961. "Resistance to Persuasion Conferred by Active and Passive Prior Refutation of the Same and Alternative Counterarguments." *Journal of Abnormal and Social Psychology* 63: 326–32.

McGuire, W. J. 1969. "The Nature of Attitudes and Attitude Change," in *The Handbook of Social Psychology* (2nd ed.). Edited by G. Lindsey and E. Aronson. Vol. 3, pp. 136–14. Reading, MA: Addison-Wesley.

McHugh, T.-L. F., and K. C. Kowalski. 2011. "'A New View of Body Image': A School-Based Participatory Action Research Project with Young Aboriginal Women." *Action Research* 9:220–41.

McIntyre, A. 2000. "Constructing Meaning about Violence, School, and Community: Participatory Action Research with Urban Youth." *The Urban Review* 32:123–54.

McKay, M. M., K. T. Chasse, R. Paikoff, L. D. McKinney, D. Baptiste, D. Coleman, S. Madison, and C. C. Bell. 2004. "Family-Level Impact of the CHAMP Family Program: A Community Collaborative Effort to Support Urban Families and Reduce Youth HIV Risk Exposure." *Family Process* 43:79–93.

Mclure, R., and M. Sotelo. 2004. "Youth Gangs in Nicaragua: Gang Membership as Structured Individualization." *Journal of Youth Studies* 7:417–32.

McNeilly, R. 1994. "Solution-Oriented Counselling. A 20-Minute Format for Medical Practice." *Australian Family Physician* 23:228–30.

Mead, M. 1928. *Coming of Age in Samoa.* New York: William Morrow and Company.

Merrifield, J. 1997. "Knowing, Learning, Doing: Participatory Action Research." *Focus on Basics: Connecting Research and Practice* 1. http://www.ncsall.net/index.html@id=479.html.

Metcalf, S. S., M. E. Northridge, and I. B. Lamster. 2011. "A Systems Perspective for Dental Health in Older Adults." *American Journal of Public Health* 101:1820–23.

Miles, M. B., and A. M. Huberman. 1994. *Qualitative Data Analysis* (2nd ed.). Newbury Park, CA: Sage.

Miller, M. L., J. Kaneko, P. Bartram, J. Marks, and D. D. Brewer. 2004. "Cultural Consensus Analysis and Environmental Anthropology: Yellowfin Tuna Fishery Management in Hawaii." *Cross-Cultural Research* 38:289–314.

Milstein, B., J. Homer, and G. Hirsch. 2010. "Analyzing National Health Reform Strategies with a Dynamic Simulation Model." *American Journal of Public Health* 100:811.

Minkler, M., and N. Wallerstein. 2010. *Community-Based Participatory Research for Health: From Process to Outcomes*. San Francisco: Jossey-Bass.

Minkler, M., N. Wallerstein, and N. Wilson. 1997. "Improving Health through Community Organization and Community Building." *Health Behavior and Health Education: Theory, Research, and Practice* 3:279–311.

Mohatt, N. V. 2014. "Forward to Ecological Description of a Multi-Level Community-Based Cultural Intervention: Reflections on Culturally-Situated Participatory Research." *American Journal of Community Psychology* 54:81–82.

Morgan, D., C. Pacheco, C. Rodriguez, E. Vazquez, M. Berg, and J. Schensul. 2004. "Youth Participatory Action Research on Hustling and Its Consequences: A Report from the Field." *Children, Youth and Environments* 14:202–28.

Morsillo, J., and I. Prilleltensky. 2007. "Social Action with Youth: Interventions, Evaluation and Psychopolitical Validity." *Journal of Community Psychology* 35:725–40.

Mosher, H. I. 2010. "Participatory Action Research with Dignity Village: An Action Tool for Empowerment within a Homeless Community." ProQuest, UMI Dissertations Publishing.

Mosher, H. I., and J. Schensul, J. 2014. *The Institute for Community Research's Youth Participatory Action Research Curriculum Adapted for Oregon*. Portland: Oregon Health Authority, State of Oregon.

Mugavero, M. J., K. R. Amico, T. Horn, and M. A. Thompson. 2013. "The State of Engagement in HIV Care in the United States: From Cascade to Continuum to Control." *Clinical Infectious Diseases* 57:1164–71.

Murphy, T. 2013. "Where Are They Now? ACT UP AIDS Activists 25 Years Later." *New York*, June 25.

Murukutla, N., T. Turk, C. V. S. Prasad, R. Saradhi, J. Kaur, S. Gupta, S. Mullin, F. Ram, P. C. Gupta, and M. Wakefield. 2012. "Results of a National Mass Media Campaign in India to Warn against the Dangers of Smokeless Tobacco Consumption." *Tobacco Control* 21:12–17.

Nagler, E. M., et al. 2013. "Designing in the Social Context: Using the Social Contextual Model of Health Behavior Change to Develop a Tobacco Control Intervention for Teachers in India." *Health Education Research* 28:113–29.

Nassaney, M. S. 2004. "Implementing Community Service Learning through Archaeological Practice." *Michigan Journal of Community Service Learning* 10:88–99.

Nastasi, B. K., and M. Berg. 1999. "Using Ethnography to Strengthen and Evaluate Intervention Programs," in *Using Ethnographic Data: Interventions, Public Programming, and Public Policy*. Edited by J. J. Schensul, M. D. LeCompte, A. Hess, Jr., B. K. Nastasi, M. Berg, and L. Williamson, pp. 1–56. Walnut Creek, CA: AltaMira.

Nastasi, B. K., and D. M. DeZolt. 1994. *School Interventions for Children of Alcoholics*. New York: Guilford Press.

Nastasi, B. K., and J. Hitchcock. 2009. "Challenges of Evaluating Multilevel Interventions." *American Journal of Community Psychology* 43:360–76.

Nastasi, B. K., K. Pluymert, K. Varjas, and R. Bernstein. 2002. *Exemplary Mental Health Programs: School Psychologists as Mental Health Service Providers* (3rd ed.). Bethesda, MD: National Association of School Psychologists.

Nastasi, B. K., J. Schensul, S. L. Schensul, A. Mekki-Berrada, P. J. Pelto, S. Maitra, R. Verma, and N. Saggurti. 2014. "A Model for Translating Ethnography and Theory into Culturally Constructed Clinical Practices." *Culture, Medicine, and Psychiatry* 29(1):1–29.

Nastasi, B. K., J. J. Schensul, C. T. Balkcom, and F. Cintrón-Moscoso. 2004. "Integrating Research and Practice to Facilitate Implementation across Multiple Contexts: Illustration from an Urban Middle School Drug and Sexual Risk Prevention Program," in *Advances in School-Based Mental Health: Best Practices and Program Models.* Edited by K. E. Robinson, pp. 13–22. Kingston: NJ: Civic Research Institute.

Nastasi, B. K., J. J. Schensul, M. W. A. De Silva, K. Varjas, K. T. Silva, P. Ratnayake, and S. L. Schensul. 1998. "Community-Based Sexual Risk Prevention Program for SRI Lankan Youth: Influencing Sexual-Risk Decision Making." *International Quarterly of Community Health Education* 18:139–55.

Nastasi, B. K., and S. L. Schensul. 2005. "Contributions of Qualitative Research to the Validity of Intervention Research." *Journal of School Psychology* 43:177–95.

Needle, R. H., R. T. Trotter, II, M. Singer, C. Bates, J. B. Page, D. Metzger, and L. H. Marcelin. 2003. "Rapid Assessment of the HIV/AIDS Crisis in Racial and Ethnic Minority Communities: An Approach for Timely Community Interventions." *American Journal of Public Health* 93:970–79.

Nichter, M. 1981. "Idioms of Distress: Alternatives in the Expression of Psychosocial Distress: A Case Study from South India." *Culture, Medicine and Psychiatry* 5:379–408.

NIH. August 18, 2011. "NIH Commissioned Study Identifies Gaps in NIH Funding Success Rates for Black Researchers." *NIH News: National Institutes of Health, Office of the Director.*

Nkoane, M. M. 2010. "Listening to Voices of the Voiceless: A Critical Consciousness for Academic Industrial Complex." *South African Journal of Higher Education* 24:317.

Nyden, P. W. 2010. "Social Problems or Social Solution? The Role of Public Sociology in Addressing Contemporary Crises." *Michigan Sociological Review* 24:5–18.

———, ed. 2012. *Public Sociology: Research, Action and Change.* Thousand Oaks, CA: Pineforge Press, Sage.

Nygreen, K. 2009–2010. "Critical Dilemmas in PAR: Toward a New Theory of Engaged Research for Social Change." *Social Justice* 36:14–35.

O'Fallon, L. R., F. L. Tyson, and A. Dearry. 2000. *Successful Models of Community-Based Participatory Researrch.* Washington, DC: NIEHS.

Osborn, C. Y., K. Rivet Amico, W. A. Fisher, L. E. Egede, and J. D. Fisher. 2010. "An Information-Motivation-Behavioral Skills Analysis of Diet and Exercise Behavior in Puerto Ricans with Diabetes." *Journal of Health Psychology* 15:1201–13.

Ozer, E., M. Ritterman, and M. Wanis. 2010. "Participatory Action Research (PAR) in Middle School: Opportunities, Constraints, and Key Processes." *American Journal of Community Psychology* 46:152–66.

Parker, E., S. Batterman, T. Robins, C. Godwin, S. Grant, L. Du, Z. Rowe, T. Lewis, and A. O'Toole. 2011. "Factors Affecting Air Filter Usage In Homes Of Children With Asthma In Detroit, Mi." *American Journal of Respiratory and Critical Care Medicine* 183:A3905.

Parker, E. A., B. A. Israel, M. Williams, W. Brakefield-Caldwell, T. C. Lewis, T. Robins, E. Ramirez, Z. Rowe, and G. Keeler. 2003. "Community Action against Asthma." *Journal of General Internal Medicine* 18:558–67.

Parker, E., T. Robins, S. Batterman, B. Mukherjee, G. Mentz, X. Ren, C. Godwin, A. O'Toole, S. Grant, and T. Lewis. 2011. "Suitability of Homes of Asthmatic Children in Detroit for Installation of Window Unit Air Conditioners." *American Journal of Respiratory and Critical Care Medicine* 183:A3909.

Patton, M. Q. 2005. "The View from Evaluation." *NAPA Bulletin* 24:31–40.

———. 2010. *Developmental Evaluation Applying Complexity Concepts to Enhance Innovation and Use.* Guilford, CT: Guilford Books.

Peak, B. J. 2015. "Militarization of School Police: One Route on the School-to-Prison Pipeline." *Arkansas Law Review (1968–present)* 68:195–229.

Peattie, L. R. 1968. *Reflections on Advocacy Planning*: http://www.worldcat.org/title/reflec tions-on-advocacy-planning/oclc/40178448?referer=di&ht=edition.

Pedrana, A. E., M. E. Hellard, P. Higgs, J. Asselin, C. Batrouney, and M. Stoovè. 2014. "No Drama: Key Elements to the Success of an HIV/STI-Prevention Mass-Media Campaign." *Qualitative Health Research* 24:695–705.

Pelto, P. J., and G. H. Pelto. 1978. *Anthropological Research: The Structure of Inquiry* (2nd ed.). Cambridge, UK: Cambridge University Press.

Pelto, P. J., and R. Singh. 2010. "Community Street Theatre as a Tool for Interventions on Alcohol Use and Other Behaviors Related to HIV Risks." *AIDS and Behavior* 14:147–57.

Pemberton, G. C. 2012. "How are Implementation and Adaptation of Evidence-Based Interventions Applied in Community Practice Settings? Lessons from the Modelo de Intervencion Psicomedica." PhD dissertation, University of North Carolina, Chapel Hill.

Penuel, W. R., and B. J. Fishman. 2012. "Large-Scale Science Education Intervention Research We Can Use." *Journal of Research in Science Teaching* 49:281–304.

Pérez-Escamilla, R., G. Damio, J. Chhabra, M. L. Fernandez, S. Segura-Pérez, S. Vega-López, G. Kollannor-Samuel, M. Calle, F. M. Shebl, and D. D'Agostino. 2015. "Impact of a Community Health Workers-Led Structured Program on Blood Glucose Control Among Latinos With Type 2 Diabetes: The DIALBEST Trial." *Diabetes Care* 38:197–205.

Pérez-Escamilla, R., J. Garcia, and D. Song. 2010. "Health Care Access among Hispanic Immigrants. ¿Alguien esta escuchando? Is Anybody Listening?" *NAPA Bulletin* 34:47–67.

Perkins, D. D., and M. A. Zimmerman. 1995. "Empowerment Theory, Research, and Application." *American Journal of Community Psychology* 23:569–79.

Pfeffer, J., and K. M. Carley. 2013. "The Importance of Local Clusters for the Diffusion of Opinions and Beliefs in Interpersonal Communication Networks." *International Journal of Innovation and Technology Management* 10:1–17.

Phillips, E. N., M. J. Berg, C. Rodriguez, and D. Morgan. 2010. "A Case Study of Participatory Action Research in a Public New England Middle School: Empowerment, Constraints and Challenges." *American Journal of Community Psychology* 46:179–94.

Pimple, S., M. Pednekar, P. Majmudar, N. Ingole, S. Goswami, and S. Shastri. 2012. "An Integrated Approach to Worksite Tobacco Use Prevention and Oral Cancer Screening among Factory Workers in Mumbai, India." *Asian Pacific Journal of Cancer Prevention* 13:527–32.

Polin, D. K., and A. S. Keene. 2010. "Bringing an Ethnographic Sensibility to Service-Learning Assessment." *Michigan Journal of Community Service Learning* 16(2):22–37.

Porter, T. R. 2015. "The School-to-Prison Pipeline: The Business Side of Incarcerating, Not Educating, Students in Public Schools." *Arkansas Law Review* 68: 55–81.

Prochaska, J. M., J. O. Prochaska, and D. A. Levesque. 2001. "A Transtheoretical Approach to Changing Organizations." *Administration and Policy in Mental Health* 28:247.

Proctor, E. K., B. J. Power, and C. M. McMillen. 2013. "Implementation Strategies: Recommendations for Specifying and Reporting." *Implementation Science* 139.

Quinn, N. 2005. "How to Reconstruct Schemas People Share, from What They Say," in *Finding Culture in Talk: A Collection of Methods.* Edited by N. Quinn. New York: Palgrave Macmillan.

Quintana, S. M., and T. A. Segura-Herrera. 2003. "Developmental Transformations of Self and Identity in the Context of Oppression." *Self and Identity* 2:269–85.

Raby, R. 2005. "What Is Resistance?" *Journal of Youth Studies* 8:151–71.

Radda, K. E., and J. J. Schensul. 2011. "Building Living Alliances: Community Engagement and Community-Based Partnerships to Address the Health of Community Elders." *Annals of Anthropological Practice* 35:154–73.

Rael, R. 2009. "Social Justice Radio: A Strategy for Long-Term Change," in *Youth Media Reporter*, pp. 167–70. Open Society Initiative, Open Society Foundations.

Rapkin, B., and E. Trickett. 2005. "Comprehensive Dynamic Trial Designs for Behavioral Prevention Research with Communities: Overcoming Inadequacies of the Randomized Controlled Trial Paradigm." *Community Interventions and AIDS*: 249–77.

Rasmus, S. M. 2014. "Indigenizing CBPR: Evaluation of a Community-Based and Participatory Research Process Implementation of the Elluam Tungiinun (Towards Wellness) Program in Alaska." *American Journal of Community Psychology* 54:170–79.

Rasmus, S. M., B. Charles, and G. V. Mohatt. 2014. "Creating Qungasvik (A Yup'ik Intervention "Toolbox"): Case Examples from a Community-Developed and Culturally-Driven Intervention." *American Journal of Community Psychology* 54:140–52.

Reason, P., and H. Bradbury, eds. 2006. *Handbook of Action Research: Concise Paperback Edition.* London: Sage.

———, eds. 2008. *Sage Handbook of Action Research: Participative Inquiry and Practice* (2nd ed.). London: Sage.

Redfield, R. 1930. *Tepoztlan, a Mexican Village: A Study of Folk Life.* Chicago: University of Chicago Press.

Register, R., and S. Hyland. 1978. "Black Social Institutions for a Just American Society: A Dialogue between Demitri Shimkin and Nkosi Ajanaku." *Anthropological Research Center Occasional Papers* 8:74.

Richardson, G. P. 2013. "Concept Models in Group Model Building." *System Dynamics Review* 29:42–55.

Rigg, K. K., H. H. Cook, and J. W. Murphy. 2014. "Expanding the Scope and Relevance of Health Interventions: Moving beyond Clinical Trials and Behavior Change Models." *International Journal of Qualitative Studies on Health and Well-Being* 9(1).

Ritterbusch, A. 2012. "Bridging Guidelines and Practice: Toward a Grounded Care Ethics in Youth Participatory Action Research." *Professional Geographer* 64:16–24.

Robins, T., S. Batterman, E. Parker, W. Brakefield-Caldwell, S. Grant, A. Weigl, R. de Majo, and G. Lewis. 2010. "Recruitment Design for a Study of Health Effects of Diesel Exhaust among Children with Asthma: A Blend of Geographic Information Systems and Community-Based Participatory Research Methods." *America* 4:5.

Robison, J., J. J. Schensul, E. Coman, G. J. Diefenbach, K. E. Radda, S. Gaztambide, and W. B. Disch. 2009. "Mental Health in Senior Housing: Racial/Ethnic Patterns and Correlates of Major Depressive Disorder." *Aging & Mental Health* 13:659–73.

Rodríguez, L. F., and T. M. Brown. 2009. "From Voice to Agency: Guiding Principles for Participatory Action Research with Youth." *New Directions for Youth Development* 2009:19–34.

Rogers, E. M. 2003. "Diffusion of Innovations" (5th ed.). New York: Free Press.

Rogoff, B. 2003. "The Cultural Nature of Human Development." New York: Oxford University Press.

Roland, M., and D. J. Torgerson. 1998. "Understanding Controlled Trials: What Are Pragmatic Trials?" *BMJ* 316:285.

Romani, M. E. T., V. Vanlerberghe, D. Perez, P. Lefevre, E. Ceballos, and D. Bandera. 2007. "Achieving Sustainability of Community-Based Dengue Control in Santiago de Cuba." *Social Science and Medicine* 64:976–88.

Romero-Daza, N., M. Weeks, and M. Singer. 2003. "'Nobody Gives a Damn if I Live or Die': Violence, Drugs, and Street-Level Prostitution in Inner-City Hartford, Connecticut." *Medical Anthropology* 22:233–59.

Romney, A. K., W. H. Batchelder, and S. C. Weller. 1987. "Recent Applications of Consensus Theory." *American Behavioral Science* 31:163–77.

Romney, A. K., J. P. Boyd, C. C. Moore, W. H. Batchelder, and T. J. Brazill. 1996. "Culture as Shared Cognitive Representations." *Proceedings of the National Academy of Sciences of the United States* 93(10):4699–4705.

Romney, A. K., S. C. Weller, and W. H. Batchelder. 1986. "Culture as Consensus: A Theory of Cultural and Informant Accuracy." *American Anthropologist* 88:313–38.

Roth, W. D., and J. D. Mehta. 2002. "The Rashomon Effect: Combining Positivist and Interpretivist Approaches in the Analysis of Contested Events." *Sociological Methods & Research* 31:131–73.

Rouwette, E. J., A. Vennix, and T. V. Mullekom. 2002. "Group Model Building Effectiveness: A Review of Assessment Studies." *System Dynamics Review* 18:5–45.

Rubak, S., A. Sandbæk, T. Lauritzen, and B. Christensen. 2005. "Motivational Interviewing: A Systematic Review and Meta-Analysis." *The British Journal of General Practice* 55:305.

Rubin, B. C., and M. Jones. 2007. "Student Action Research: Reaping the Benefits for Students and School Leaders." *NASSP Bulletin* 91:363–78.

Rylko-Bauer, B., M. Singer, and J. van Willigen. 2006. "Reclaiming Applied Anthropology: Its Past, Present and Future." *American Anthropologist* 108:178–90.

Sabo, K. 2004. "Youth Participatory Evaluation: A Field in the Making." *Children, Youth and Environments* 14:1–4.

Saggurti, N., S. L. Schensul, B. K. Nastasi, R. Singh, J. A. Burleson, and R. K. Verma. 2013. "Effects of a Health Care Provider Intervention in Reduction of Sexual Risk and Related Outcomes in Economically Marginal Communities in Mumbai, India." *Sexual Health* 10:502–11.

Salovey, P., and J. D. Mayer. 1989. "Emotional Intelligence." *Imagination, Cognition and Personality* 9:185–211.

Sánchez, P. 2009. "Chicana Feminist Strategies in a Participatory Action Research Project with Transnational Latina Youth." *New Directions for Youth Development* 2009:83–97.

Sanjek, R. 2004. "Going Public: Responsibilities and Strategies in the Aftermath of Ethnography." *Human Organization* 63:444–56.

Schank, R. C., and R. P. Abelson. 1977. *Scripts, Plans, Goals, and Understanding: An Inquiry into Human Knowledge Structures.* Hillsdale, NJ: Lawrence Erlbaum Associates.

Scheirer, M. A. 2005. "Is Sustainability Possible? A Review and Commentary on Empirical Studies of Program Sustainability." *American Journal of Evaluation* 26:320–47.

Schensul, J. 1985. "Systems Consistency in Field Research, Dissemination, and Social Change." *American Behavioral Scientist* 29(2):186–204.

———. 1998. "Community-Based Risk Prevention with Urban Youth." *School Psychology Review* 27:233.

———. 1999. "Building Community Research Partnerships in the Struggle Against AIDS." *Health Education & Behavior* 26:266–83.

———. 2002. "Democratizing Science through Social Science Research Partnerships." *Bulletin of Science, Technology & Society* 22:190–202.

———. 2005. "Strengthening Communities through Research Partnerships for Social Change: Perspectives from the Institute for Community Research," in *Community Building in the Twenty-First Century* (1st ed.). School of American Research advanced seminar series. Edited by S. Hyland, pp. 191–218. Santa Fe, NM: School of American Research.

———. 2009. "Community, Culture and Sustainability in Multilevel Dynamic Systems Intervention Science." *American Journal of Community Psychology* 43:241–56.

———. 2010. "Engaged Universities, Community Based Research Organizations and Third Sector Science in a Global System." *Human Organization* 69:307–20.

———. 2012. "Building a Systems Dynamic Model of Smokeless Tobacco Use in Mumbai." *Practicing Anthropology* 35:24–28.

———. 2015. "Community-Based Organizations: Co-constructing knowledge and Bridging Knowledge/Action Communities through Participatory Action Research," in *Public Anthropology in a Borderless World*. Edited by S. Beck and C. Maida. New York: Berghahn Books.

Schensul, J., and M. Berg. 2004. "Youth Participatory Action Research: A Transformative Approach to Service-Learning." *Michigan Journal of Community Service Learning* 10(3):76–88.

Schensul, J., M. Berg, and S. Nair. 2012. "Using Ethnography in Participatory Community Assessment," in *Methods for Conducting Community-Based Participatory Research for Health*. Edited by B. Israel, E. Eng, E. Parker, and A. Schultz, pp. 161–88. New York: Jossey Bass.

Schensul, J., M. Berg, and K. Williamson. 2008. "Challenging Hegemonies: Advancing Collaboration in Community-Based Participatory Action Research." *Collaborative Anthropologies* 1:102–38.

Schensul, J., C. Coleman, S. Diamond, R. Pino, A. R. Bermudez, O. Velazco, R. Blake, and N. Bessette. 2012. "'Rollin' n Dustin': Using Installation and Film for Interactive Dissemination of Drug Study Results to Youth in Participant Communities," in *Popularizing Research: Engaging New Genres, Media, and Audiences*. Edited by P. Vannini, pp. 161–88. New York: Peter Lang.

Schensul, J., and C. Dalglish. 2015. "A Hard Way Out: Improvisational Video and Youth Participatory Action Research," in *Participatory Visual and Digital Research in Action*. Edited by A. C. Gubrium, Amy L. Hill, Sarah Flicker, K. Harper, and M. Otanez, pp. 115–28. Walnut Creek, CA: LeftCoast Press.

Schensul, J., D. Dennelli-Hess, M. Borrero, and M. P. Bhavati. 1987. "Urban Comadronas: Maternal and Child Health Research and Policy Forumulation in a Puerto Rican Community," in *Collaborative Research and Social Change: Applied Anthropology in Action*. Edited by D. D. Stull and J. J. Schensul, pp. 8–32. Boulder, CO: Westview Press.

Schensul, J., S. Diamond, W. Disch, R. Pino, and R. Bermudez. 2005. "The Diffusion of Ecstasy through Urban Youth Networks." *Journal of Ethnicity in Substance Abuse* 4:39–71.

Schensul, J., and E. M. Eddy, guest eds. 1985. "Applying Educational Anthropology." *Anthropology & Education Quarterly* 16.

Schensul, J., J. A. Levy, and W. B. Disch. 2003. "Individual, Contextual, and Social Network Factors Affecting Exposure to HIV/AIDS Risk Among Older Residents Living in Low-Income Senior Housing Complexes." *Journal of Acquired Immune Deficiency Syndromes* 33:S138.

Schensul, J., I. Nieves, and M. D. Martinez. 1982. "The Crisis Event in the Puerto Rican Community: Research and Intervention in the Community/Institution Interface." *Urban Anthropology* 11:101–28.

Schensul, J., K. Radda, E. Coman, and E. Vazquez. 2009. "Multi-Level Intervention to Prevent Influenza Infections in Older Low Income and Minority Adults." *American Journal of Community Psychology* 43:313–29.

Schensul, J., J. Robison, C, Y. Reyes, K. Radda, S. Gaztambide, and W. B. Disch. 2006. "Building Interdisciplinary/Intersectoral Research Partnerships for Community-Based Mental Health Research with Older Minority Adults." *American Journal of Community Psychology* 38:79–93.

Schensul, J. , and S. Schensul. 1992. "Collaborative research: Methods of inquiry for social change," in *The Handbook of Qualitative Research in Education*. Edited by M. D. LeCompte, W. L. Millroy, and J. Preissle, pp. 161–200. New York: Academic Press.

Schensul, J., M. Singer, G. Burke, M. Torres, and ACRG. 1989. *AIDS Knowledge Attitudes and Behaviors Survey in a Multi-Ethnic Neighborhood of Hartford: Volumes I and II*. Hartford, CT: Institute for Community Research.

Schensul, J., and G. Stern. 1985. "Collaborative Research and Social Policy." *American Behavioral Scientist* 29:133–38.

Schensul, J., S. Sydlo, M. Berg, D. Schensul, K. Wiley, S. Schensul, M. Brase, and D. Owens. 2004. *Participatory Action Research: A Curriculum for Empowering Youth*. Hartford, CT: Institute for Community Research.

Schensul, J., and E. Trickett. 2009. "Introduction to Multi-Level Community Based Culturally Situated Interventions." *American Journal of Community Psychology* 43:232–40.

Schensul, S. 1974. "Skills Needed in Applied Anthropology: Lessons from El Centro de la Causa." *Human Organization* 33:203–8.

———. 1978. "Commando Research: Innovative Approaches to Anthropological Research." *Practicing Anthropology* 1:13–14.

———. 1979. "Medical Anthropology in the Community." *Medical Anthropology* 3.

———. 1980. "Anthropological Fieldwork and Sociopolitical Change." *Social Problems* 27:309–19.

Schensul, S., and M. Borrero. 1982. "Introduction to the Hispanic Health Council." *Urban Anthropology* 11:1–8.

Schensul, S., M. Borrero, V. Barrera, J. Backstrand, and P. Guarnaccia. 1982. "A Model of Fertility Control in a Puerto Rican Community." *Urban Anthropology* 11:81–99.

Schensul, S., N. Saggurti, R. Singh, R. Verma, B. Nastasi, and P. Mazumder. 2009. "Multilevel Perspectives on Community Intervention: An Example from an Indo-US HIV Prevention Project in Mumbai, India." *American Journal of Community Psychology* 43:277–91.

Schensul, S., and J. Schensul. 1978. "Advocacy and Applied Anthropology," in *Social Scientists as Advocates: Views from the Applied Disciplines*. Edited by G. Weber and G. McCall. Beverly Hills, CA: Sage.

———. 1982. "Helping Resource Use in a Puerto Rican Community." *Urban Anthropology* 11:59–79.

Schensul, S., J. J. Schensul, and M. D. LeCompte. 2012. *Initiating Ethnographic Research: Models, Methods and Measurement*. Vol. 2. *Ethnographer's Toolkit*. Lanham, MD: AltaMira.

Schensul, S., J. Schensul, M. Singer, M. Weeks, and M. Brault. 2014. "Participatory Methods and Community Based Collaborations," in *Research Methods in Anthropology* (2nd ed.). Edited by H. R. Bernard and C. Gravlee, pp. 185–212. Lanham, MD: Roman & Littlefield.

Schensul, S., R. K. Verma, and B. K. Nastasi. 2004. "Responding to Men's Sexual Concerns: Research and Intervention in Slum Communities in Mumbai, India." *International Journal of Men's Health* 3:197–220.

Scherer, C. W., and H. Cho. 2003. "A Social Network Contagion Theory of Risk Perception." *Risk Analysis* 23:261–67.

Schulz, A., D. Williams, B. Israel, A. Becker, E. Parker, S. A. James, and J. Jackson. 2000. "Unfair Treatment, Neighborhood Effects, and Mental Health in the Detroit Metropolitan Area." *Journal of Health & Social Behavior* 41:314–32.

Schutte, N. S., et al. 2007. "A Meta-Analytic Investigation of the Relationship between Emotional Intelligence and Health." *Personality and Individual Differences* 42:921–33.

Scrimshaw, N., and G. Gleason, eds. 1992. *Rapid Assessment Procedures: Qualitative Methodologies for Planning and Evaluation of Health Related Programs.* Boston: INFDC.

Shah, A., and E. Treby. 2006. "Using a Community Based Project to Link Teaching and Research: The Bourne Stream Partnership." *Journal of Geography in Higher Education* 30:33–48.

Shankman, P. 2009. *The Trashing of Margaret Mead: Anatomy of an Anthropological Controversy.* Madison: University of Wisconsin Press.

Shediac-Rizkallah, M. C., and L. R. Bone. 1998. "Planning for the Sustainability of Community-Based Health Programs: Conceptual Frameworks and Future Directions for Research, Practice and Policy. *Health Education Research* 13:87–108.

Shimkin, D. B., N. Ajanaku, R. Register, and S. Hyland. 1978. *Black Social Institutions in the Mid-South: A Dialogue between Demitri Shimkin and Nkosi Ajanaku.* Memphis: Memphis State University, Anthropological Research Center.

Simon, W., and J. H. Gagnon. 1984. "Sexual Scripts." *Society & Natural Resources* 22.

———. 1986. "Sexual Scripts: Permanence and Change." *Archives of Sexual Behavior* 15:97–120.

———. 1987. "A Sexual Scripts Approach," in *Theories of Human Sexuality.* Edited by J. H. Greer and W. T. O'Donohue, pp. 363–83. New York: Plenum.

Simonds, V. W. S., and S. P. Christopher. 2013. "Adapting Western Research Methods to Indigenous Ways of Knowing." *American Journal of Public Health* 103:2185–92.

Simonds, V. W., S. Christopher, T. D. Sequist, G. A. Colditz, and R. E. Rudd. 2011. "Exploring Patient-Provider Interactions in a Native American Community." *Journal of Health Care for the Poor and Underserved* 22:836–52.

Simonelli, J., and D. Earle. 2001. "Help without Hurt: Community Goals, NGO Interventions and Lasting aid Lessons in Chiapas, Mexico." *Urban Anthropology,* 29:97–144.

Simonelli, J., D. Earle, and E. Story. 2004. "Acompañar Obediciendo: Learning to Help in Collaboration with Zapatista Communities." *Michigan Journal of Community Service Learning* 10(3)43–56.

Singer, M., L. Davison, and F. Yalin. 1987. "Conference Proceedings: Alcohol Use and Abuse among Hispanic Adolescents: State of Knowledge, State of Need." Hartford, CT: Hispanic Health Council.

Singer, M., J. Simmons, M. Duke, and L. Broomhall. 2001. "The Challenges of Street Research on Drug Use, Violence and HIV Risk." *Addiction Research & Theory* 9:365–402.

Singer, M., and M. Weeks. 2005. "The Hartford Model of AIDS Practice/Research Collaboration," in *Community Interventions and AIDS.* Edited by E. Trickett and W. Peguegnat. Oxford, UK: Oxford University Press.

Slater, M. D., L. Snyder, and A. F. Hayes. 2006. "Thinking and Modeling at Multiple Levels: The Potential Contribution of Multilevel Modeling to Communication Theory and Research." *Human Communication Research* 32:375–84.

Smith, C. S., W. Hill, C. Francovich, M. Morris, F. Langlois-Winkle, K. Caverzagie, and W. Iobst. 2011. "Developing a Cultural Consensus Analysis Based on the Internal Medicine Milestones (M-CCA)." *Journal of Graduate Medical Education* 3:246–48.

Smith, L. T. 2012. *Decolonizing Methodologies*. New York: Zed Books.

Smith, S. S., L. M. Rouse, M. Caskey, J. Fossum, R. Strickland, J. K. Culhane, and J. Waukau. 2014. "Culturally Tailored Smoking Cessation for Adult American Indian Smokers: A Clinical Trial." *The Counseling Psychologist* 42:852–86.

Snyder, L. B. 2007. "Health Communication Campaigns and Their Impact on Behavior." *Journal of Nutrition Education and Behavior* 39:S32–S40.

Sohng, S. S. L. 1996. "Participatory Research and Community Organizing." *Society and Social Welfare* 77:77–97.

Sorensen, G., P. C. Gupta, D. N. Sinha, S. Shastri, M. Kamat, M. S. Pednekar, and S. Ramakrishnan. "Teacher Tobacco Use and Tobacco Use Prevention in Two Regions in India: Qualitative Research Findings." *American Journal of Preventive Medicine* 41(2):424–32.

Springston, J. 2005. "Public Health Campaign," in *Encyclopedia of public relations*. Edited by R. Heath, pp. 670–74. Thousand Oaks, CA: Sage.

Stall, S., and R. Stoecker. 1998. "Community Organizing or Organizing Community? Gender and the Crafts of Empowerment." *Gender and Society, Special Issue: Gender and Social Movements, Part 1,* 12:729–56.

Sterman, J. D. 2000. *Business Dynamics: Systems Thinking and Modeling for a Complex World*. New York: McGraw Hill.

———. 2002. "All Models Are Wrong: Reflections on Becoming a Systems Scientist." *System Dynamics Review* 18:501–31.

Sternberg, R. J. 1985. *Beyond IQ: A Triarchic Theory of Intelligence*. Cambridge: Cambridge University Press.

Stocking, V. B., and N. Cutforth. 2006. "Managing the Challenges of Teaching Community-Based Research Courses: Insights from Two Instructors." *Michigan Journal of Community Service Learning* 13:56.

Stoecker, R. 1999. "Are Academics Irrelevant? Roles for Scholars in Participatory Research." *American Behavioral Science* 425:840–54.

Stopka, T. J., M. Singer, C. Santelices, and J. Eiserman. 2003. "Public Health Interventionists, Penny Capitalists, or Sources of Risk? Assessing Street Syringe Sellers in Hartford, Connecticut." *Substance Use & Misuse* 38:1345.

Stoudt. Brett G., M. Fox, and M. Fine. 2012. "Contesting Privilege with Critical Participatory Action Research." *Journal of Social Issues* 68:178–93.

Stovall, D., and N. Delgado. 2009. "Knowing the Ledge": Participatory Action Research as Legal Studies for Urban High School Youth. *New Directions for Youth Development* 2009:67–81.

Strand, K., S. Marullo, N. Cutforth, R. Stoecker, and P. Donohue. 2003. *Community-Based Research and Higher Education: Principles and Practices*. San Francisco: Jossey-Bass.

Stull, D. D., and J. J. Schensul, eds. 1987. *Collaborative Research and Social Change. Special Studies in Applied Anthropology*. Boulder CO: Westview Press/Praeger.

Swain, R., A. Berger, J. Bongard, and P. Hines. 2015. "Participation and Contribution in Crowdsourced Surveys." *PLoS ONE* 10:1–21.

Tandon, R. 1981. "Dialogue as Inquiry and Intervention," in *Human Inquiry: A Sourcebook of New Paradigm Research*. Edited by P. Reason and J. Rowan. New York: John Wiley and Sons.

Tax, S. 1958. "The Fox Project." *Human Organization* 17:17–19.

Tayabas, L. M. T., L. T. Castillo, and J. M. Espino. 2014. "Qualitative Evaluation: A Critical and Interpretative Complementary Approach to Improve Health Programs and Services." *International Journal of Qualitative Studies on Health and Well Being*, http://dx.doi.org/10.3402/qhw.v9.24417:1–6.

Thomas, A. J., R. Barrie, J. Brunner, A. Clawson, A. Hewitt, G. Jeremie-Brink, and M. Rowe-Johnson. 2014. "Assessing Critical Consciousness in Youth and Young Adults." *Journal of Research on Adolescence* 24:485–96.

Thompson, S. 1995. *Going All The Way: Teenage Girls Tales of Sex, Romance and Pregnancy*. New York: Hill and Wang.

Thompson, W. W., D. K. Shay, E. Weintraub, L. Brammer, C. B. Bridges, N. J. Cox, and K. Fukuda. 2004. "Influenza-Associated Hospitalizations in the United States." *JAMA* 292:1333–40.

Thompson, W. W., D. K. Shay, E. Weintraub, L. Brammer, N. Cox, L. J. Anderson, and K. J. Fukuda. 2003. "Mortality Associated with Influenza and Respiratory Syncytial Virus in the United States." *JAMA* 289:79–86.

Toba, S. 1992. "Rites of Passage: An Aspect of Rai Culture" (1st ed.). Kathmandu: Royal Nepal Academy.

Torre, M. E., C. Cahill, and M. Fox. 2015. "Participatory Action Research in Social Research," in *International Encyclopedia of the Social & Behavioral Sciences* (2nd ed.). Edited by J. D. Wright, pp. 540–44. Oxford: Elsevier.

Trickett, E. J., S. Beehler, C. Deutsch, L. W. Green, P. Hawe, K. McLeroy, R. Lin Miller, B. D. Rapkin, J. J. Schensul, A. J. Schulz, and J. E. Trimble. 2011. "Advancing the Science of Community-Level Interventions." *American Journal of Public Health* 101:1410–19.

Trotter, R. T. 1997. "Anthropological Midrange Theories in Mental Health Research: Selected Theory, Methods, and Systematic Approaches to At-Risk Populations." *Ethos* 25:259–74.

Trotter, R. T., J. Schensul, and K. Kostick. 2014. *Theories and Methods in Applied Anthropology*. Edited by H. R. Bernard and L. Gravlee, pp. 661–94. Lanham, MD: Rowman & Littlefield.

Tuck, E. 2009. "Re-Visioning Action: Participatory Action Research and Indigenous Theories of Change." *Urban Review* 41:47–65.

Turk, T., N. Murukutla, S. Gupta, J. Kaur, S. Mullin, R. Saradhi, and P. Chaturvedi. 2012. "Using a Smokeless Tobacco Control Mass Media Campaign and Other Synergistic Elements to Address Social Inequalities in India." *Cancer Causes & Control* 23:81–90.

Vanderbroek, I., V. Reyes-Garcia, U. P. de Albuqueque, R. Bussmann, and A. Pieroni. 2011. "Local Knowledge: Who Cares?" *Journal of Ethnobiology and Ethnomedicine* 7:1–7.

Van Willigen, J. 2005. "Community Assets and the Community Building Process: Historical Perspectives," in *Community Building in the 21st Century*. Edited by L. Hyland, pp. 25–44. Santa Fe, NM: School for Advanced Research Press.

Vennix, J. A. M., D. F. Andersen, G. P. Richardson, and J. Rohrbaugh. 1992. "Model-Building for Group Decision Support: Issues and Alternatives in Knowledge Elicitation." *European Journal of Operational Research* 59:28–41.

Viswanathan, M., A. Ammerman, E. Eng, G. Gartlehner, K. N. Lohr, D. Griffith, S. Rhodes, C. Samuel-Hodge, S. Mary, L. Lux, L. Webb, S. F. Sutton, T. Swinson, A. Jackman, and L. Whitener. 2004. *Community-Based Participatory Research: Assessing the Evidence*. RTI: University of North Carolina Evidence-Based Practice Center.

Voordouw, B. C. G., P. D. van der Linden, S. Simonian, J. van der Lei, M. C. J. Sturkenboom, and B. H. C. Stricker. 2003. "Influenza Vaccination in Community-Dwelling Elderly: Impact on Mortality and Influenza-Associated Morbidity." *Archives of Internal Medicine* 163:1089–94.

Vygotsky, L. S. 1978. *Mind in Society: The Development of Higher Psychological Processes*. Cambridge, MA: Harvard University Press.

Wakefield, M. A., B. Loken, and R. C. Hornik. 2010. CSU 169/2011: "Use of Mass Media Campaigns to Change Health Behavior." *The Lancet* 376:1261–71.

Wandersman, A., P. Imm, M. Chinman, and S. Kaftarian. 2000. "Getting to Outcomes: A Results-Based Approach to Accountability." *Evaluation and Program Planning* 23.389–95.

Ward, E. G., W. B. Dioch, J. A. Levy, and J. J. Schensul. 2004. "Perception of HIV/AIDS Risk among Urban, Low-Income Senior-Housing Residents." *AIDS Education & Prevention* 16:571–88.

Ward, K., and L. Wolf-Wendel. 2000. "Community-Centered Service Learning." *American Behavioral Scientist* 43:767–80.

Waree, C. 2013. "A Development of the Multiple Intelligences Measurement of Elementary Students." *International Journal of Social, Education, Economics and Management Engineering* 7:870–75.

Warner, R. E. 2013. *Solution Focused Interviewing: Applying Positive Psychology A Manual for Practitioners*. Toronto: University of Toronto Press.

Watts, R. J., M. A. Diemer, and A. M. Voight. 2011. "Critical Consciousness: Current Status and Future Directions." *New Directions for Child and Adolescent Development* 2011:43–57.

Watts, R. J., D. M. Griffith, and J. Abdul-Adil. 1999. "Sociopolitical Development as an Antidote for Oppression-Theory and Action." *American Journal of Community Psychology*, 27:255–71.

Weeks, M. R., S. Clair, S. P. Borgatti, K. Radda, and J. J. Schensul. 2002. "Social Networks of Drug Users in High-Risk Sites: Finding the Connections." *AIDS & Behavior* 6:193–206.

Weeks, M. R., S. Clair, M. Singer, K. Radda, J. J. Schensul, D. S. Wilson, M. Martinez, G. Scott, and G. Knight. 2001. "High-Risk Drug Use Sites, Meaning and Practice: Implications for AIDS Prevention." *Journal of Drug Issues* 31:781–808.

Weeks, M. R., M. Convey, J. Dickson-Gomez, J. Li, K. Radda, M. Martinez, and E. Robles. 2009. "Changing Drug Users' Risk Environments: Peer Health Advocates as Multi-level Community Change Agents." *American Journal of Community Psychology* 43:330–44.

Weeks, M. R., M. Grier, N. Romero-Daza, M. J. Puglisi-Vasquez, and M. Singer. 1998. "Streets, Drugs, and the Economy of Sex in the Age of AIDS." *Women & Health* 27:205–29.

Weeks, M. R., D. A. Himmelgreen, M. Singer, S. Woolley, N. Romero-Daza, and M. Grier. 1996. "Community-Based Aids Prevention: Preliminary Outcomes of a Program for African American and Latino Injection Drug Users." *Journal of Drug Issues* 26:561–90.

Weeks, M. R., J. Li, E. Coman, M. Abbott, L. Sylla, M. Corbett, and J. Dickson-Gomez. 2010. "Multilevel Social Influences on Female Condom Use and Adoption among Women in the Urban United States." *AIDS Patient Care and STDs* 24:297–309.

Weeks, M. R., J. Li, J. Dickson-Gomez, M. Convey, M. Martinez, K. Radda, and S. Clair. 2009. "Outcomes of a Peer HIV Prevention Program with Injection Drug and Crack Users: The Risk Avoidance Partnership." *Substance Use & Misuse* 44:253–81.

Weidlich, W. 2005. "Thirty Years of Sociodynamics. An Integrated Strategy of Modelling in the Social Sciences: Applications to Migration and Urban Evolution." *Chaos Solitons & Fractals* 24:45–56.

Weiss, M. 1997. "Explanatory Model Interview Catalogue (EMIC): Framework for Comparative Study of Illness." *Transcultural Psychiatry* 34:235–63.

Weller, S. C., and A. K. Romney. 1988. *Systematic Data Collection*. Newbury Park, CA: Sage.

Wenger, E. 1998. *Communities of Practice: Learning, Meaning and Identity*. Cambridge: Cambridge University Press.

Wertsch, J. V. 1985. "Vygotsky and the Social Formation of Mind." Cambridge, MA: Harvard University Press.

West, S. G., N. Duan, W. Pequegnat, P. Gaist, D. C. D. Jarlais, D. Holtgrave, J. Szapocznik, M. Fishbein, B. Rapkin, M. Clatts, and P. D. Mullen. 2008. "Alternatives to the Randomized Controlled Trial." *American Journal of Public Health* 98:1359–66.

WHO/UNFPA/UNICEF. 1992. "Traditional Birth Attendants: A Joint WHO/UNFPA/UNICEF Statement." Geneva: World Health Organization.

Whyte, W. F. 1991. *Participatory Action Research*. Newberry Park, CA: Sage.

Wiggins, A., and K. Crowston. 2011. "From Conservation to Crowdsourcing: A Typology of Citizen Science," in *Crowdsourcing*. Edited by D. C. Brabham. Cambridge, MA: MIT Press.

Wilby, J. 2005. "Combining a Systems Framework with Epidemiology in the Study of Emerging Infectious Disease." *Systems Research and Behavioral Science*, 22:385–98.

Williamson, K. M., and K. Brown. 2014. "Collective Voices: Engagement of Hartford Community Residents through Participatory Action Research." *The Qualitative Report* 19:1–14.

Williamson, L., J. Brecher, R. Glasser, and J. J. Schensul. 1999. "Using Ethnography to Enhance Public Programming," in *Using Ethnographic Data*, vol. 7. Edited by J. J. Schensul and M. D. LeCompte, pp. 115–78. Walnut Creek, CA: AltaMira.

Wilson, A., I. D. Gallos, N. Plana, D. Lissauer, K. S. Khan, J. Zamora, C. MacArthur, and A. Coomarasamy. 2011. *Effectiveness of Strategies Incorporating Training and Support of Traditional Birth Attendants on Perinatal and Maternal Mortality: Meta-Analysis. BMJ*, vol. 343. Published online 2011 December 1. DOI: 10.1136/bmj.d7102.

Wilson, H. 2014. "Turning Off the School-to-Prison Pipeline." *Reclaiming Children & Youth* 23:49–53.

Wilson, N., S. Dasho, A. C. Martin, N. Wallerstein, C. C. Wang, and M. Minkler. 2007. "Engaging Young Adolescents in Social Action through Photovoice: The Youth Empowerment Strategies (YES!) Project." *The Journal of Early Adolescence* 27:241–61.

Wilson, P. M., M. Petticrew, M. W. Calnan, and I. Nazareth. 2010. "Disseminating Research Findings: What Should Researchers Do? A Systematic Scoping Review of Conceptual Frameworks." *Implementation Science* 5.

Winskell, K., and D. Enger. 2009. "A New Way of Perceiving the Pandemic: The Findings from a Participatory Research Process on Young African Americans' Stories about HIV/AIDS." *Culture, Health and Sexuality* 11(4): 453–67.

Wood, S. D., and R. Samuel. 2012. "History as Community-Based Research and the Pedagogy of Discovery: Teaching Racial Inequality, Documenting Local History and Building Links between Students and Communities in Mississippi and Tennessee." *Journal of Rural Social Sciences* 27:32–49.

Xie, X. F., M. Wang, R. G. Zhang, J. Li, and Q. Y. Yu. 2011. "The Role of Emotions in Risk Communication." *Risk Analysis* 31:450–65.

Yosso, T. 2005. "Whose Culture Has Capital? A Critical Race Theory Discussion of Community Cultural Wealth." *Race, Ethnicity & Education* 8:69–91.

INDEX

ABOUT THE AUTHORS

 **Jean J. Schensul**, founding director, and now senior scientist, Institute for Community Research, Hartford, is an interdisciplinary medical/educational anthropologist with a lifelong commitment to the conduct and use of research in collaboration with local communities to address issues of social, health, and cultural injustice. Born in Canada, she completed her BA in archaeology at the University of Manitoba and her MA and PhD in anthropology at the University of Minnesota. From 1978 to 1987, as deputy director and cofounder of the Hispanic Health Council in Hartford, Connecticut, she built its research and training infrastructure. In 1987, she became the founding director of the Institute for Community Research, an innovative, multi-million-dollar community research organization, conducting collaborative and participatory applied research and intervention in health, education, cultural studies, and folklore in the United States, China, Sri Lanka, and India. Dr. Schensul's research cuts across the developmental spectrum, addressing contributions of ethnography to disparities and structural inequities in early childhood development, adolescent and young adult substance use and sexual risk, reproductive health, and chronic diseases of older adulthood. She is the recipient of more than twenty National Institutes of Health research grants for work with local communities and coalitions, as well as other federal, state, and foundation grants. In addition to conferences, workshops, over eighty peer-reviewed journal articles, many edited substantive special issues of journals including *Anthropology and Education Quarterly*, *AIDS and Behavior*, *American Behavioral Scientist*, and the *American Journal of Community Psychiatry*, her collaborative work in research methodology is reflected in a book (with Don Stull), *Collaborative Research and Social Change*, the widely celebrated seven-volume series, the *Ethnographer's Toolkit*, first and second editions, with Margaret LeCompte, and in other articles and book chapters on ethnography and advocacy, community building, and sustainability of interventions. Dr. Schensul has served as reviewer on various NSF, NIH, and other federal committees and has reviewed for many established peer reviewed journals. She has served as

president of the Society for Applied Anthropology and the Council on Anthropology and Education, was an elected board member of the American Anthropological Association (2010–2013), elected treasurer of the Association on Anthropology and Gerontology, and appointed member and chair of the AAA Committee on Applied and Practicing Anthropology. In recognition of her work as a scholar-activist she has been awarded two senior anthropology awards, the Solon T. Kimball Award for anthropology and policy (with Stephen Schensul) and the 2010 Malinowski Award for lifetime contribution to the use of anthropology for the solution of human problems. She has been active in the Society for Prevention Research and the American Public Health Association, for both of which she has organized oral and poster sessions on diverse topics including multilevel interventions, tobacco use, and oral health. Dr. Schensul is research professor, School of Dental Medicine, was director of Qualitative Research, Interdisciplinary Research Methods Core, Yale Center for Interdisciplinary Research on AIDS, and holds an Honorary Doctorate from North Carolina State University.

Margaret D. LeCompte received her BA from Northwestern University in political science and, after serving as a civil rights worker in Mississippi and a Peace Corps volunteer in the Somali Republic, earned her MA and PhD from the University of Chicago. She then taught at the Universities of Houston and Cincinnati, with visiting appointments at the University of North Dakota and the Universidad de Monterrey, Mexico, before moving to the School of Education at the University of Colorado, Boulder, in 1990. She also served for five years as executive director for research and evaluation for the Houston Independent School District. She is internationally known as a pioneer in the use of qualitative and ethnographic research and evaluation in education. Fluent in Spanish, she has consulted throughout Latin America on educational research issues. Her publications include many articles and book chapters on research methods in the social sciences, as well as her cowritten (with Judith Preissle) *Ethnography and Qualitative Design in Educational Research* (1984, 1993) and coedited (with Wendy Millroy and Judith Preissle) *The Handbook of Qualitative Research in Education* (1992), the first textbook and handbook published on ethnographic and qualitative methods in education. Her collaborative work in research methodology continues with this second edition of the *Ethnographer's Toolkit*. Dr. LeCompte is deeply interested in the educational success of linguistically and culturally different students from kindergarten through university, as well as reform initiatives for schools and communities serving such students. Her books in these areas include *The Way Schools Work: A Sociological Analysis of Education*

(1990, 1995, and 1999) with K. DeMarrais and *Giving Up on School: Teacher Burnout and Student Dropout* (1991) with A. G. Dworkin. Her diverse interests as a researcher, evaluator, and consultant to school districts, museums, communities, and universities have led to publications on dropouts, artistic and gifted students, school reform efforts, schools serving American Indian students, and the impact of strip mining on the social environment of rural communities. Her most recent research involves explorations in the politics and finance of public universities. Winner of the Council on Anthropology and Education's 2011 Spindler Award for lifetime contributions to educational anthropology, she is an elected Fellow of the American Educational Research Association, the American Anthropological Association, and the Society for Applied Anthropology, and has been president of the Council on Anthropology and Education of the American Anthropology Association and editor of the journals *Review of Educational Research* and *Youth and Society*. A founding member and the first president of the University of Colorado, Boulder, chapter of the American Association of University Professors, she also served as vice president of the Colorado Conference of the AAUP and was active in faculty governance at the University of Colorado. As professor emerita, she continues to use action research strategies in the service of improving the intellectual life in higher education.